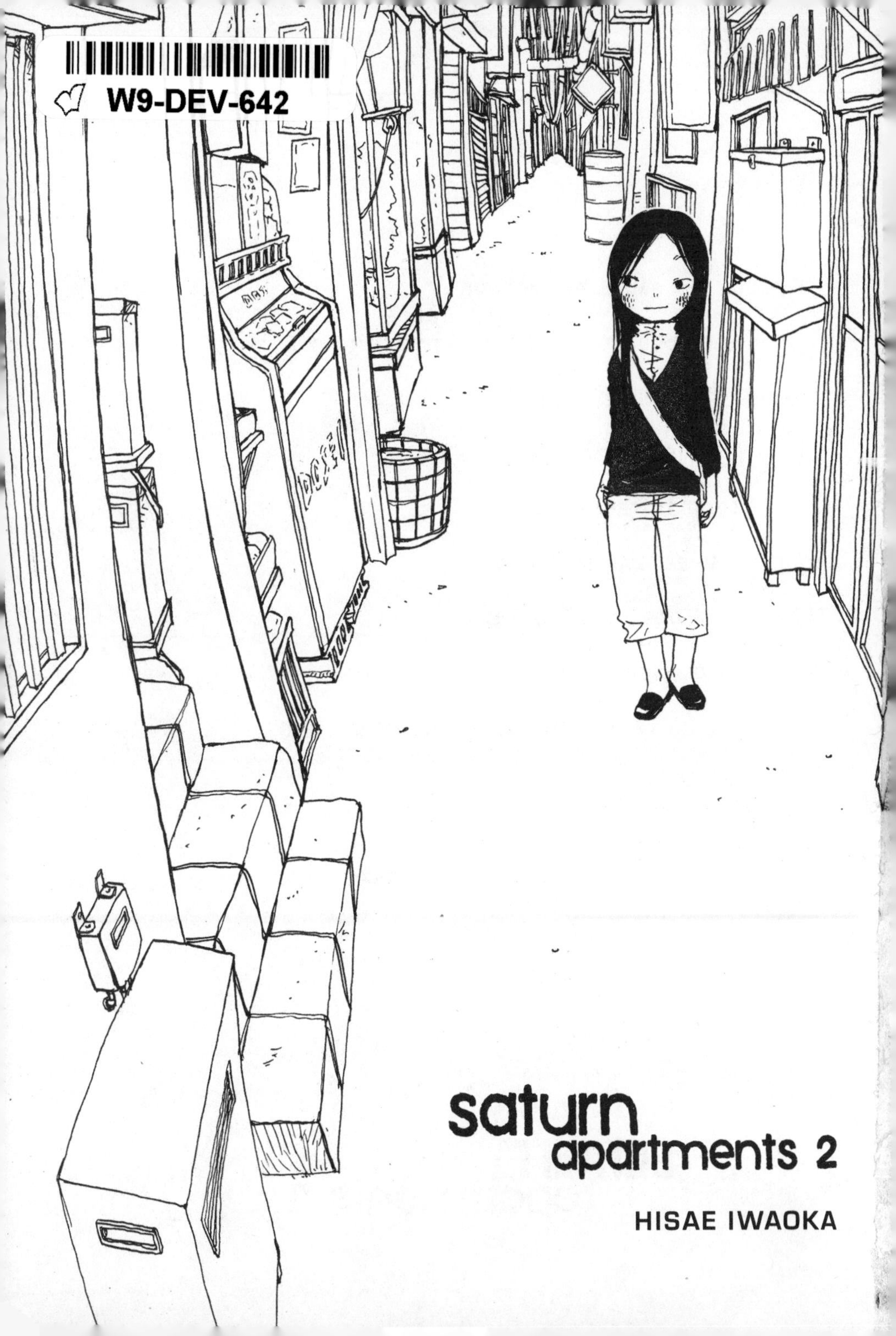

saturn apartments 2

HISAE IWAOKA

saturn
apartments 2

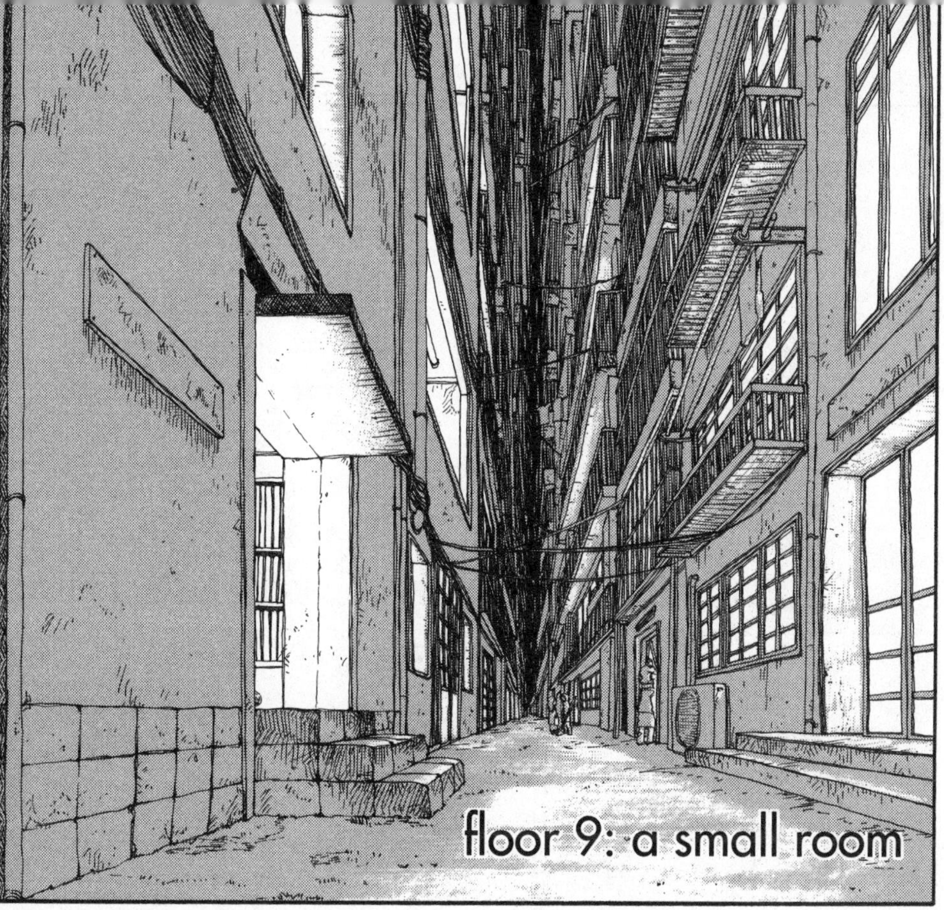
floor 9: a small room

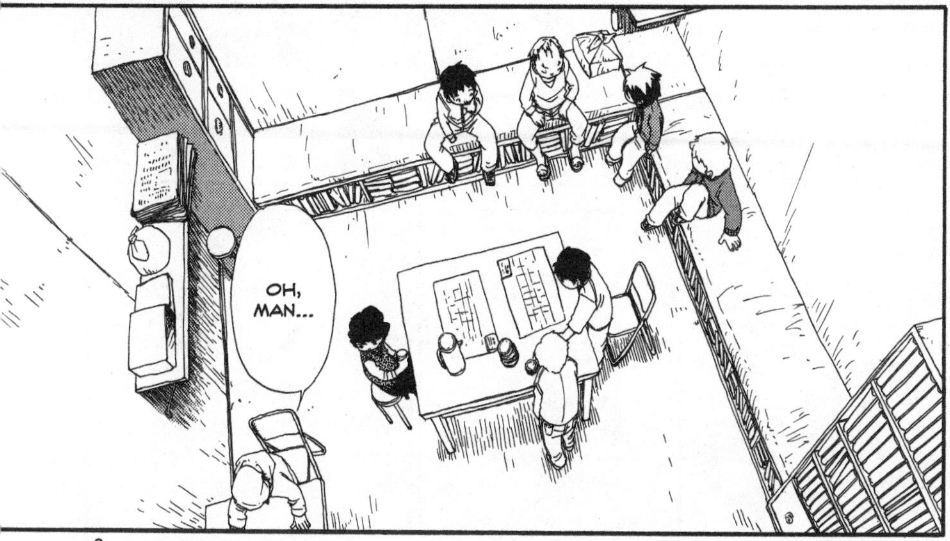
OH, MAN...

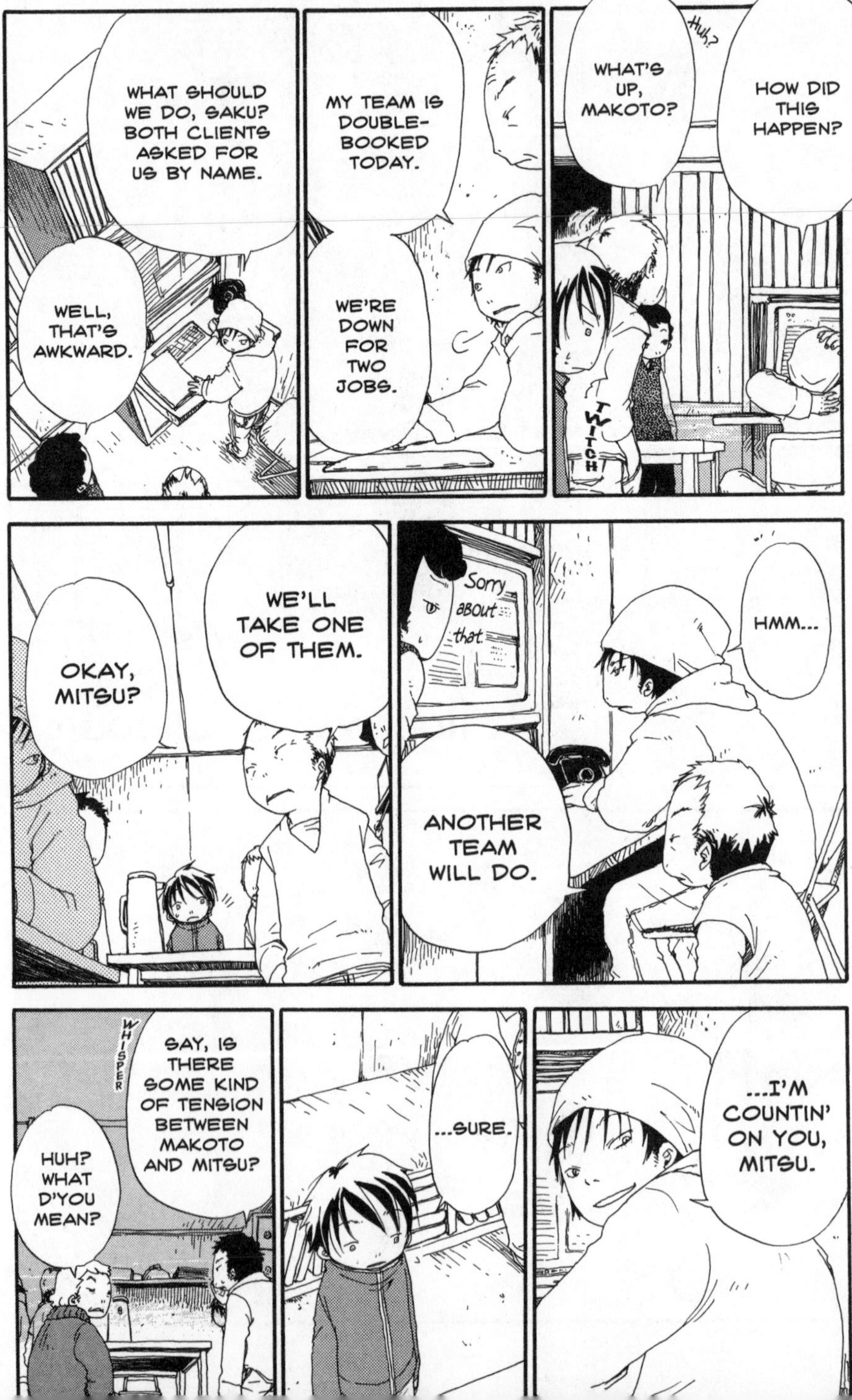
HOW DID THIS HAPPEN?
Huh?
WHAT'S UP, MAKOTO?
TWITCH
MY TEAM IS DOUBLE-BOOKED TODAY.
WE'RE DOWN FOR TWO JOBS.
WHAT SHOULD WE DO, SAKU? BOTH CLIENTS ASKED FOR US BY NAME.
WELL, THAT'S AWKWARD.
HMM...
Sorry about that.
ANOTHER TEAM WILL DO.
WE'LL TAKE ONE OF THEM.
OKAY, MITSU?
...I'M COUNTIN' ON YOU, MITSU.
...SURE.
WHISPER
SAY, IS THERE SOME KIND OF TENSION BETWEEN MAKOTO AND MITSU?
HUH? WHAT D'YOU MEAN?

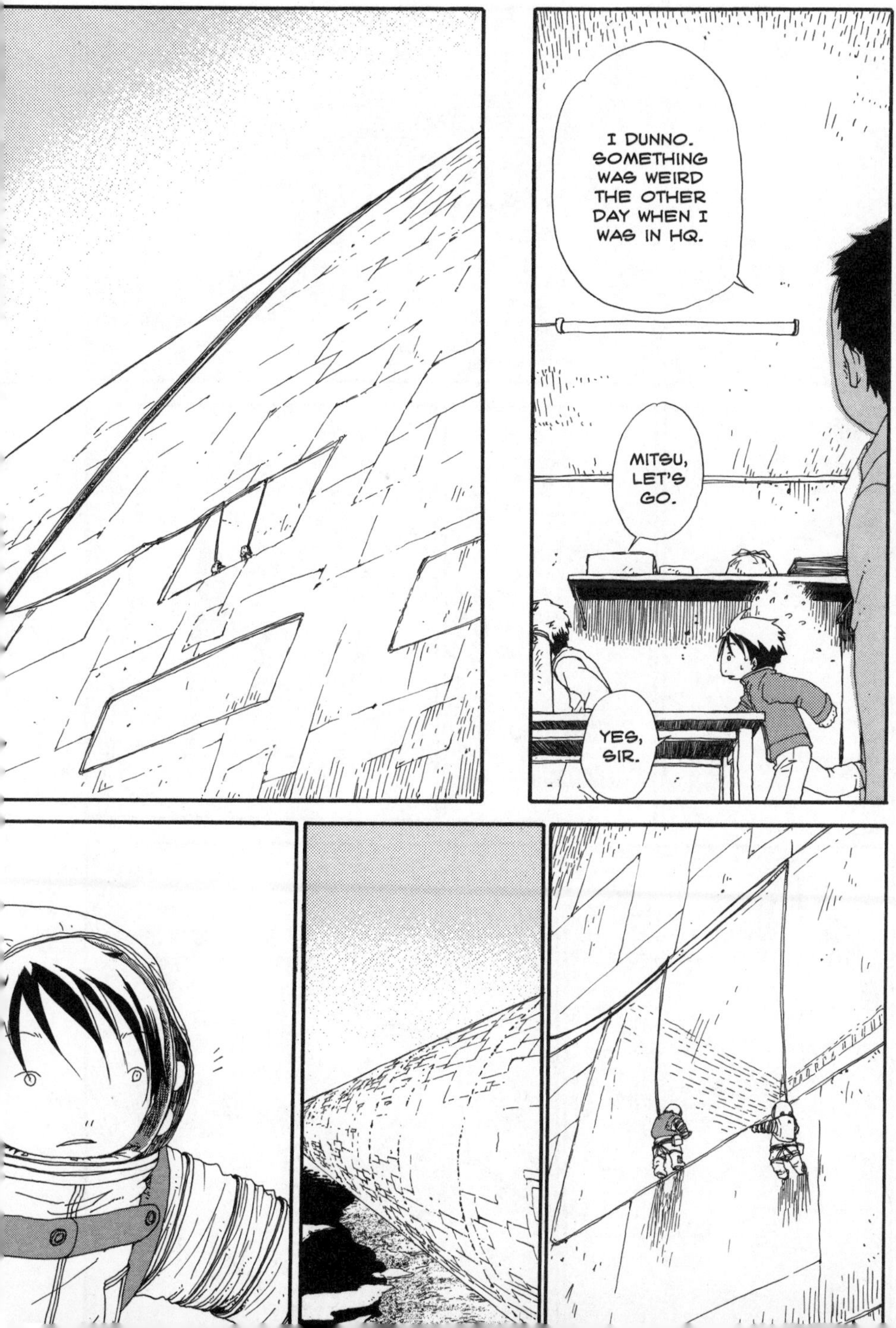
I DUNNO. SOMETHING WAS WEIRD THE OTHER DAY WHEN I WAS IN HQ.
MITSU, LET'S GO.
YES, SIR.

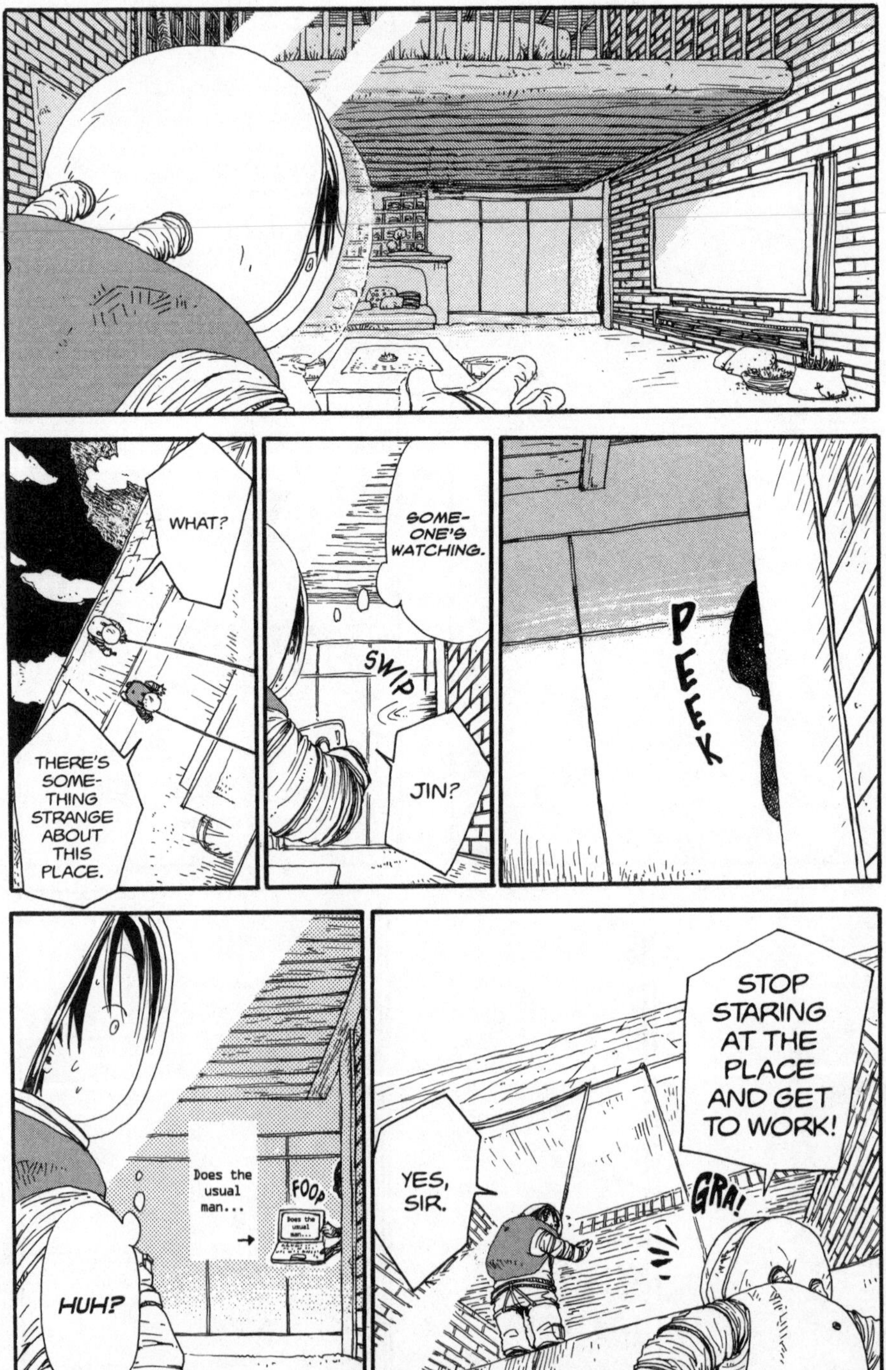
PEEK
SOME-ONE'S WATCHING.
SWIP
JIN?
WHAT?
THERE'S SOME-THING STRANGE ABOUT THIS PLACE.
STOP STARING AT THE PLACE AND GET TO WORK!
GRA!
YES, SIR.
Does the usual man...
FOOP
Does the usual man...
HUH?

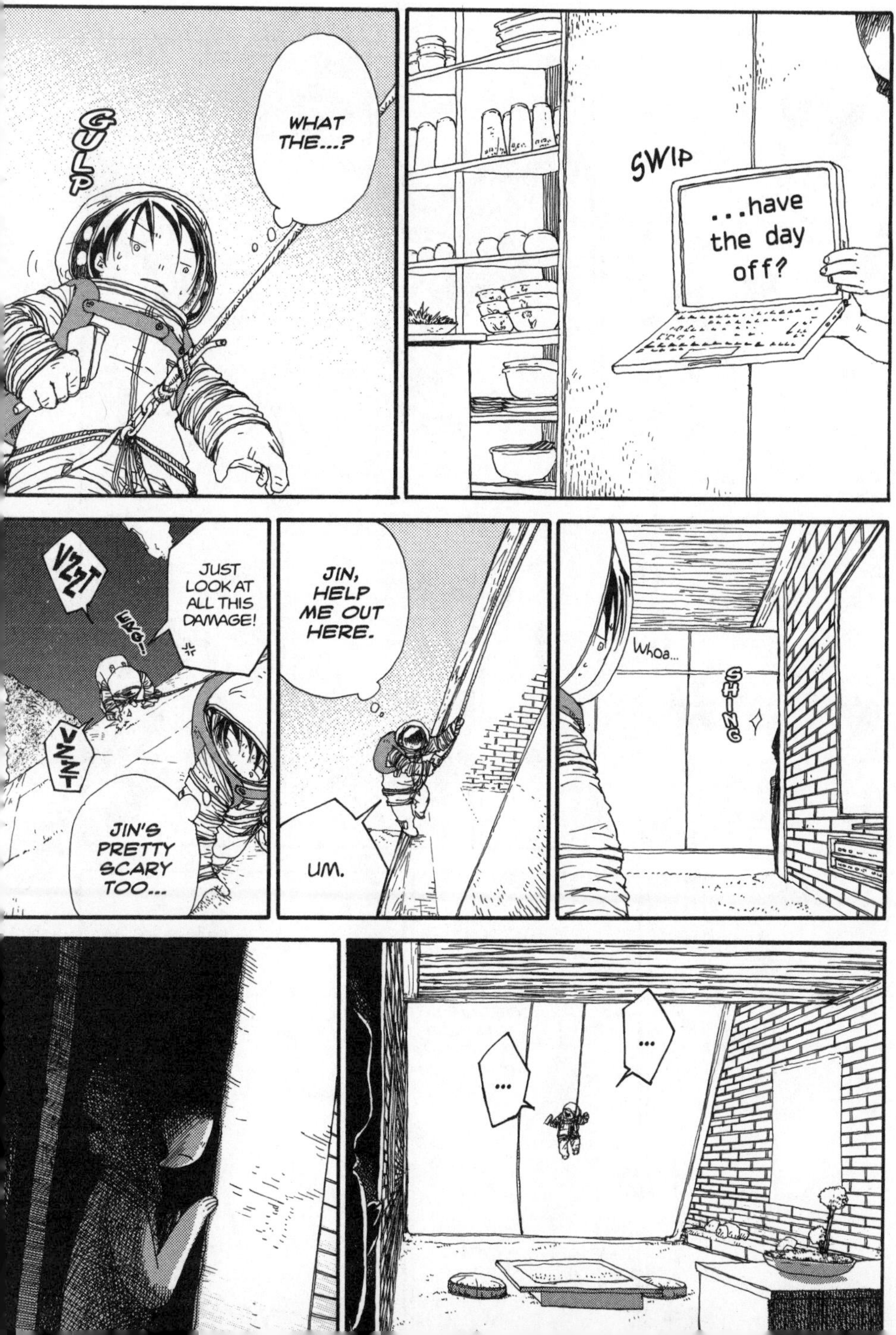
SWIP
...have the day off?
WHAT THE...?
GULP
Whoa...
SHING
JIN, HELP ME OUT HERE.
UM.
JUST LOOK AT ALL THIS DAMAGE!
VZZT
ERG-
VZZT
JIN'S PRETTY SCARY TOO...
...
...

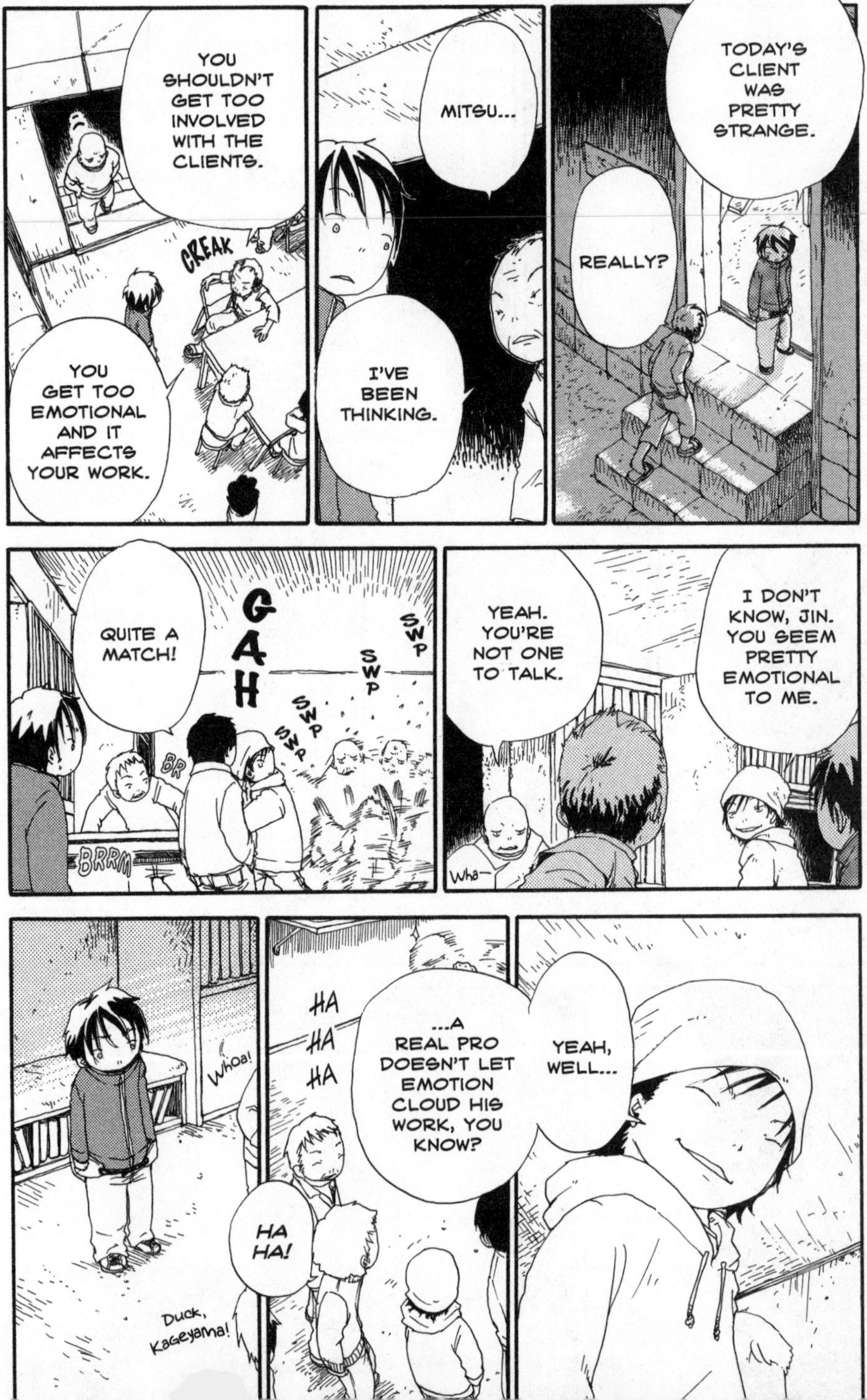
TODAY'S CLIENT WAS PRETTY STRANGE.
REALLY?
MITSU...
I'VE BEEN THINKING.
YOU SHOULDN'T GET TOO INVOLVED WITH THE CLIENTS.
CREAK
YOU GET TOO EMOTIONAL AND IT AFFECTS YOUR WORK.
I DON'T KNOW, JIN. YOU SEEM PRETTY EMOTIONAL TO ME.
YEAH. YOU'RE NOT ONE TO TALK.
Wha—
GAH
SWP
SWP
SWP
SWP
QUITE A MATCH!
BR
BRRM
YEAH, WELL...
...A REAL PRO DOESN'T LET EMOTION CLOUD HIS WORK, YOU KNOW?
HA HA HA
HA HA!
Whoa!
Duck, Kageyama!

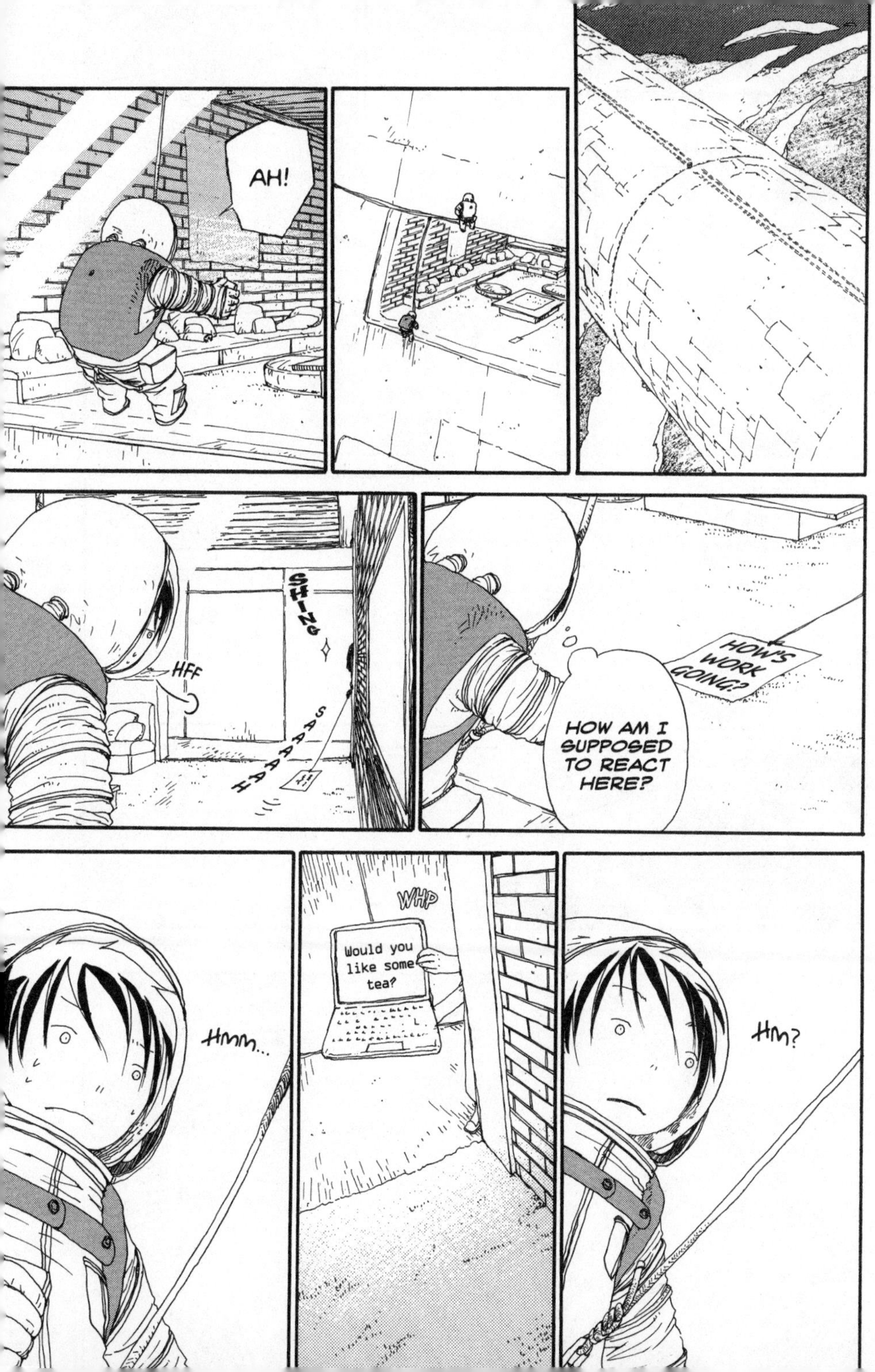
AH!
HOW'S WORK GOING?
HOW AM I SUPPOSED TO REACT HERE?
SHING
HFF
SAAAAAH
Hm?
WHP
Would you like some tea?
Hmm...

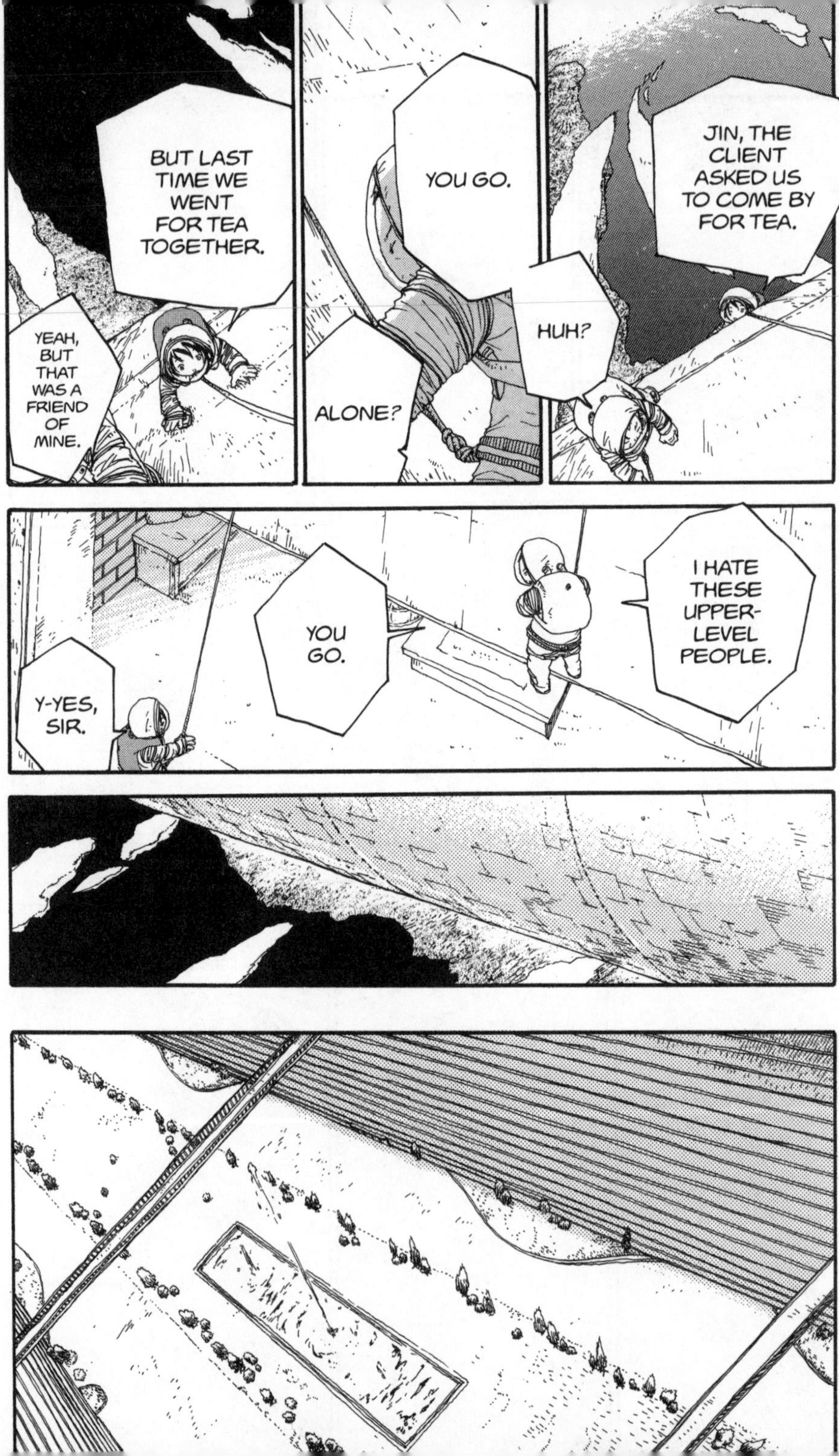
JIN, THE CLIENT ASKED US TO COME BY FOR TEA.
HUH?
YOU GO.
ALONE?
BUT LAST TIME WE WENT FOR TEA TOGETHER.
YEAH, BUT THAT WAS A FRIEND OF MINE.
I HATE THESE UPPER-LEVEL PEOPLE.
YOU GO.
Y-YES, SIR.

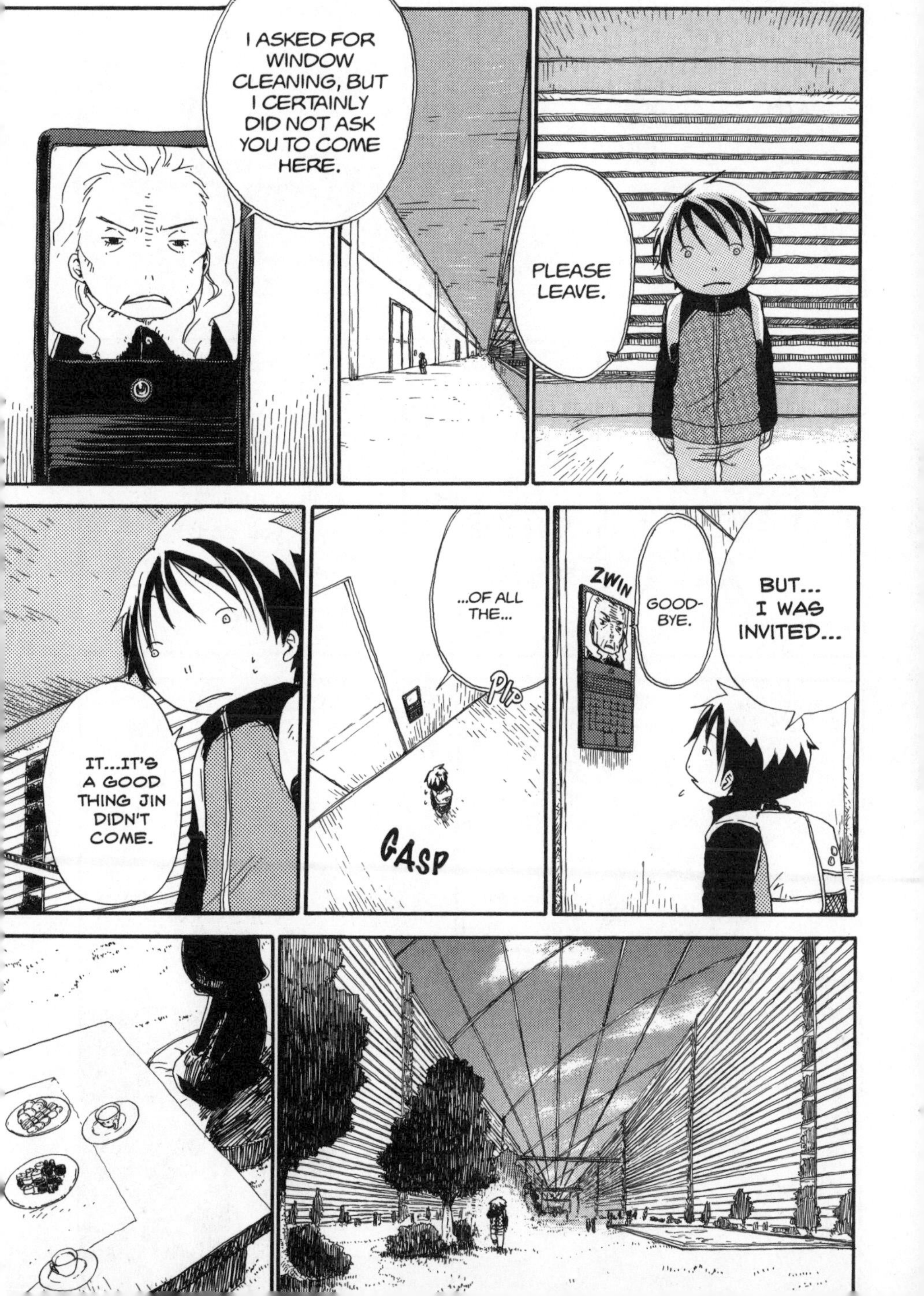
PLEASE LEAVE.
I ASKED FOR WINDOW CLEANING, BUT I CERTAINLY DID NOT ASK YOU TO COME HERE.
BUT... I WAS INVITED...
GOOD-BYE.
ZWIN
...OF ALL THE...
PIP
GASP
IT...IT'S A GOOD THING JIN DIDN'T COME.

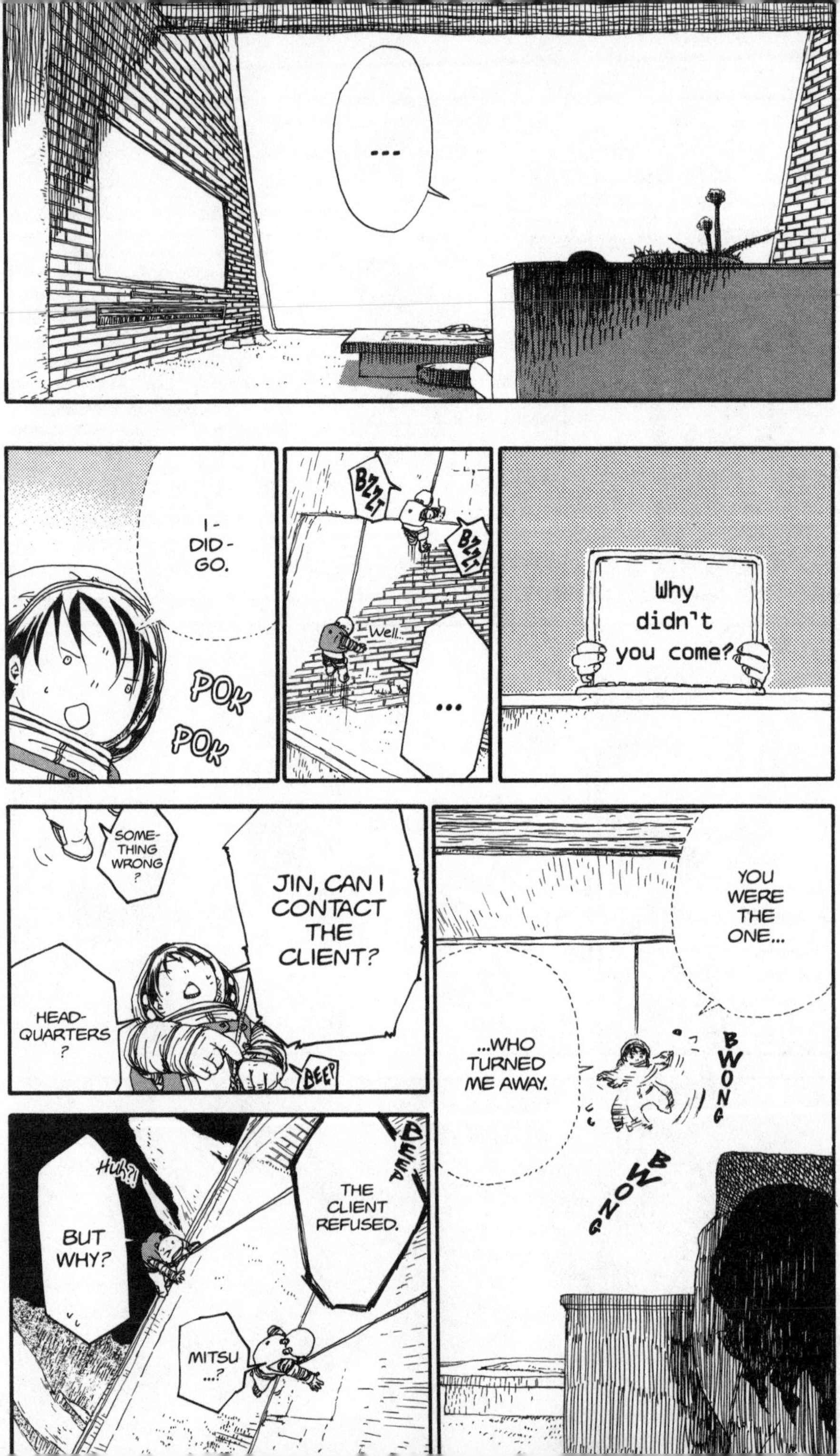
...
Why didn't you come?
BZZT
BZZT
Well...
I...
...
I- DID- GO.
POK
POK
YOU WERE THE ONE...
...WHO TURNED ME AWAY.
BWONG
BWONG
JIN, CAN I CONTACT THE CLIENT?
SOME-THING WRONG?
HEAD-QUARTERS?
BEEP
BEEP
THE CLIENT REFUSED.
HUH?!
BUT WHY?
MITSU...?

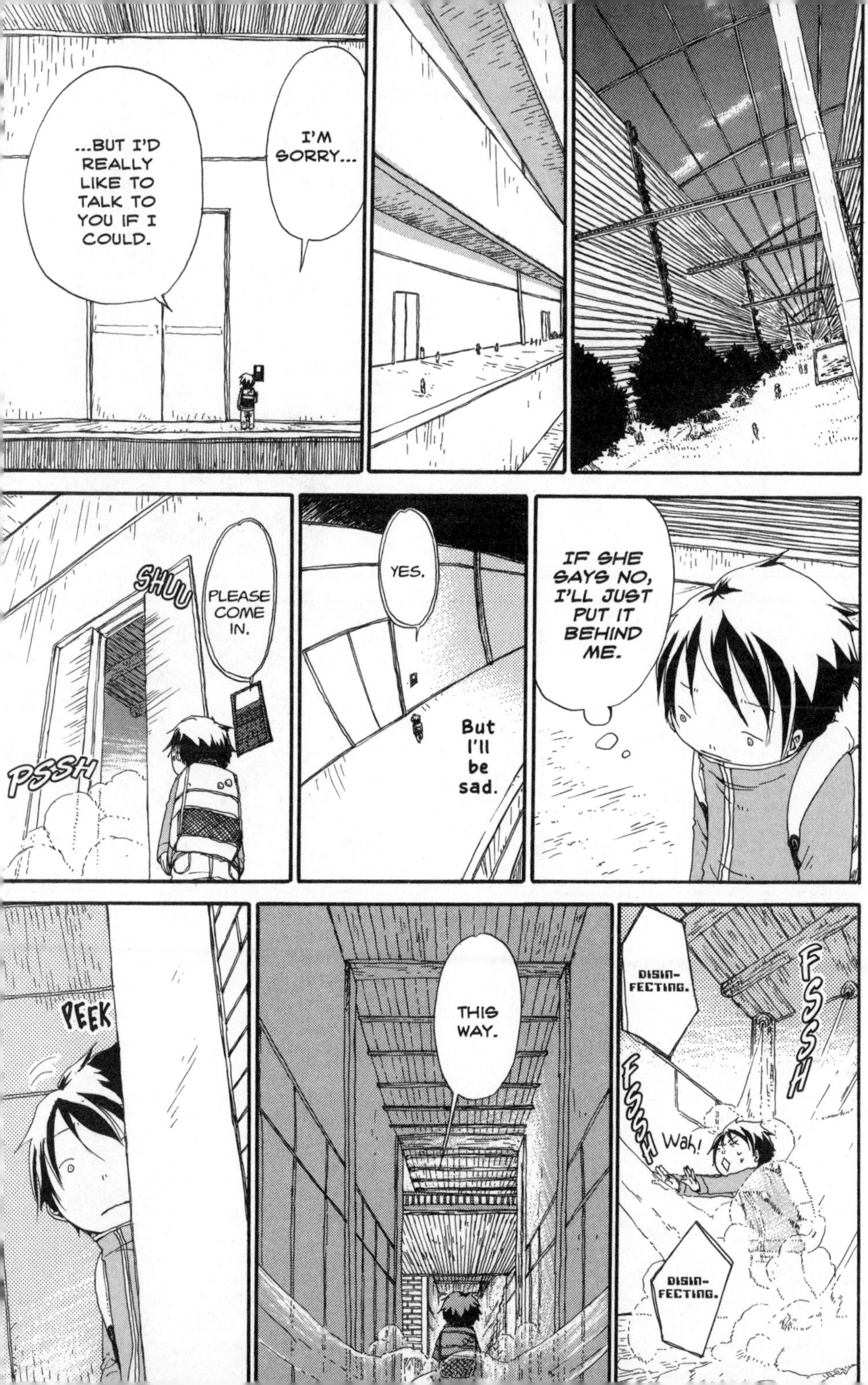
I'M SORRY...
...BUT I'D REALLY LIKE TO TALK TO YOU IF I COULD.
IF SHE SAYS NO, I'LL JUST PUT IT BEHIND ME.
YES.
But I'll be sad.
SHUU
PLEASE COME IN.
PSSH
DISIN-FECTING.
FSSSH
FSSSH
Wah!
DISIN-FECTING.
THIS WAY.
PEEK

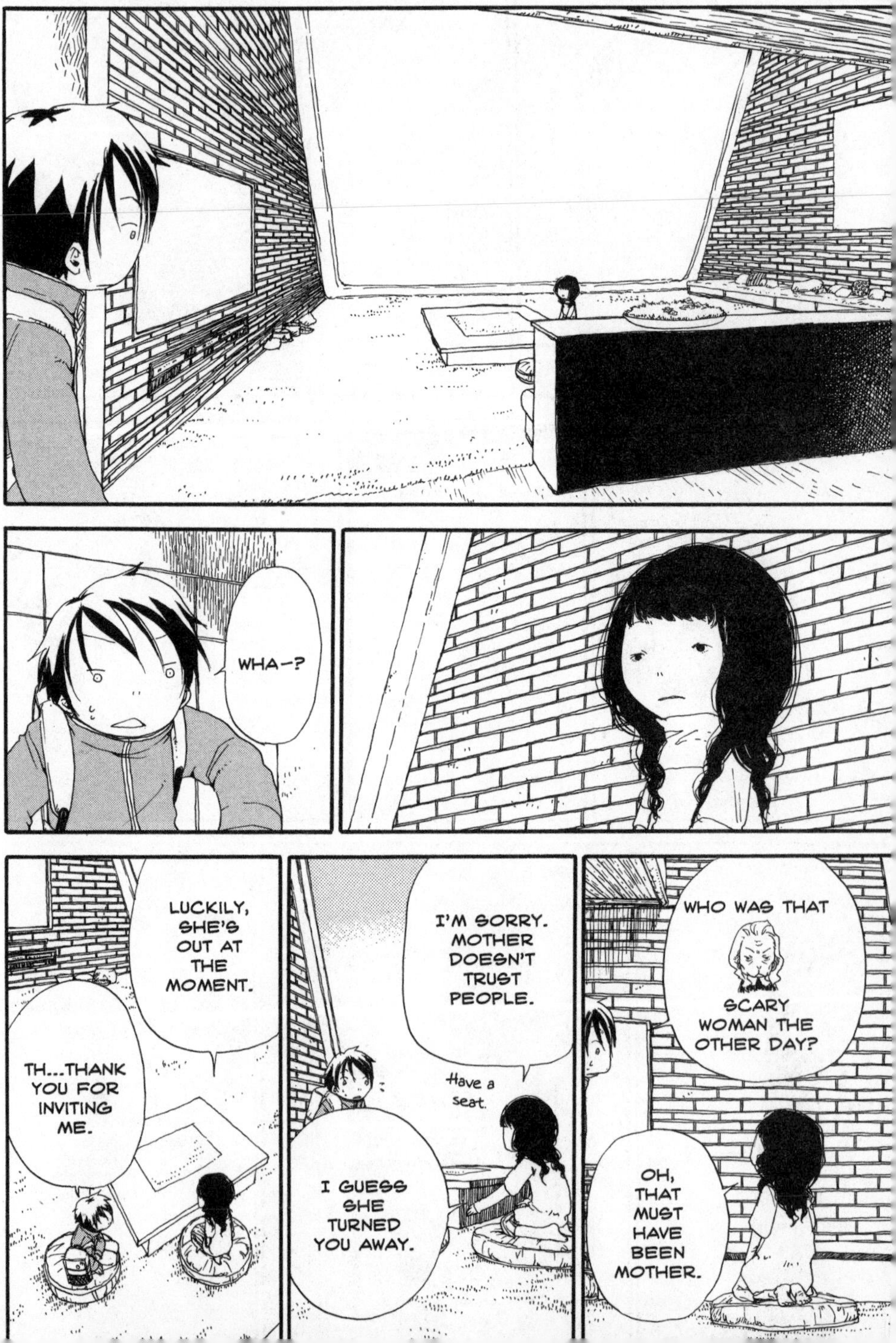
WHA-?
WHO WAS THAT SCARY WOMAN THE OTHER DAY?
OH, THAT MUST HAVE BEEN MOTHER.
I'M SORRY. MOTHER DOESN'T TRUST PEOPLE.
Have a seat.
I GUESS SHE TURNED YOU AWAY.
LUCKILY, SHE'S OUT AT THE MOMENT.
TH...THANK YOU FOR INVITING ME.

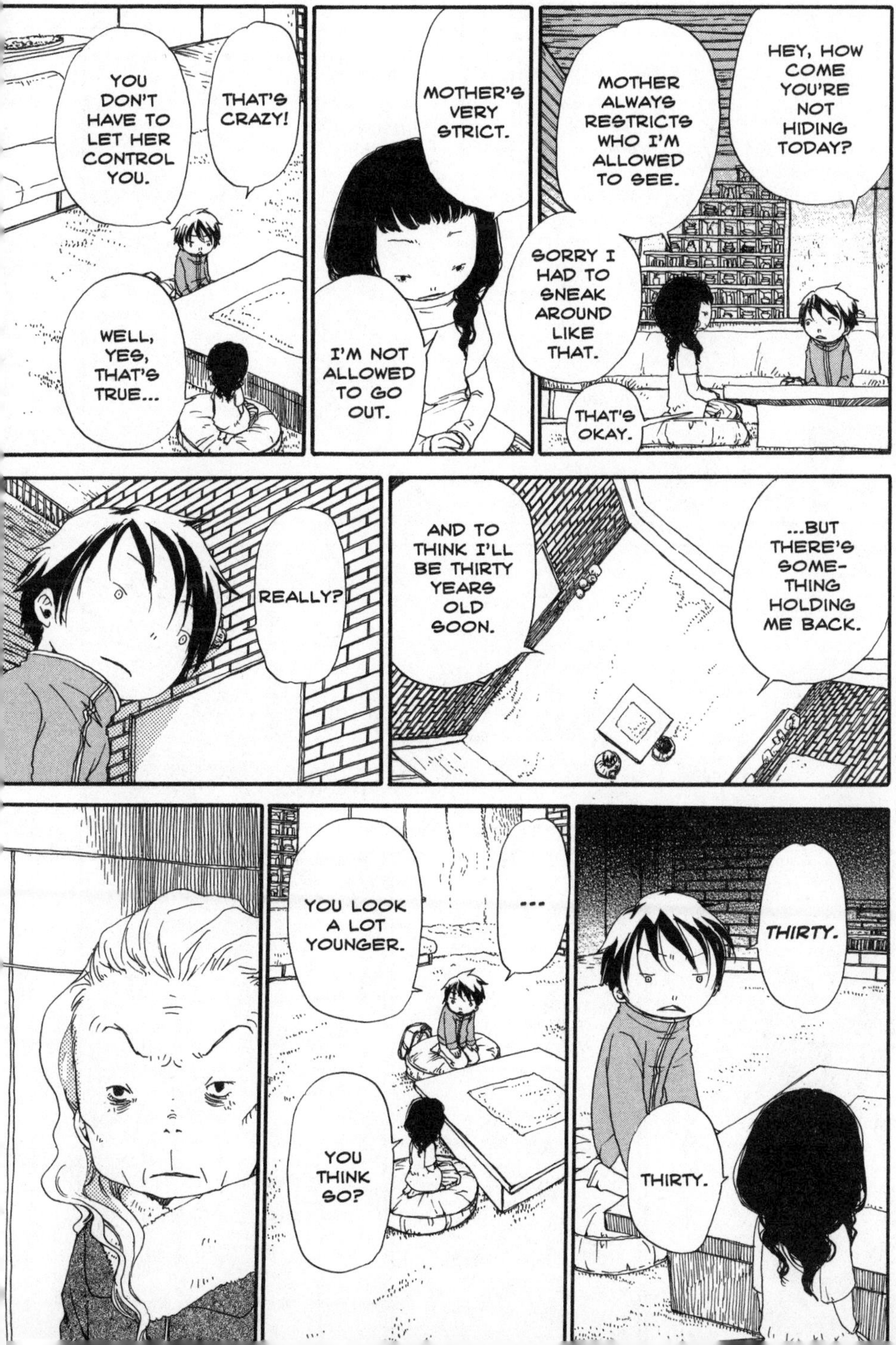
HEY, HOW COME YOU'RE NOT HIDING TODAY?
MOTHER ALWAYS RESTRICTS WHO I'M ALLOWED TO SEE.
SORRY I HAD TO SNEAK AROUND LIKE THAT.
THAT'S OKAY.
MOTHER'S VERY STRICT.
I'M NOT ALLOWED TO GO OUT.
THAT'S CRAZY!
YOU DON'T HAVE TO LET HER CONTROL YOU.
WELL, YES, THAT'S TRUE...
...BUT THERE'S SOME-THING HOLDING ME BACK.
AND TO THINK I'LL BE THIRTY YEARS OLD SOON.
REALLY?
THIRTY.
THIRTY.
...
YOU LOOK A LOT YOUNGER.
YOU THINK SO?

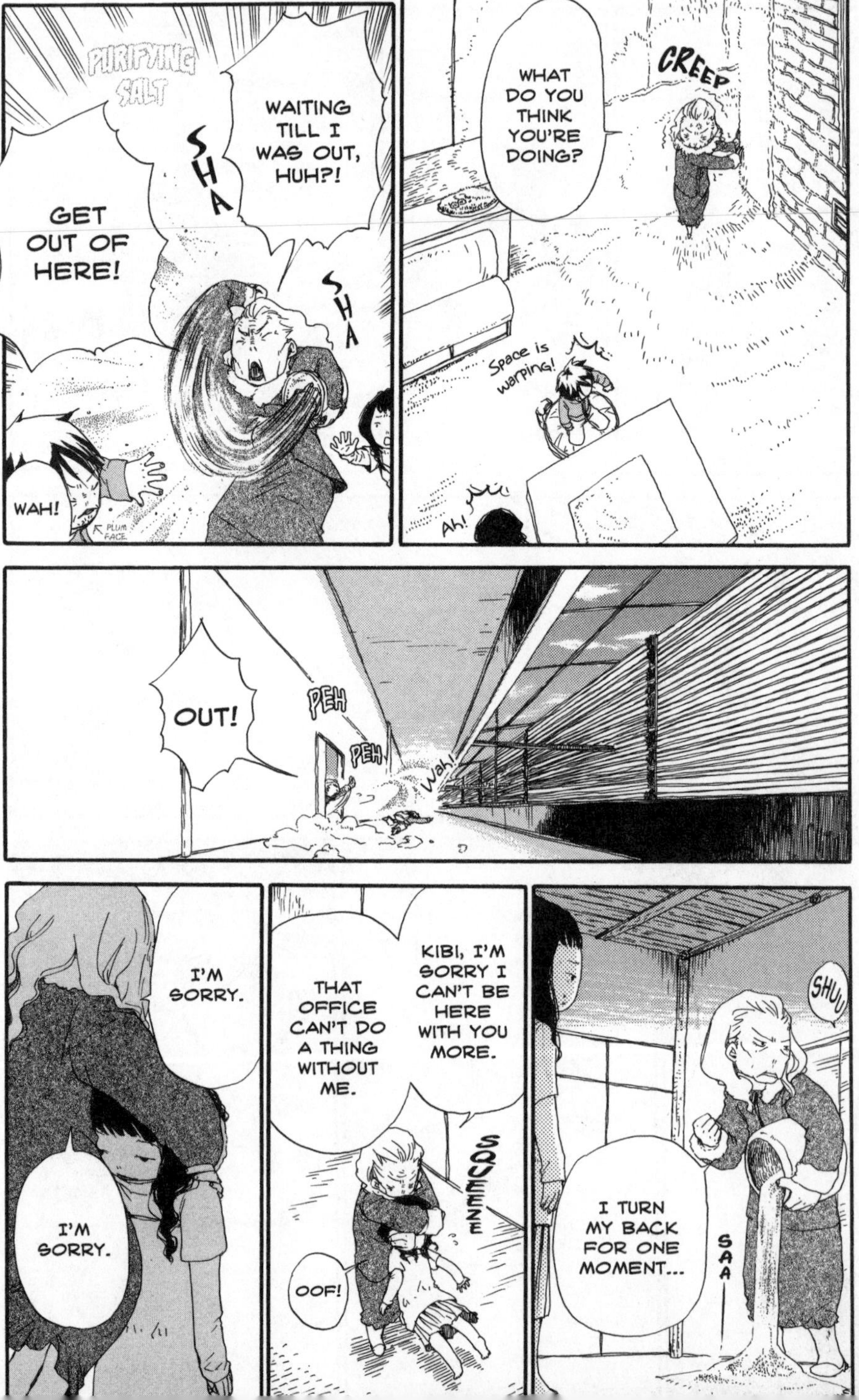
CREEP
WHAT DO YOU THINK YOU'RE DOING?
Space is warping!
Ah!
PURIFYING SALT
WAITING TILL I WAS OUT, HUH?!
SHA
GET OUT OF HERE!
SHA
WAH!
PLUM FACE
OUT!
PEH
PEH
Wah!
SHUU
I TURN MY BACK FOR ONE MOMENT...
SAA
KIBI, I'M SORRY I CAN'T BE HERE WITH YOU MORE.
THAT OFFICE CAN'T DO A THING WITHOUT ME.
SQUEEZE
OOF!
I'M SORRY.
I'M SORRY.

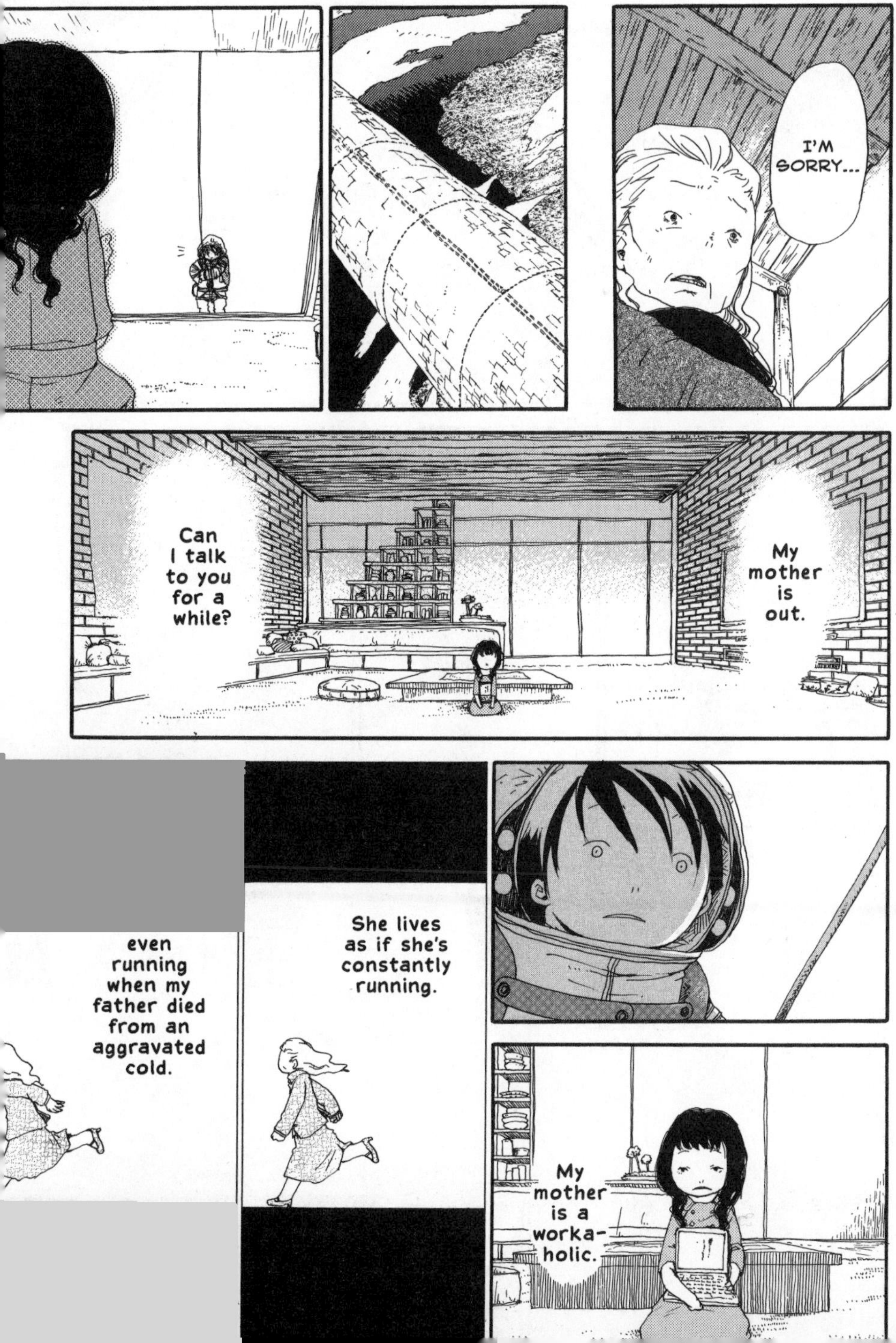
I'M SORRY...
My mother is out.
Can I talk to you for a while?
My mother is a workaholic.
She lives as if she's constantly running.
even running when my father died from an aggravated cold.

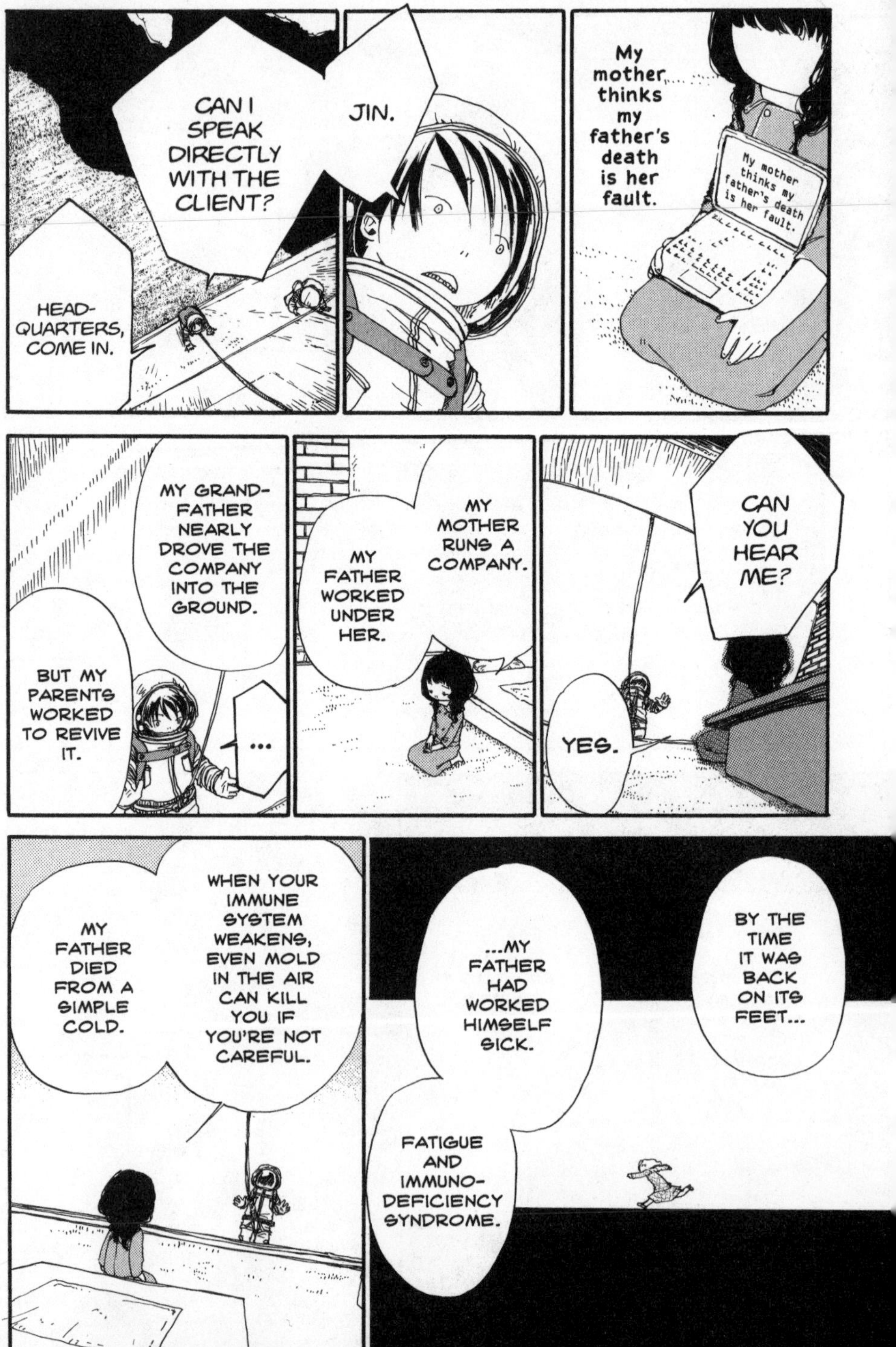

My mother thinks my father's death is her fault.
My mother thinks my father's death is her fault.
JIN.
CAN I SPEAK DIRECTLY WITH THE CLIENT?
HEAD-QUARTERS, COME IN.
CAN YOU HEAR ME?
YES.
MY MOTHER RUNS A COMPANY.
MY FATHER WORKED UNDER HER.
MY GRAND-FATHER NEARLY DROVE THE COMPANY INTO THE GROUND.
...
BUT MY PARENTS WORKED TO REVIVE IT.
BY THE TIME IT WAS BACK ON ITS FEET...
...MY FATHER HAD WORKED HIMSELF SICK.
FATIGUE AND IMMUNO-DEFICIENCY SYNDROME.
WHEN YOUR IMMUNE SYSTEM WEAKENS, EVEN MOLD IN THE AIR CAN KILL YOU IF YOU'RE NOT CAREFUL.
MY FATHER DIED FROM A SIMPLE COLD.

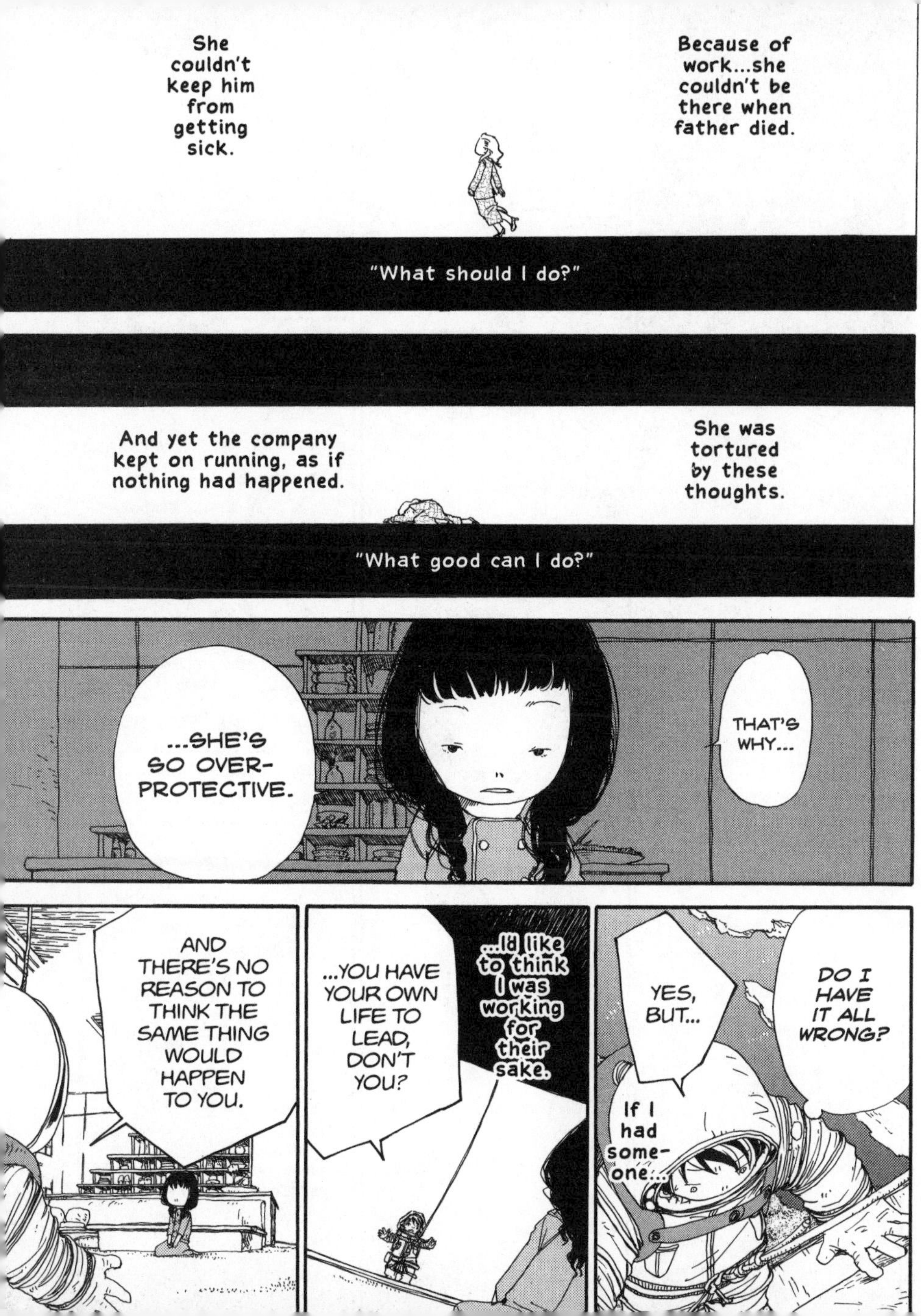
Because of work...she couldn't be there when father died.
She couldn't keep him from getting sick.
"What should I do?"
She was tortured by these thoughts.
And yet the company kept on running, as if nothing had happened.
"What good can I do?"
THAT'S WHY...
...SHE'S SO OVER-PROTECTIVE.
DO I HAVE IT ALL WRONG?
YES, BUT...
If I had some-one...
...I'd like to think I was working for their sake.
...YOU HAVE YOUR OWN LIFE TO LEAD, DON'T YOU?
AND THERE'S NO REASON TO THINK THE SAME THING WOULD HAPPEN TO YOU.

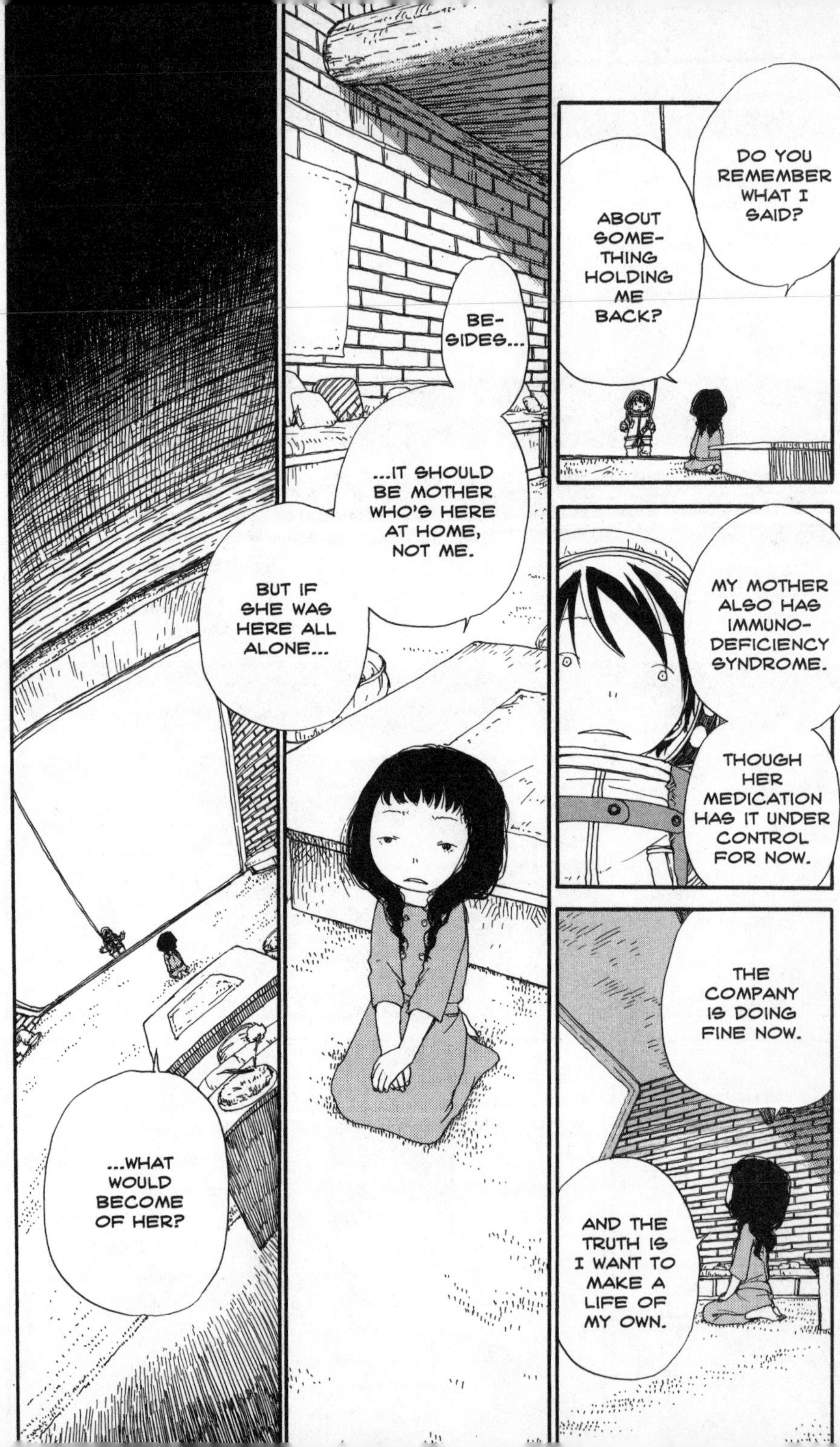
DO YOU REMEMBER WHAT I SAID?
ABOUT SOME-THING HOLDING ME BACK?
MY MOTHER ALSO HAS IMMUNO-DEFICIENCY SYNDROME.
THOUGH HER MEDICATION HAS IT UNDER CONTROL FOR NOW.
THE COMPANY IS DOING FINE NOW.
AND THE TRUTH IS I WANT TO MAKE A LIFE OF MY OWN.
BE-SIDES...
...IT SHOULD BE MOTHER WHO'S HERE AT HOME, NOT ME.
BUT IF SHE WAS HERE ALL ALONE...
...WHAT WOULD BECOME OF HER?

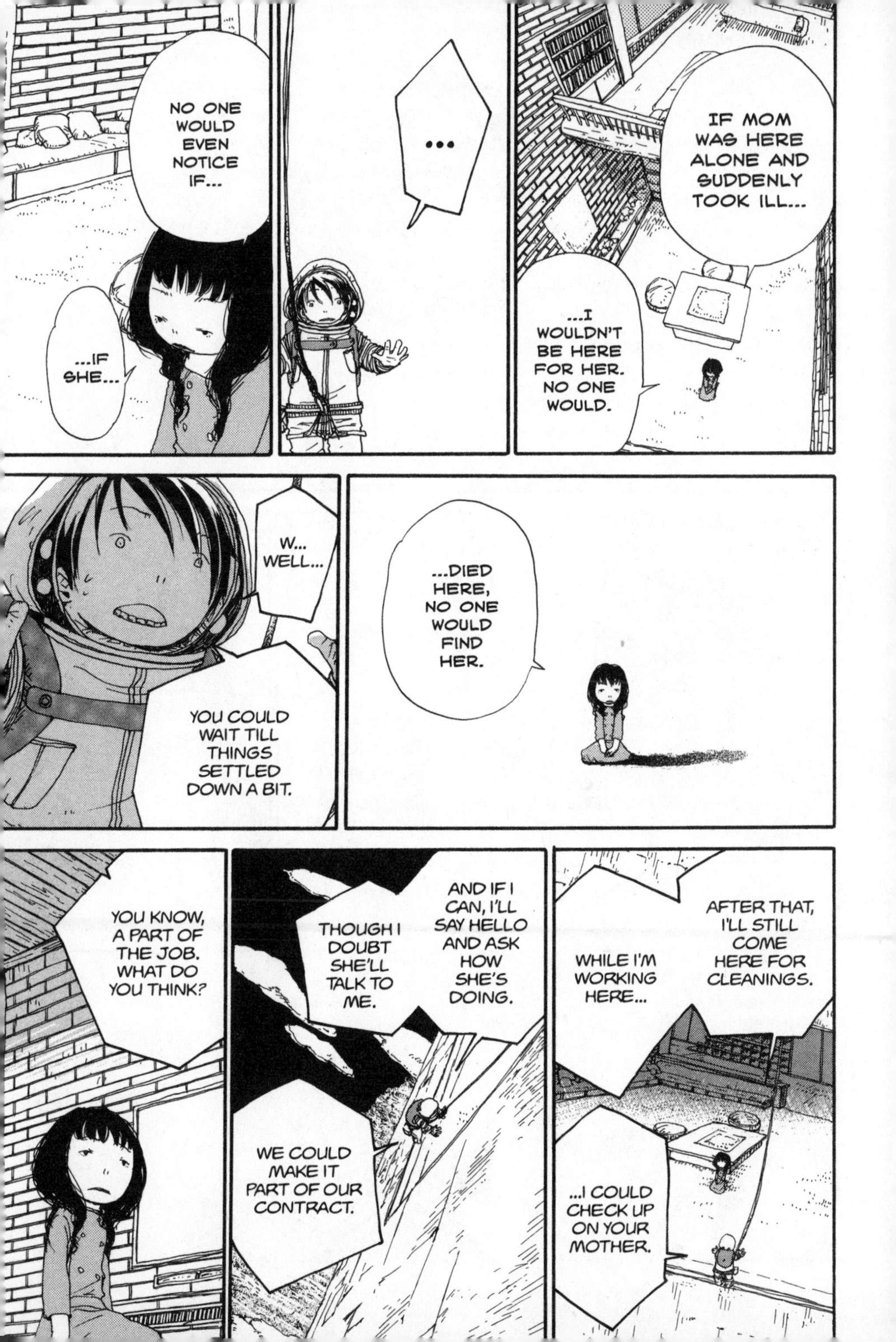
IF MOM WAS HERE ALONE AND SUDDENLY TOOK ILL...
...I WOULDN'T BE HERE FOR HER. NO ONE WOULD.
...
NO ONE WOULD EVEN NOTICE IF...
...IF SHE...
...DIED HERE, NO ONE WOULD FIND HER.
W... WELL...
YOU COULD WAIT TILL THINGS SETTLED DOWN A BIT.
AFTER THAT, I'LL STILL COME HERE FOR CLEANINGS.
WHILE I'M WORKING HERE...
...I COULD CHECK UP ON YOUR MOTHER.
AND IF I CAN, I'LL SAY HELLO AND ASK HOW SHE'S DOING.
THOUGH I DOUBT SHE'LL TALK TO ME.
WE COULD MAKE IT PART OF OUR CONTRACT.
YOU KNOW, A PART OF THE JOB. WHAT DO YOU THINK?

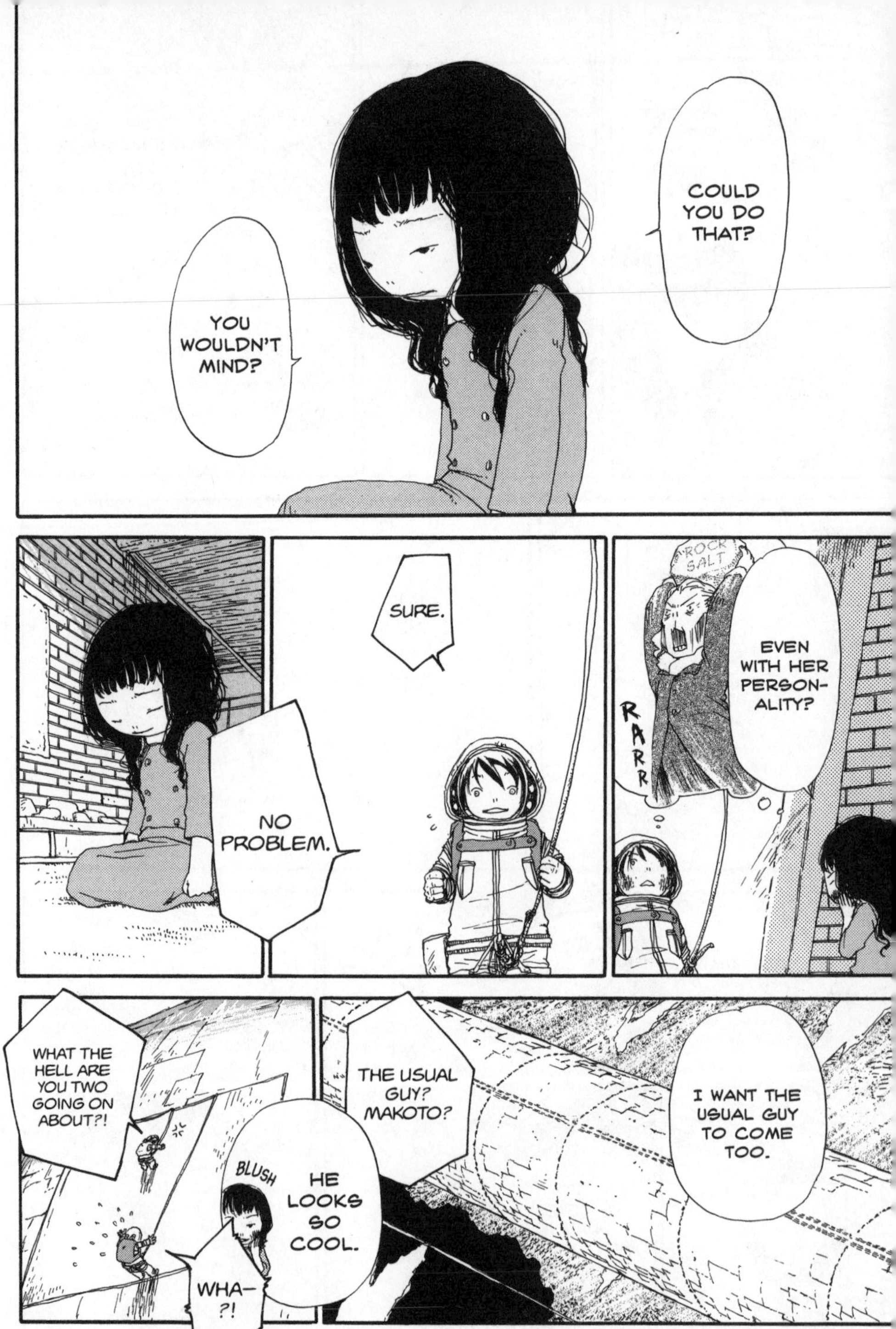
COULD YOU DO THAT?
YOU WOULDN'T MIND?
ROCK SALT
EVEN WITH HER PERSONALITY?
RARR
SURE.
NO PROBLEM.
I WANT THE USUAL GUY TO COME TOO.
THE USUAL GUY? MAKOTO?
BLUSH
HE LOOKS SO COOL.
WHA- ?!
WHAT THE HELL ARE YOU TWO GOING ON ABOUT?!

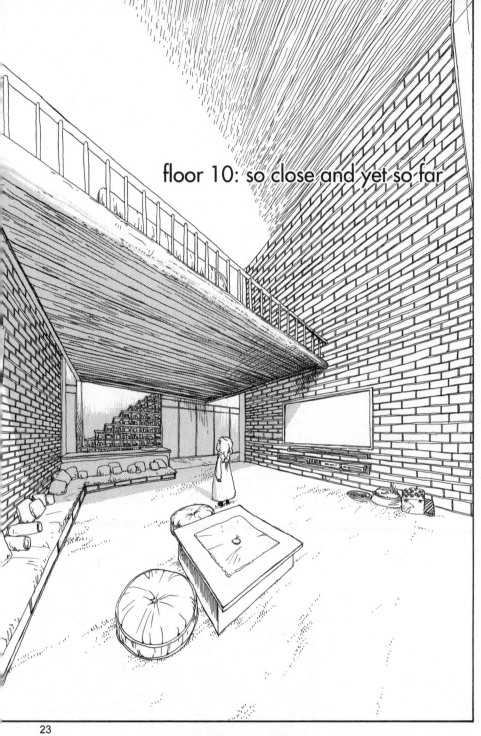

floor 10: so close and yet so far

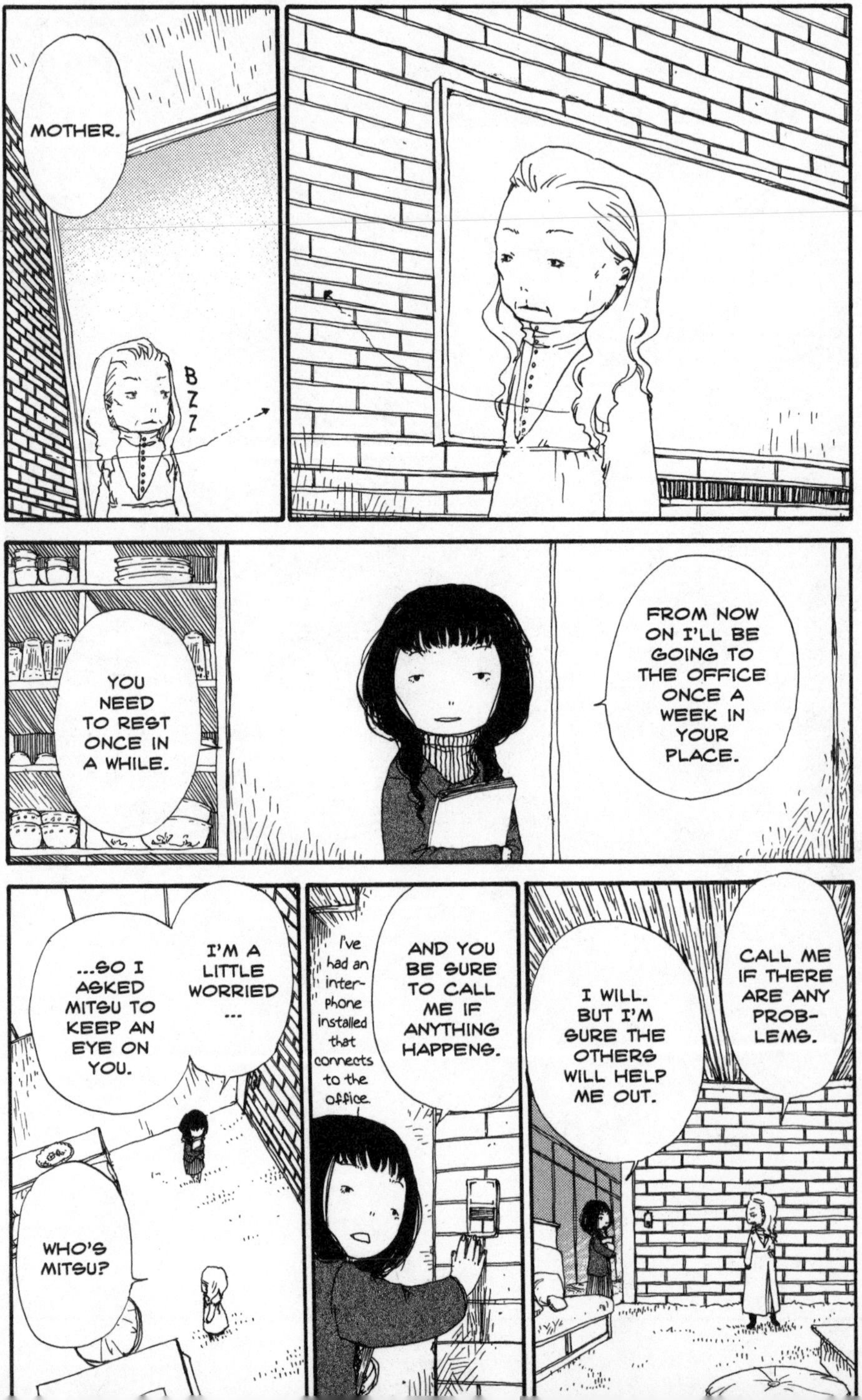
MOTHER.
BZZ
FROM NOW ON I'LL BE GOING TO THE OFFICE ONCE A WEEK IN YOUR PLACE.
YOU NEED TO REST ONCE IN A WHILE.
CALL ME IF THERE ARE ANY PROB-LEMS.
I WILL. BUT I'M SURE THE OTHERS WILL HELP ME OUT.
AND YOU BE SURE TO CALL ME IF ANYTHING HAPPENS.
I've had an inter-phone installed that connects to the office.
I'M A LITTLE WORRIED ...
...SO I ASKED MITSU TO KEEP AN EYE ON YOU.
WHO'S MITSU?

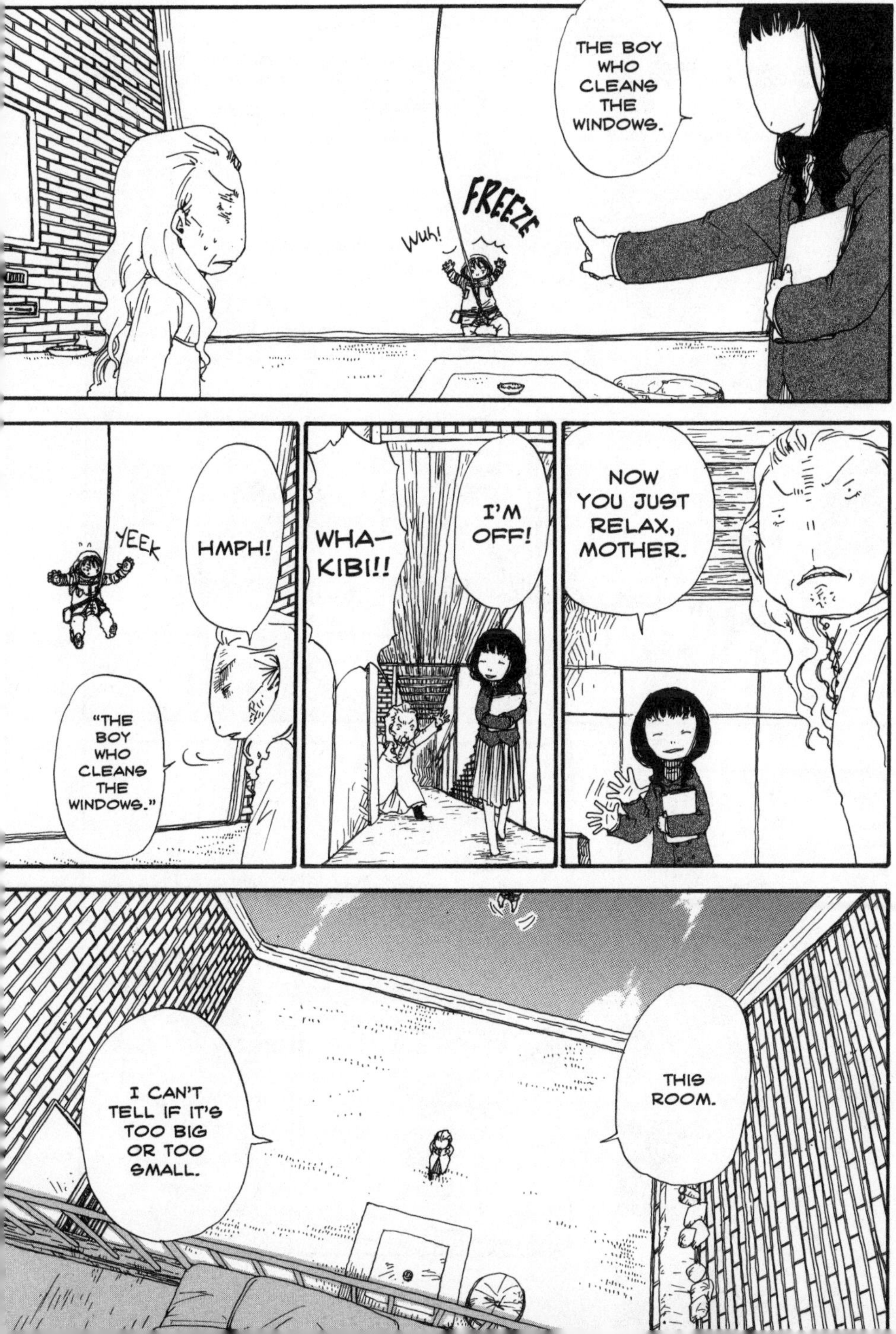
THE BOY WHO CLEANS THE WINDOWS.
FREEZE
WUH!
NOW YOU JUST RELAX, MOTHER.
I'M OFF!
WHA- KIBI!!
HMPH!
YEEK
"THE BOY WHO CLEANS THE WINDOWS."
THIS ROOM.
I CAN'T TELL IF IT'S TOO BIG OR TOO SMALL.

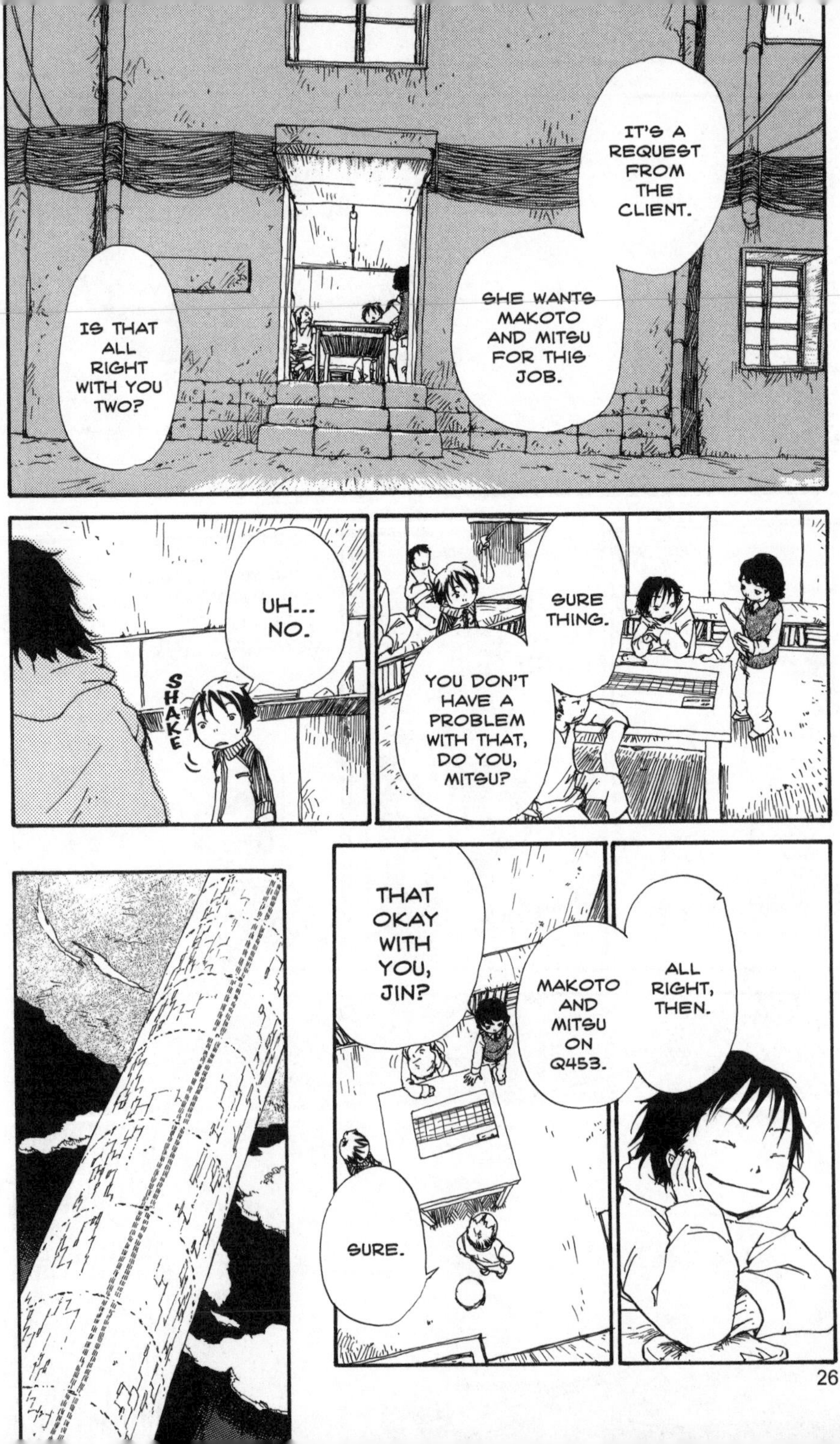
IT'S A REQUEST FROM THE CLIENT.
SHE WANTS MAKOTO AND MITSU FOR THIS JOB.
IS THAT ALL RIGHT WITH YOU TWO?
SURE THING.
YOU DON'T HAVE A PROBLEM WITH THAT, DO YOU, MITSU?
UH... NO.
SHAKE
ALL RIGHT, THEN.
MAKOTO AND MITSU ON Q453.
THAT OKAY WITH YOU, JIN?
SURE.

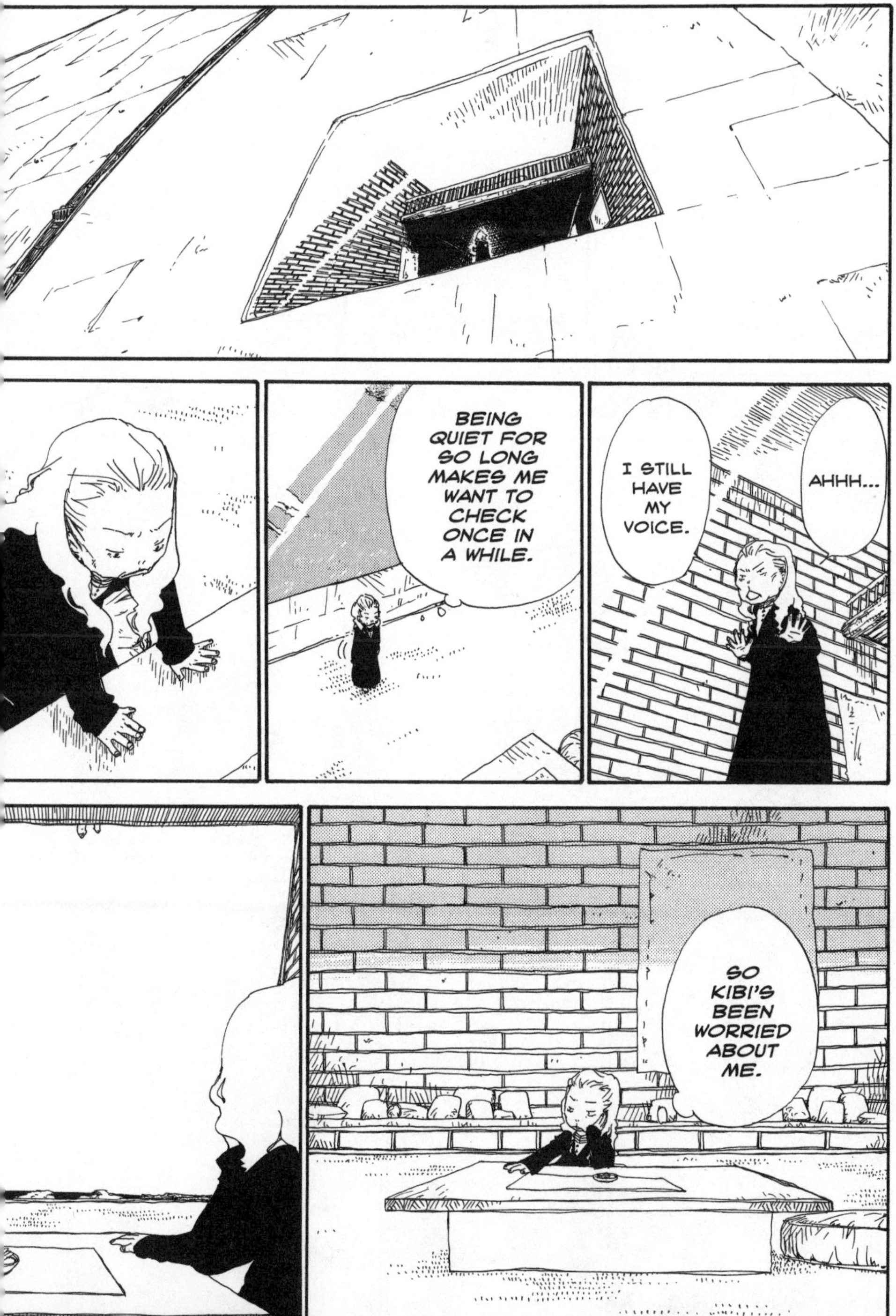
AHHH...
I STILL HAVE MY VOICE.
BEING QUIET FOR SO LONG MAKES ME WANT TO CHECK ONCE IN A WHILE.
SO KIBI'S BEEN WORRIED ABOUT ME.

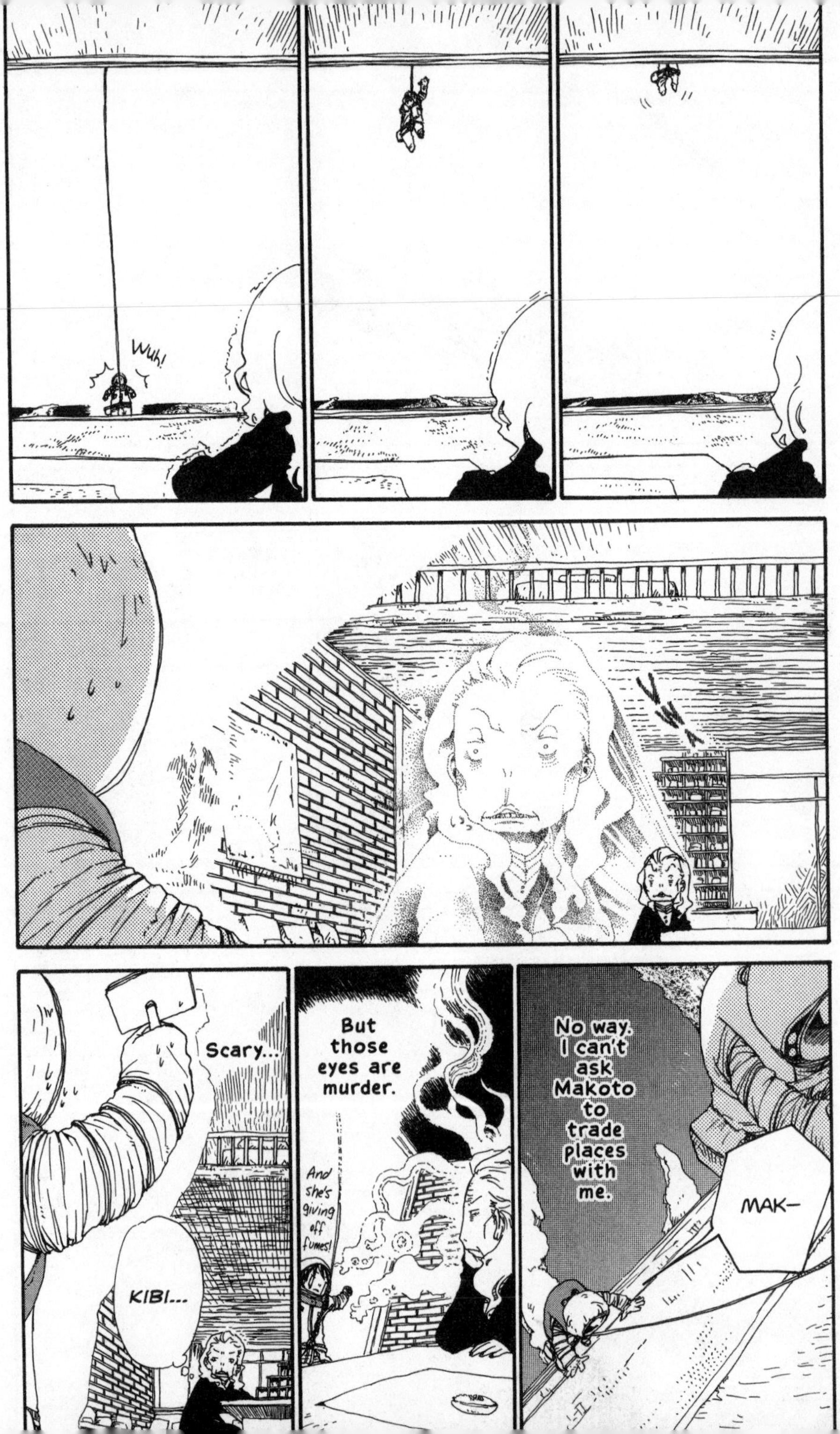
Wuh!
No way. I can't ask Makoto to trade places with me.
MAK—
But those eyes are murder.
And she's giving off fumes!
Scary...
KIBI...

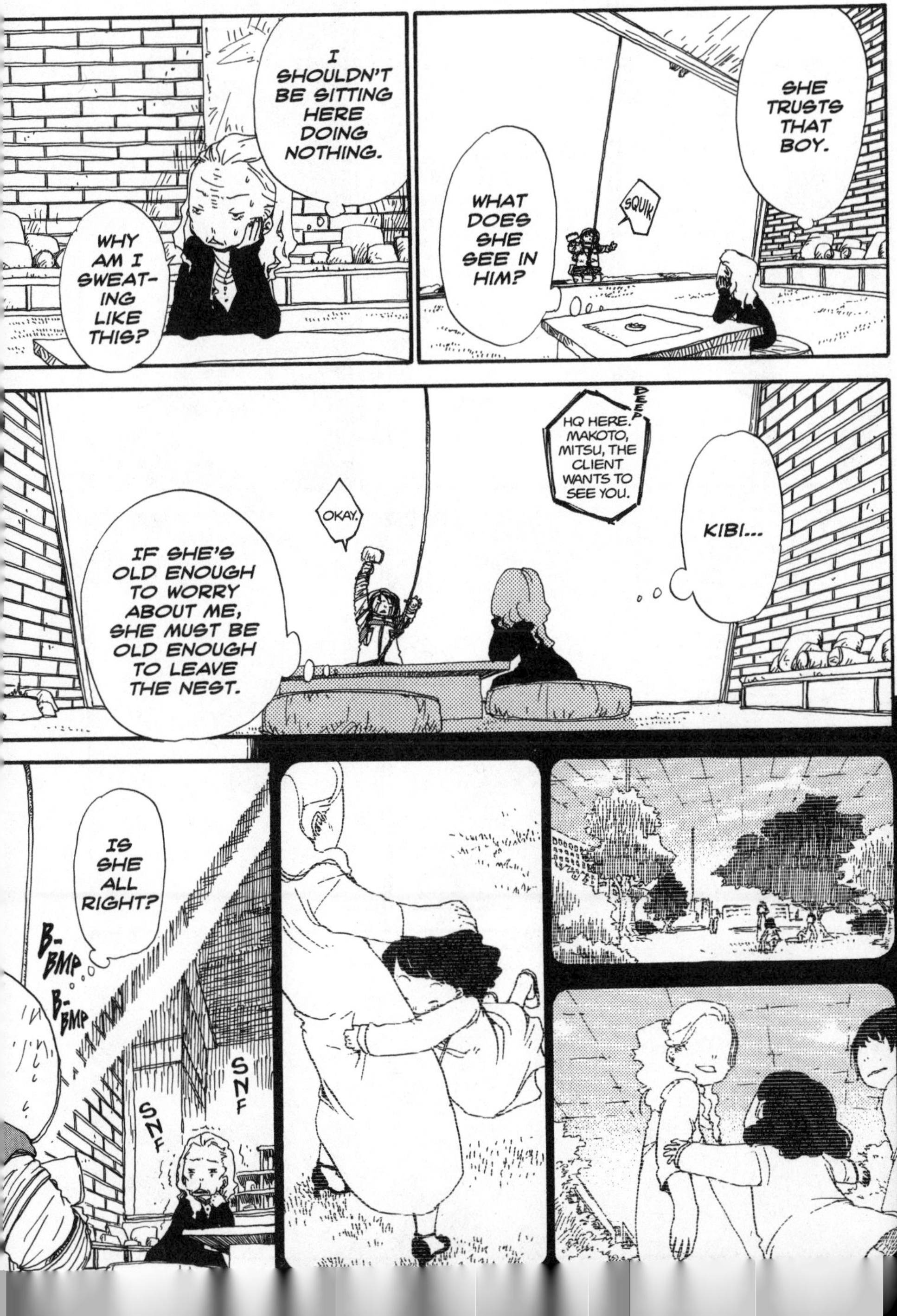
SHE TRUSTS THAT BOY.
SQUIK
WHAT DOES SHE SEE IN HIM?
I SHOULDN'T BE SITTING HERE DOING NOTHING.
WHY AM I SWEAT-ING LIKE THIS?
BEEP
HQ HERE. MAKOTO, MITSU, THE CLIENT WANTS TO SEE YOU.
KIBI...
OKAY.
IF SHE'S OLD ENOUGH TO WORRY ABOUT ME, SHE MUST BE OLD ENOUGH TO LEAVE THE NEST.
IS SHE ALL RIGHT?
B-BMP
B-BMP
SNF
SNF

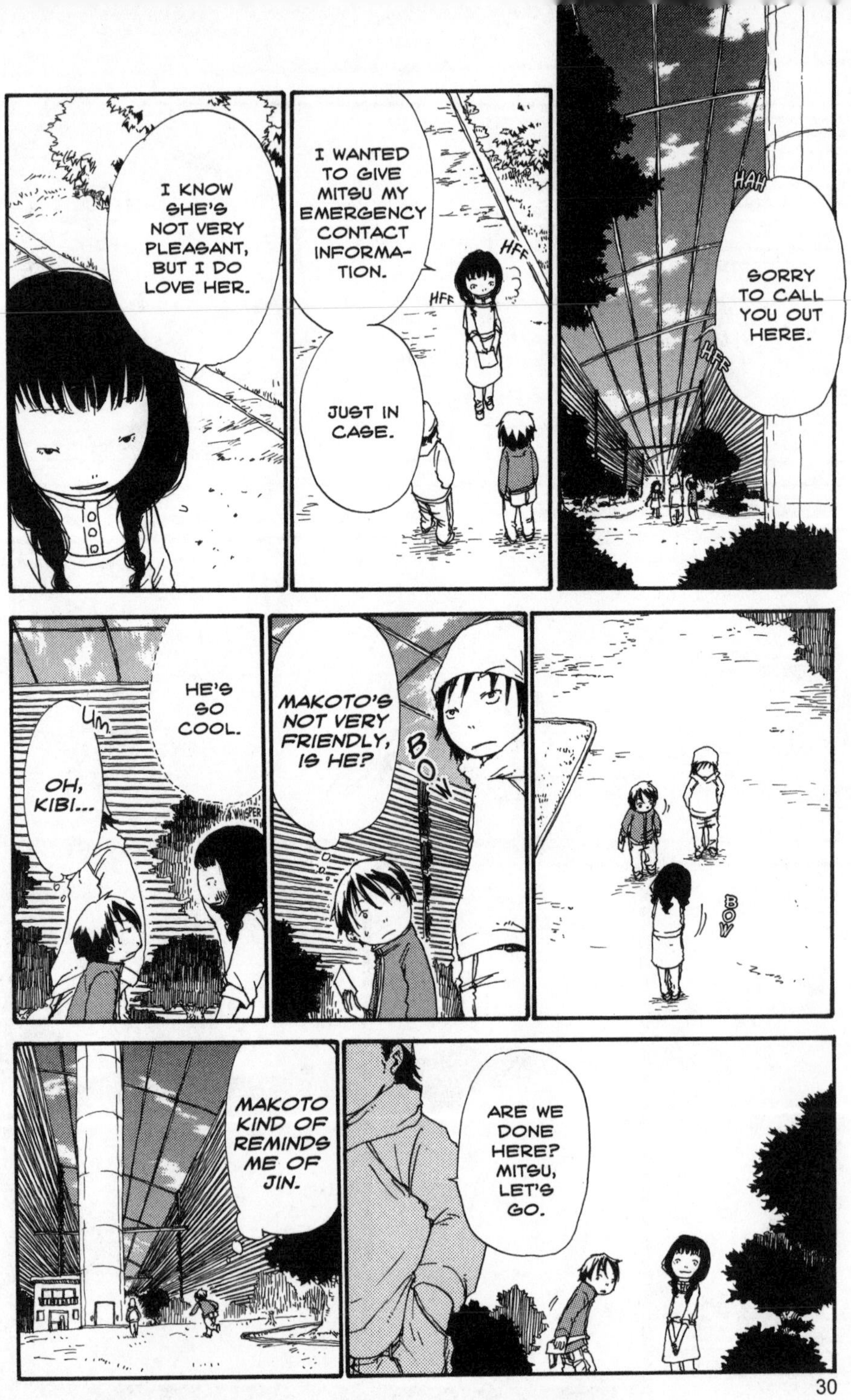
HAH
SORRY TO CALL YOU OUT HERE.
HFF
I WANTED TO GIVE MITSU MY EMERGENCY CONTACT INFORMATION.
JUST IN CASE.
HFF
HFF
I KNOW SHE'S NOT VERY PLEASANT, BUT I DO LOVE HER.
BOW
MAKOTO'S NOT VERY FRIENDLY, IS HE?
BOW
HE'S SO COOL.
Um.
OH, KIBI...
WHISPER
ARE WE DONE HERE? MITSU, LET'S GO.
MAKOTO KIND OF REMINDS ME OF JIN.

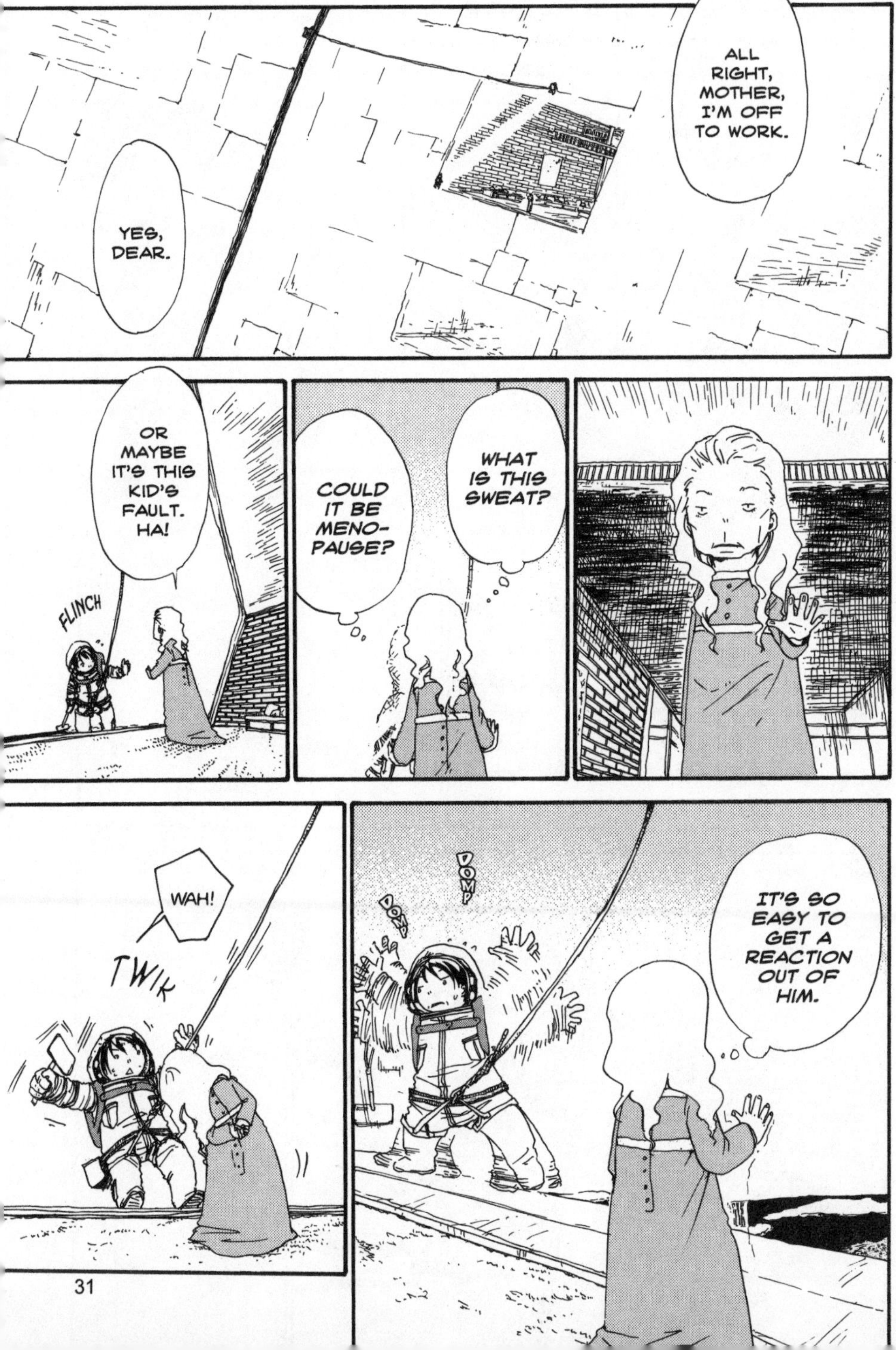
ALL RIGHT, MOTHER, I'M OFF TO WORK.
YES, DEAR.
WHAT IS THIS SWEAT?
COULD IT BE MENOPAUSE?
OR MAYBE IT'S THIS KID'S FAULT. HA!
FLINCH
IT'S SO EASY TO GET A REACTION OUT OF HIM.
DOMP
DOMP
WAH!
TWIK

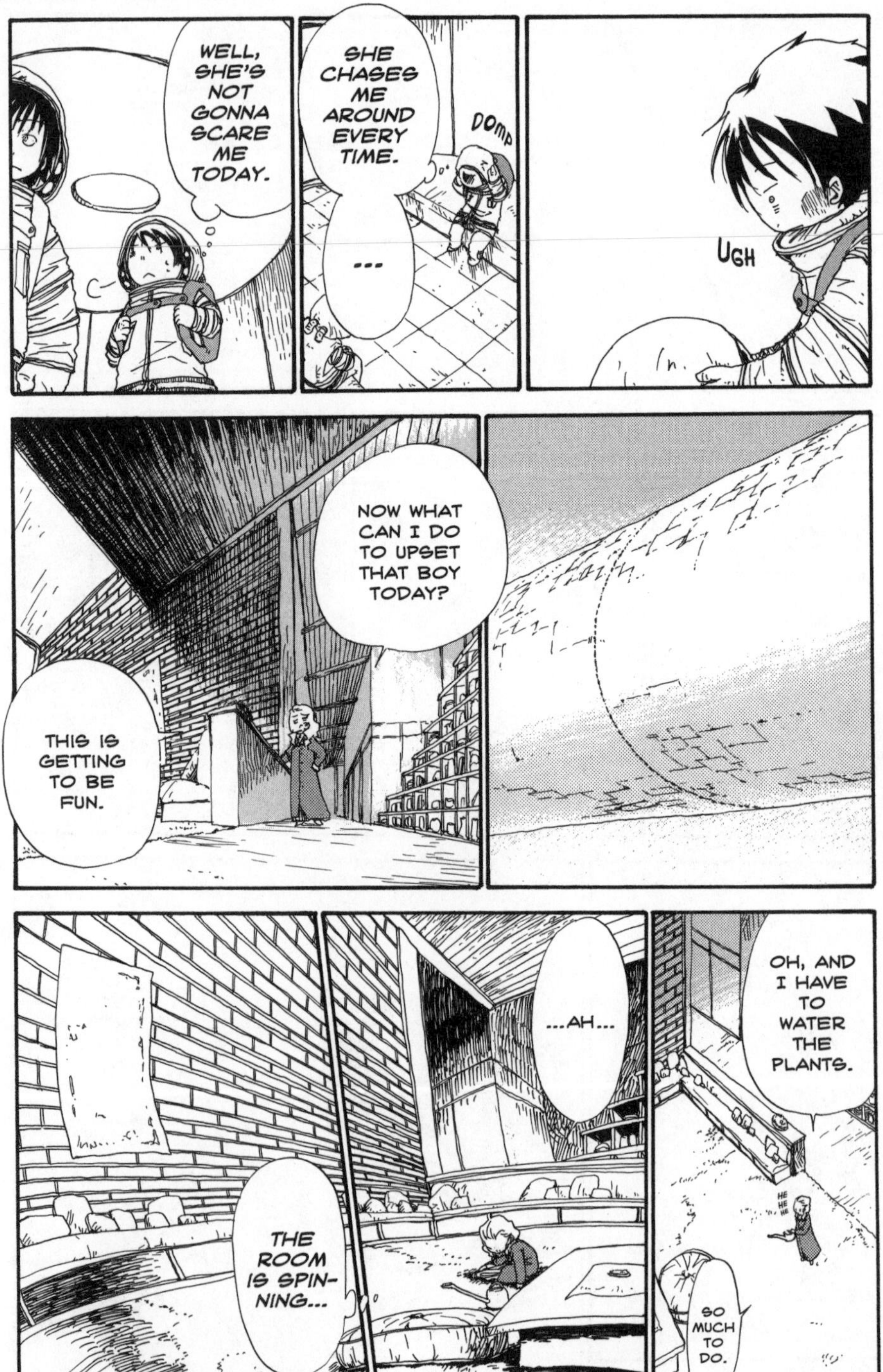
UGH
SHE CHASES ME AROUND EVERY TIME.
DOMP
...
WELL, SHE'S NOT GONNA SCARE ME TODAY.
NOW WHAT CAN I DO TO UPSET THAT BOY TODAY?
THIS IS GETTING TO BE FUN.
OH, AND I HAVE TO WATER THE PLANTS.
HE HE HE
SO MUCH TO DO.
...AH...
THE ROOM IS SPINNING...

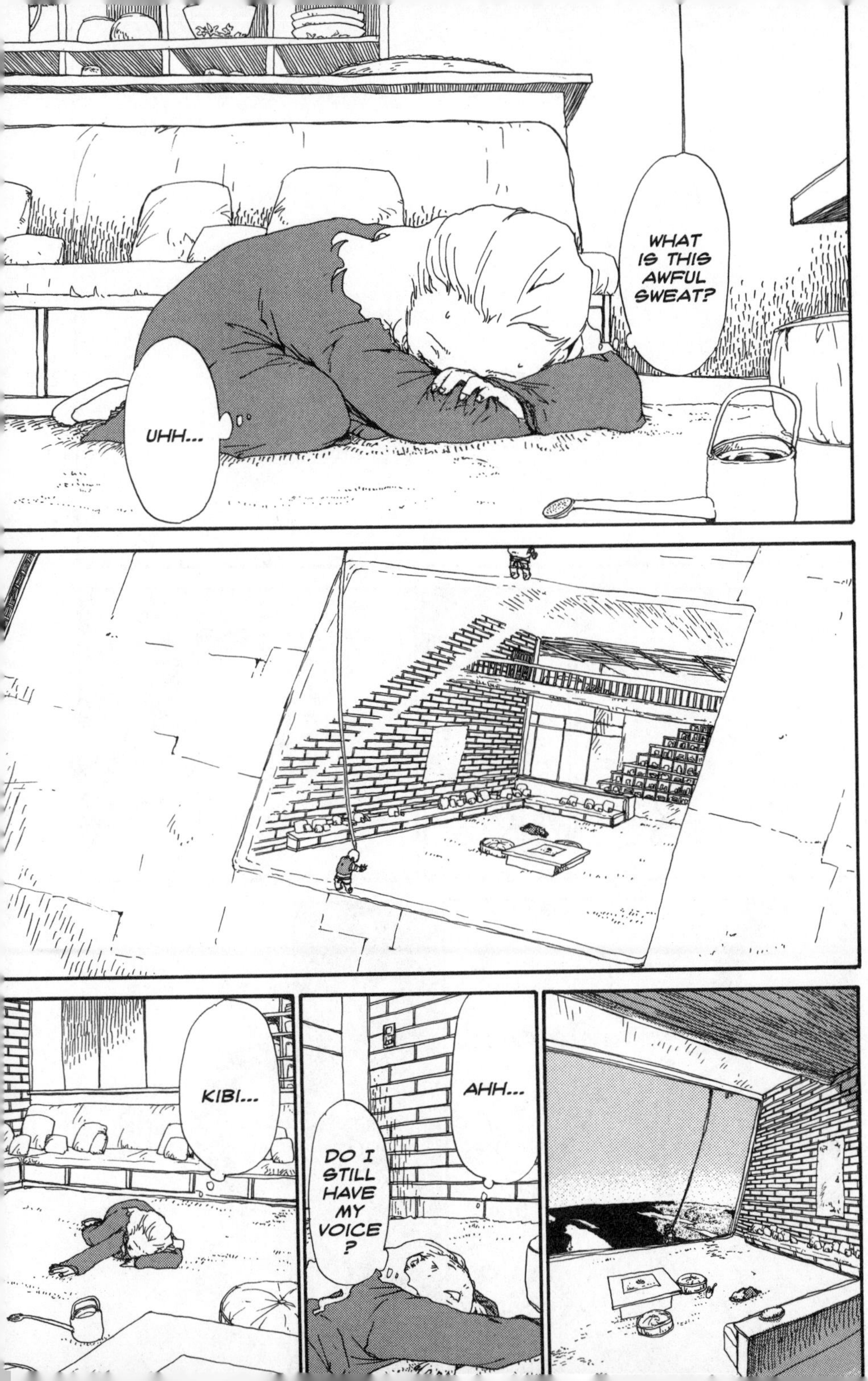
WHAT IS THIS AWFUL SWEAT?
UHH...
AHH...
DO I STILL HAVE MY VOICE?
KIBI...

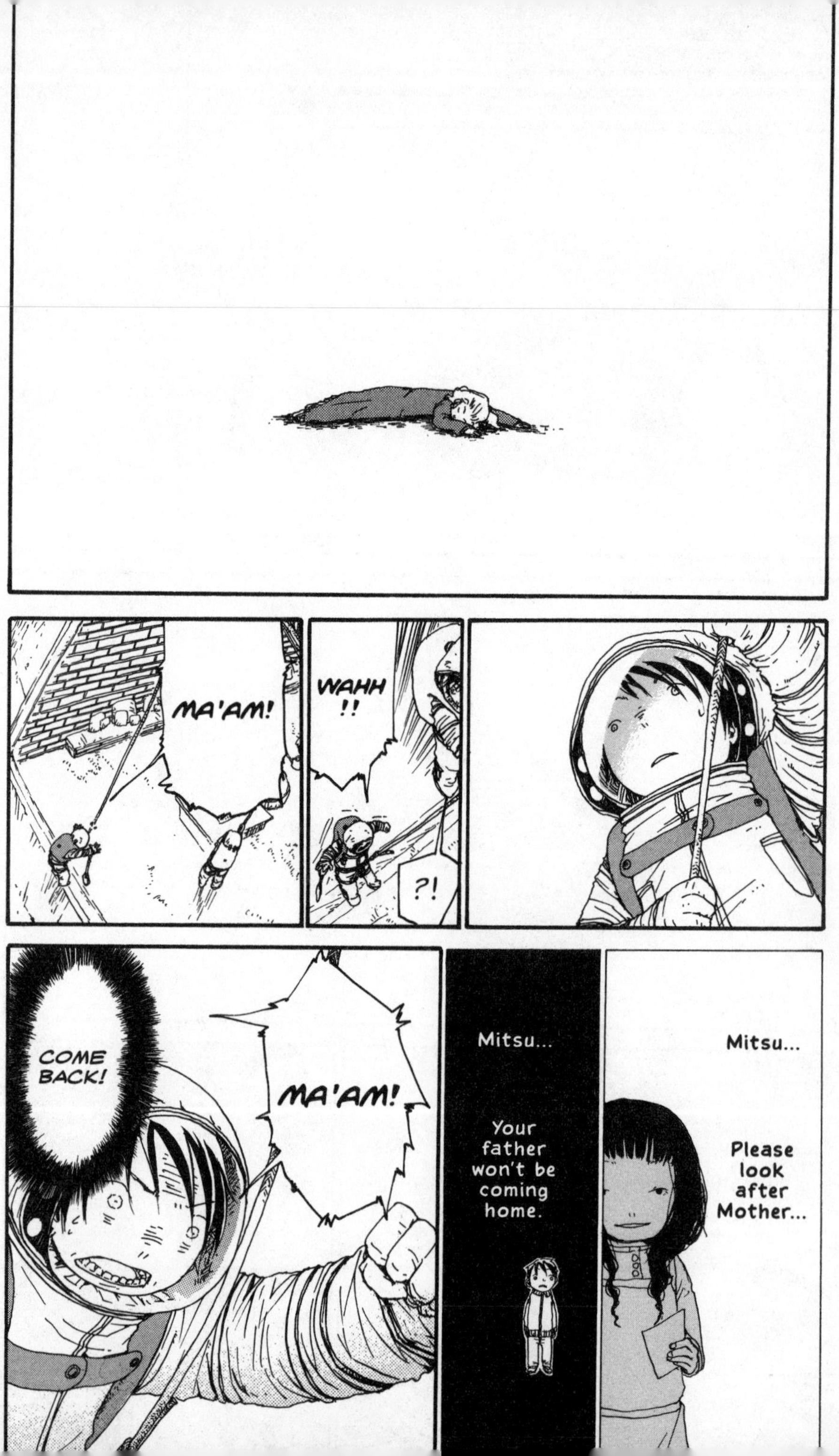
WAHH !!
?!
MA'AM!
Mitsu...
Please look after Mother...
Mitsu...
Your father won't be coming home.
MA'AM!
COME BACK!

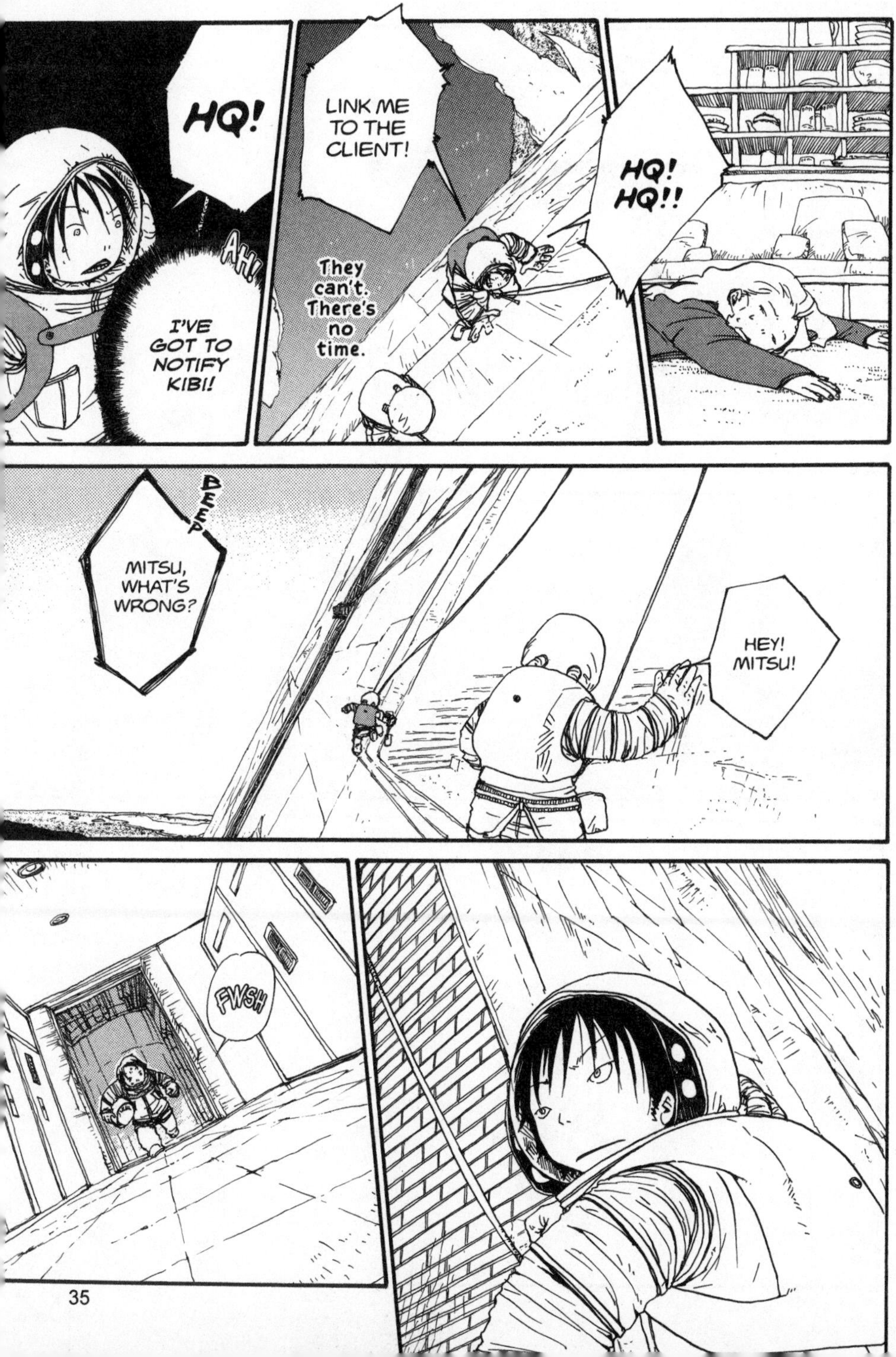
HQ! HQ!!
LINK ME TO THE CLIENT!
They can't. There's no time.
HQ!
AH!
I'VE GOT TO NOTIFY KIBI!!
HEY! MITSU!
BEEEP
MITSU, WHAT'S WRONG?
FWSH

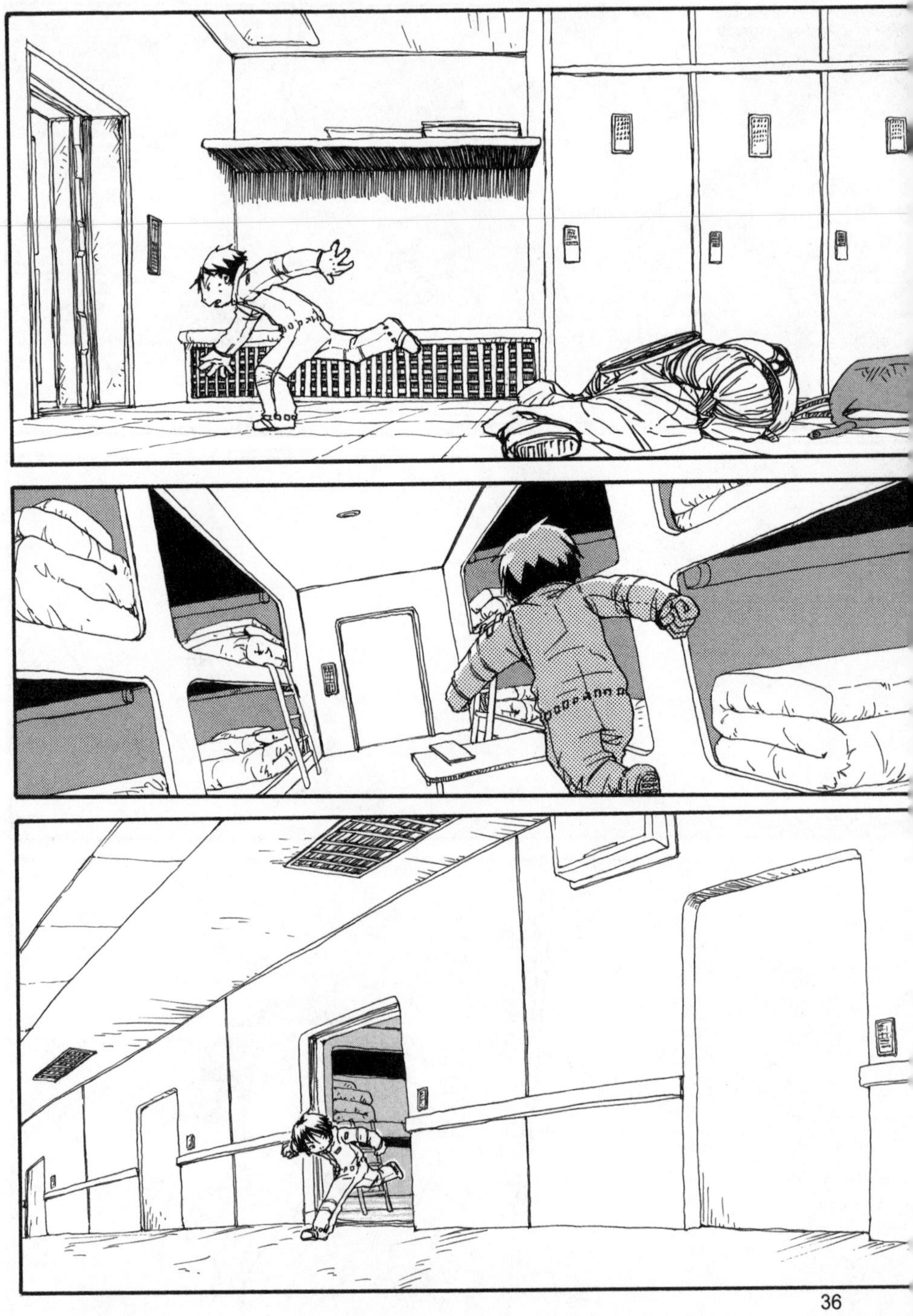

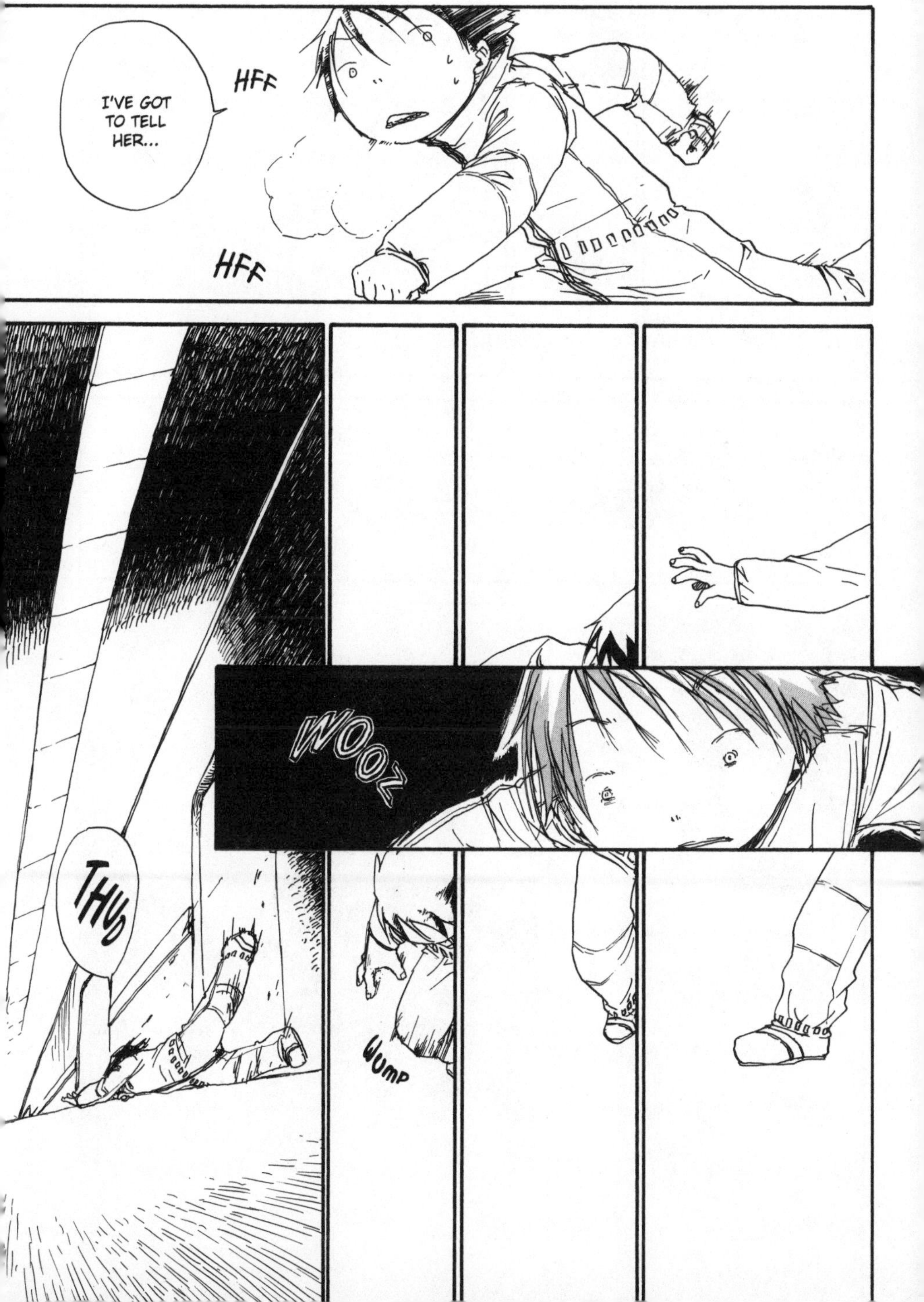
HFF
I'VE GOT TO TELL HER...
HFF
WOOZ
WUMP
THUD

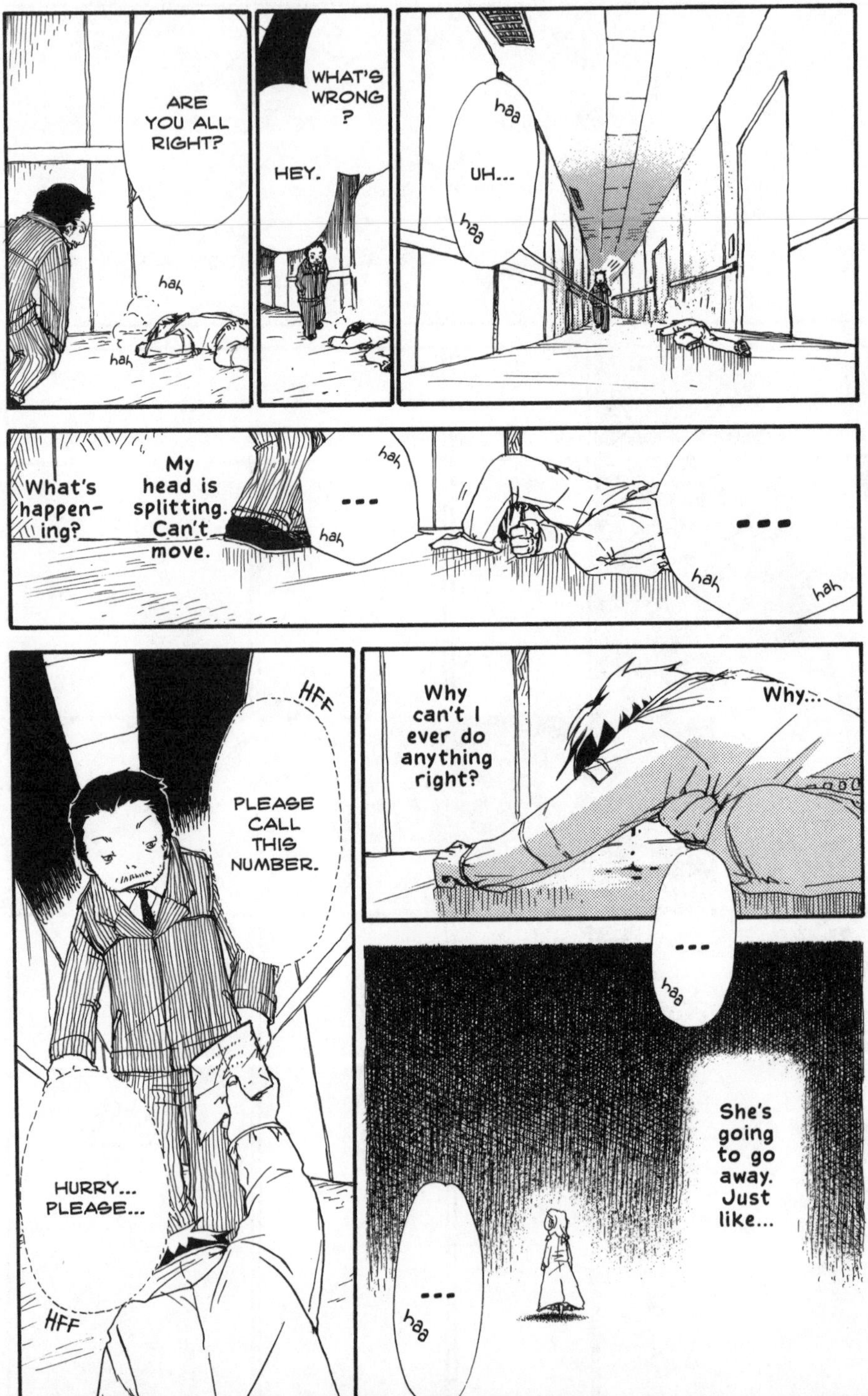
haa
UH...
haa
WHAT'S WRONG?
HEY.
ARE YOU ALL RIGHT?
hah
hah
...
hah
hah
hah
...
hah
My head is splitting. Can't move.
What's happening?
Why...
Why can't I ever do anything right?
...
haa
She's going to go away. Just like...
...
haa
HFF
PLEASE CALL THIS NUMBER.
HURRY... PLEASE...
HFF

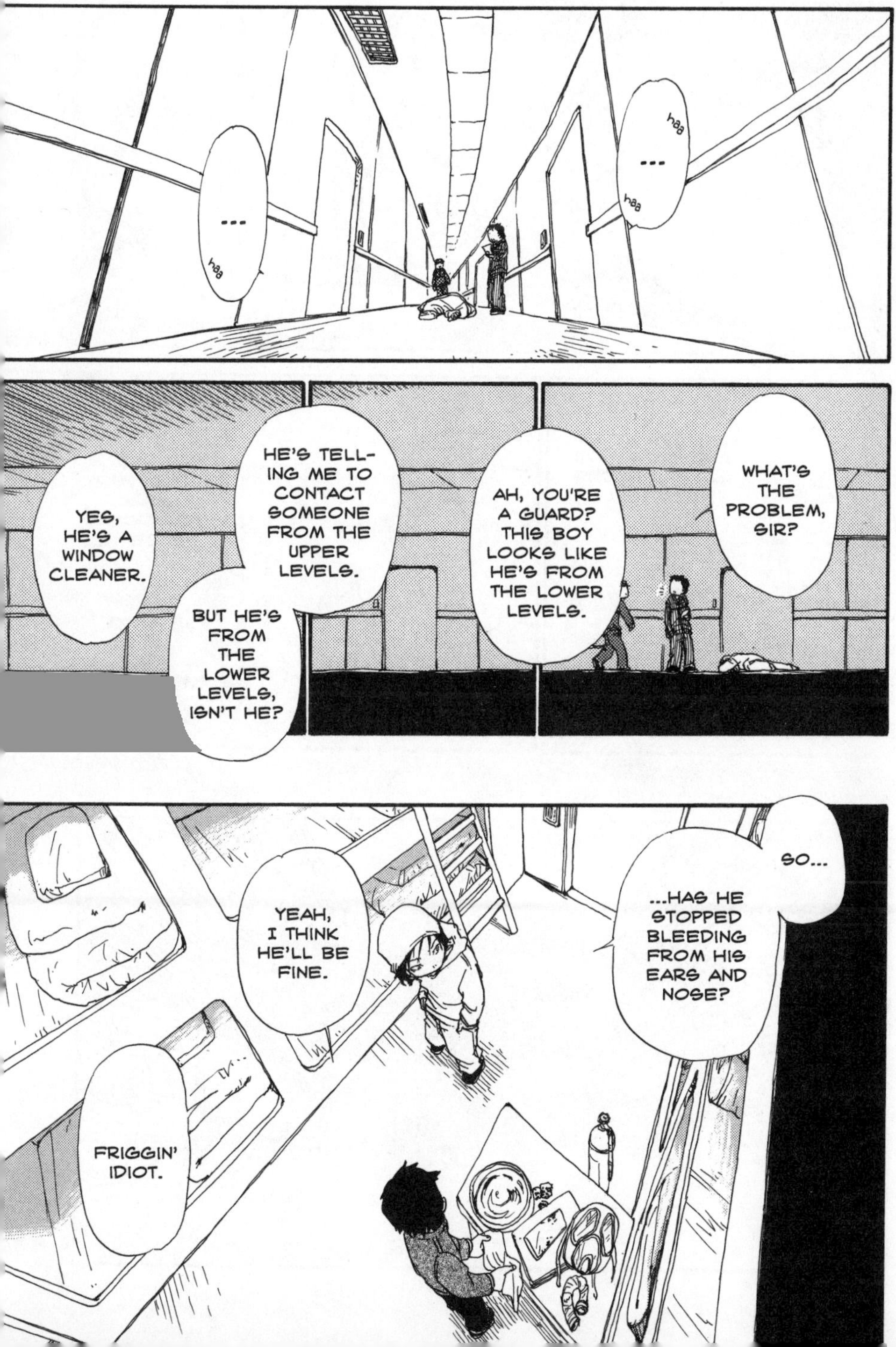
haa --- haa
--- haa
WHAT'S THE PROBLEM, SIR?
AH, YOU'RE A GUARD? THIS BOY LOOKS LIKE HE'S FROM THE LOWER LEVELS.
HE'S TELLING ME TO CONTACT SOMEONE FROM THE UPPER LEVELS.
BUT HE'S FROM THE LOWER LEVELS, ISN'T HE?
YES, HE'S A WINDOW CLEANER.
SO...
...HAS HE STOPPED BLEEDING FROM HIS EARS AND NOSE?
YEAH, I THINK HE'LL BE FINE.
FRIGGIN' IDIOT.

WHAT THE HELL WAS HE THINKING?
WHAT KIND OF WINDOW CLEANER FORGETS ABOUT DEPRESSUR-IZATION?
SHARP EAR PAIN, NOSE BLEED—ALL CLASSIC SIGNS OF DECOM-PRESSION SICKNESS.
HE DROPPED WORK, ABANDONED HIS GEAR...
COME ON, MAKOTO.
HE CAN'T EVEN HANDLE THE BASICS.
WHERE WOULD HE BE IF THAT GUARD HADN'T ALERTED US?
QUIET, MAKOTO. YOU'LL WAKE HIM UP.

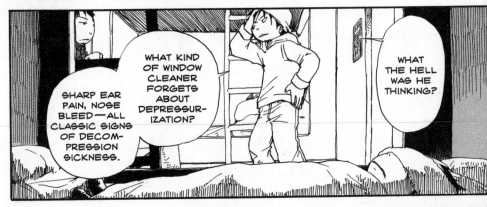

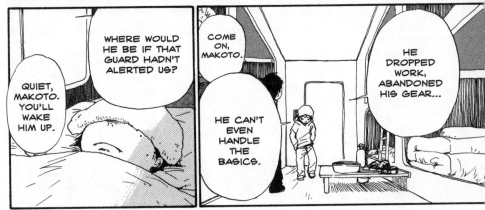

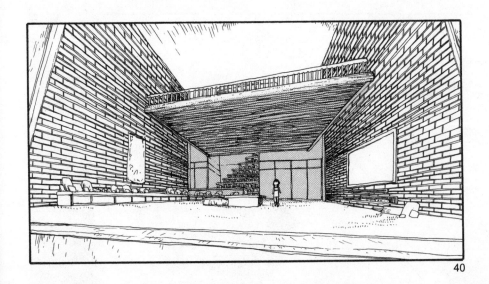

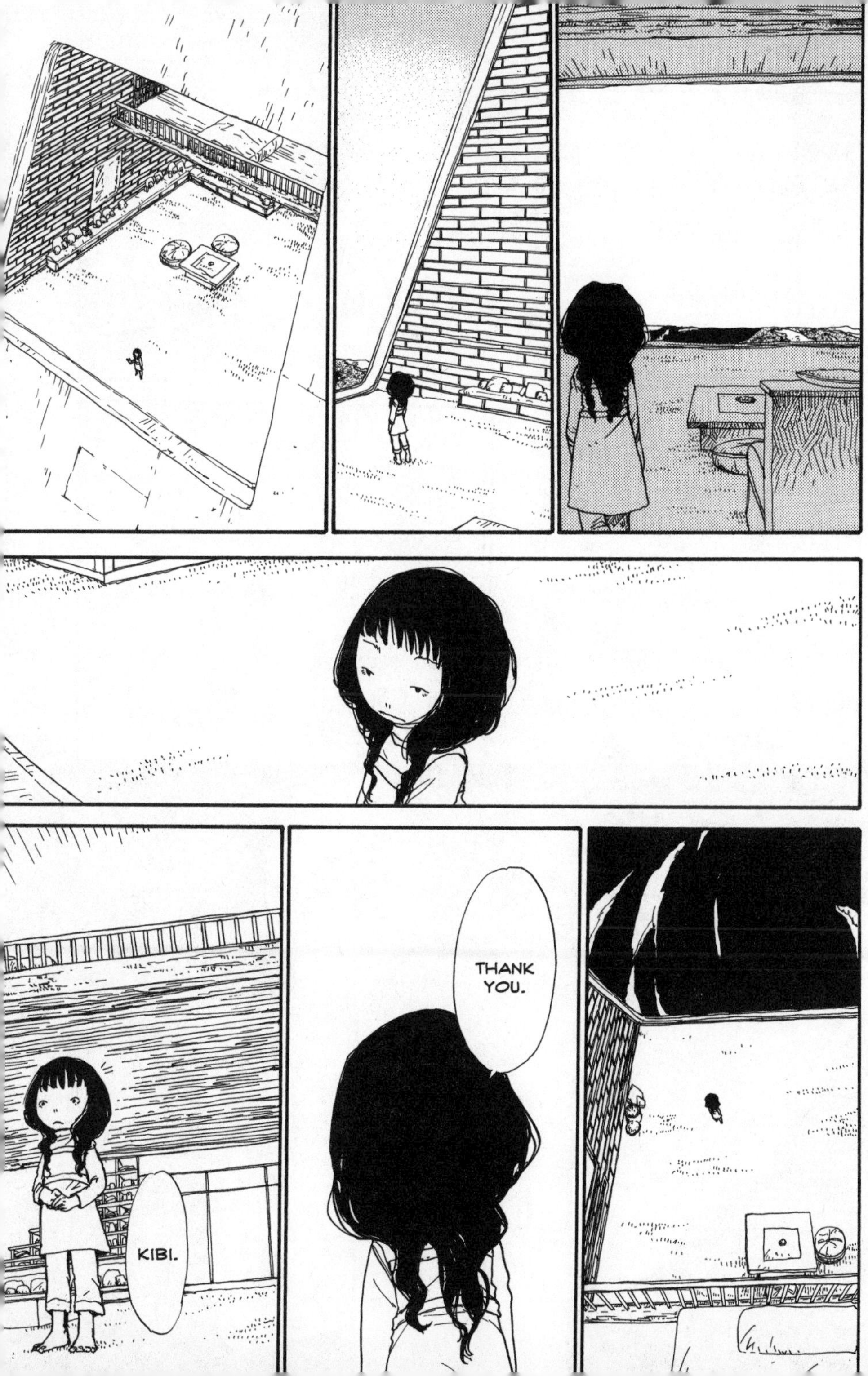
THANK YOU.
KIBI.

IS THAT BOY BACK YET?
SQUEEK
MOTHER, YOU SHOULDN'T BE OUT OF BED.
SQUEEK
SQUEEK
OH, I HOPE HE COMES BACK SOON.
MOTHER, DO YOU REALIZE YOU ALMOST DIED?
OH, I KNOW. I STILL CAN'T WALK PROPERLY.
I'm trying not to put any strain on my heart.
THAT BOY SAW ME LYING THERE AND CAME RUNNING.
IF HE HADN'T GOTTEN IN TOUCH WITH YOU...
I didn't hear about this conversation until much later.
I CAN'T JUST LOLL AROUND LIKE THIS.
But while she was saying such nice things about me...
...I was on leave from work and wouldn't be back for a while.

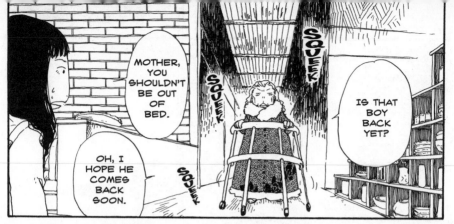

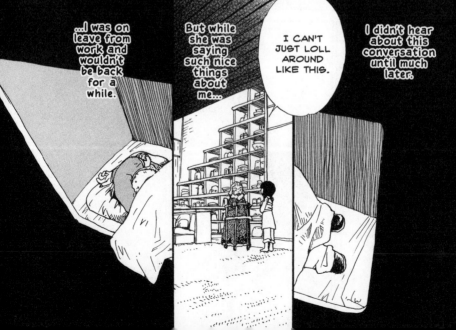

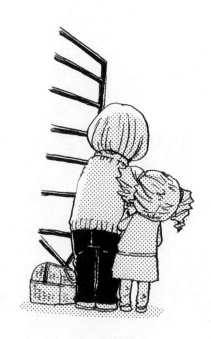

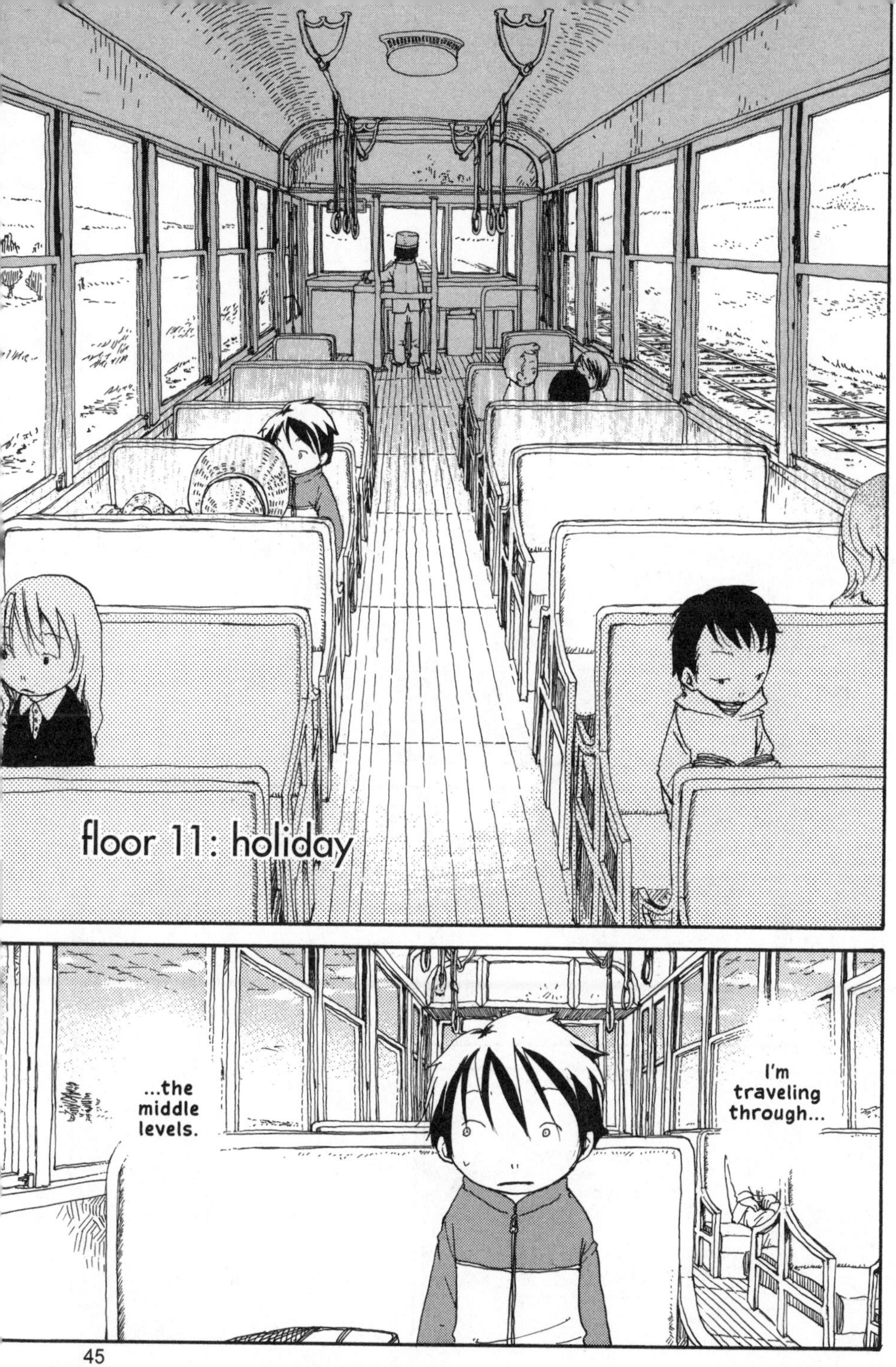
floor 11: holiday
I'm traveling through...
...the middle levels.

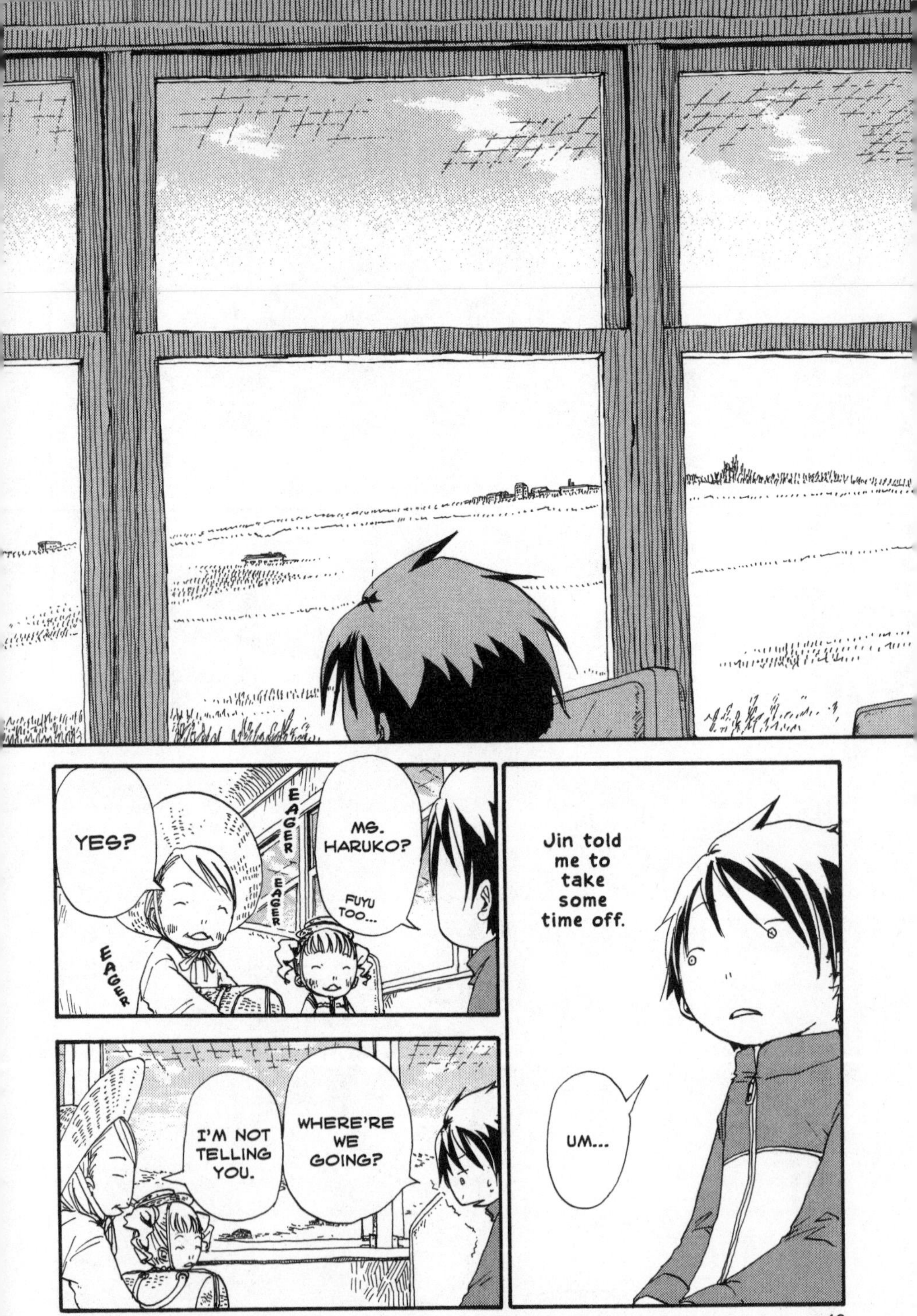
Jin told me to take some time off.
UM...
MS. HARUKO?
FUYU TOO...
EAGER
EAGER
YES?
EAGER
WHERE'RE WE GOING?
I'M NOT TELLING YOU.

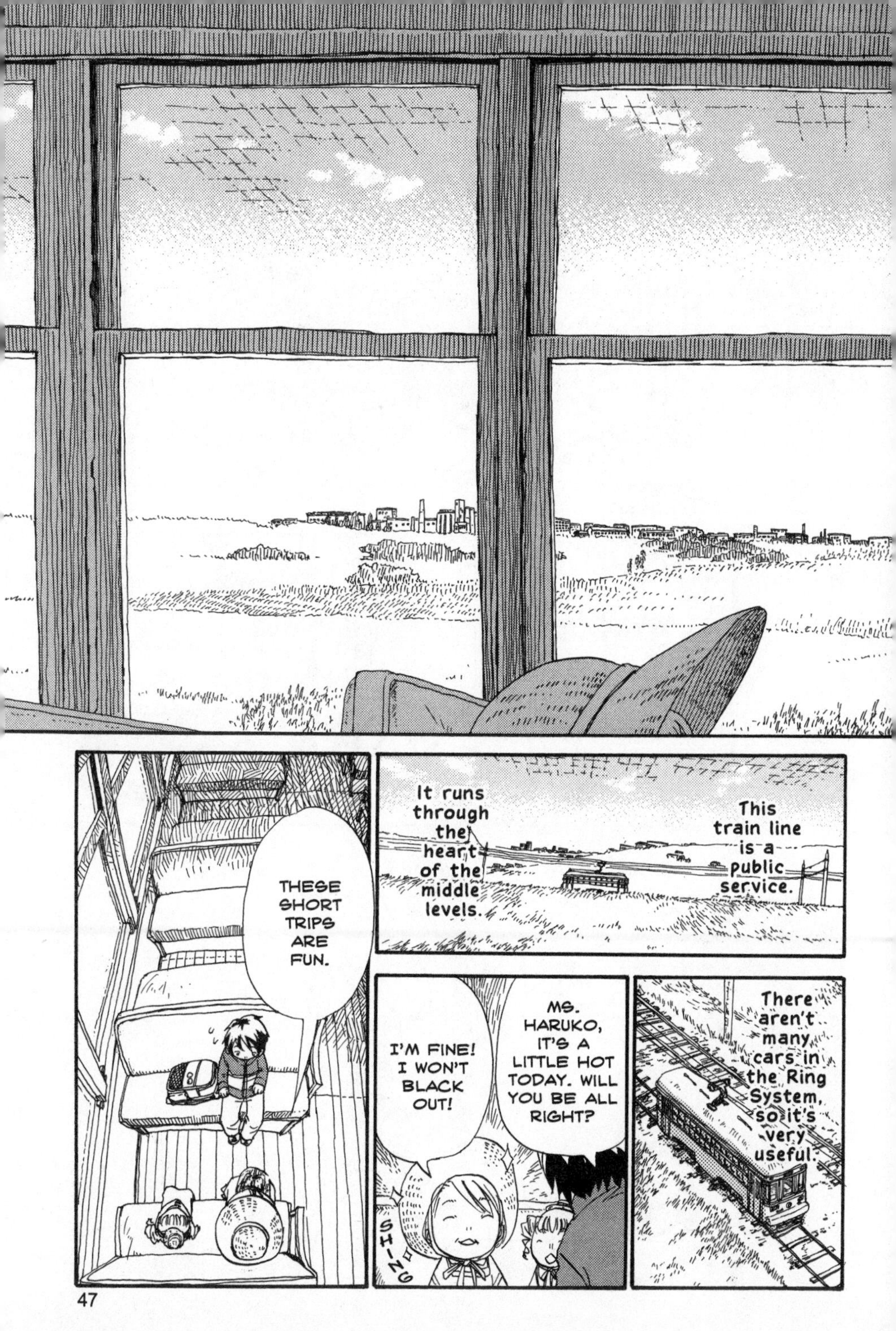
This train line is a public service.
It runs through the heart of the middle levels.
There aren't many cars in the Ring System, so it's very useful.
MS. HARUKO, IT'S A LITTLE HOT TODAY. WILL YOU BE ALL RIGHT?
I'M FINE! I WON'T BLACK OUT!
SHING
THESE SHORT TRIPS ARE FUN.

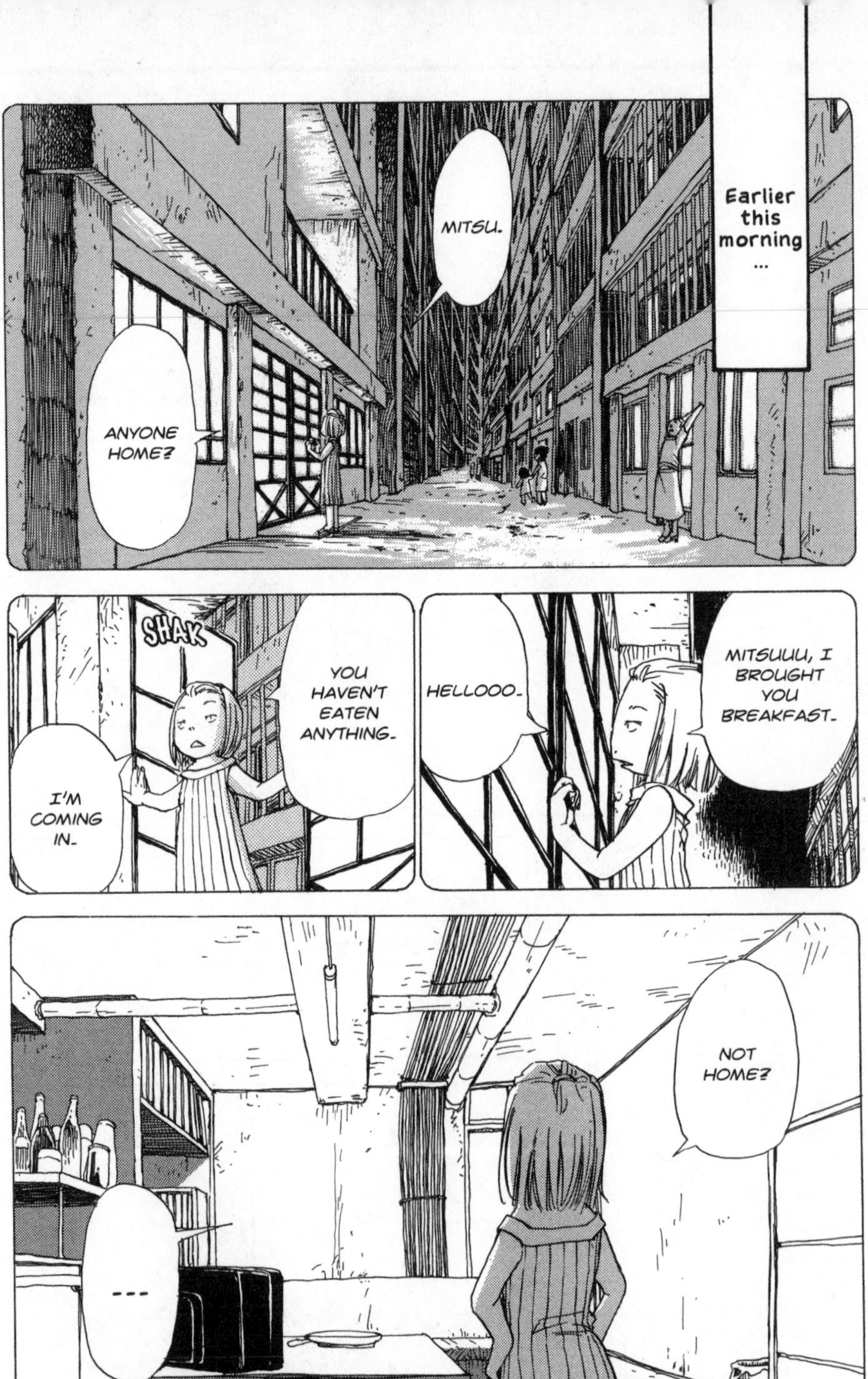
Earlier this morning ...
MITSU.
ANYONE HOME?
MITSUUU, I BROUGHT YOU BREAKFAST.
HELLOOO.
SHAK
YOU HAVEN'T EATEN ANYTHING.
I'M COMING IN.
NOT HOME?
...

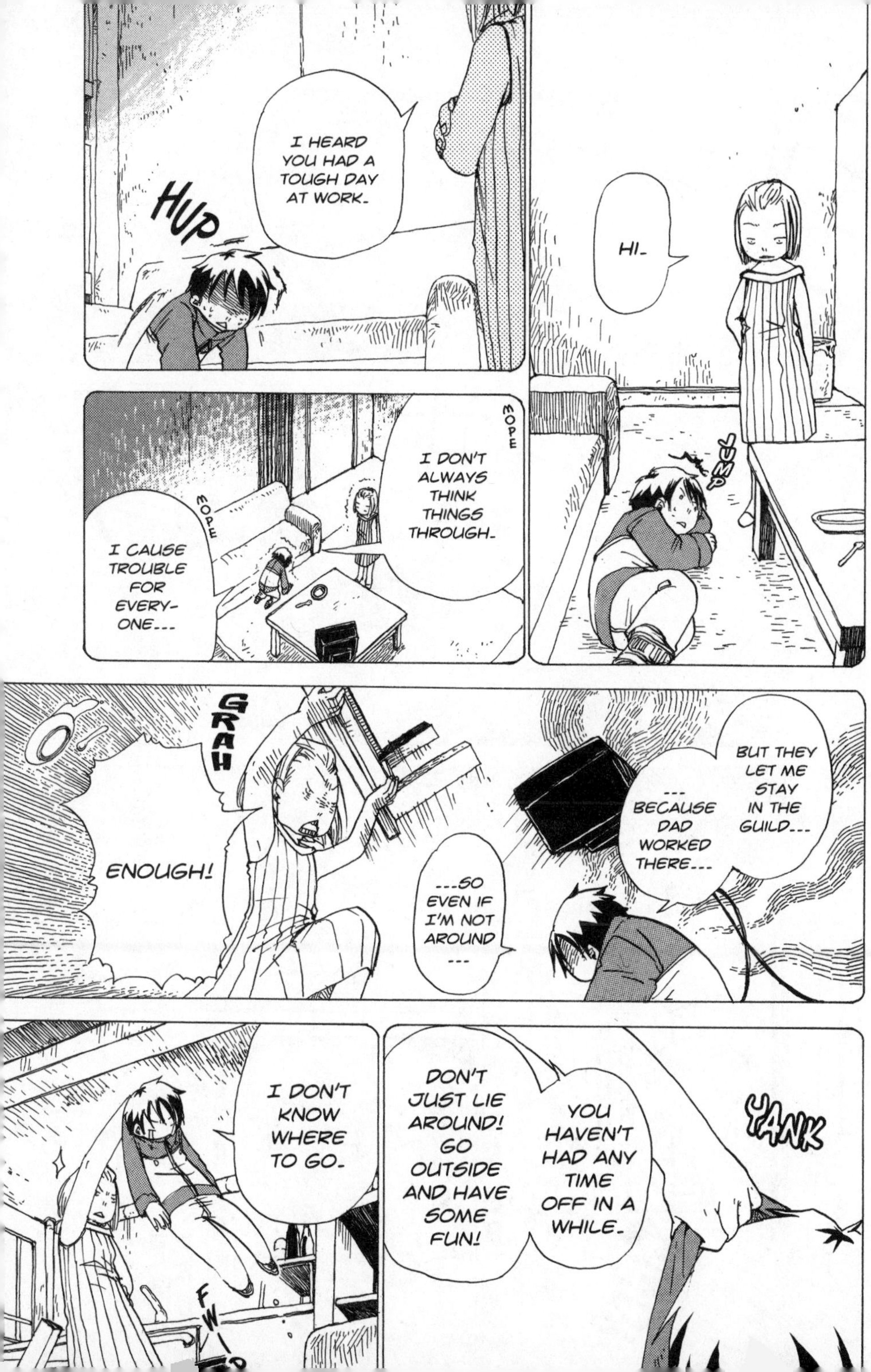
HI.
JUMP
I HEARD YOU HAD A TOUGH DAY AT WORK.
HUP
MOPE
I DON'T ALWAYS THINK THINGS THROUGH.
MOPE
I CAUSE TROUBLE FOR EVERY-ONE...
BUT THEY LET ME STAY IN THE GUILD...
...BECAUSE DAD WORKED THERE...
...SO EVEN IF I'M NOT AROUND...
GRAH
ENOUGH!
YANK
YOU HAVEN'T HAD ANY TIME OFF IN A WHILE.
DON'T JUST LIE AROUND! GO OUTSIDE AND HAVE SOME FUN!
I DON'T KNOW WHERE TO GO.

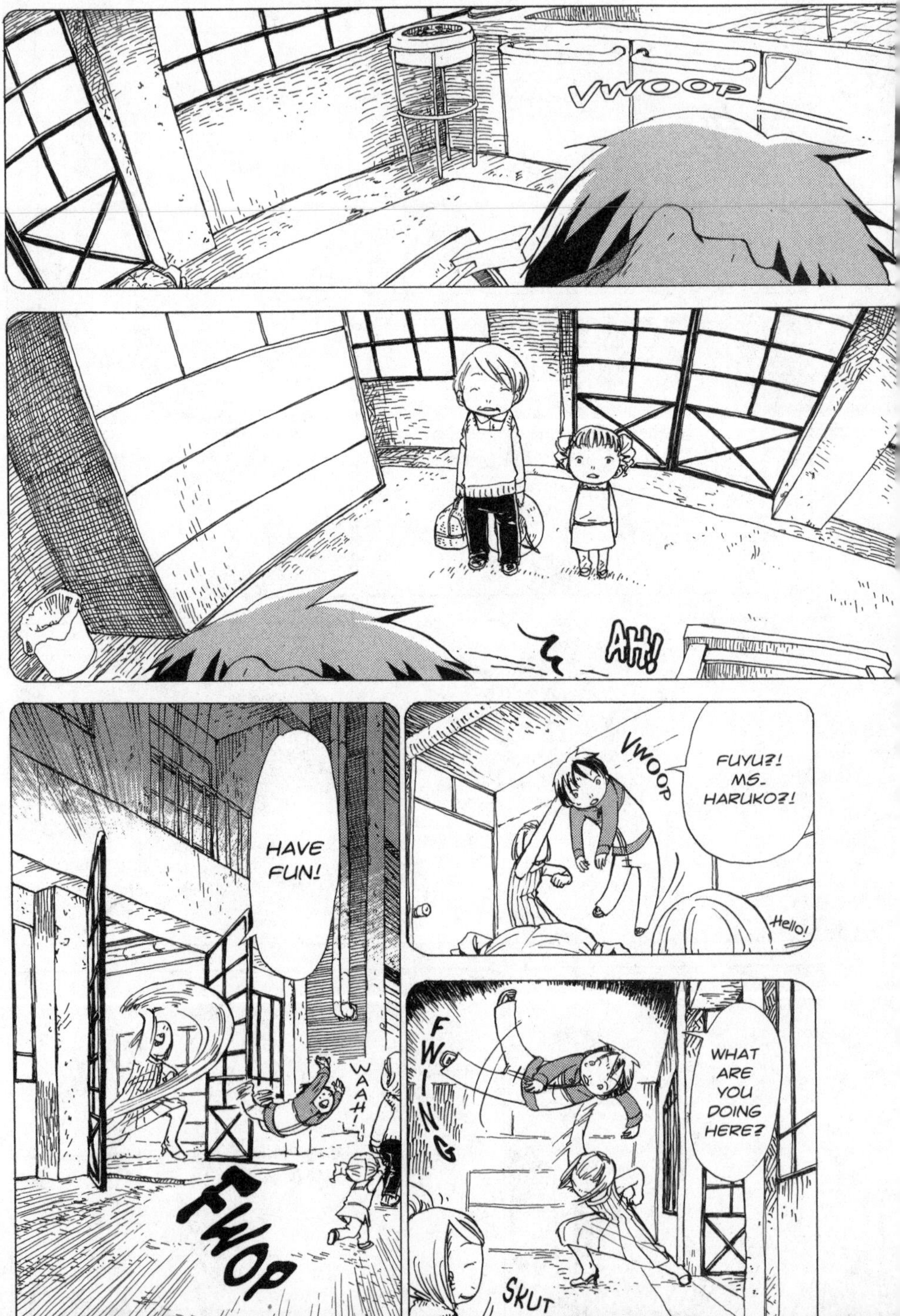
VWOOP
AH!
VWOOP
FUYU?! MS. HARUKO?!
Hello!
FWING
WHAT ARE YOU DOING HERE?
SKUT
HAVE FUN!
WAAH!
FWOP

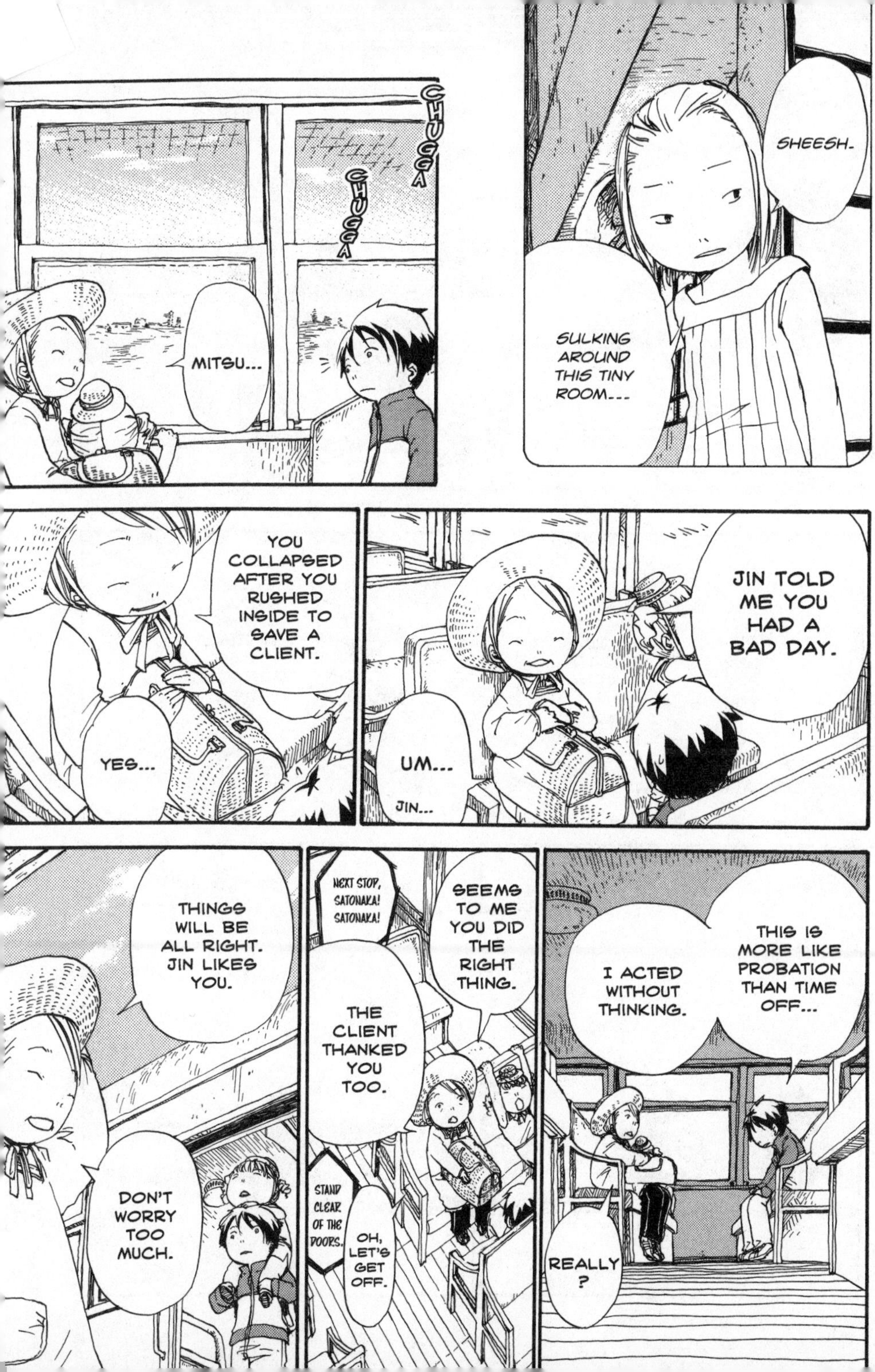
SHEESH.
SULKING AROUND THIS TINY ROOM...
CHUGGA
CHUGGA
MITSU...
JIN TOLD ME YOU HAD A BAD DAY.
UM...
JIN...
YOU COLLAPSED AFTER YOU RUSHED INSIDE TO SAVE A CLIENT.
YES...
THIS IS MORE LIKE PROBATION THAN TIME OFF...
I ACTED WITHOUT THINKING.
REALLY?
SEEMS TO ME YOU DID THE RIGHT THING.
NEXT STOP, SATONAKA! SATONAKA!
THE CLIENT THANKED YOU TOO.
OH, LET'S GET OFF.
STAND CLEAR OF THE DOORS.
THINGS WILL BE ALL RIGHT. JIN LIKES YOU.
DON'T WORRY TOO MUCH.

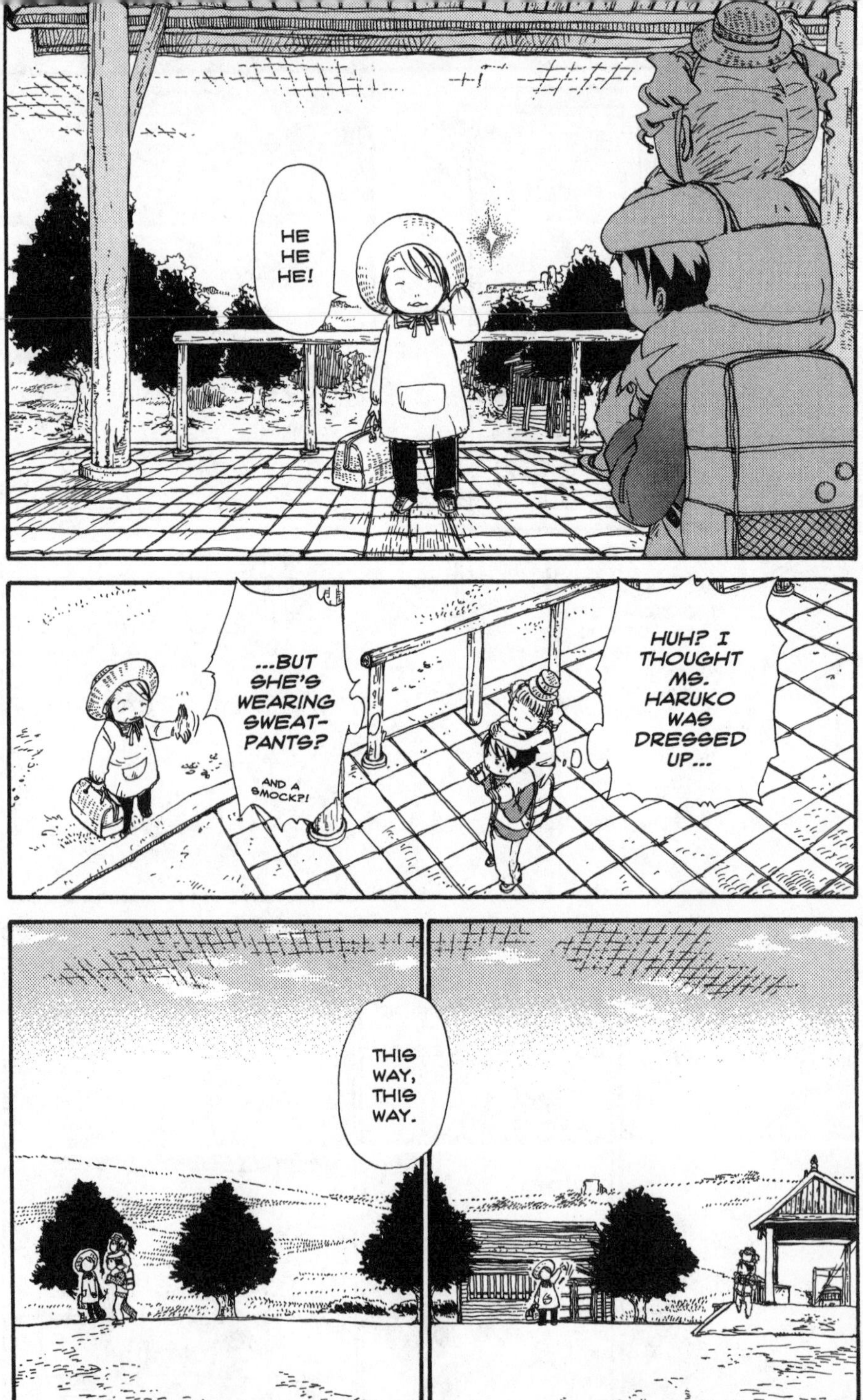
HE HE HE!
HUH? I THOUGHT MS. HARUKO WAS DRESSED UP...
...BUT SHE'S WEARING SWEAT-PANTS?
AND A SMOCK?!
THIS WAY, THIS WAY.

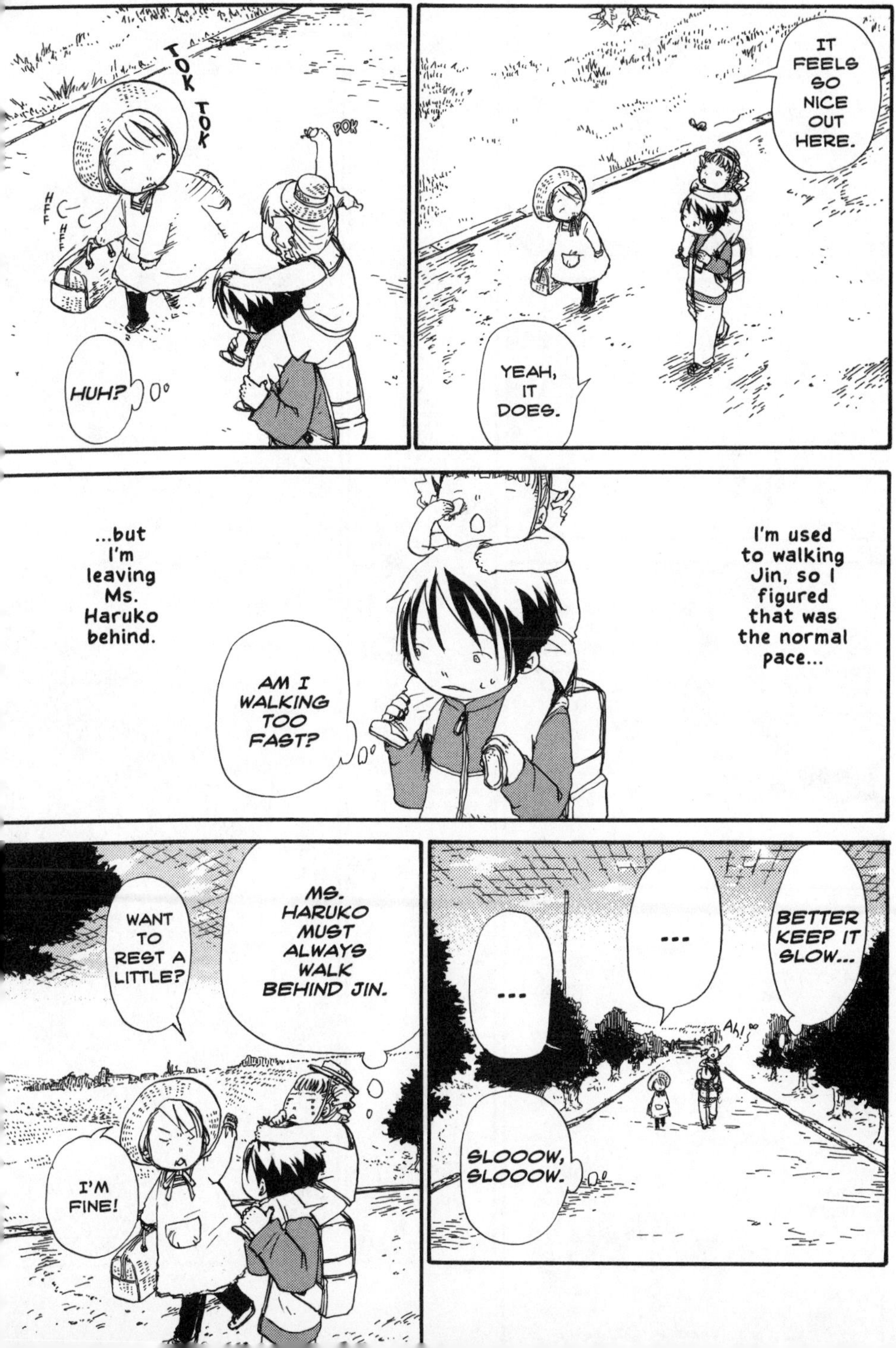
IT FEELS SO NICE OUT HERE.
YEAH, IT DOES.
TOK TOK
POK
HFF HFF
HUH?
I'm used to walking Jin, so I figured that was the normal pace...
...but I'm leaving Ms. Haruko behind.
AM I WALKING TOO FAST?
BETTER KEEP IT SLOW...
...
Ah!
...
SLOOOW, SLOOOW.
MS. HARUKO MUST ALWAYS WALK BEHIND JIN.
WANT TO REST A LITTLE?
I'M FINE!

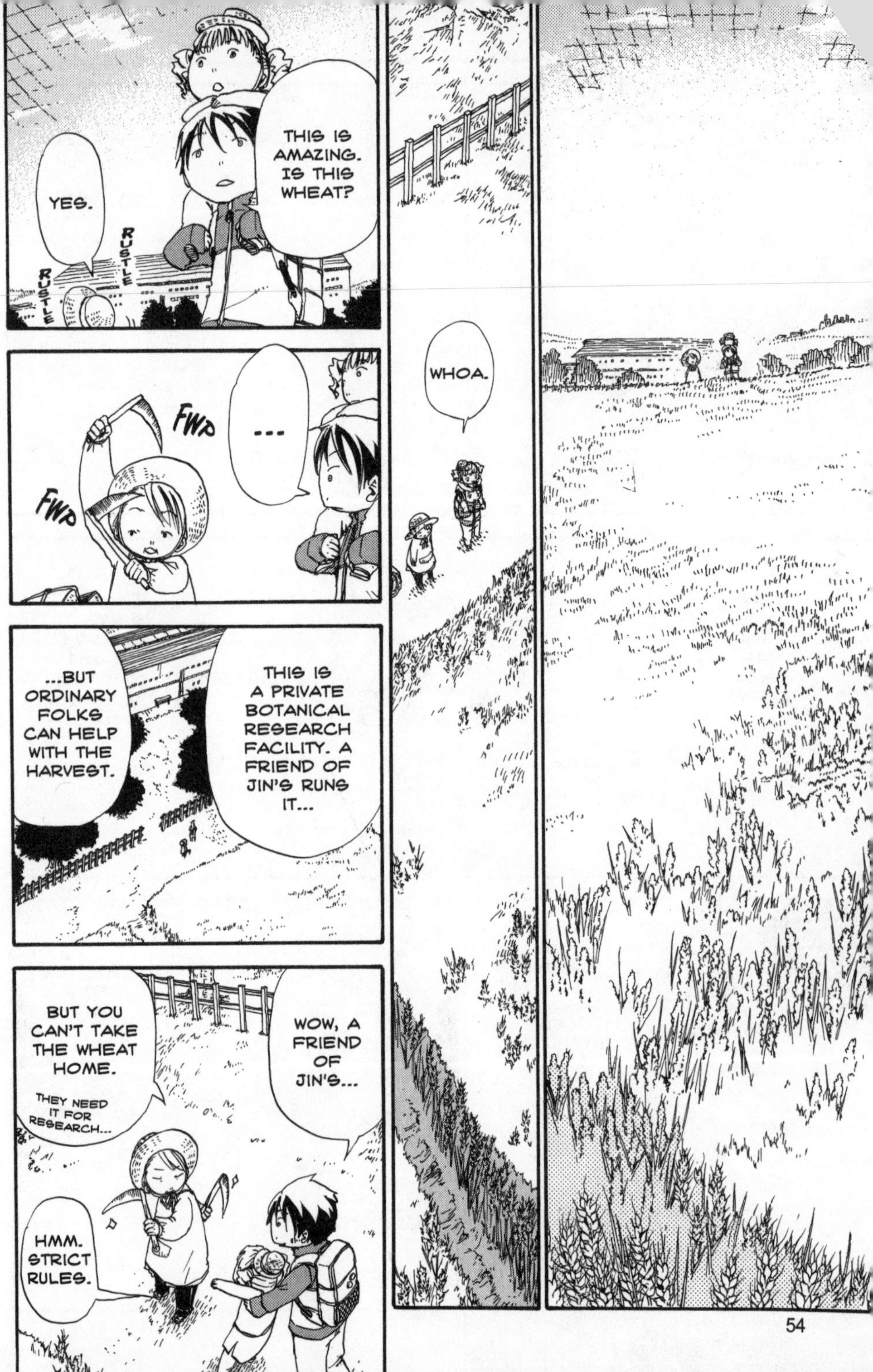
WHOA.
THIS IS AMAZING. IS THIS WHEAT?
YES.
RUSTLE
RUSTLE
...
FWP
FWP
THIS IS A PRIVATE BOTANICAL RESEARCH FACILITY. A FRIEND OF JIN'S RUNS IT...
...BUT ORDINARY FOLKS CAN HELP WITH THE HARVEST.
WOW, A FRIEND OF JIN'S...
BUT YOU CAN'T TAKE THE WHEAT HOME.
THEY NEED IT FOR RESEARCH...
HMM. STRICT RULES.

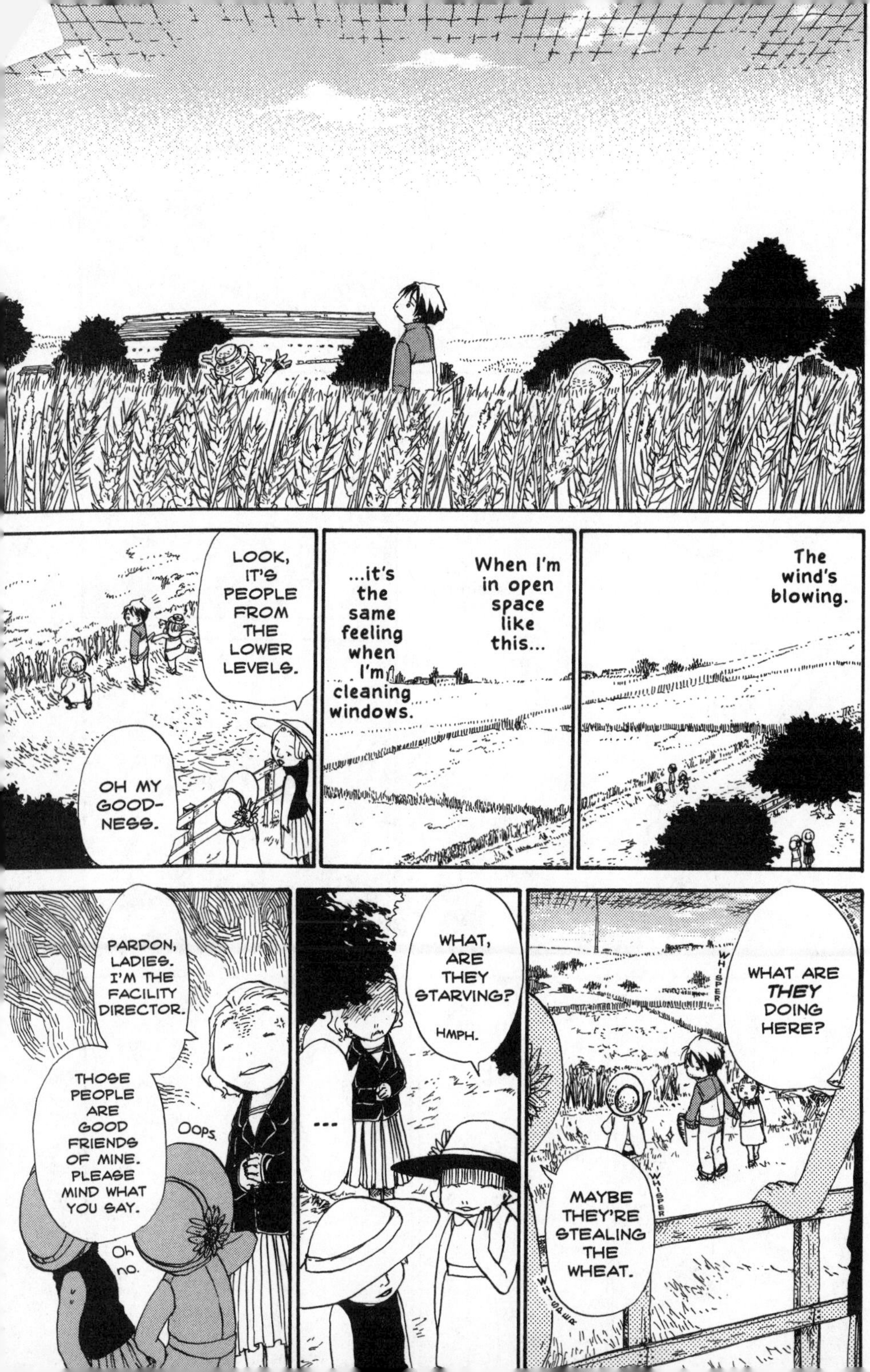

The wind's blowing.
When I'm in open space like this...
...it's the same feeling when I'm cleaning windows.
LOOK, IT'S PEOPLE FROM THE LOWER LEVELS.
OH MY GOODNESS.
WHAT ARE *THEY* DOING HERE?
WHISPER
MAYBE THEY'RE STEALING THE WHEAT.
WHISPER
WHAT, ARE THEY STARVING?
HMPH.
...
PARDON, LADIES. I'M THE FACILITY DIRECTOR.
THOSE PEOPLE ARE GOOD FRIENDS OF MINE. PLEASE MIND WHAT YOU SAY.
OOPS.
Oh no.

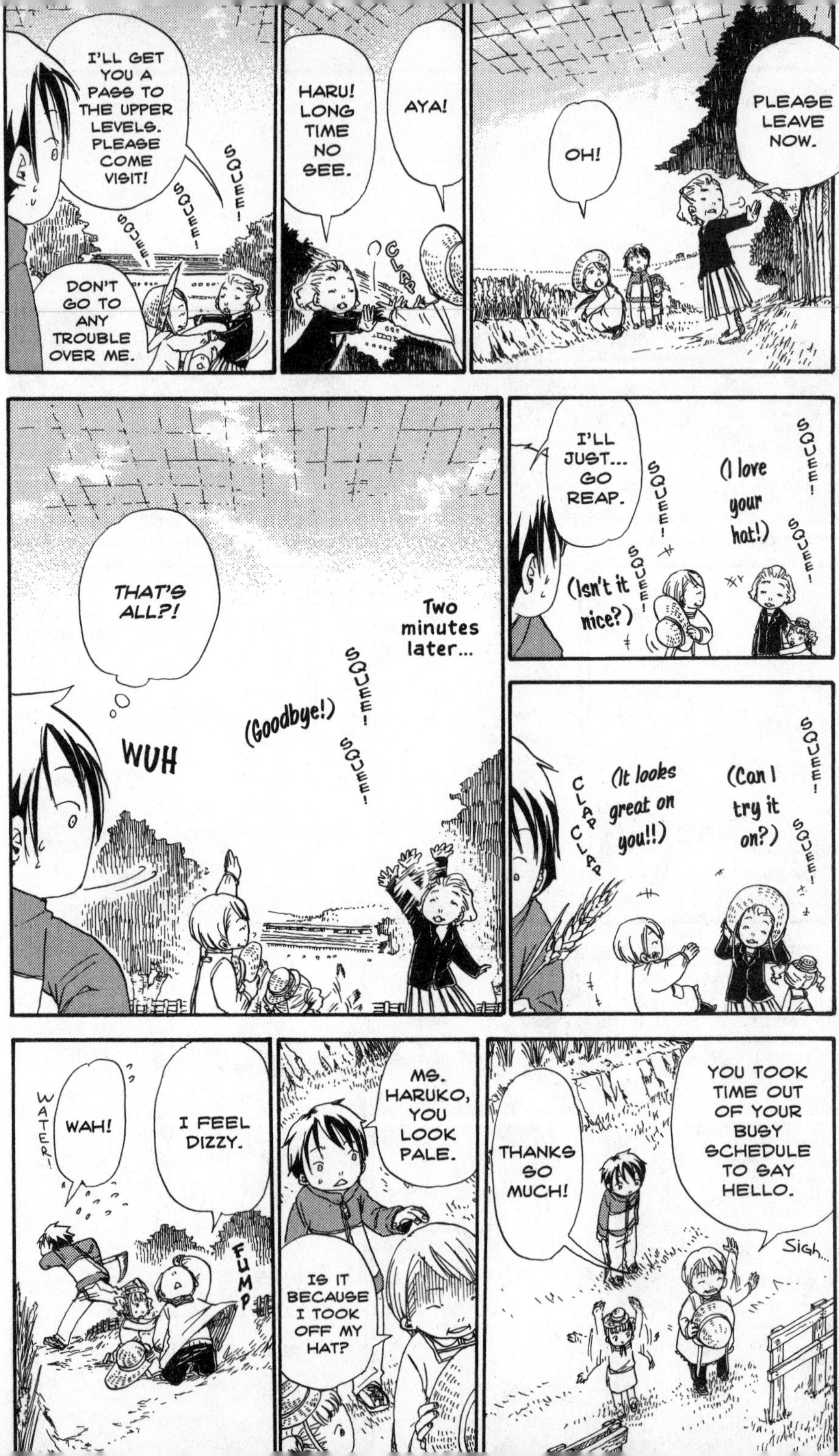
PLEASE LEAVE NOW.
OH!
AYA!
HARU! LONG TIME NO SEE.
CLAP
I'LL GET YOU A PASS TO THE UPPER LEVELS. PLEASE COME VISIT!
SQUEE!
SQUEE!
DON'T GO TO ANY TROUBLE OVER ME.
SQUEE!
(I love your hat!)
SQUEE!
I'LL JUST... GO REAP.
SQUEE!
SQUEE!
(Isn't it nice?)
SQUEE!
(Can I try it on?)
SQUEE!
(It looks great on you!!)
CLAP CLAP
Two minutes later...
SQUEE!
(Goodbye!)
SQUEE!
THAT'S ALL?!
WUH
YOU TOOK TIME OUT OF YOUR BUSY SCHEDULE TO SAY HELLO.
Sigh...
THANKS SO MUCH!
MS. HARUKO, YOU LOOK PALE.
IS IT BECAUSE I TOOK OFF MY HAT?
I FEEL DIZZY.
FUMP
WAH!
WATER!

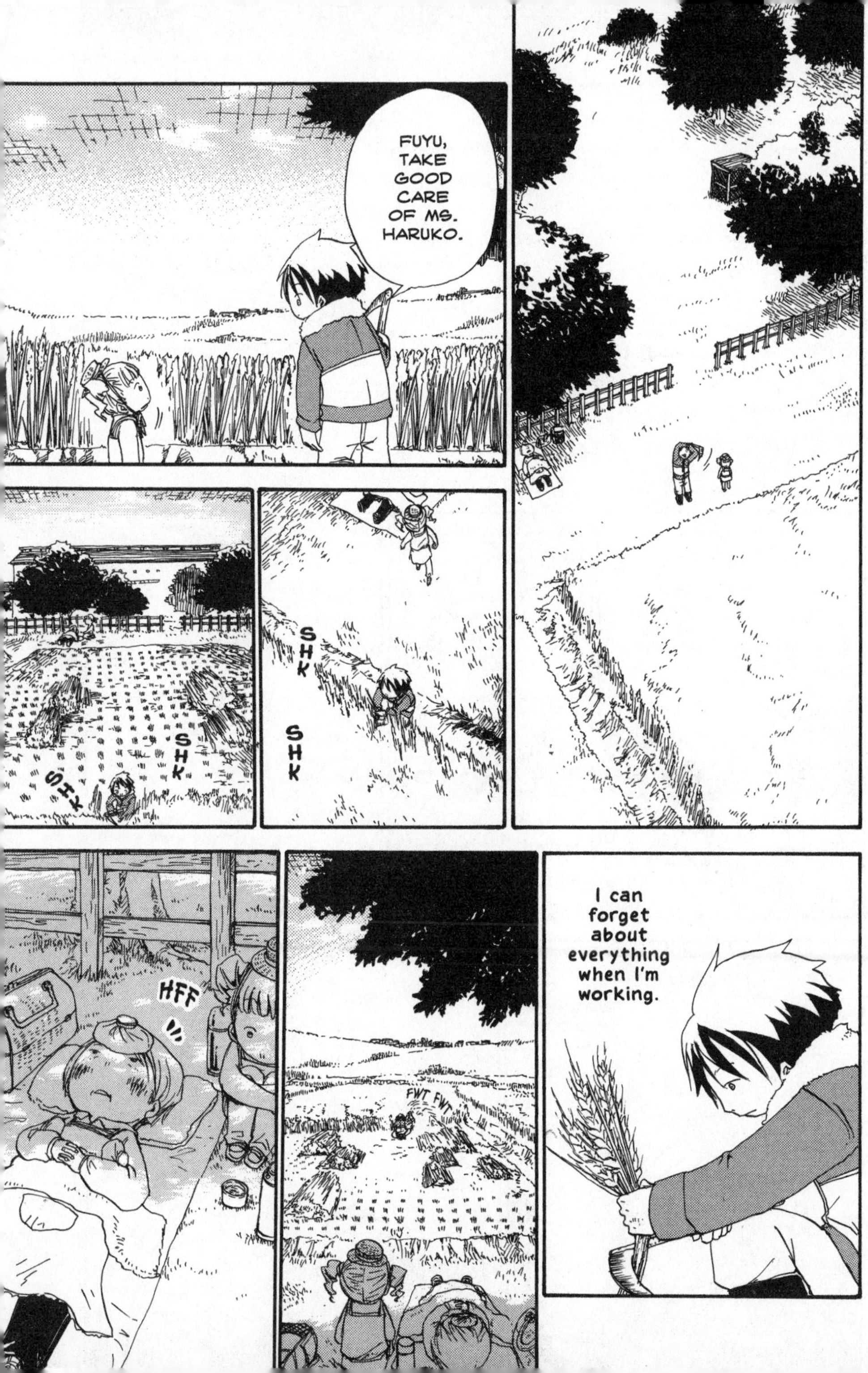
FUYU, TAKE GOOD CARE OF MS. HARUKO.
SHK
SHK
SHK
SIK
I can forget about everything when I'm working.
FWT FWT
HFF

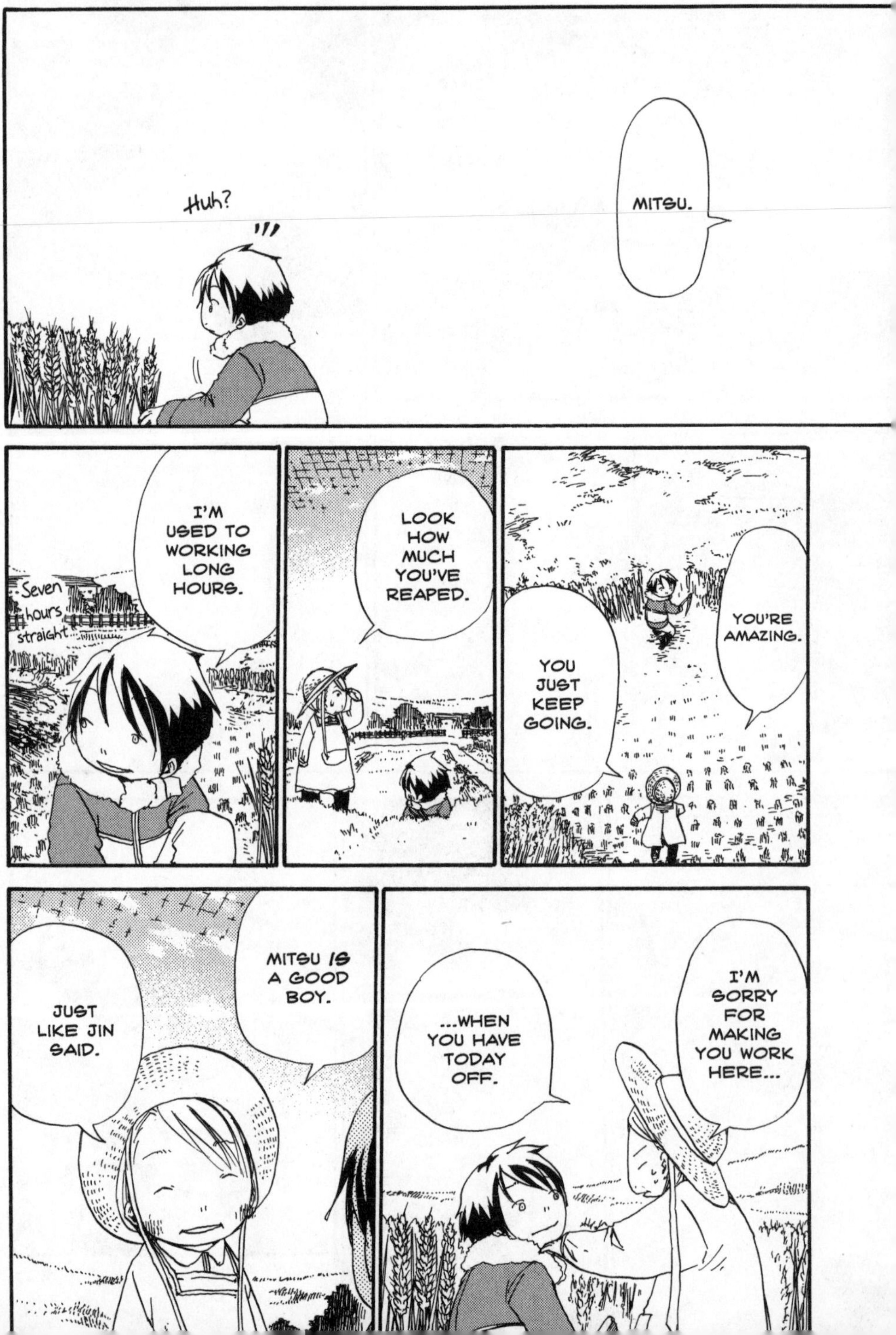
MITSU.
Huh?
YOU'RE AMAZING.
YOU JUST KEEP GOING.
LOOK HOW MUCH YOU'VE REAPED.
I'M USED TO WORKING LONG HOURS.
Seven hours straight...
I'M SORRY FOR MAKING YOU WORK HERE...
...WHEN YOU HAVE TODAY OFF.
MITSU *IS* A GOOD BOY.
JUST LIKE JIN SAID.

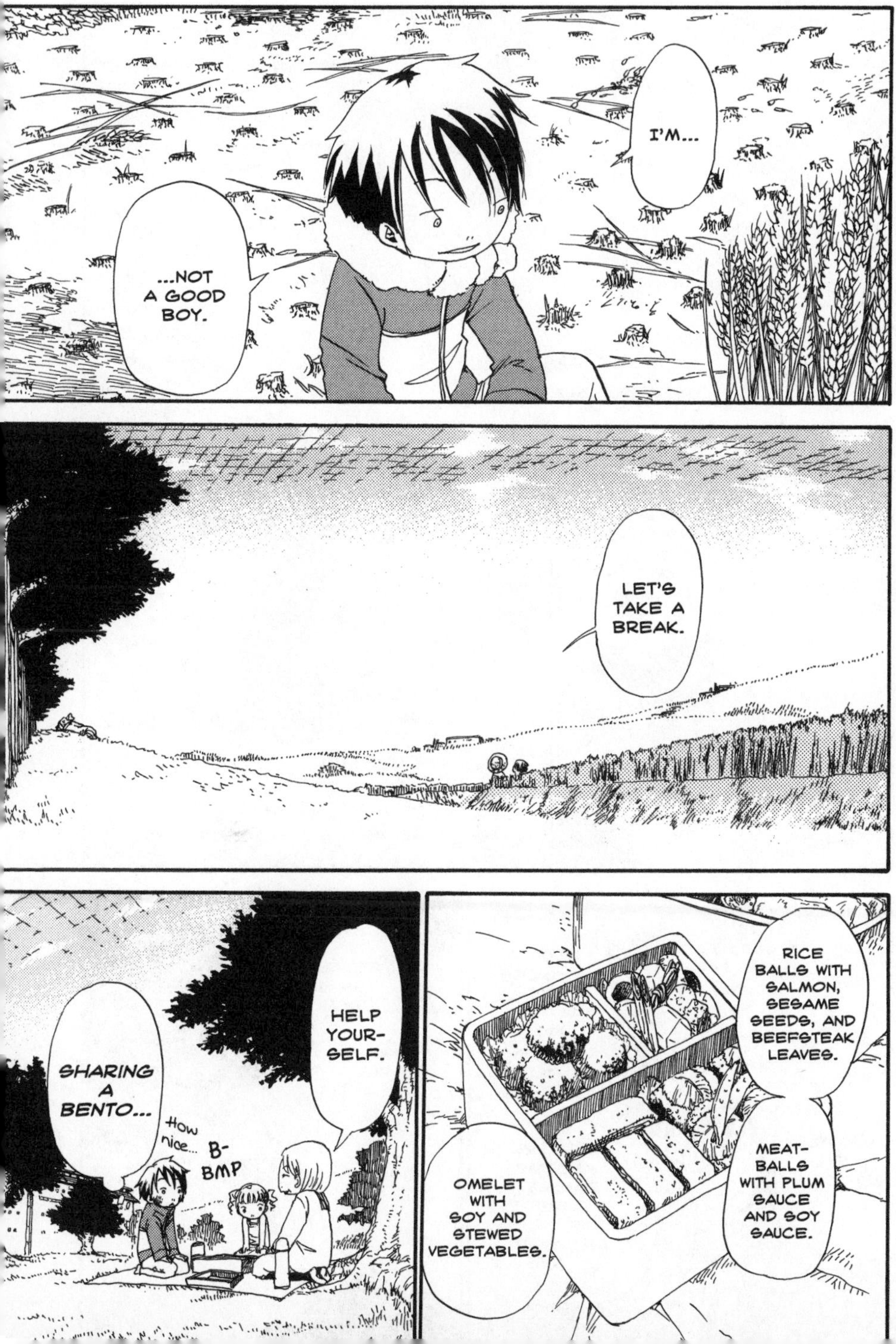
I'M...
...NOT A GOOD BOY.
LET'S TAKE A BREAK.
RICE BALLS WITH SALMON, SESAME SEEDS, AND BEEFSTEAK LEAVES.
MEAT-BALLS WITH PLUM SAUCE AND SOY SAUCE.
OMELET WITH SOY AND STEWED VEGETABLES.
HELP YOUR-SELF.
SHARING A BENTO...
How nice...
B-BMP

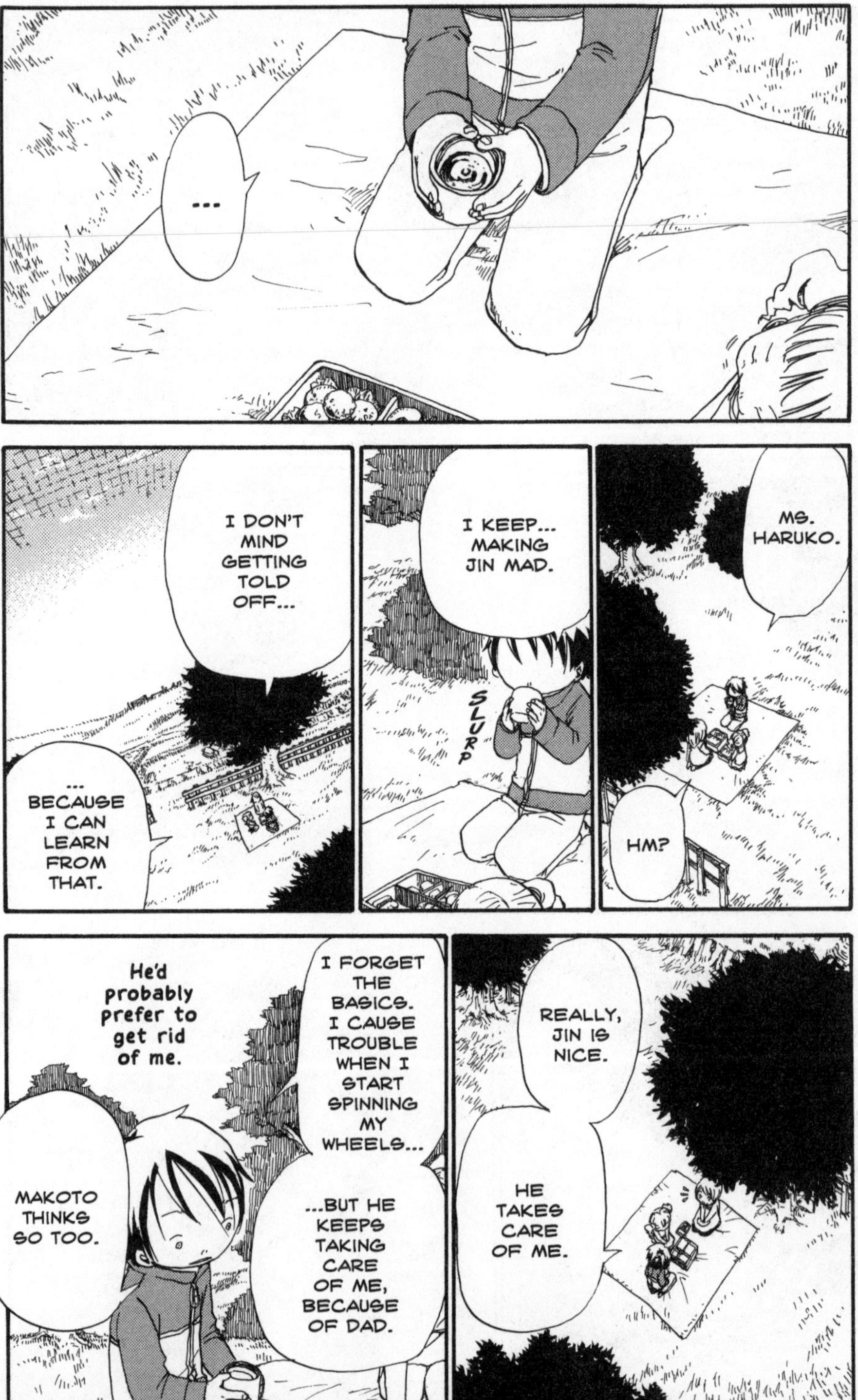
...
MS. HARUKO.
HM?
I KEEP... MAKING JIN MAD.
SLURP
I DON'T MIND GETTING TOLD OFF...
...BECAUSE I CAN LEARN FROM THAT.
REALLY, JIN IS NICE.
HE TAKES CARE OF ME.
I FORGET THE BASICS. I CAUSE TROUBLE WHEN I START SPINNING MY WHEELS...
...BUT HE KEEPS TAKING CARE OF ME, BECAUSE OF DAD.
He'd probably prefer to get rid of me.
MAKOTO THINKS SO TOO.

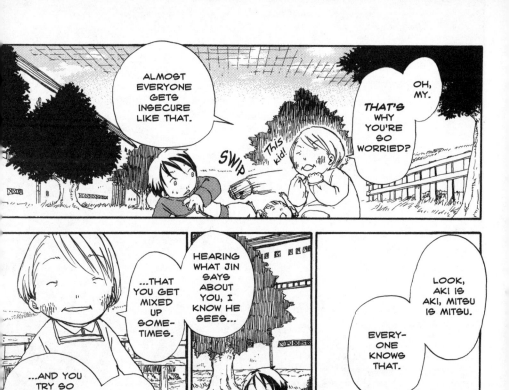

OH, MY. THAT'S WHY YOU'RE SO WORRIED?
This kid!
SWIP
ALMOST EVERYONE GETS INSECURE LIKE THAT.
LOOK, AKI IS AKI, MITSU IS MITSU.
EVERYONE KNOWS THAT.
HEARING WHAT JIN SAYS ABOUT YOU, I KNOW HE SEES...
...THAT YOU GET MIXED UP SOMETIMES.
BUT YOU'RE HONEST...
...AND YOU TRY SO HARD THAT YOU SOMETIMES FORGET WHAT'S GOING ON AROUND YOU.
HE ALSO KNOWS THAT THERE ARE THINGS ONLY YOU CAN DO.
SO STOP WORRYING.

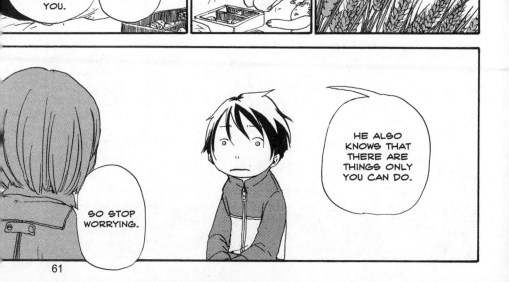

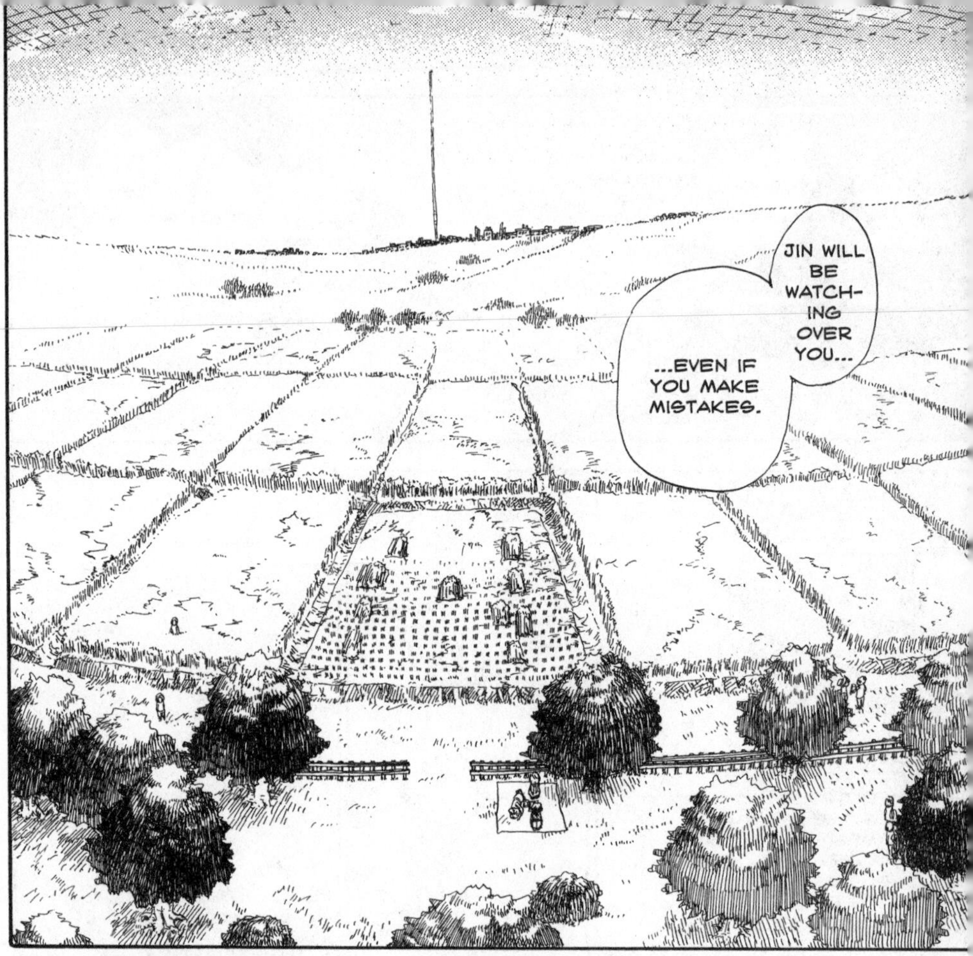
JIN WILL BE WATCHING OVER YOU...
...EVEN IF YOU MAKE MISTAKES.

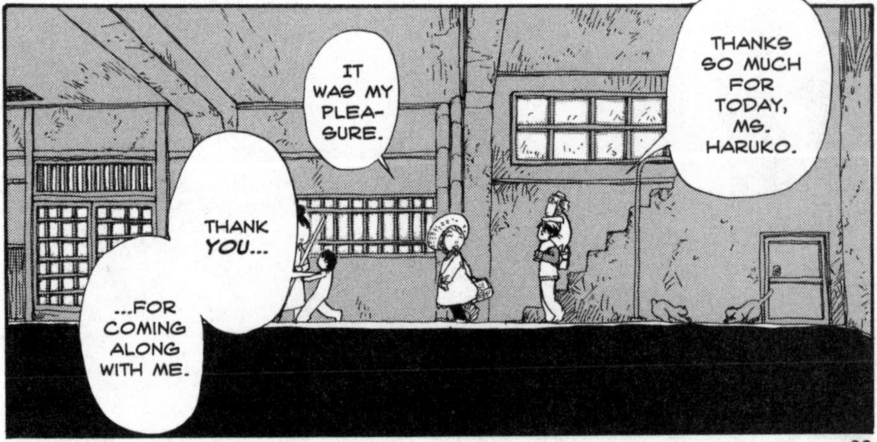
THANKS SO MUCH FOR TODAY, MS. HARUKO.
IT WAS MY PLEASURE.
THANK *YOU*...
...FOR COMING ALONG WITH ME.

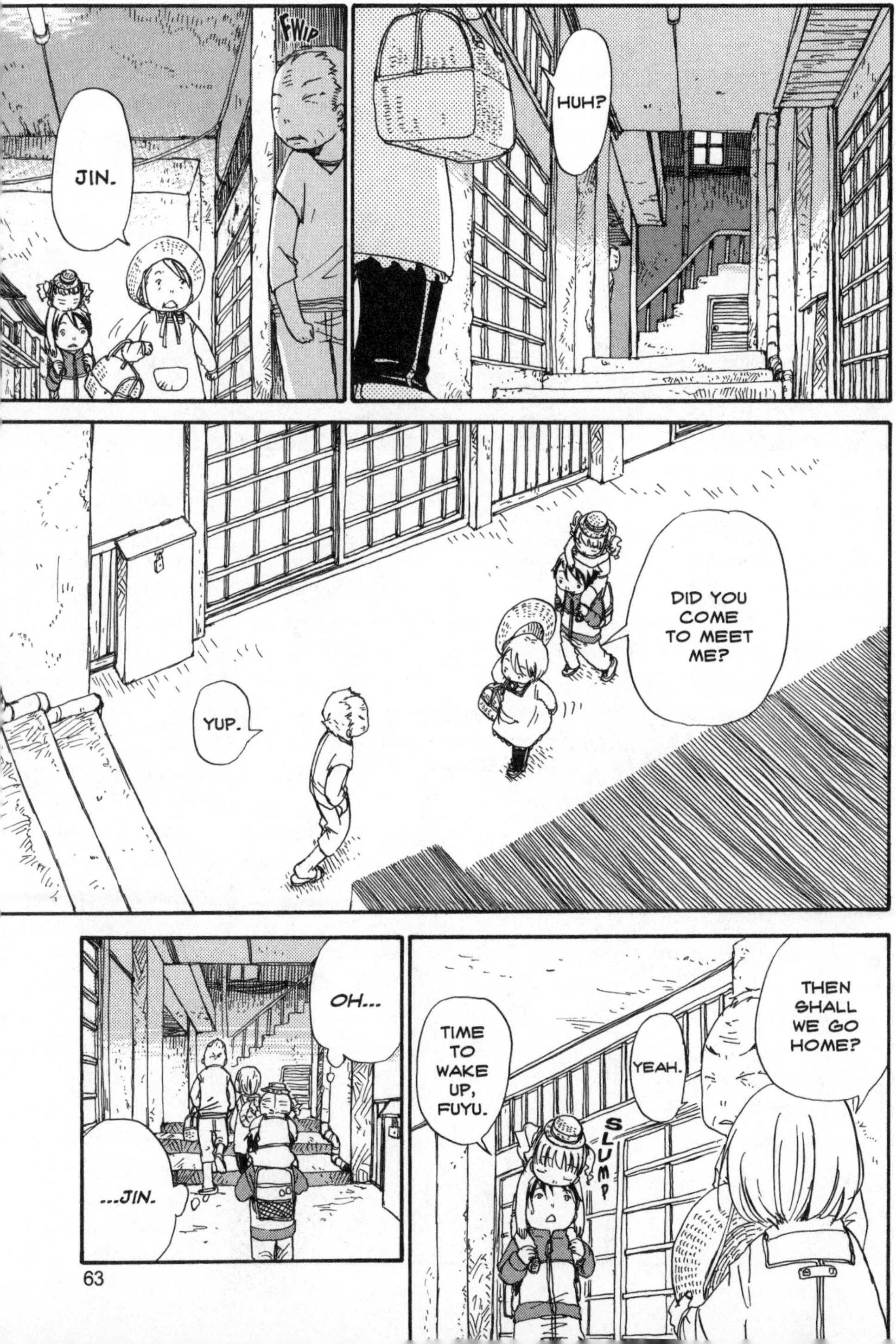
HUH?
FWIP
JIN.
DID YOU COME TO MEET ME?
YUP.
THEN SHALL WE GO HOME?
YEAH.
SLUMP
TIME TO WAKE UP, FUYU.
OH...
...JIN.

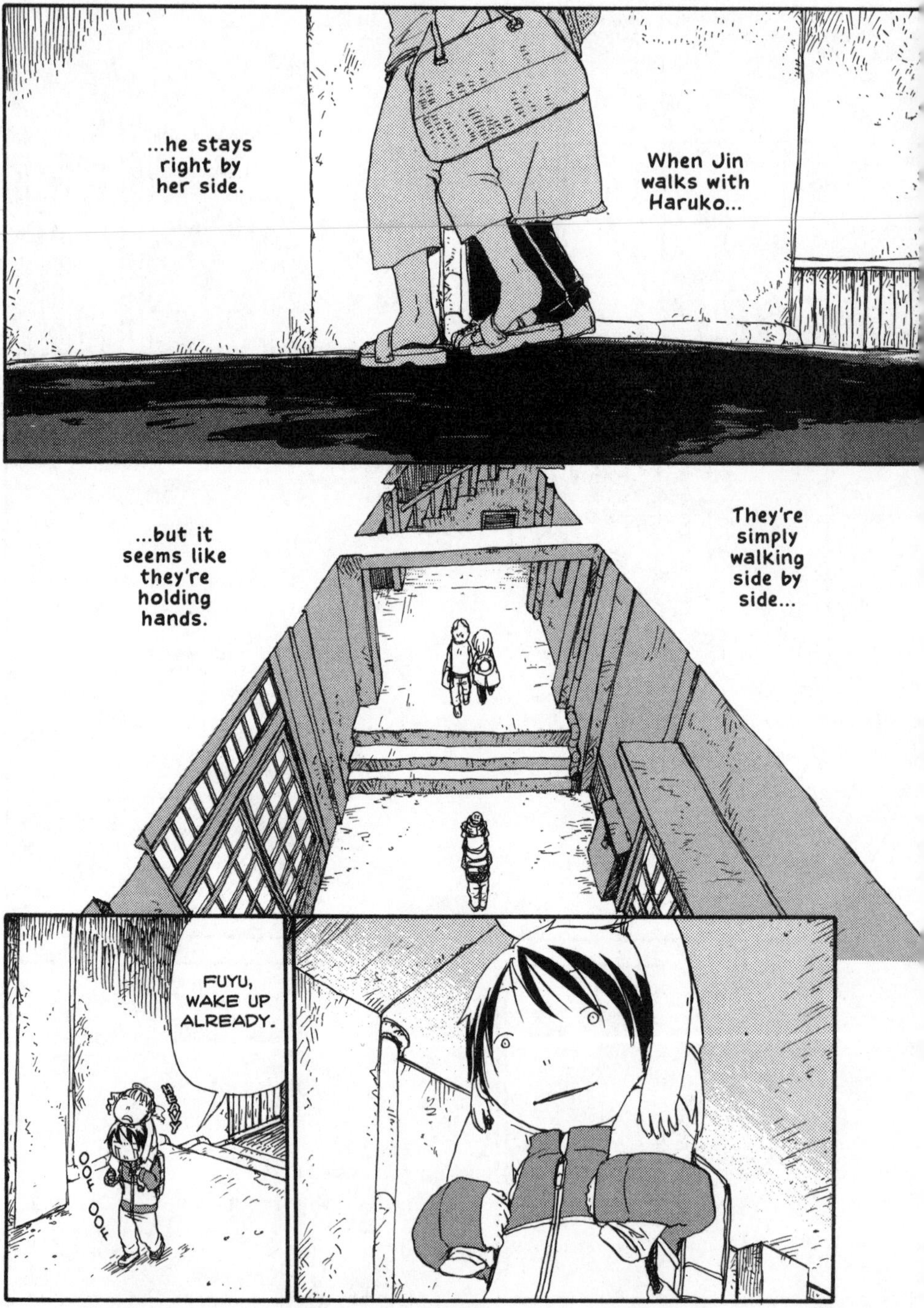
When Jin walks with Haruko...
...he stays right by her side.
They're simply walking side by side...
...but it seems like they're holding hands.
FUYU, WAKE UP ALREADY.
HEAVY
OOF OOF

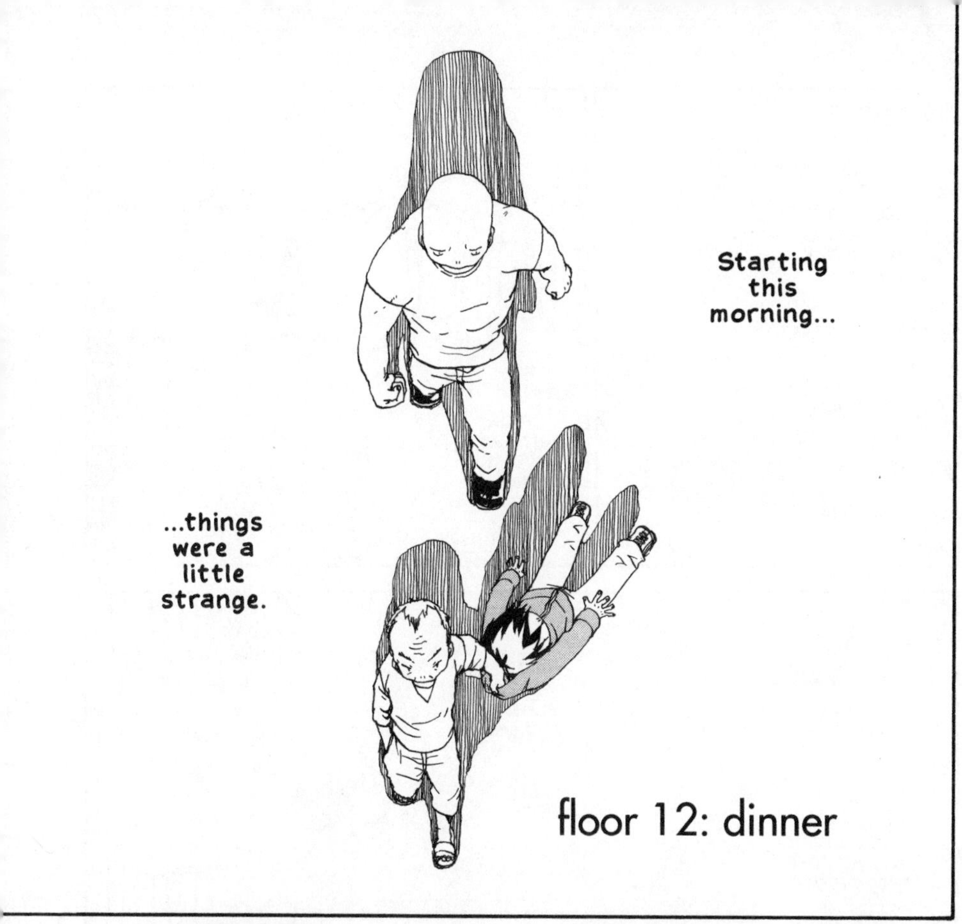
Starting this morning...
...things were a little strange.
floor 12: dinner

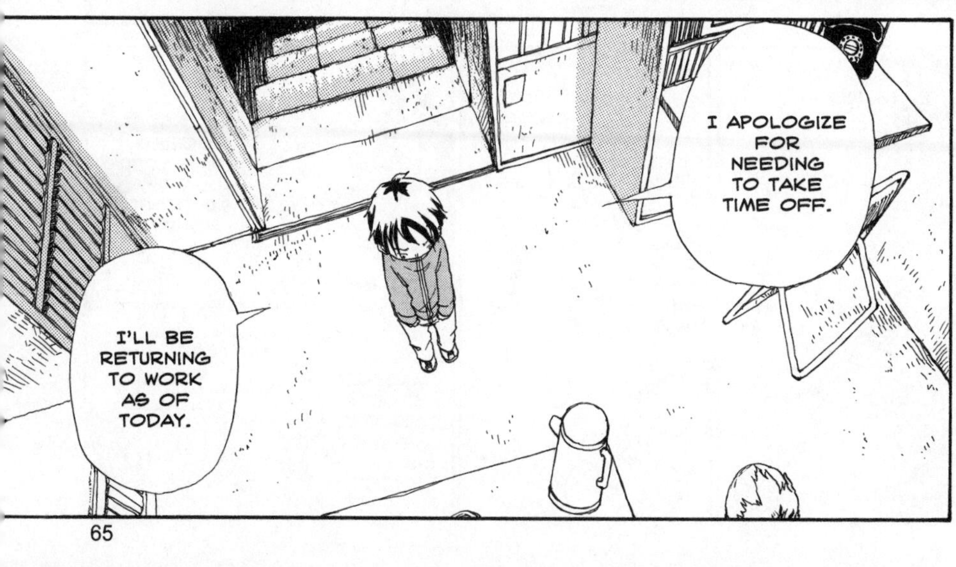
I APOLOGIZE FOR NEEDING TO TAKE TIME OFF.
I'LL BE RETURNING TO WORK AS OF TODAY.

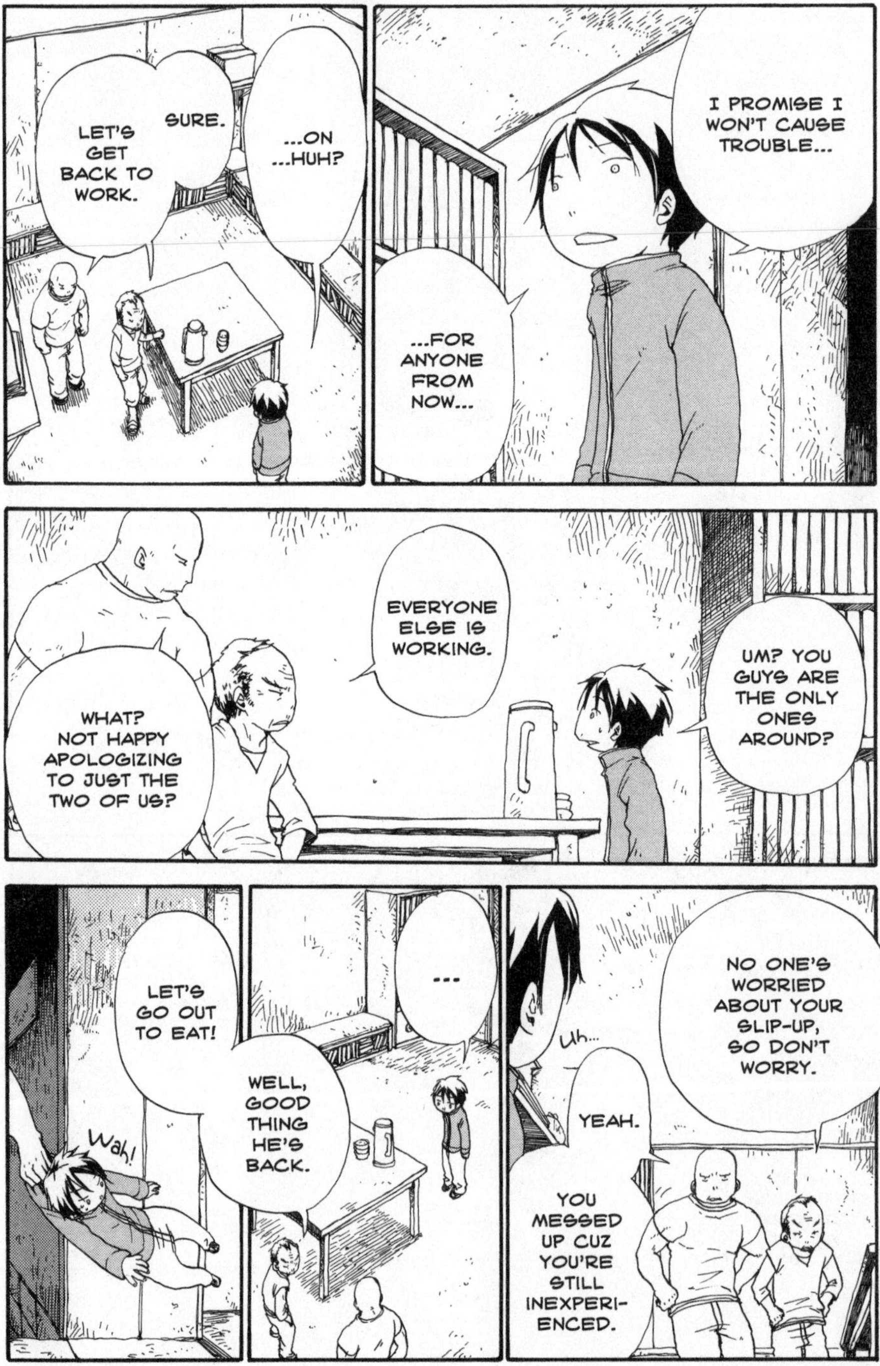
I PROMISE I WON'T CAUSE TROUBLE...
...FOR ANYONE FROM NOW...
...ON ...HUH?
SURE.
LET'S GET BACK TO WORK.
UM? YOU GUYS ARE THE ONLY ONES AROUND?
EVERYONE ELSE IS WORKING.
WHAT? NOT HAPPY APOLOGIZING TO JUST THE TWO OF US?
NO ONE'S WORRIED ABOUT YOUR SLIP-UP, SO DON'T WORRY.
Uh...
YEAH.
YOU MESSED UP CUZ YOU'RE STILL INEXPERIENCED.
...
WELL, GOOD THING HE'S BACK.
LET'S GO OUT TO EAT!
Wah!

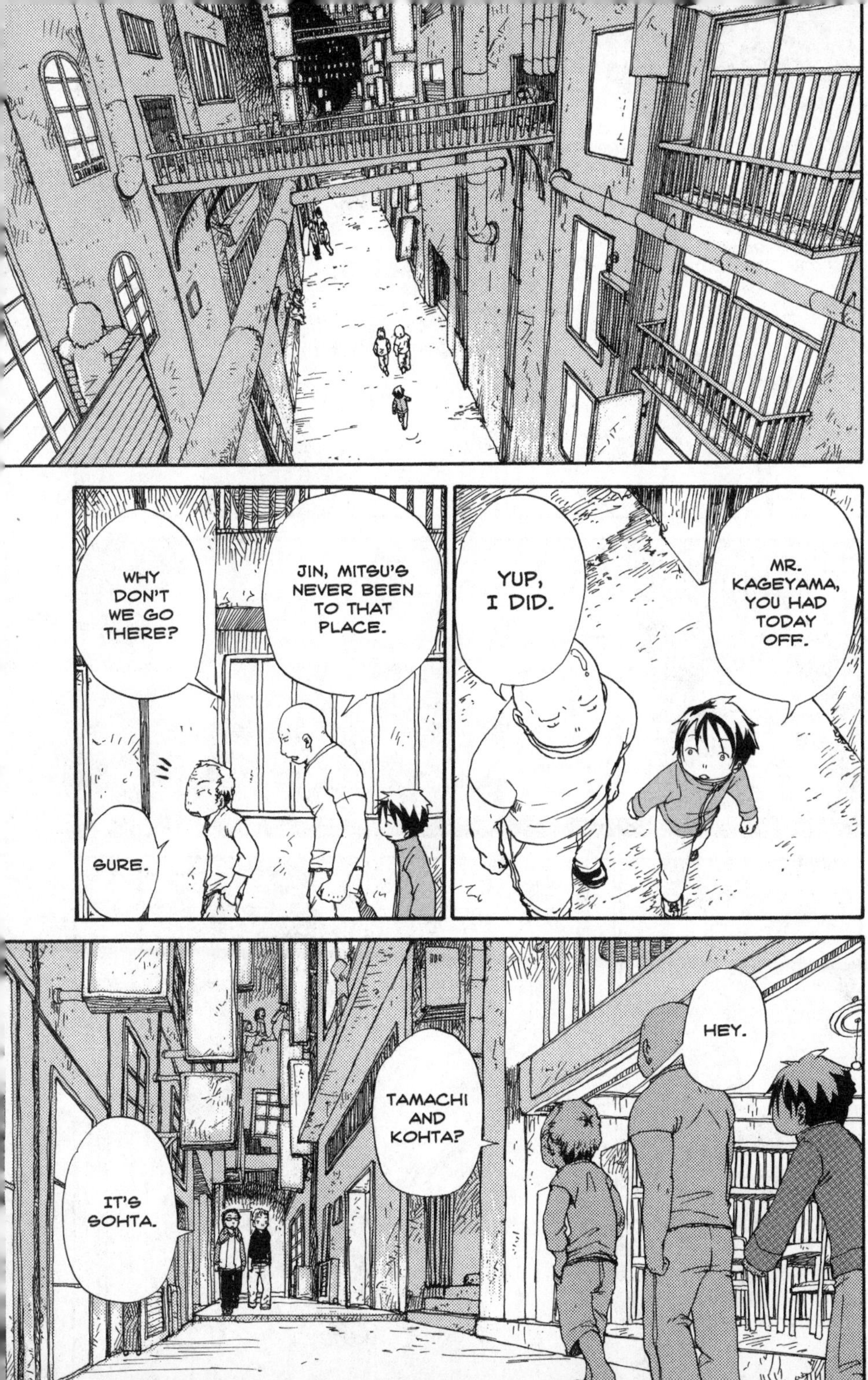
MR. KAGEYAMA, YOU HAD TODAY OFF.
YUP, I DID.
JIN, MITSU'S NEVER BEEN TO THAT PLACE.
WHY DON'T WE GO THERE?
SURE.
HEY.
TAMACHI AND KOHTA?
IT'S SOHTA.

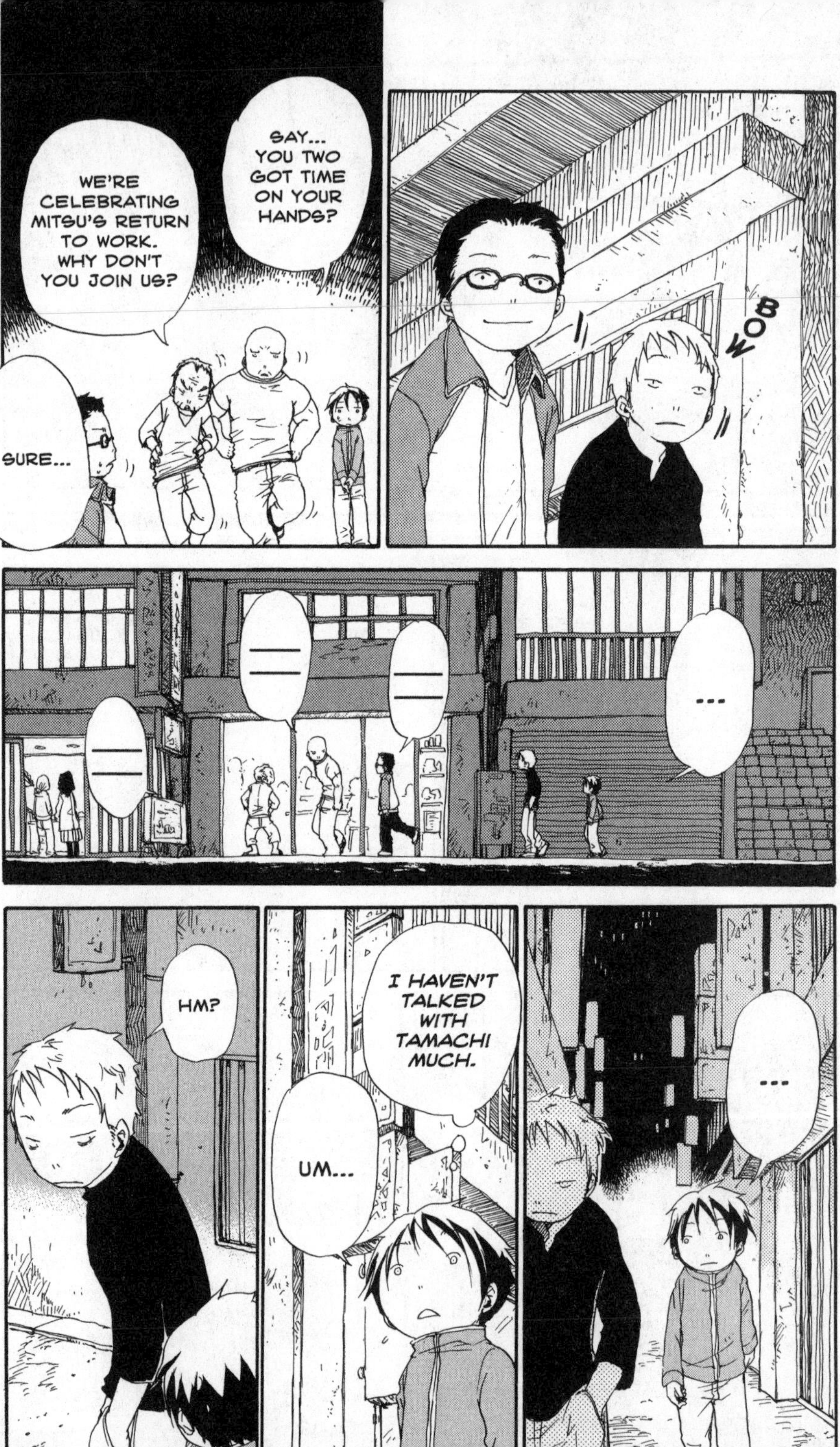
BOW
SAY... YOU TWO GOT TIME ON YOUR HANDS?
WE'RE CELEBRATING MITSU'S RETURN TO WORK. WHY DON'T YOU JOIN US?
SURE...
...
——
——
——
...
I HAVEN'T TALKED WITH TAMACHI MUCH.
UM...
HM?

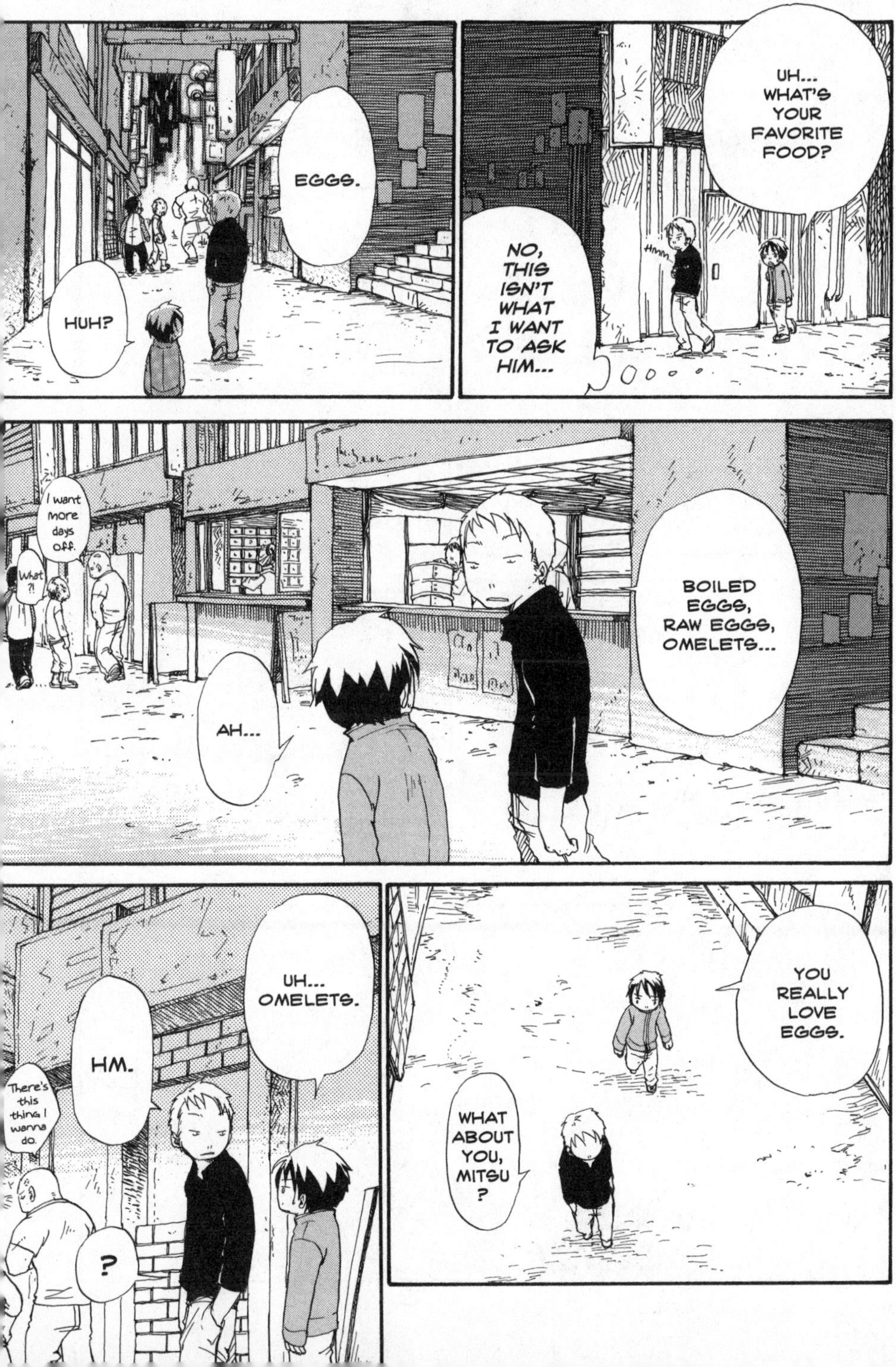
UH... WHAT'S YOUR FAVORITE FOOD?
NO, THIS ISN'T WHAT I WANT TO ASK HIM...
Hmm
EGGS.
HUH?
BOILED EGGS, RAW EGGS, OMELETS...
AH...
I want more days off.
What?!
YOU REALLY LOVE EGGS.
WHAT ABOUT YOU, MITSU?
UH... OMELETS.
HM.
There's this thing I wanna do.
?

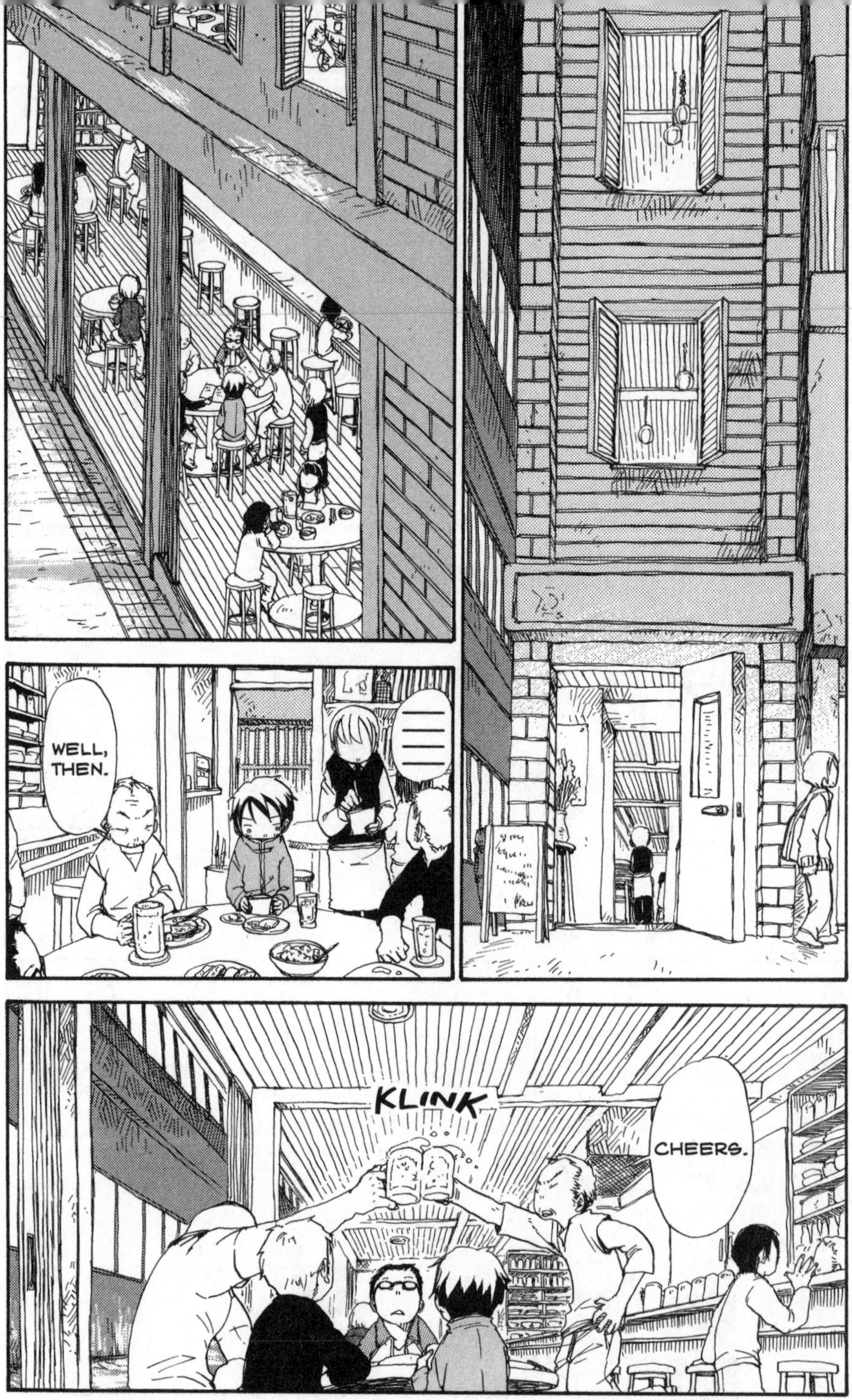
WELL, THEN.
CHEERS.
KLINK

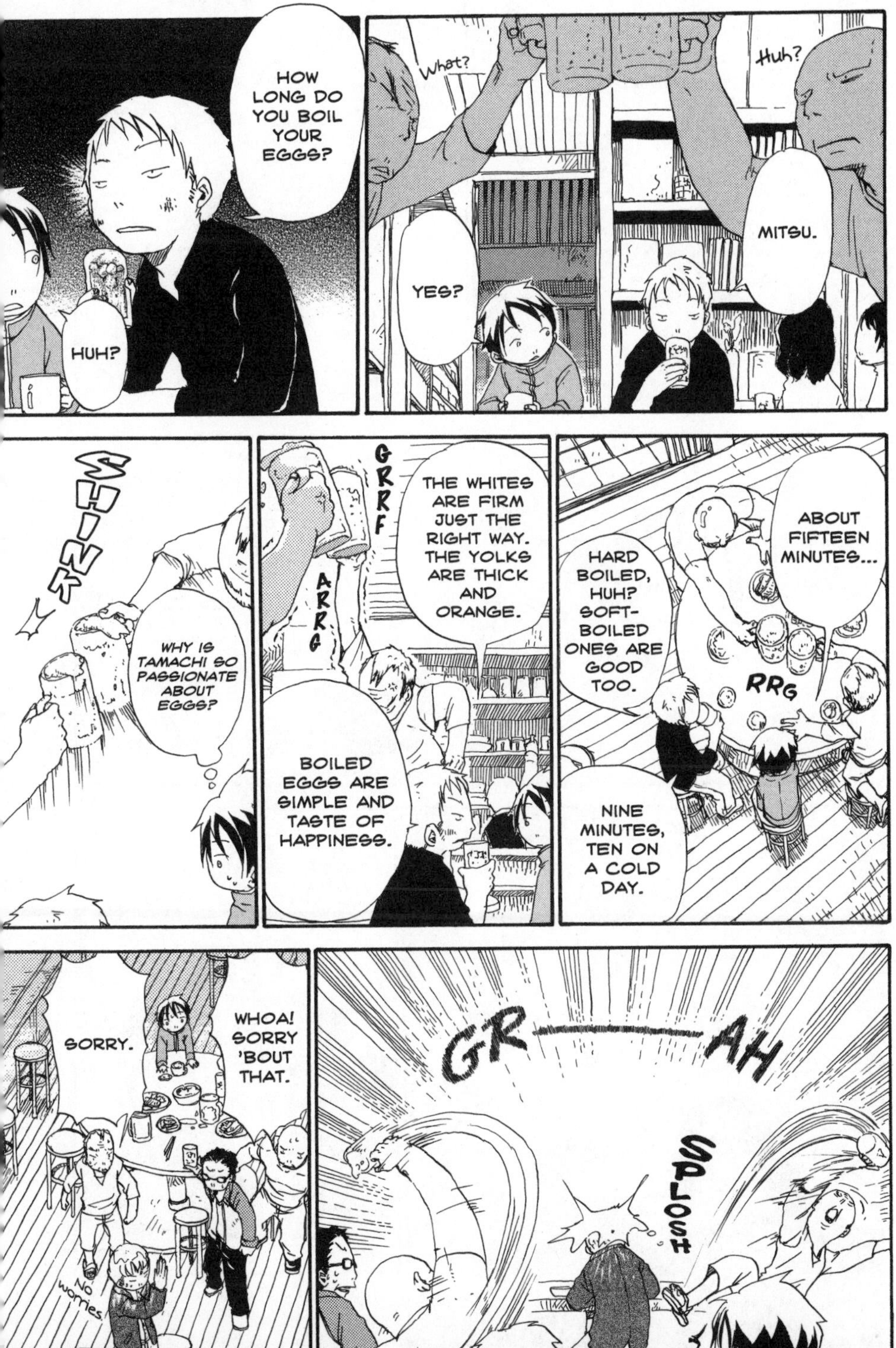
Huh?
What?
MITSU.
YES?
HOW LONG DO YOU BOIL YOUR EGGS?
HUH?
ABOUT FIFTEEN MINUTES...
HARD BOILED, HUH? SOFT-BOILED ONES ARE GOOD TOO.
RRG
NINE MINUTES, TEN ON A COLD DAY.
GRRF
THE WHITES ARE FIRM JUST THE RIGHT WAY. THE YOLKS ARE THICK AND ORANGE.
ARRG
BOILED EGGS ARE SIMPLE AND TASTE OF HAPPINESS.
SHINK
WHY IS TAMACHI SO PASSIONATE ABOUT EGGS?
GR——AH
SPLOSH
WHOA! SORRY 'BOUT THAT.
SORRY.
No worries

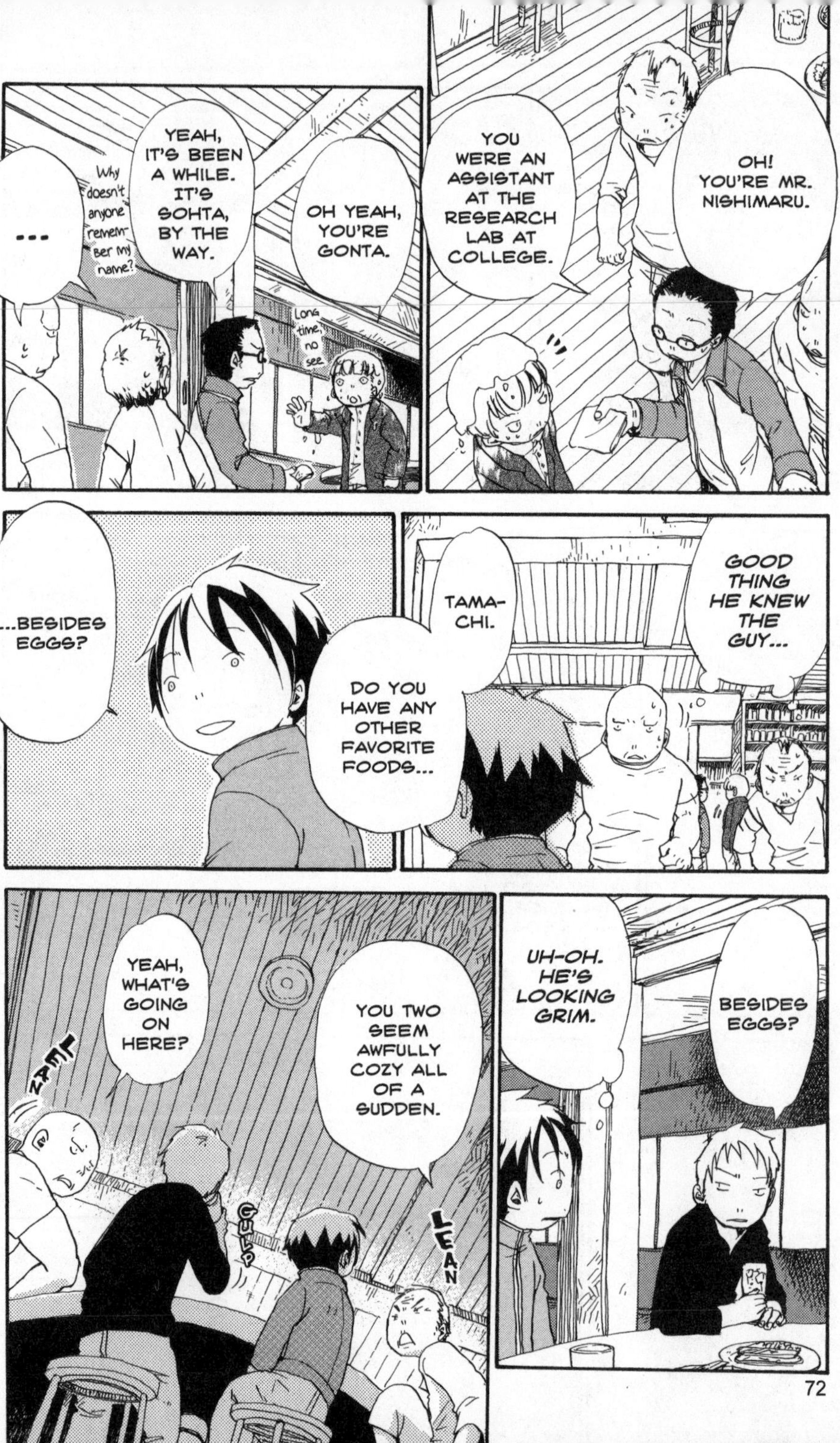
OH! YOU'RE MR. NISHIMARU.
YOU WERE AN ASSISTANT AT THE RESEARCH LAB AT COLLEGE.
OH YEAH, YOU'RE GONTA.
Long time, no see
YEAH, IT'S BEEN A WHILE. IT'S SOHTA, BY THE WAY.
Why doesn't anyone remember my name?
...
GOOD THING HE KNEW THE GUY...
TAMA-CHI.
DO YOU HAVE ANY OTHER FAVORITE FOODS...
...BESIDES EGGS?
BESIDES EGGS?
UH-OH. HE'S LOOKING GRIM.
LEAN
YOU TWO SEEM AWFULLY COZY ALL OF A SUDDEN.
GULP
YEAH, WHAT'S GOING ON HERE?

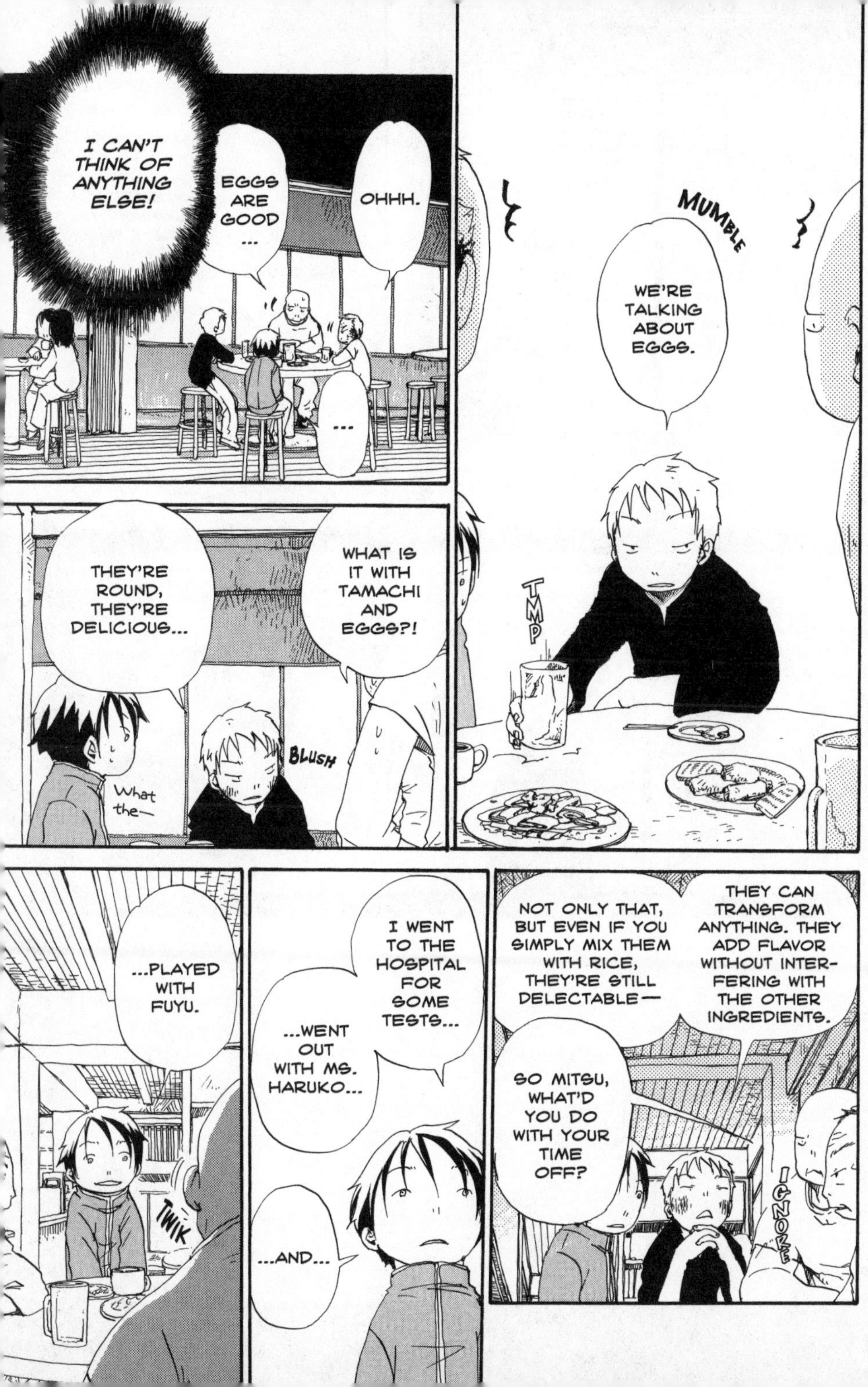
MUMBLE
WE'RE TALKING ABOUT EGGS.
TMP
OHHH.
EGGS ARE GOOD ...
I CAN'T THINK OF ANYTHING ELSE!
...
WHAT IS IT WITH TAMACHI AND EGGS?!
THEY'RE ROUND, THEY'RE DELICIOUS...
BLUSH
What the—
THEY CAN TRANSFORM ANYTHING. THEY ADD FLAVOR WITHOUT INTERFERING WITH THE OTHER INGREDIENTS.
NOT ONLY THAT, BUT EVEN IF YOU SIMPLY MIX THEM WITH RICE, THEY'RE STILL DELECTABLE—
IGNORE
SO MITSU, WHAT'D YOU DO WITH YOUR TIME OFF?
I WENT TO THE HOSPITAL FOR SOME TESTS...
...WENT OUT WITH MS. HARUKO...
...AND...
...PLAYED WITH FUYU.
TWIK

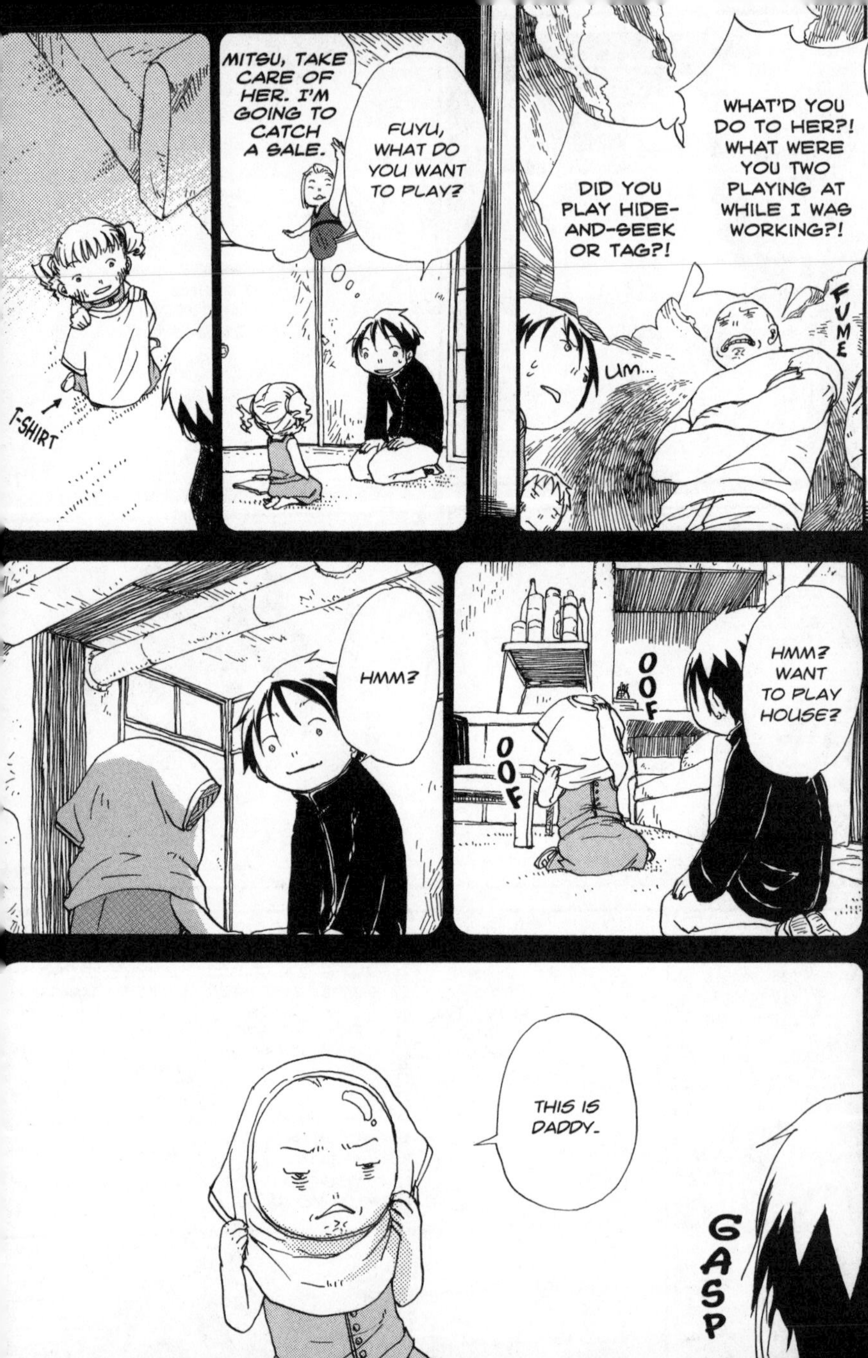
WHAT'D YOU DO TO HER?! WHAT WERE YOU TWO PLAYING AT WHILE I WAS WORKING?!
DID YOU PLAY HIDE-AND-SEEK OR TAG?!
FUME
UM...
MITSU, TAKE CARE OF HER. I'M GOING TO CATCH A SALE.
FUYU, WHAT DO YOU WANT TO PLAY?
T-SHIRT
HMM? WANT TO PLAY HOUSE?
OOF
OOF
HMM?
GASP
THIS IS DADDY.

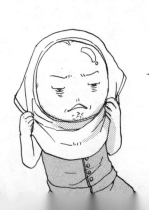

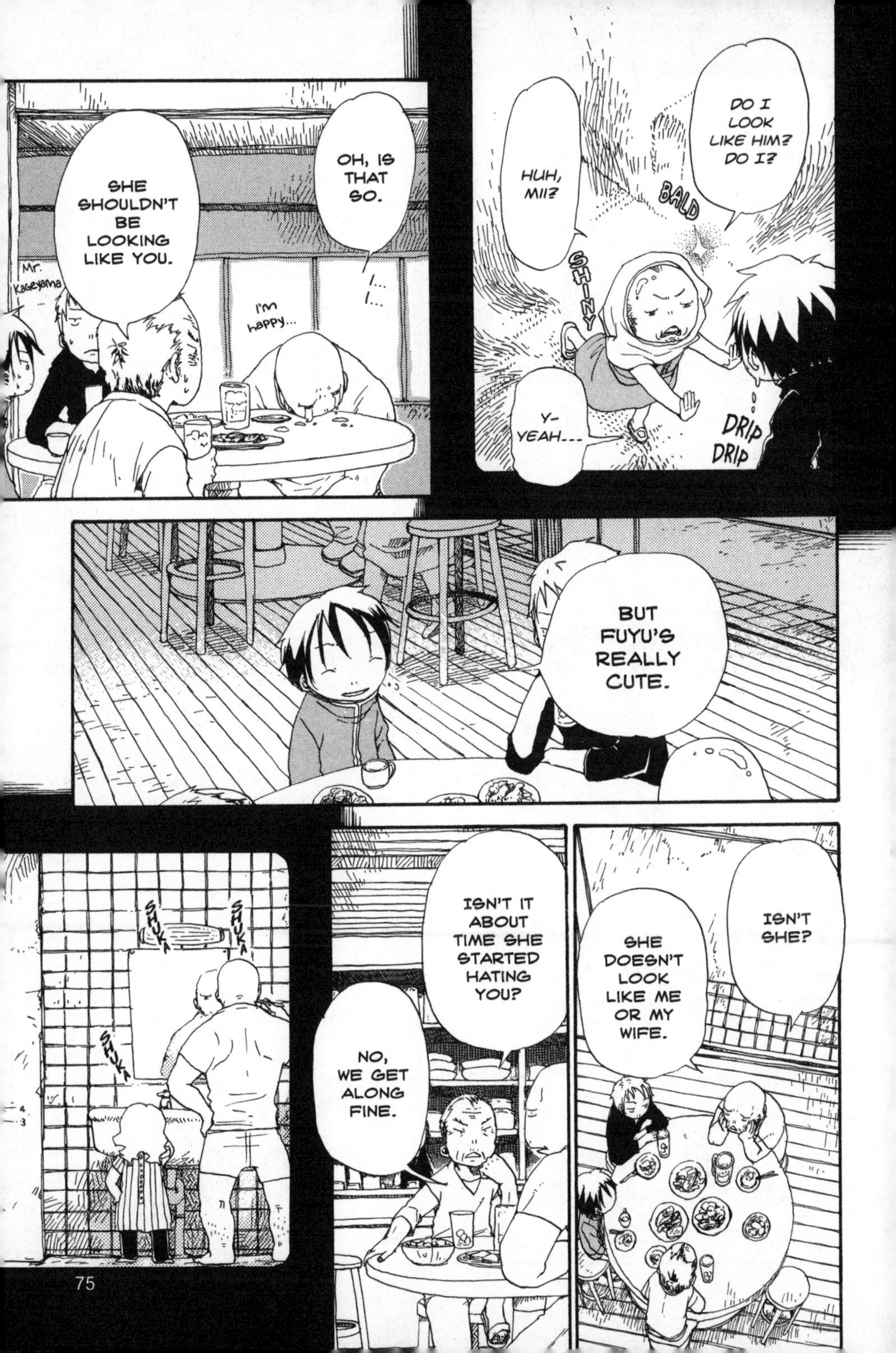
DO I LOOK LIKE HIM? DO I?
BALD
HUH, MII?
SHINY
Y-YEAH...
DRIP DRIP
OH, IS THAT SO.
SHE SHOULDN'T BE LOOKING LIKE YOU.
I... I...
I'm happy...
Mr. Kageyama ...
BUT FUYU'S REALLY CUTE.
ISN'T SHE?
SHE DOESN'T LOOK LIKE ME OR MY WIFE.
ISN'T IT ABOUT TIME SHE STARTED HATING YOU?
NO, WE GET ALONG FINE.
SHUKA
SHUKA
SHUKA

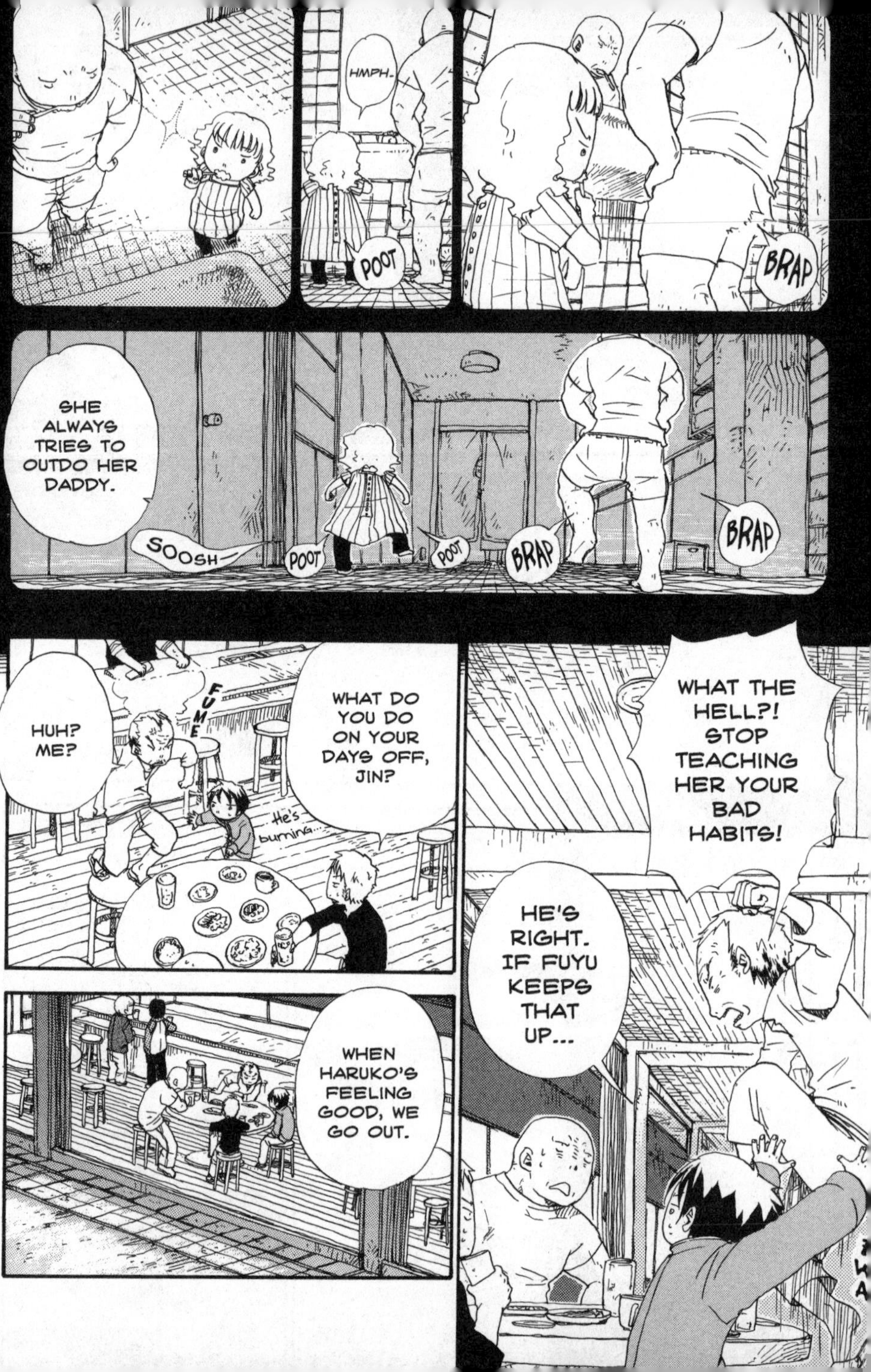
BRAP
HMPH..
POOT
SHE ALWAYS TRIES TO OUTDO HER DADDY.
BRAP
BRAP
POOT
POOT
SOOSH
WHAT THE HELL?! STOP TEACHING HER YOUR BAD HABITS!
HE'S RIGHT. IF FUYU KEEPS THAT UP...
WHAT DO YOU DO ON YOUR DAYS OFF, JIN?
FUME
He's burning...
HUH? ME?
WHEN HARUKO'S FEELING GOOD, WE GO OUT.

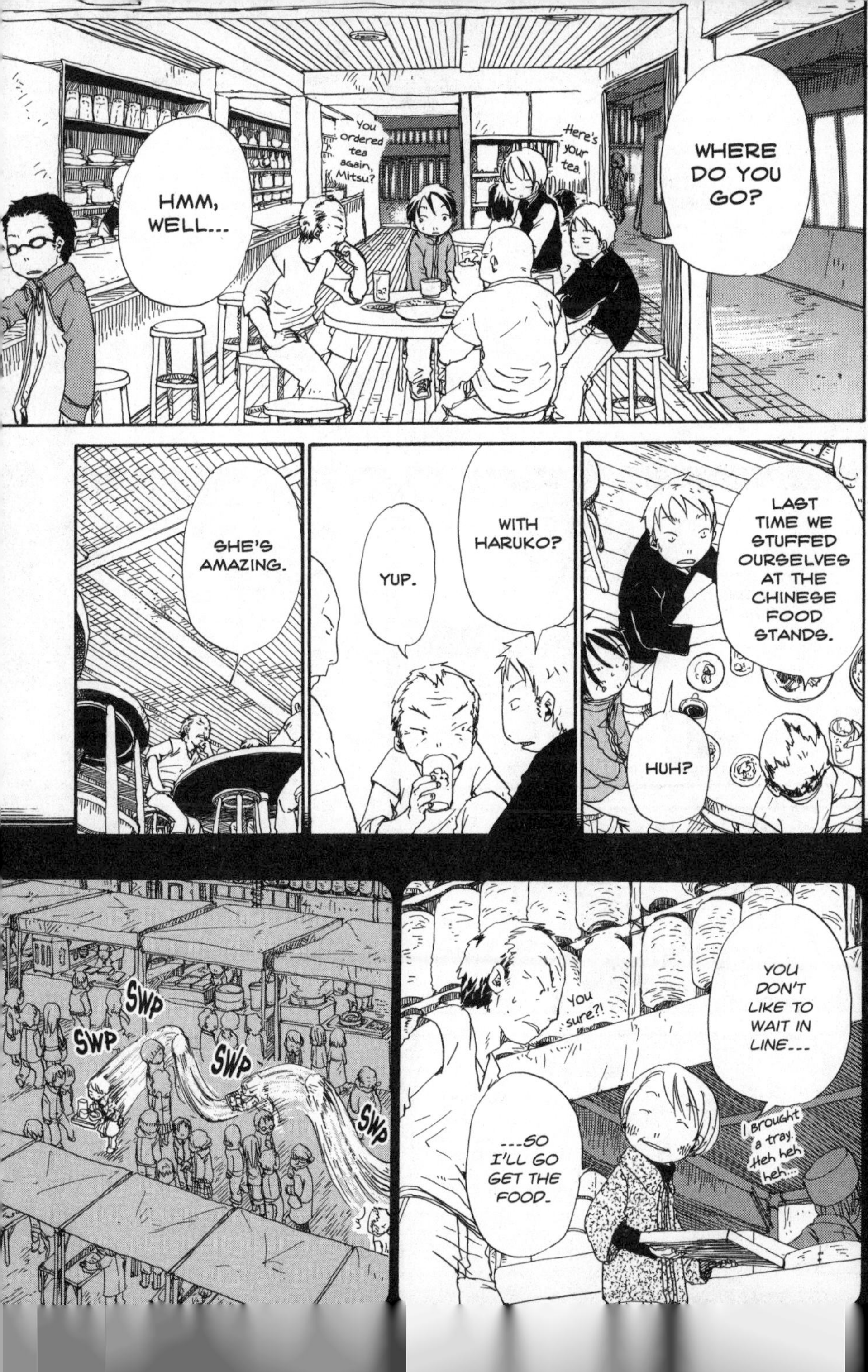
WHERE DO YOU GO?
Here's your tea.
You ordered tea again, Mitsu?
HMM, WELL...
LAST TIME WE STUFFED OURSELVES AT THE CHINESE FOOD STANDS.
HUH?
WITH HARUKO?
YUP.
SHE'S AMAZING.
YOU DON'T LIKE TO WAIT IN LINE...
You sure?!
I brought a tray. Heh heh heh...
...SO I'LL GO GET THE FOOD.
SWP
SWP
SWP
SWP

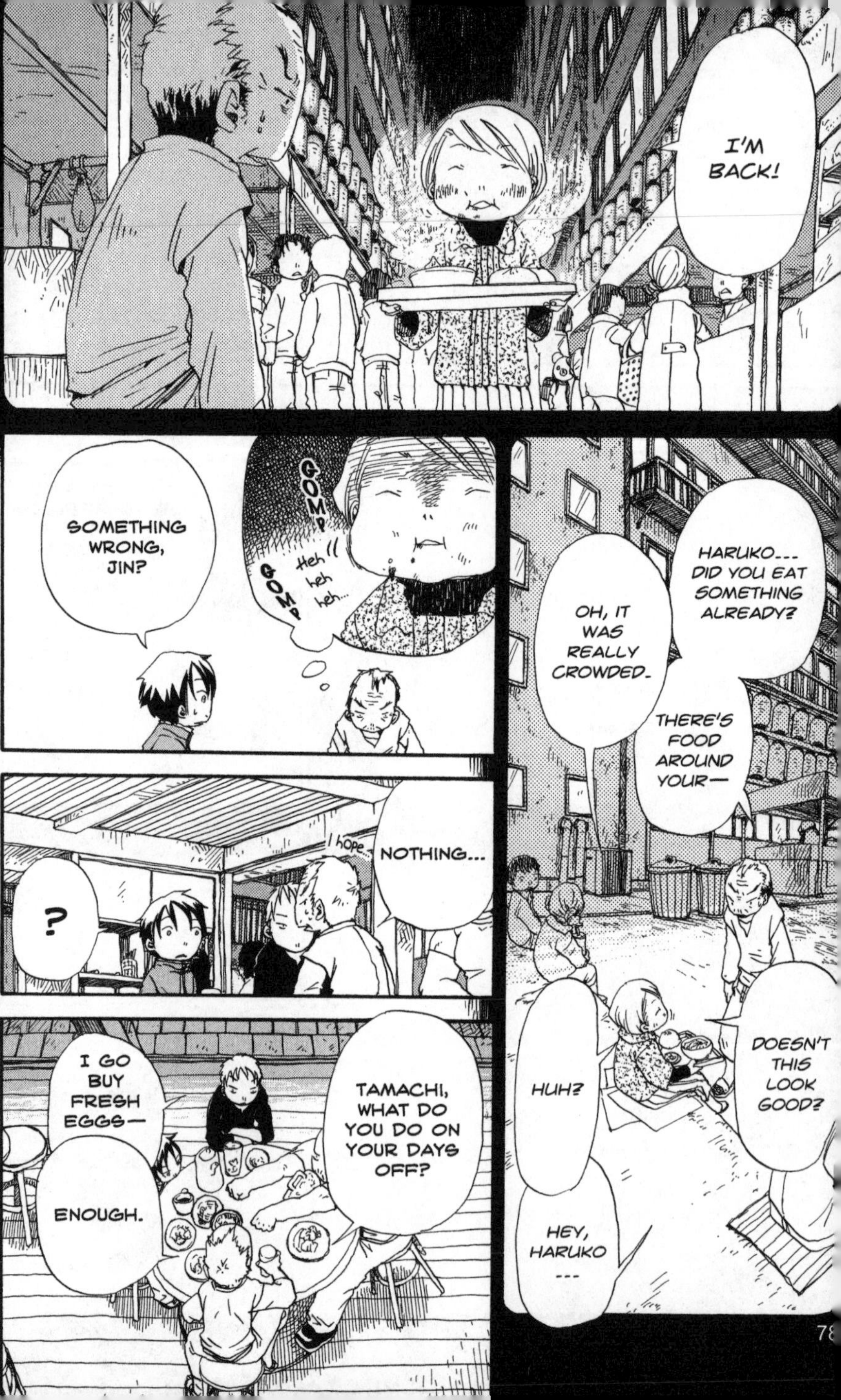

I'M BACK!
HARUKO... DID YOU EAT SOMETHING ALREADY?
OH, IT WAS REALLY CROWDED.
THERE'S FOOD AROUND YOUR—
DOESN'T THIS LOOK GOOD?
HUH?
HEY, HARUKO...
GOMP GOMP
Heh heh heh...
SOMETHING WRONG, JIN?
I hope...
NOTHING...
?
TAMACHI, WHAT DO YOU DO ON YOUR DAYS OFF?
I GO BUY FRESH EGGS—
ENOUGH.

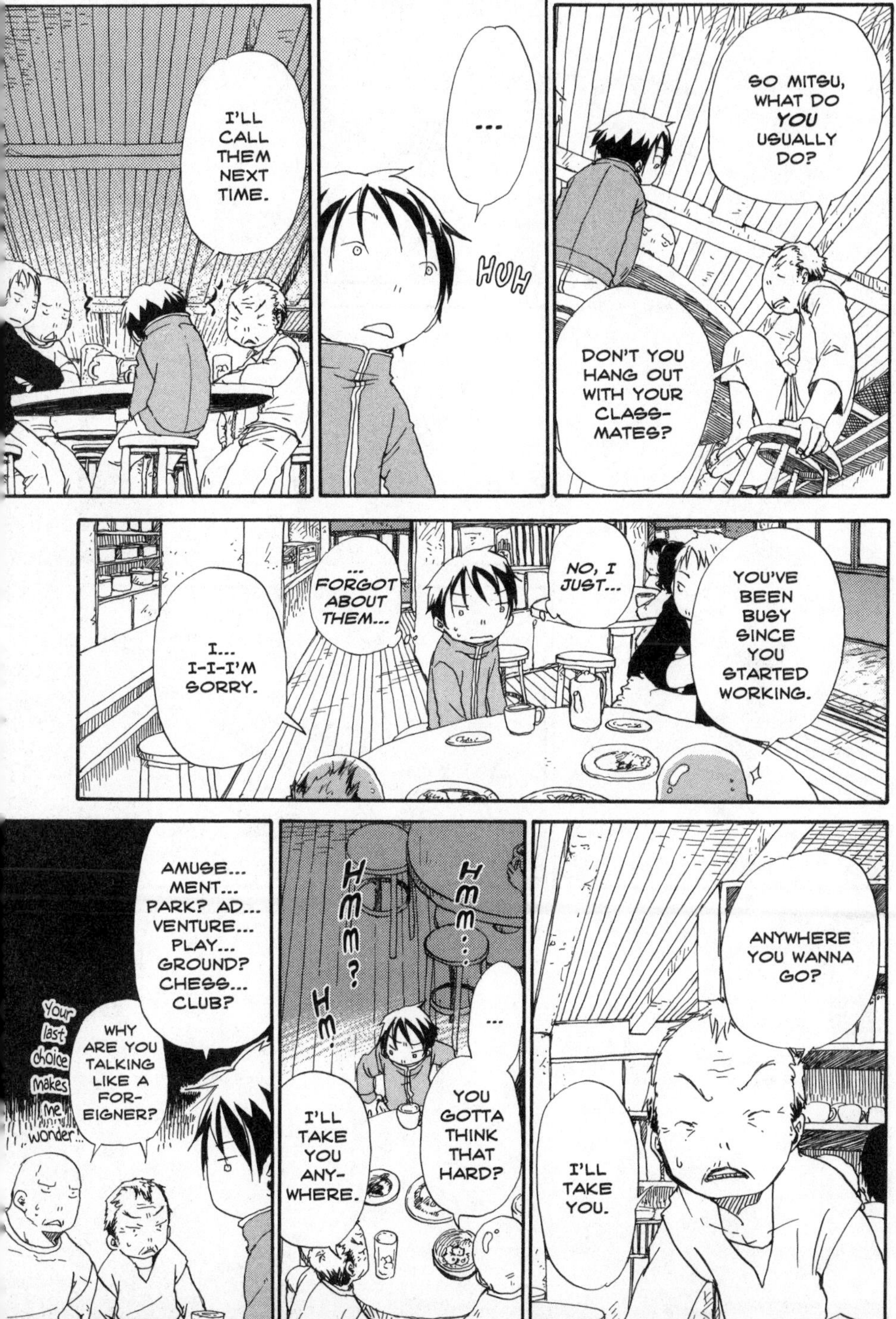
SO MITSU, WHAT DO *YOU* USUALLY DO?
DON'T YOU HANG OUT WITH YOUR CLASS-MATES?
...
HUH
I'LL CALL THEM NEXT TIME.
YOU'VE BEEN BUSY SINCE YOU STARTED WORKING.
NO, I JUST...
... FORGOT ABOUT THEM...
I... I-I-I'M SORRY.
ANYWHERE YOU WANNA GO?
I'LL TAKE YOU.
HMM...
HMM?
HM.
...
YOU GOTTA THINK THAT HARD?
I'LL TAKE YOU ANY-WHERE.
AMUSE... MENT... PARK? AD... VENTURE... PLAY... GROUND? CHESS... CLUB?
WHY ARE YOU TALKING LIKE A FOR-EIGNER?
Your last choice makes me wonder...

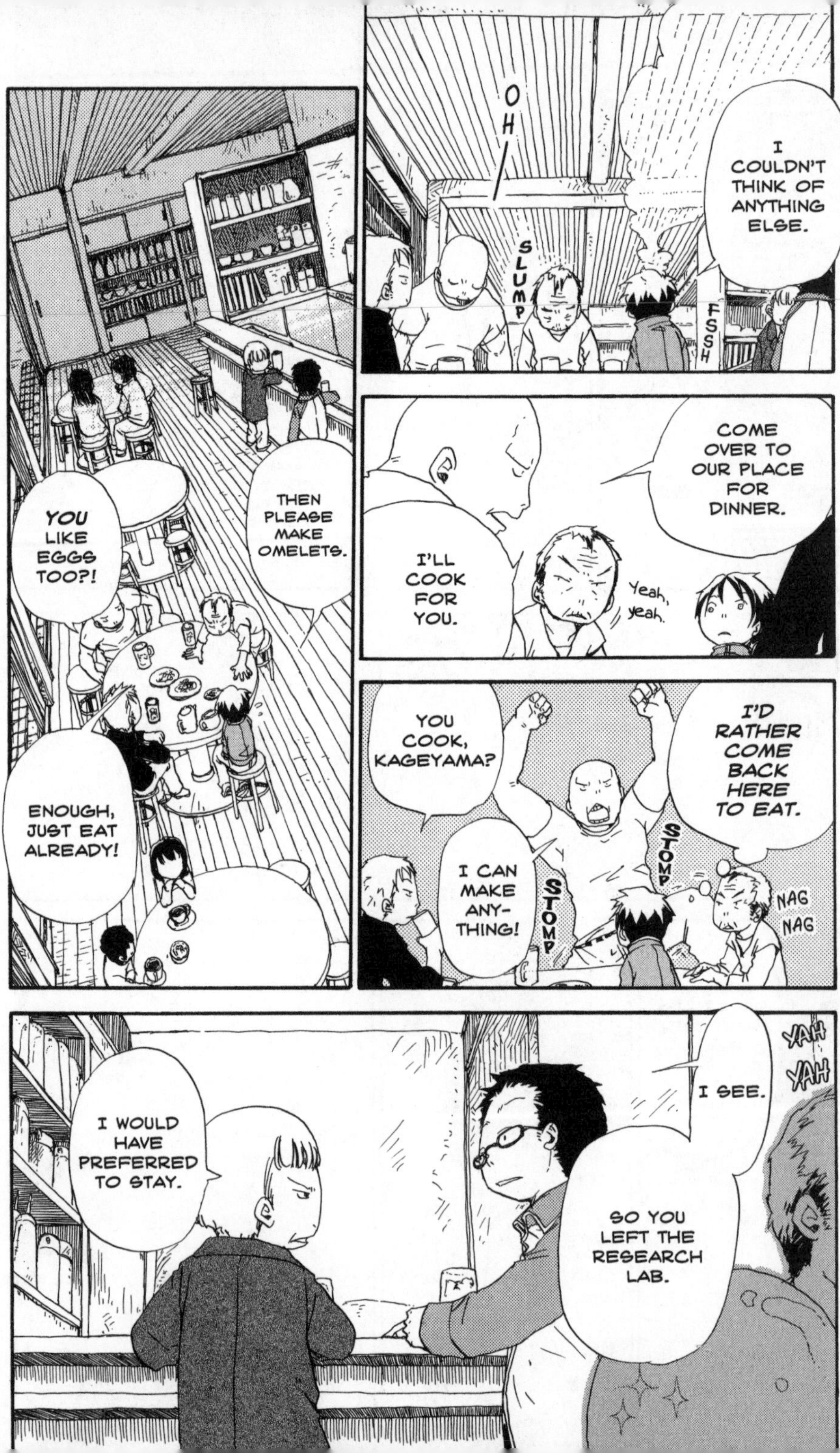
I COULDN'T THINK OF ANYTHING ELSE.
OH
FSSH
SLUMP
COME OVER TO OUR PLACE FOR DINNER.
Yeah, yeah.
I'LL COOK FOR YOU.
I'D RATHER COME BACK HERE TO EAT.
NAG NAG
STOMP
YOU COOK, KAGEYAMA?
I CAN MAKE ANY-THING!
STOMP
THEN PLEASE MAKE OMELETS.
YOU LIKE EGGS TOO?!
ENOUGH, JUST EAT ALREADY!
YAH YAH
I SEE.
SO YOU LEFT THE RESEARCH LAB.
I WOULD HAVE PREFERRED TO STAY.

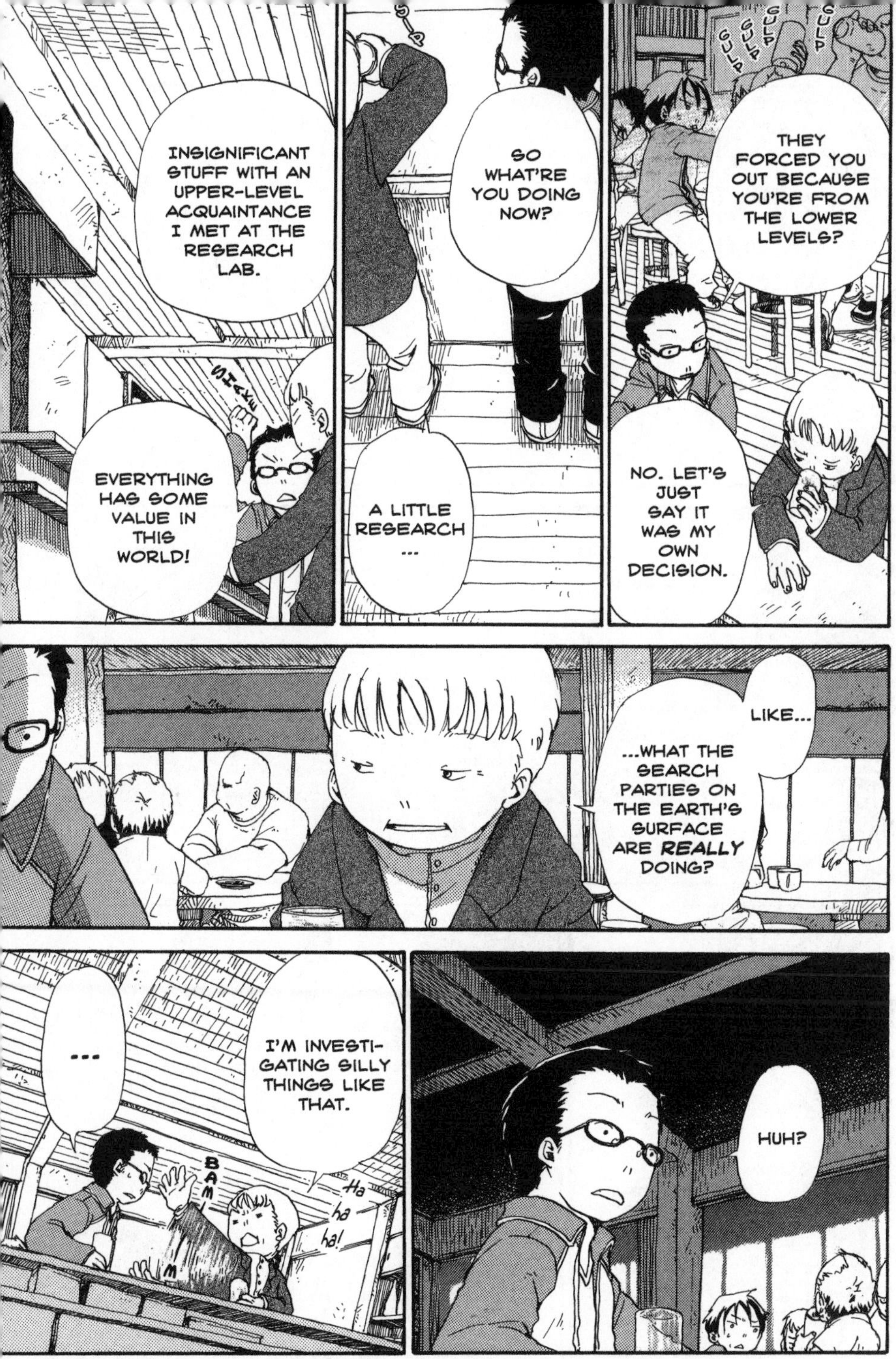
GULP GULP GULP GULP
THEY FORCED YOU OUT BECAUSE YOU'RE FROM THE LOWER LEVELS?
NO. LET'S JUST SAY IT WAS MY OWN DECISION.
SO WHAT'RE YOU DOING NOW?
A LITTLE RESEARCH ...
INSIGNIFICANT STUFF WITH AN UPPER-LEVEL ACQUAINTANCE I MET AT THE RESEARCH LAB.
EVERYTHING HAS SOME VALUE IN THIS WORLD!
LIKE...
...WHAT THE SEARCH PARTIES ON THE EARTH'S SURFACE ARE *REALLY* DOING?
HUH?
I'M INVESTI-GATING SILLY THINGS LIKE THAT.
BAM!
Ha ha ha!
...

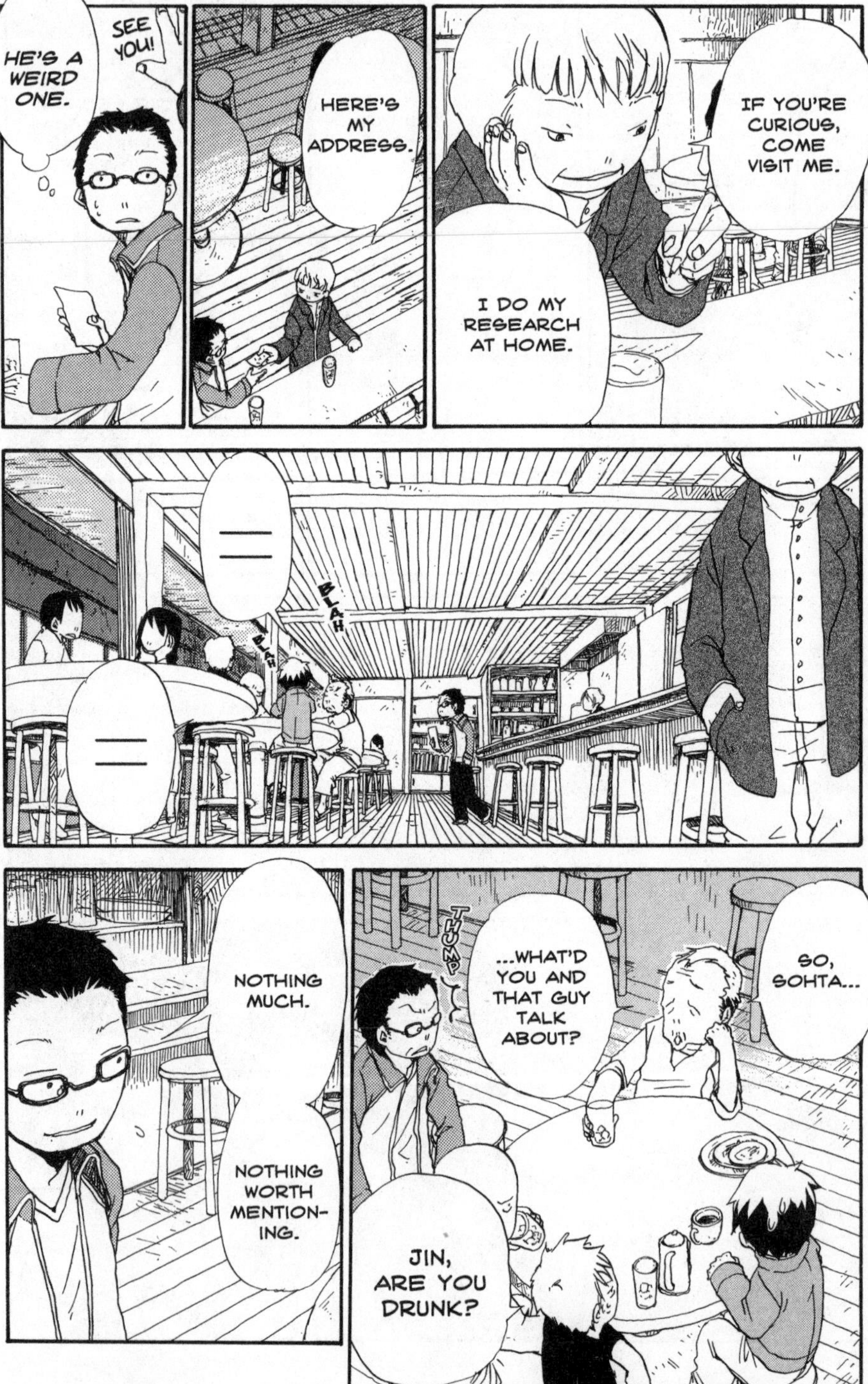
IF YOU'RE CURIOUS, COME VISIT ME.
I DO MY RESEARCH AT HOME.
HERE'S MY ADDRESS.
SEE YOU!
HE'S A WEIRD ONE.
BLAH
BLAH
SO, SOHTA...
THUMP
...WHAT'D YOU AND THAT GUY TALK ABOUT?
JIN, ARE YOU DRUNK?
NOTHING MUCH.
NOTHING WORTH MENTION-ING.

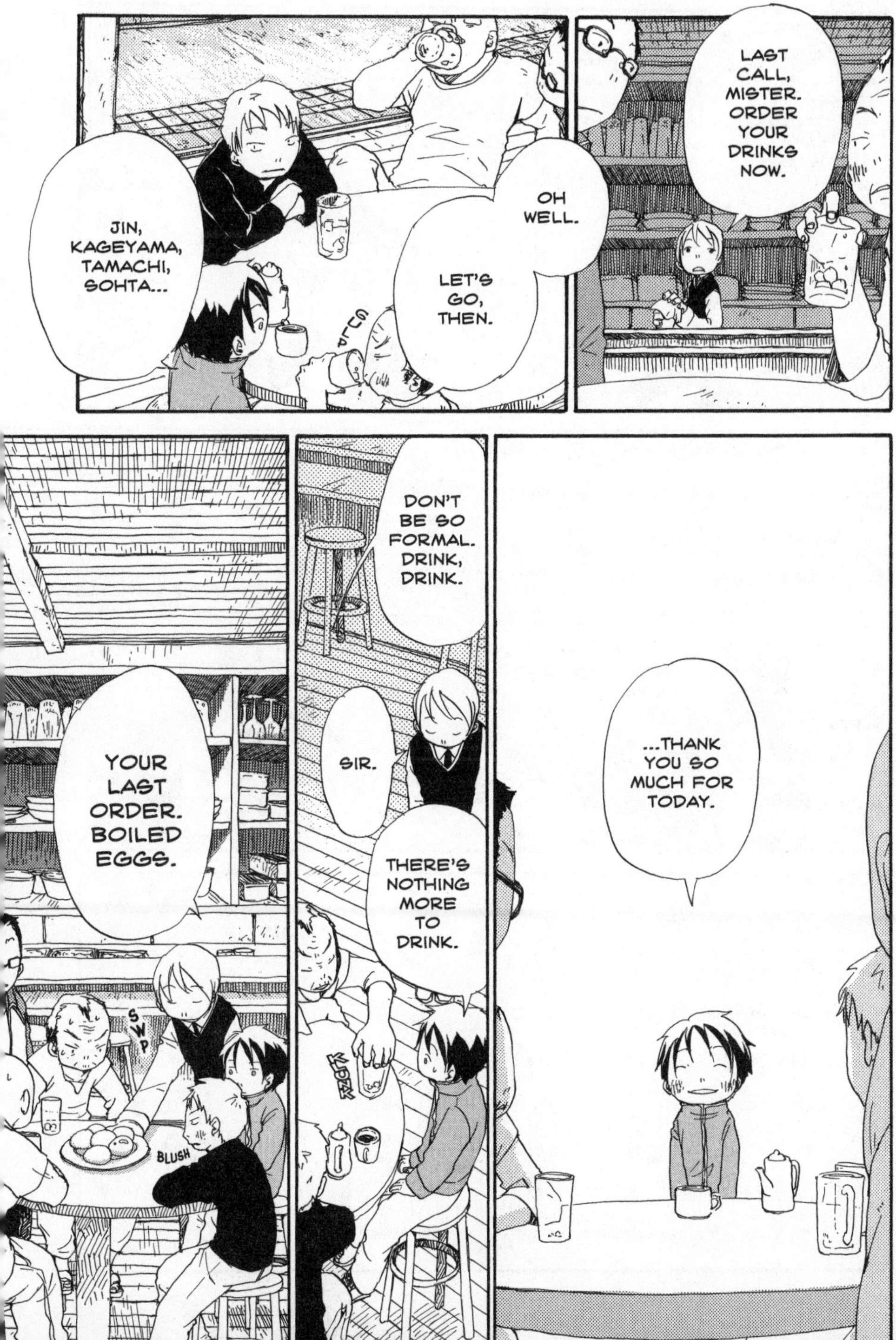
LAST CALL, MISTER. ORDER YOUR DRINKS NOW.
OH WELL.
LET'S GO, THEN.
JIN, KAGEYAMA, TAMACHI, SOHTA...
...THANK YOU SO MUCH FOR TODAY.
DON'T BE SO FORMAL. DRINK, DRINK.
SIR.
THERE'S NOTHING MORE TO DRINK.
YOUR LAST ORDER. BOILED EGGS.
SWP
BLUSH

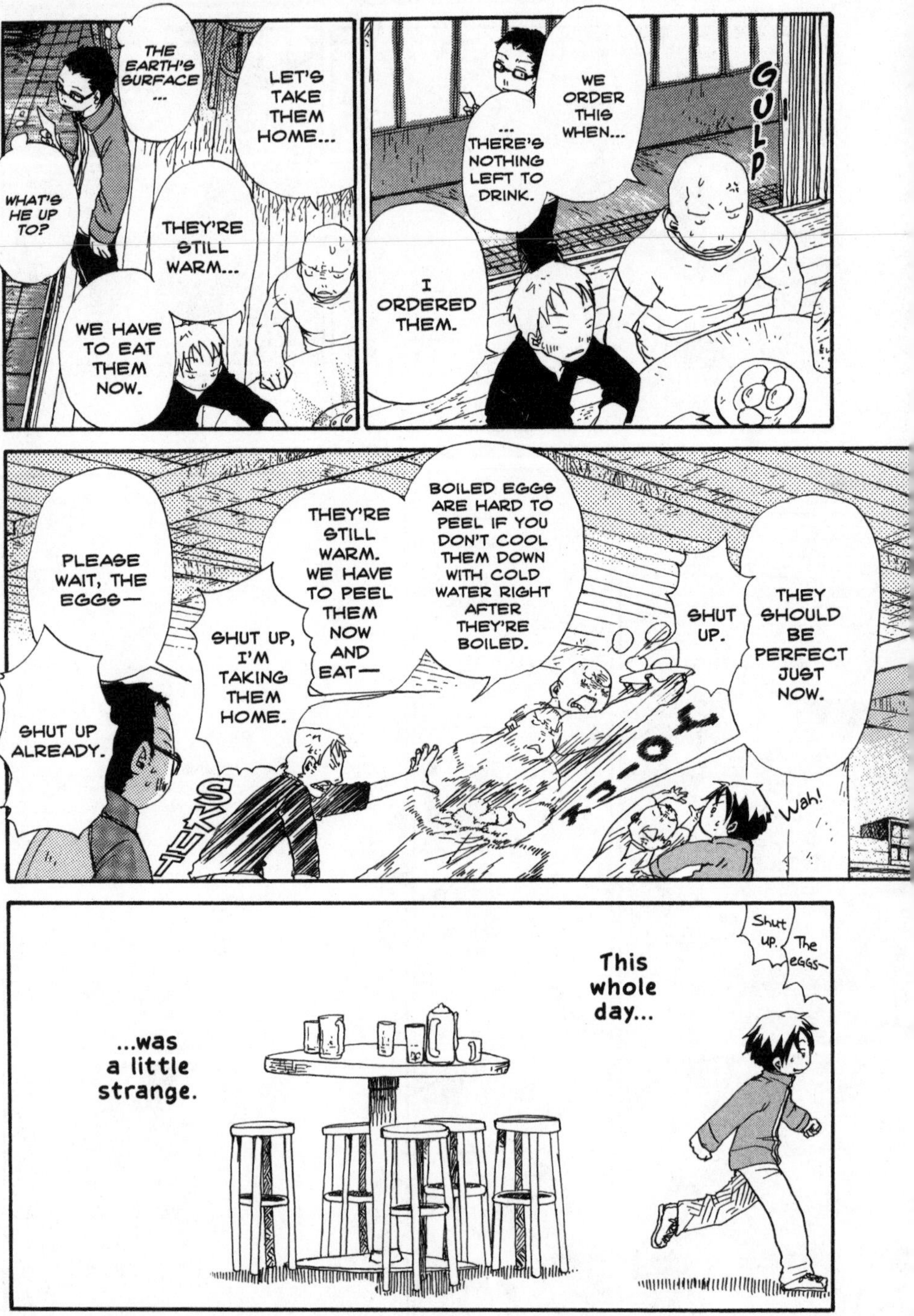
GULP
WE ORDER THIS WHEN...
...THERE'S NOTHING LEFT TO DRINK.
I ORDERED THEM.
LET'S TAKE THEM HOME...
THE EARTH'S SURFACE...
WHAT'S HE UP TO?
THEY'RE STILL WARM...
WE HAVE TO EAT THEM NOW.
THEY SHOULD BE PERFECT JUST NOW.
SHUT UP.
BOILED EGGS ARE HARD TO PEEL IF YOU DON'T COOL THEM DOWN WITH COLD WATER RIGHT AFTER THEY'RE BOILED.
THEY'RE STILL WARM. WE HAVE TO PEEL THEM NOW AND EAT—
SHUT UP, I'M TAKING THEM HOME.
PLEASE WAIT, THE EGGS—
SHUT UP ALREADY.
Wah!
SKUT
Shut up.
The eggs—
This whole day...
...was a little strange.

floor 13: night festival

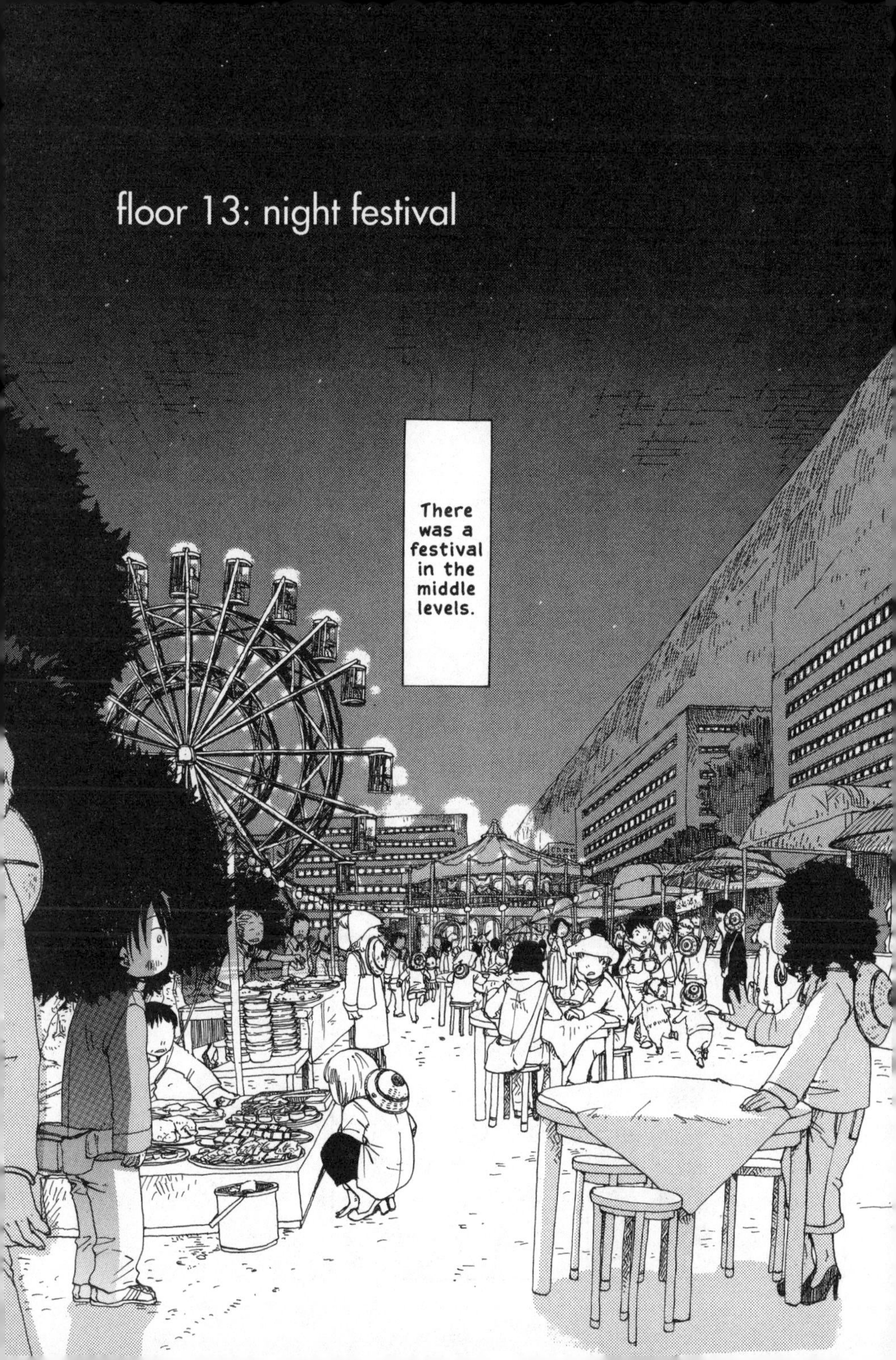
There was a festival in the middle levels.

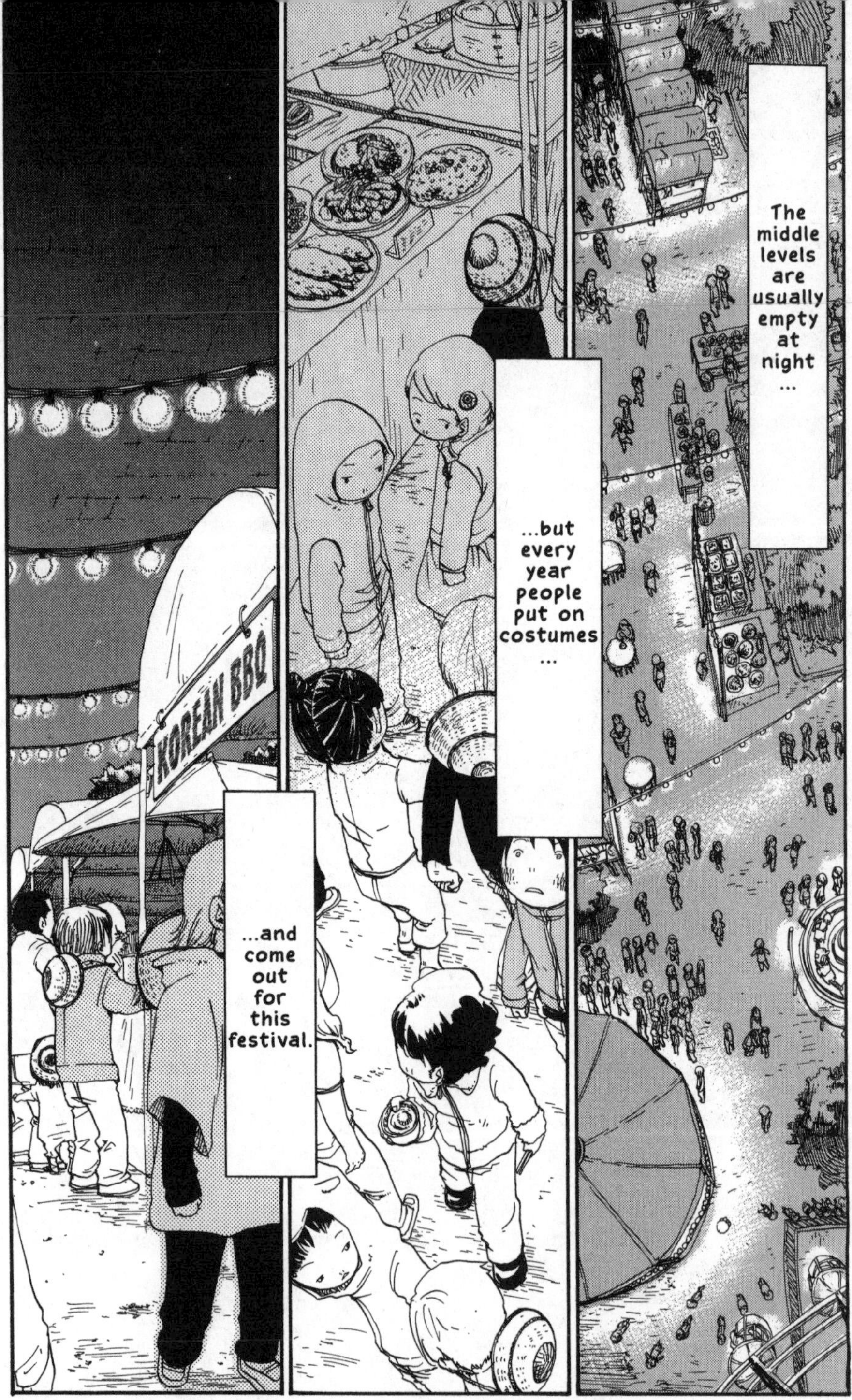
The middle levels are usually empty at night ...
...but every year people put on costumes ...
...and come out for this festival.
KOREAN BBQ

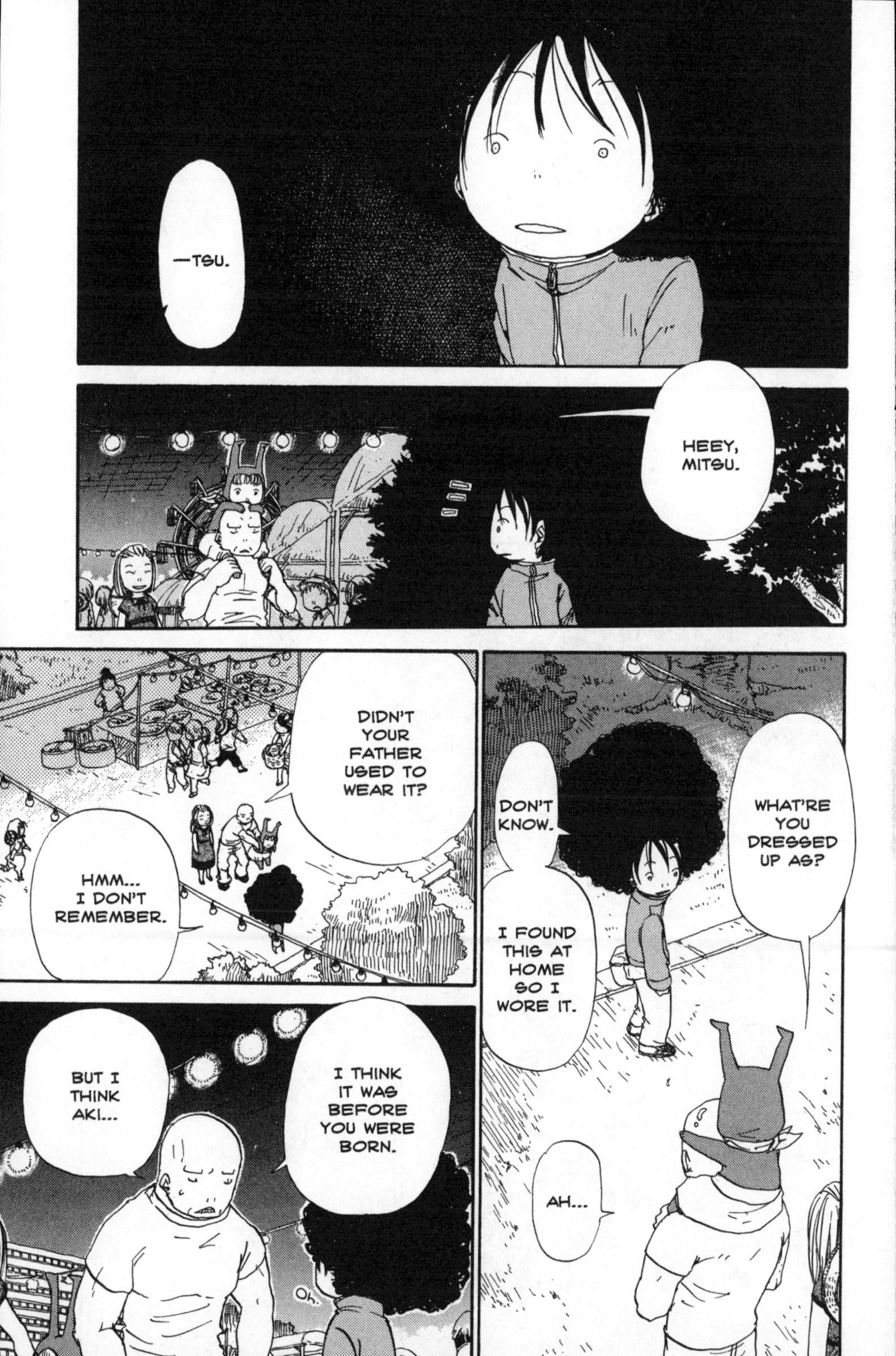
—TSU.
HEEY, MITSU.
WHAT'RE YOU DRESSED UP AS?
DON'T KNOW.
I FOUND THIS AT HOME SO I WORE IT.
AH...
DIDN'T YOUR FATHER USED TO WEAR IT?
HMM... I DON'T REMEMBER.
I THINK IT WAS BEFORE YOU WERE BORN.
BUT I THINK AKI...
Oh.

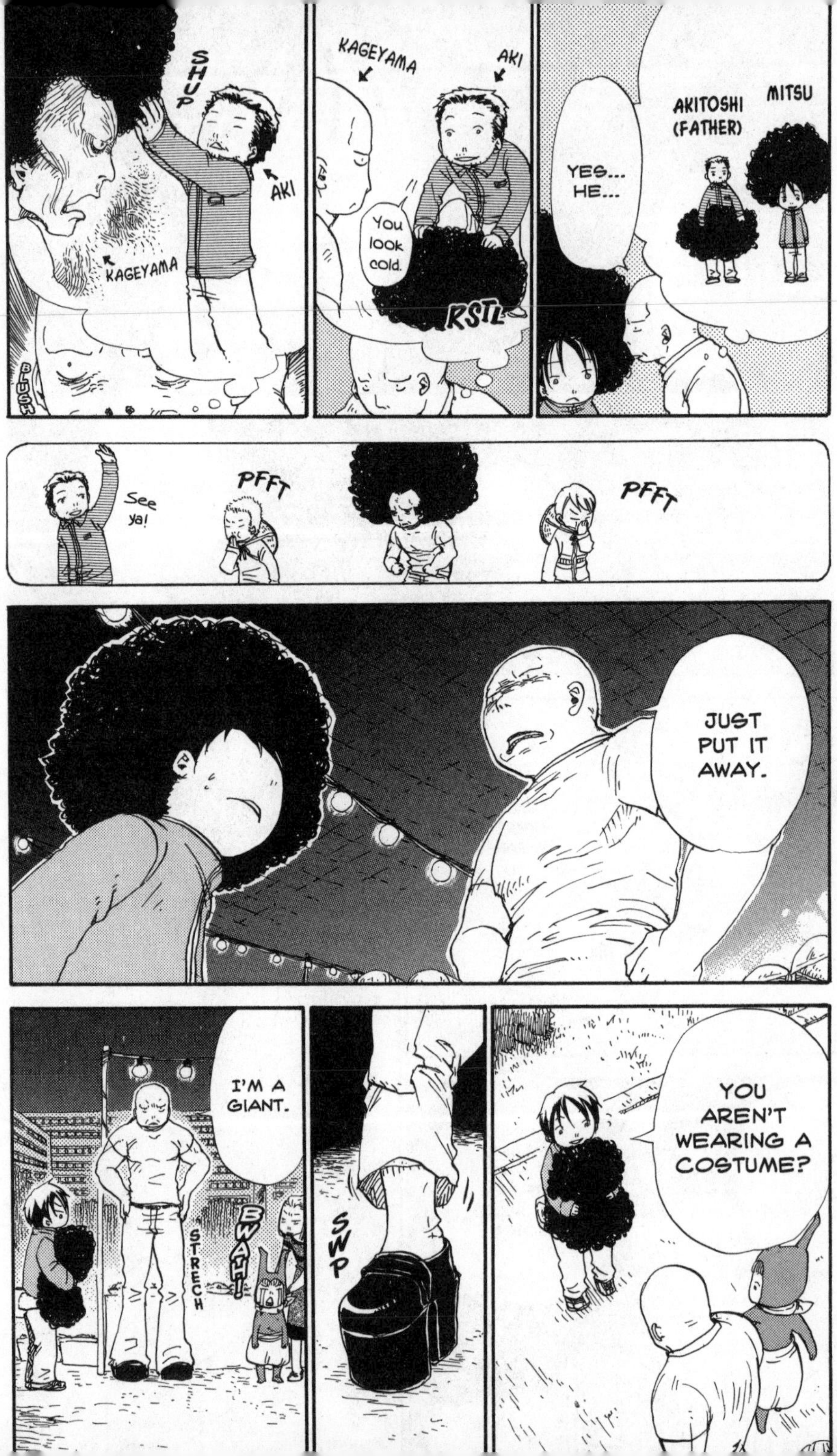
AKITOSHI (FATHER)
MITSU
YES... HE...
KAGEYAMA
AKI
You look cold.
RSTL
SHUP
AKI
KAGEYAMA
BLUSH
PFFT
PFFT
See ya!
JUST PUT IT AWAY.
YOU AREN'T WEARING A COSTUME?
SWP
I'M A GIANT.
BWAH!
STRECH

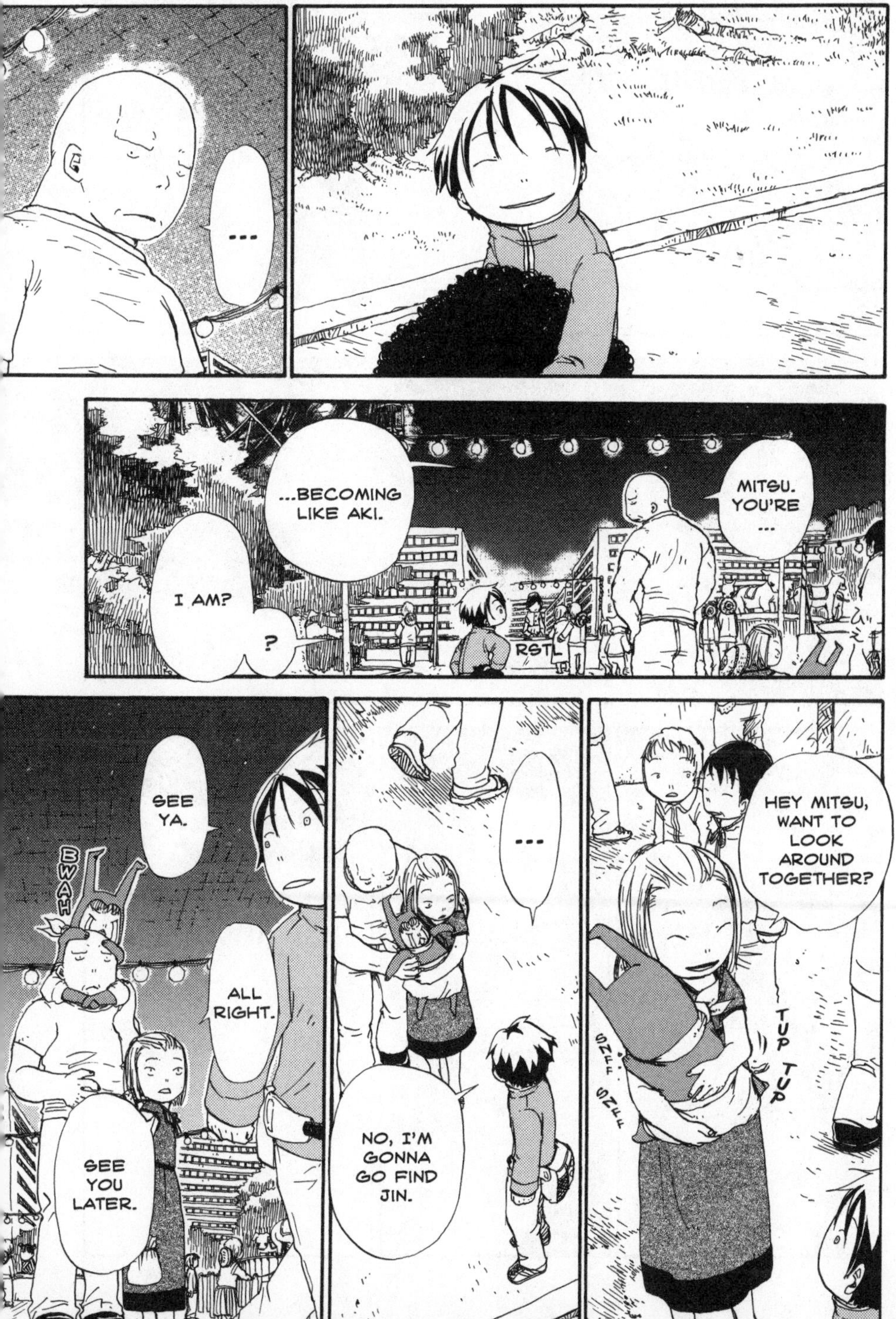
...
MITSU. YOU'RE ...
...BECOMING LIKE AKI.
I AM?
?
RSTL
HEY MITSU, WANT TO LOOK AROUND TOGETHER?
TUP TUP
SNFF SNFF
...
NO, I'M GONNA GO FIND JIN.
SEE YA.
BWAH
ALL RIGHT.
SEE YOU LATER.

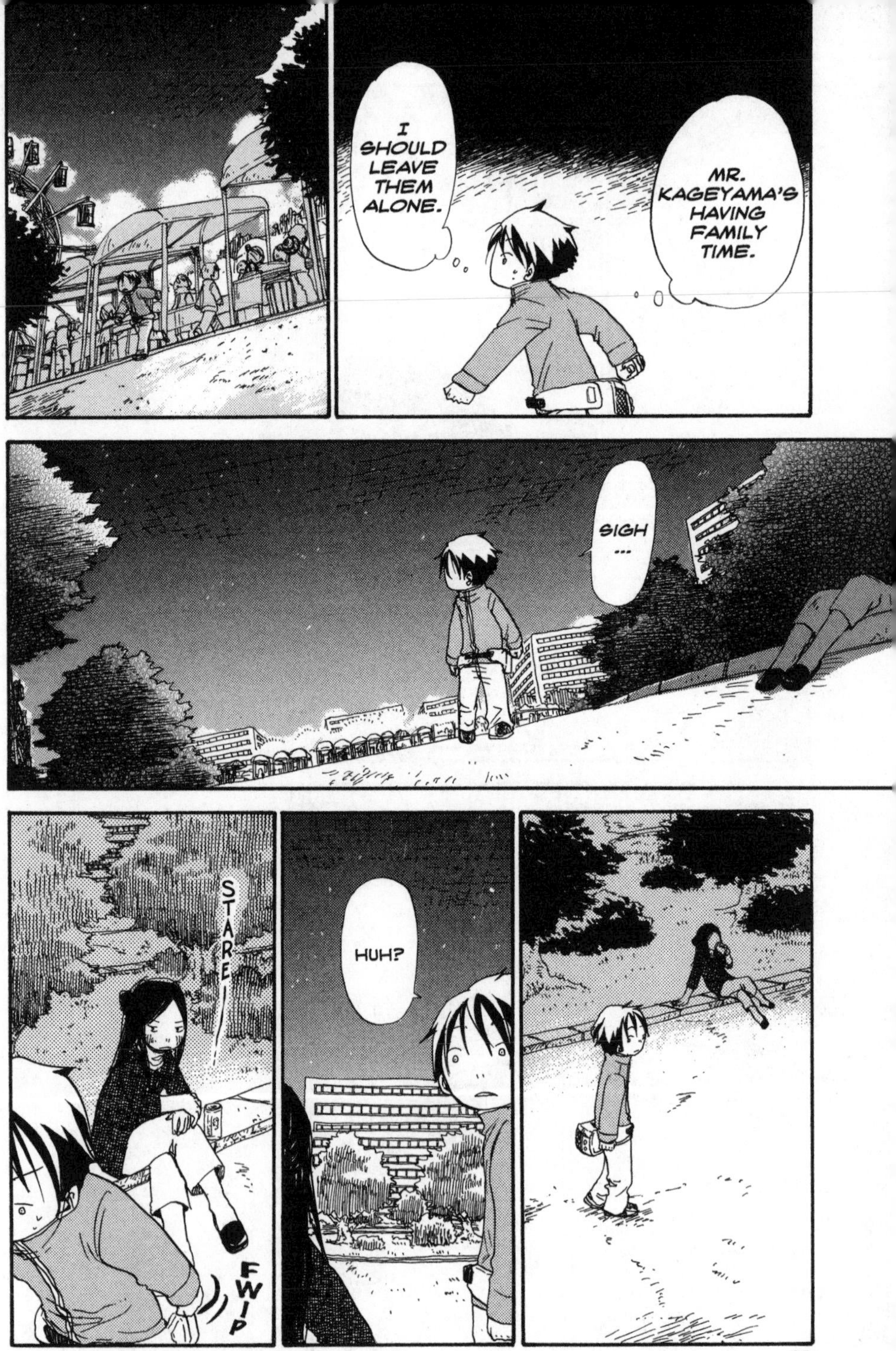
MR. KAGEYAMA'S HAVING FAMILY TIME.
I SHOULD LEAVE THEM ALONE.
SIGH...
HUH?
STARE
FWIP

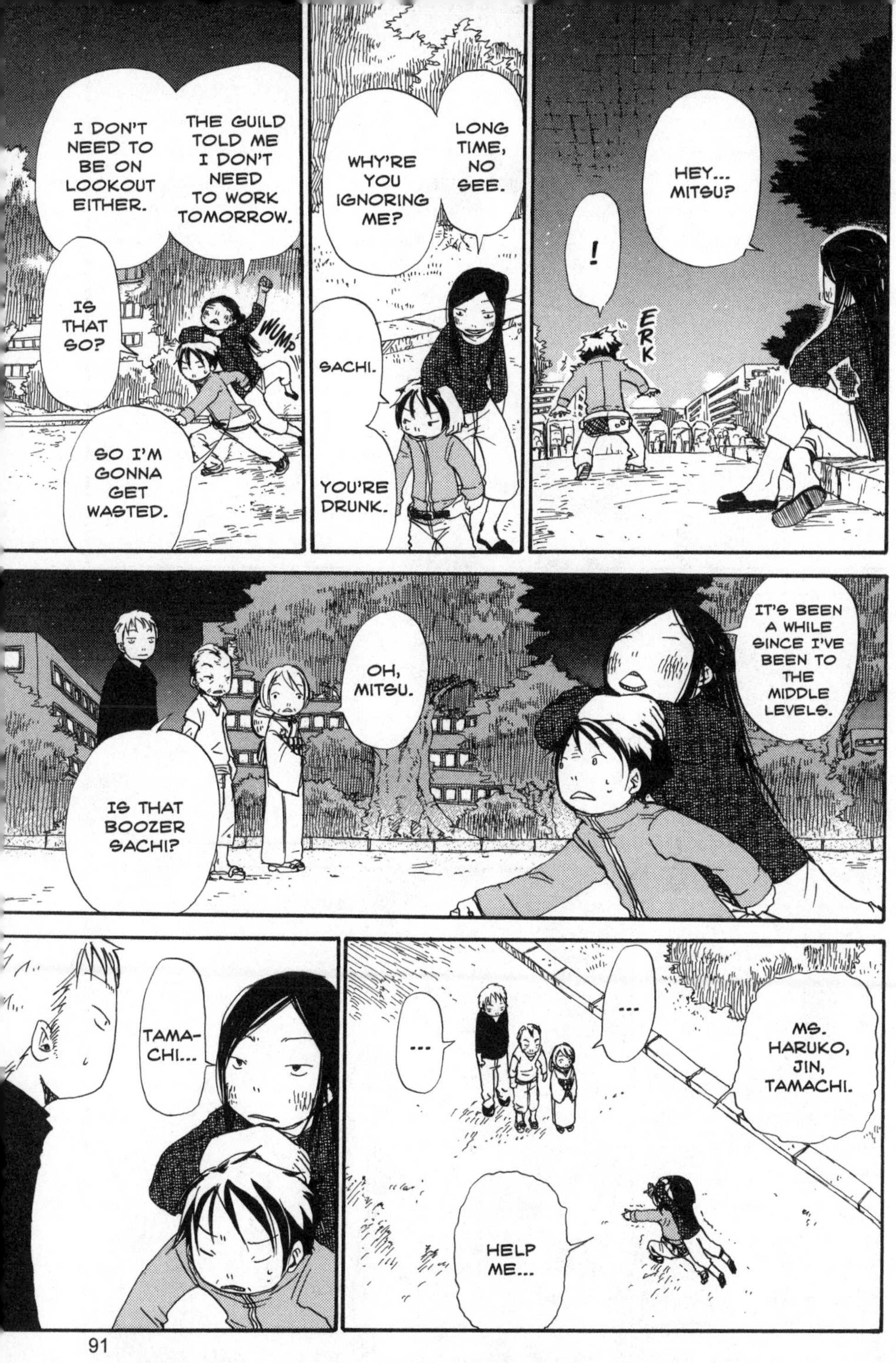
HEY... MITSU?
!
ERK
LONG TIME, NO SEE.
WHY'RE YOU IGNORING ME?
SACHI.
YOU'RE DRUNK.
THE GUILD TOLD ME I DON'T NEED TO WORK TOMORROW.
I DON'T NEED TO BE ON LOOKOUT EITHER.
IS THAT SO?
WUMP
SO I'M GONNA GET WASTED.
IT'S BEEN A WHILE SINCE I'VE BEEN TO THE MIDDLE LEVELS.
OH, MITSU.
IS THAT BOOZER SACHI?
MS. HARUKO, JIN, TAMACHI.
...
...
HELP ME...
TAMA-CHI...

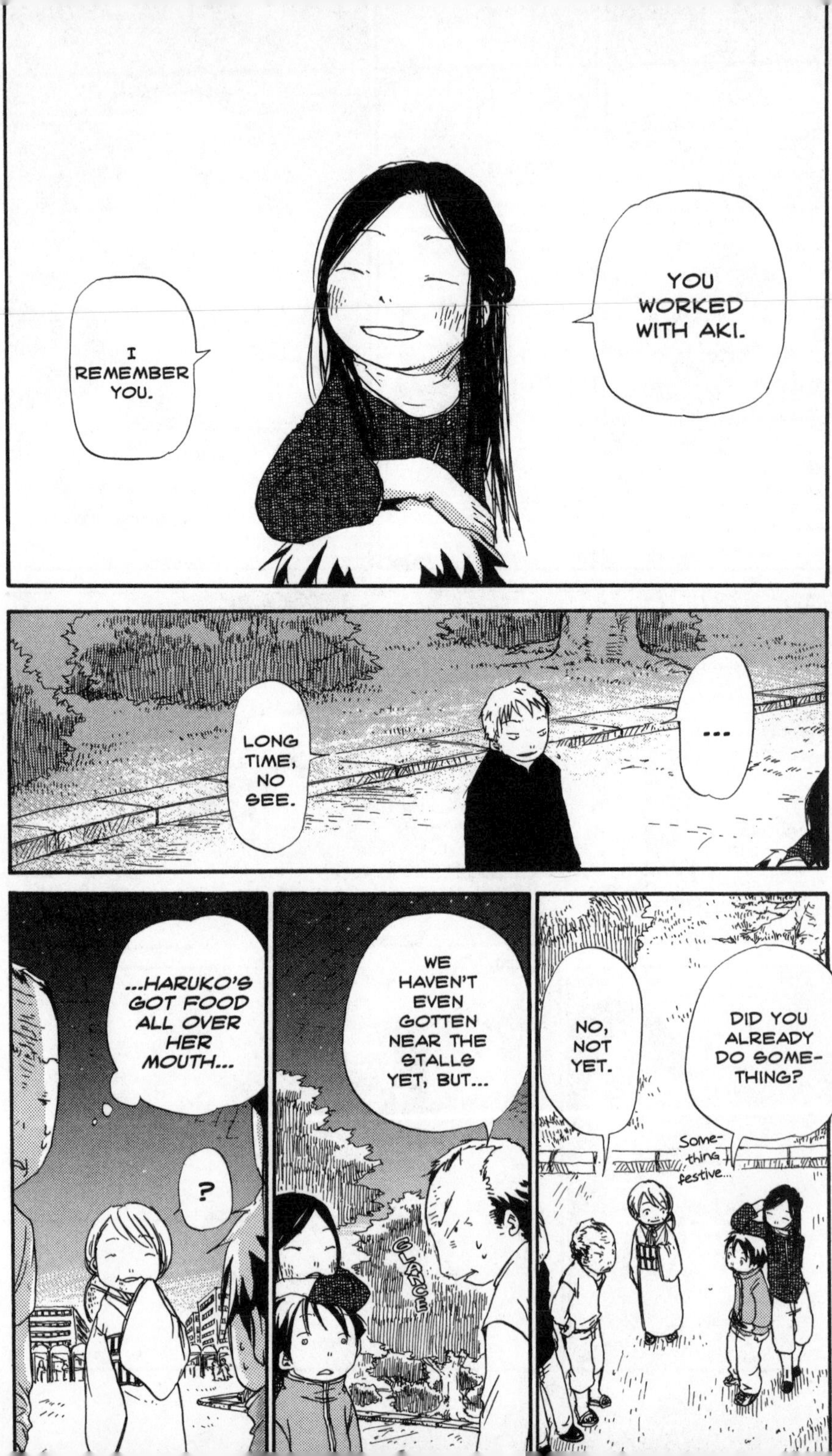
YOU WORKED WITH AKI.
I REMEMBER YOU.
...
LONG TIME, NO SEE.
DID YOU ALREADY DO SOME-THING?
Some-thing festive...
NO, NOT YET.
WE HAVEN'T EVEN GOTTEN NEAR THE STALLS YET, BUT...
GLANCE
...HARUKO'S GOT FOOD ALL OVER HER MOUTH...
?

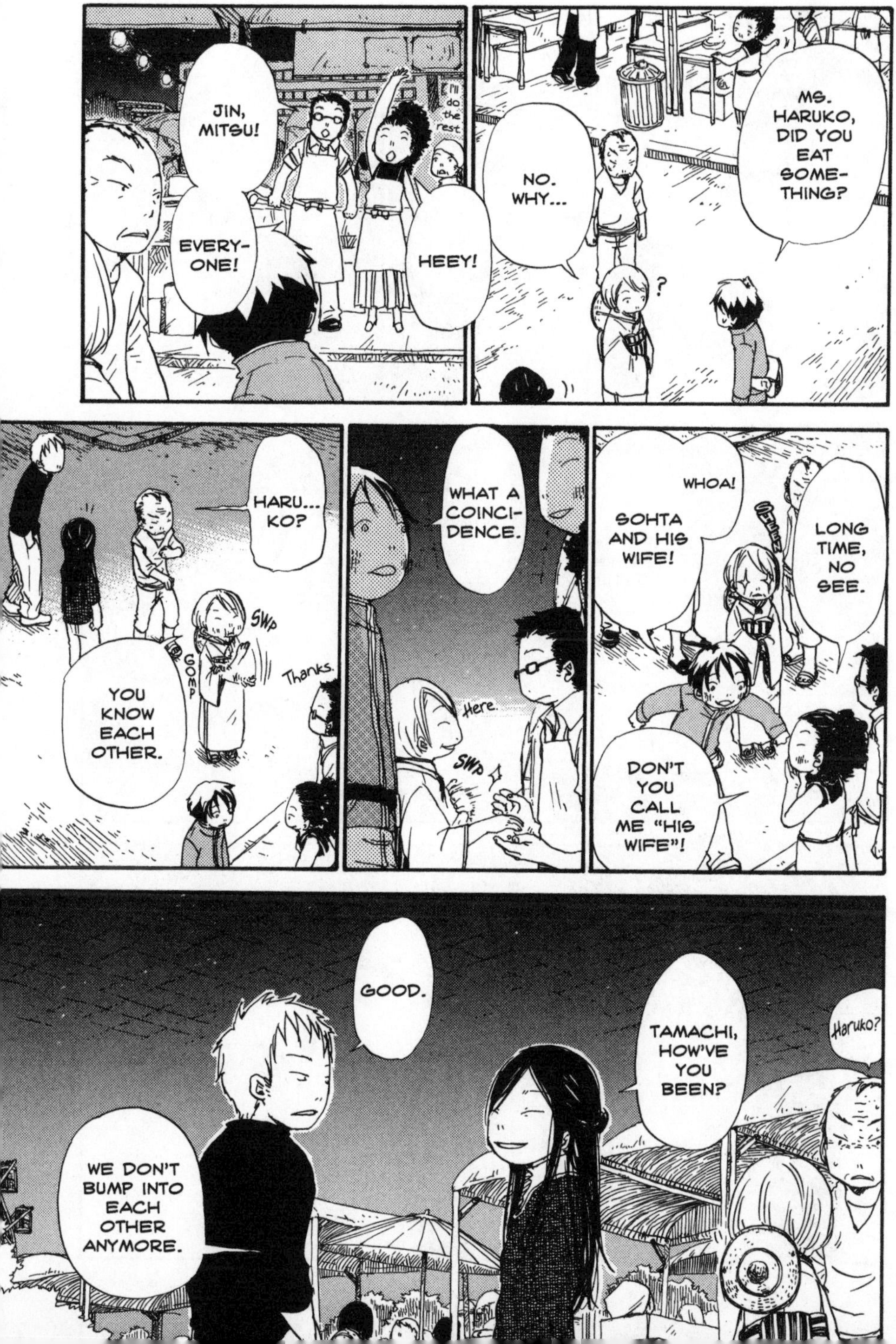
MS. HARUKO, DID YOU EAT SOME-THING?
NO. WHY...
?
I'll do the rest
JIN, MITSU!
HEEY!
EVERY-ONE!
WHOA!
LONG TIME, NO SEE.
SOHTA AND HIS WIFE!
DON'T YOU CALL ME "HIS WIFE"!
WHAT A COINCI-DENCE.
Here.
SWP
HARU... KO?
SWP
GOMP
Thanks.
YOU KNOW EACH OTHER.
Haruko?
TAMACHI, HOW'VE YOU BEEN?
GOOD.
WE DON'T BUMP INTO EACH OTHER ANYMORE.

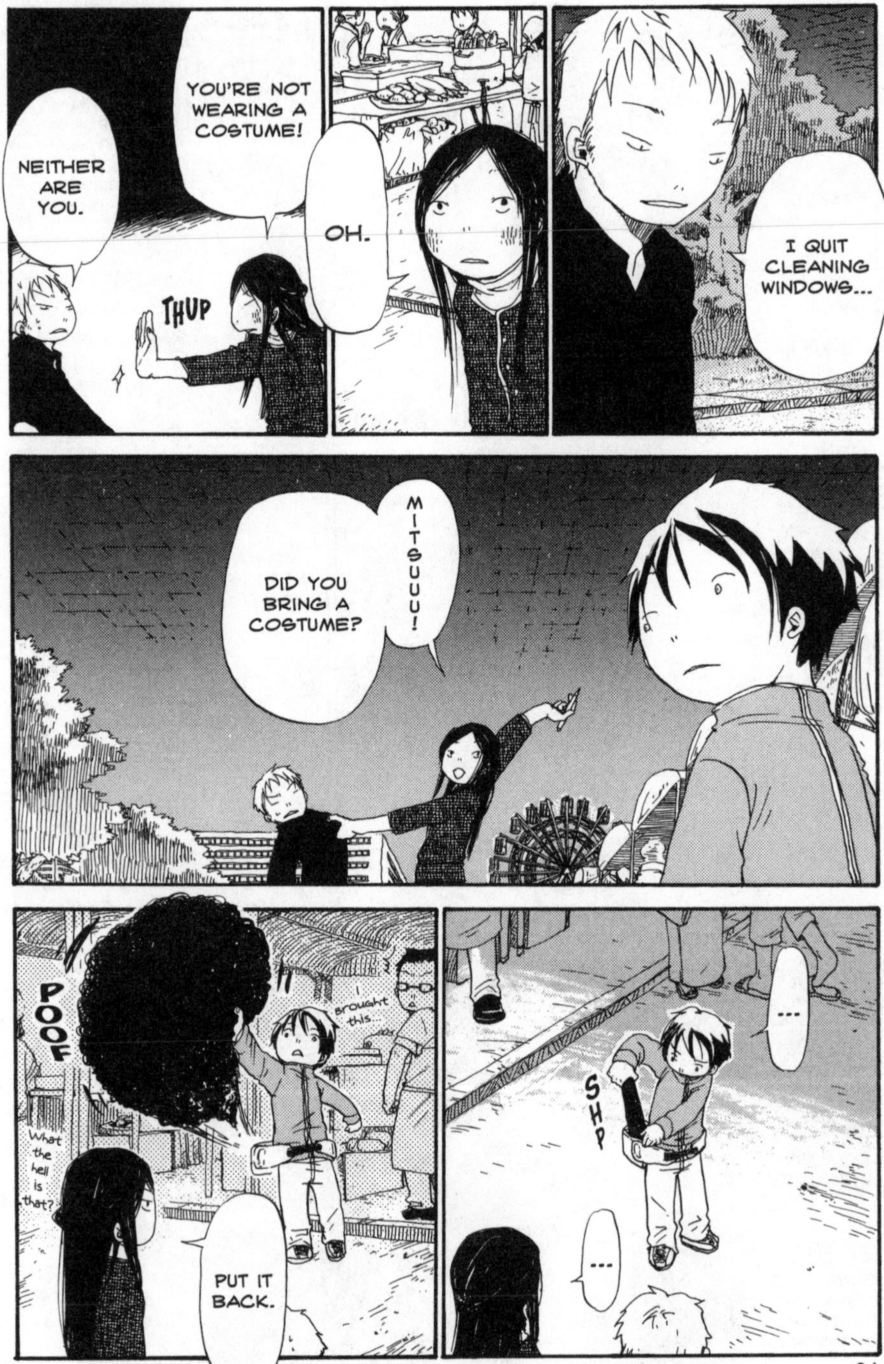

I QUIT CLEANING WINDOWS...
OH.
YOU'RE NOT WEARING A COSTUME!
NEITHER ARE YOU.
THUP
MITSUUU!
DID YOU BRING A COSTUME?
...
SHP
...
I brought this..
POOF
What the hell is that?
PUT IT BACK.

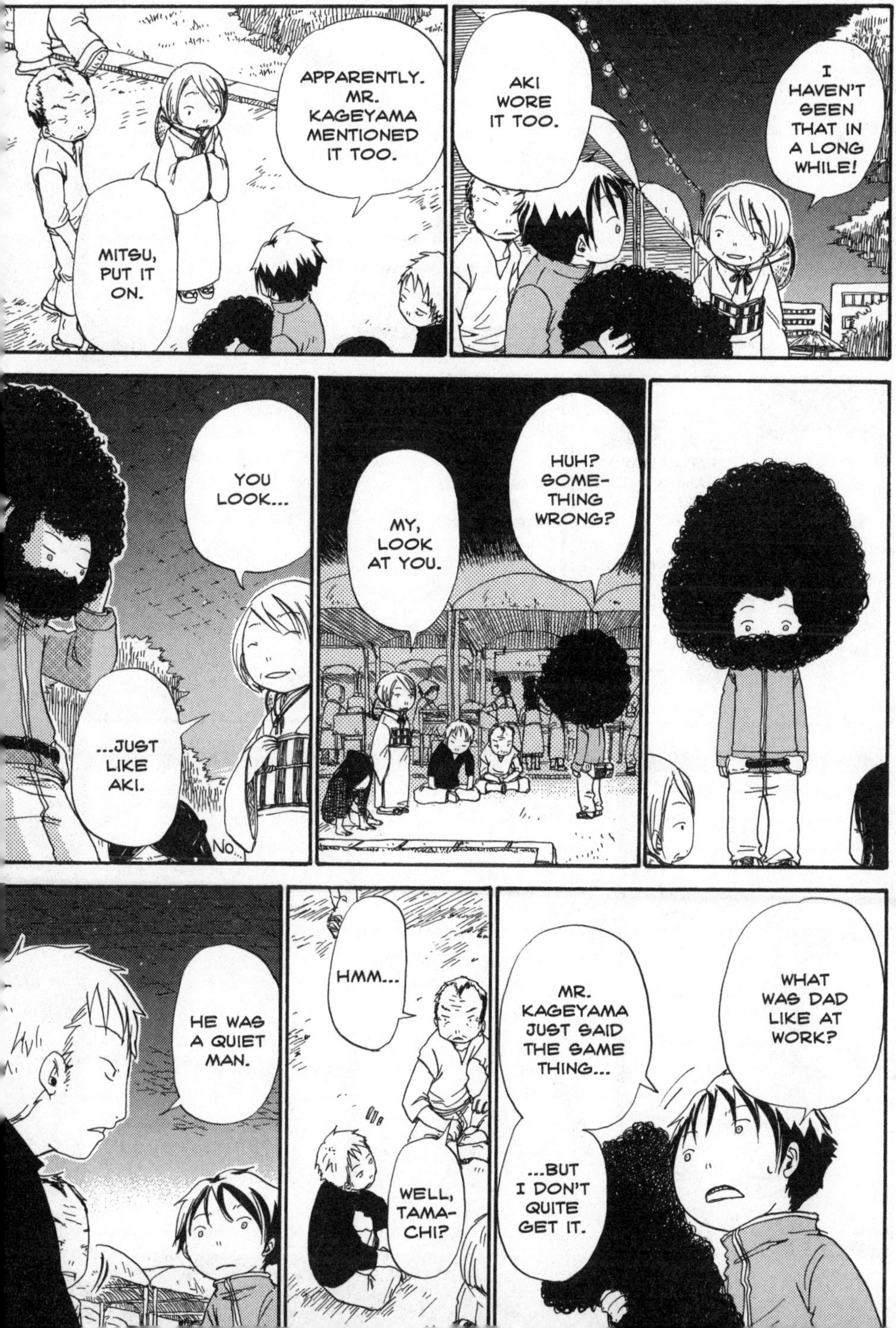
I HAVEN'T SEEN THAT IN A LONG WHILE!
AKI WORE IT TOO.
APPARENTLY. MR. KAGEYAMA MENTIONED IT TOO.
MITSU, PUT IT ON.
HUH? SOME-THING WRONG?
MY, LOOK AT YOU.
YOU LOOK...
...JUST LIKE AKI.
NO...
WHAT WAS DAD LIKE AT WORK?
MR. KAGEYAMA JUST SAID THE SAME THING...
...BUT I DON'T QUITE GET IT.
HMM...
WELL, TAMA-CHI?
HE WAS A QUIET MAN.

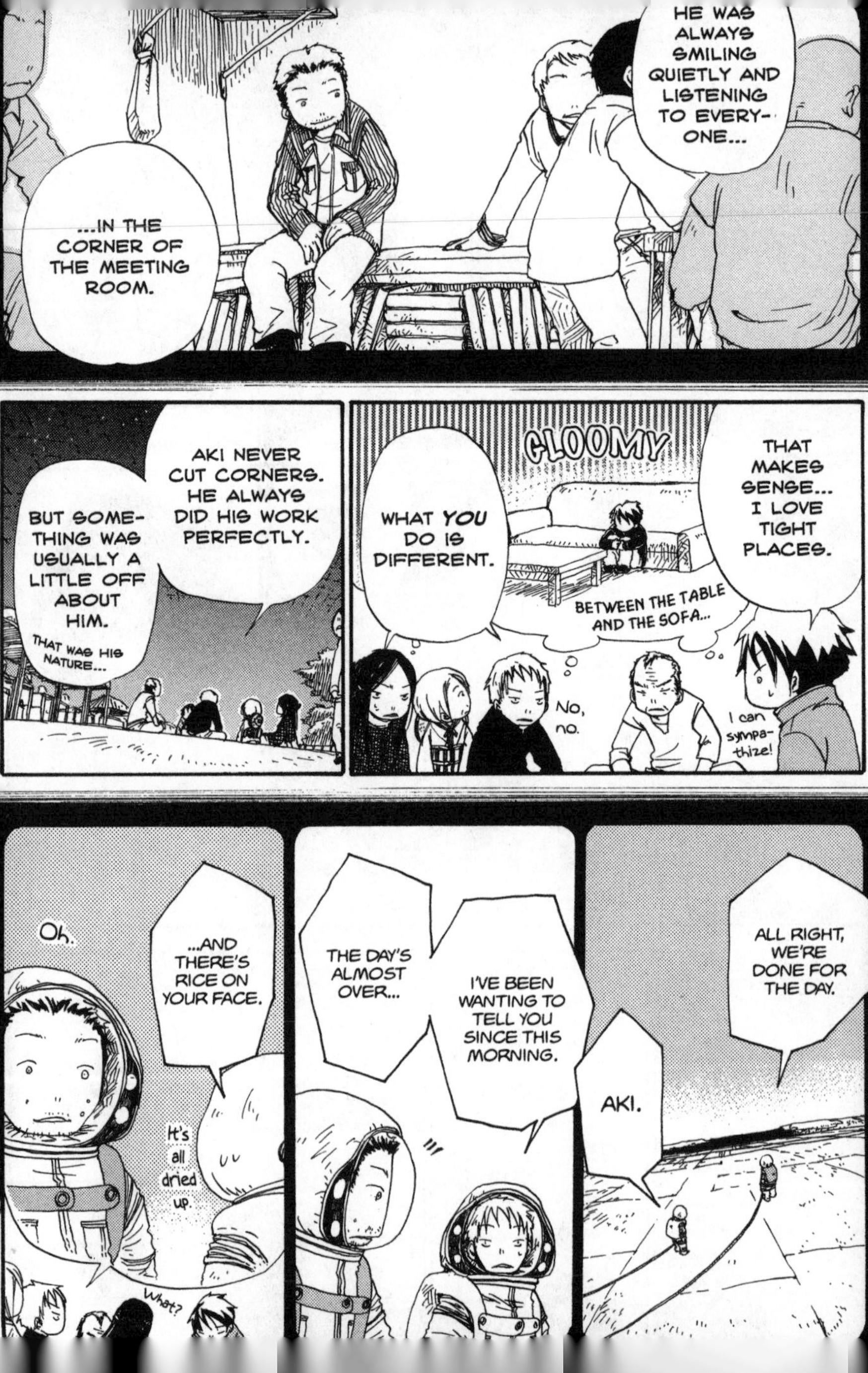
HE WAS ALWAYS SMILING QUIETLY AND LISTENING TO EVERY-ONE...
...IN THE CORNER OF THE MEETING ROOM.
THAT MAKES SENSE... I LOVE TIGHT PLACES.
GLOOMY
WHAT YOU DO IS DIFFERENT.
BETWEEN THE TABLE AND THE SOFA...
I can sympa-thize!
No, no.
AKI NEVER CUT CORNERS. HE ALWAYS DID HIS WORK PERFECTLY.
BUT SOME-THING WAS USUALLY A LITTLE OFF ABOUT HIM.
THAT WAS HIS NATURE...
ALL RIGHT, WE'RE DONE FOR THE DAY.
AKI.
THE DAY'S ALMOST OVER...
I'VE BEEN WANTING TO TELL YOU SINCE THIS MORNING.
...AND THERE'S RICE ON YOUR FACE.
Oh.
It's all dried up.
What?

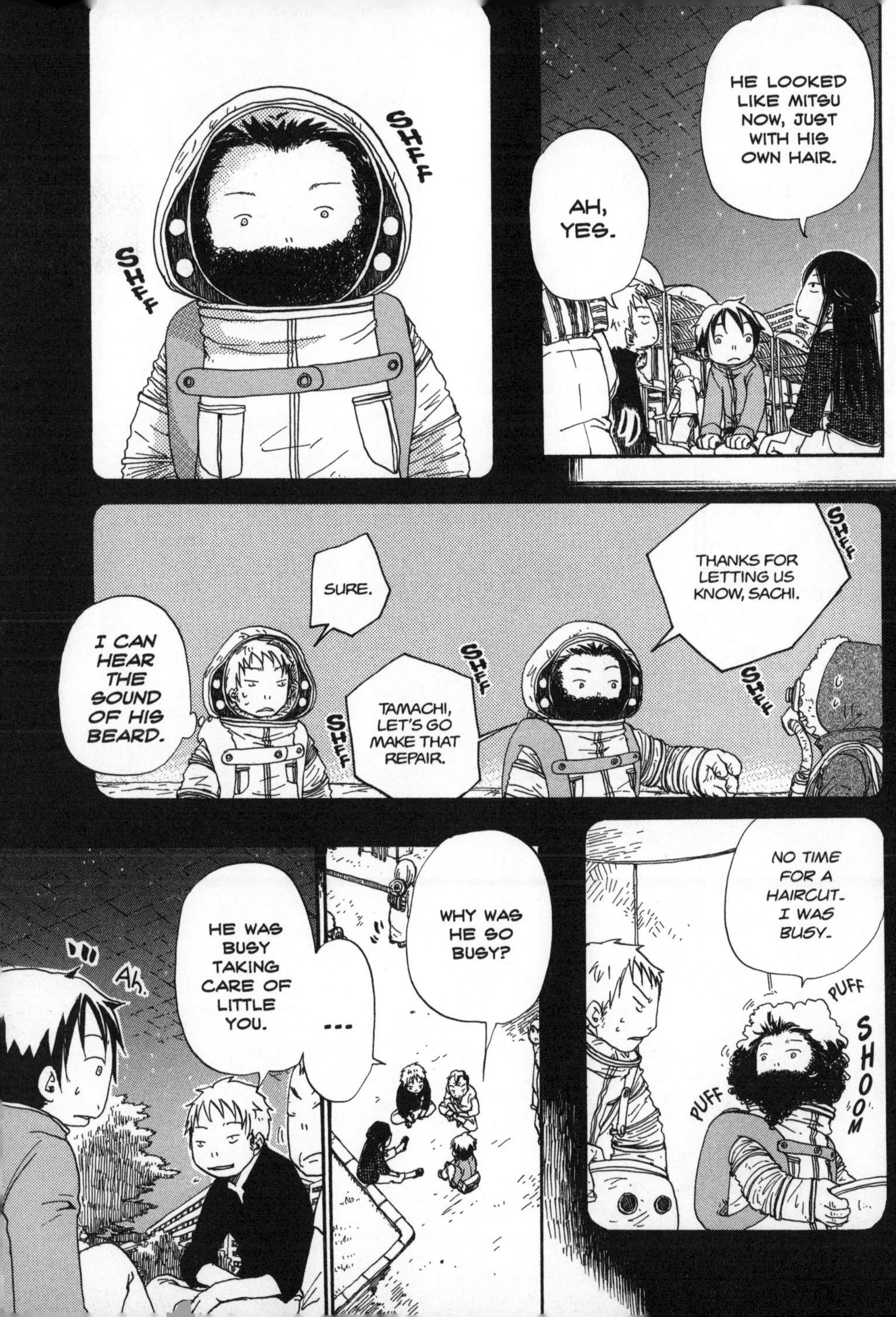
HE LOOKED LIKE MITSU NOW, JUST WITH HIS OWN HAIR.
AH, YES.
SHFF
SHFF
SHFF
THANKS FOR LETTING US KNOW, SACHI.
SHFF
SURE.
SHFF
TAMACHI, LET'S GO MAKE THAT REPAIR.
SHFF
I CAN HEAR THE SOUND OF HIS BEARD.
NO TIME FOR A HAIRCUT. I WAS BUSY.
PUFF
SHOOM
PUFF
WHY WAS HE SO BUSY?
...
HE WAS BUSY TAKING CARE OF LITTLE YOU.
Ah.

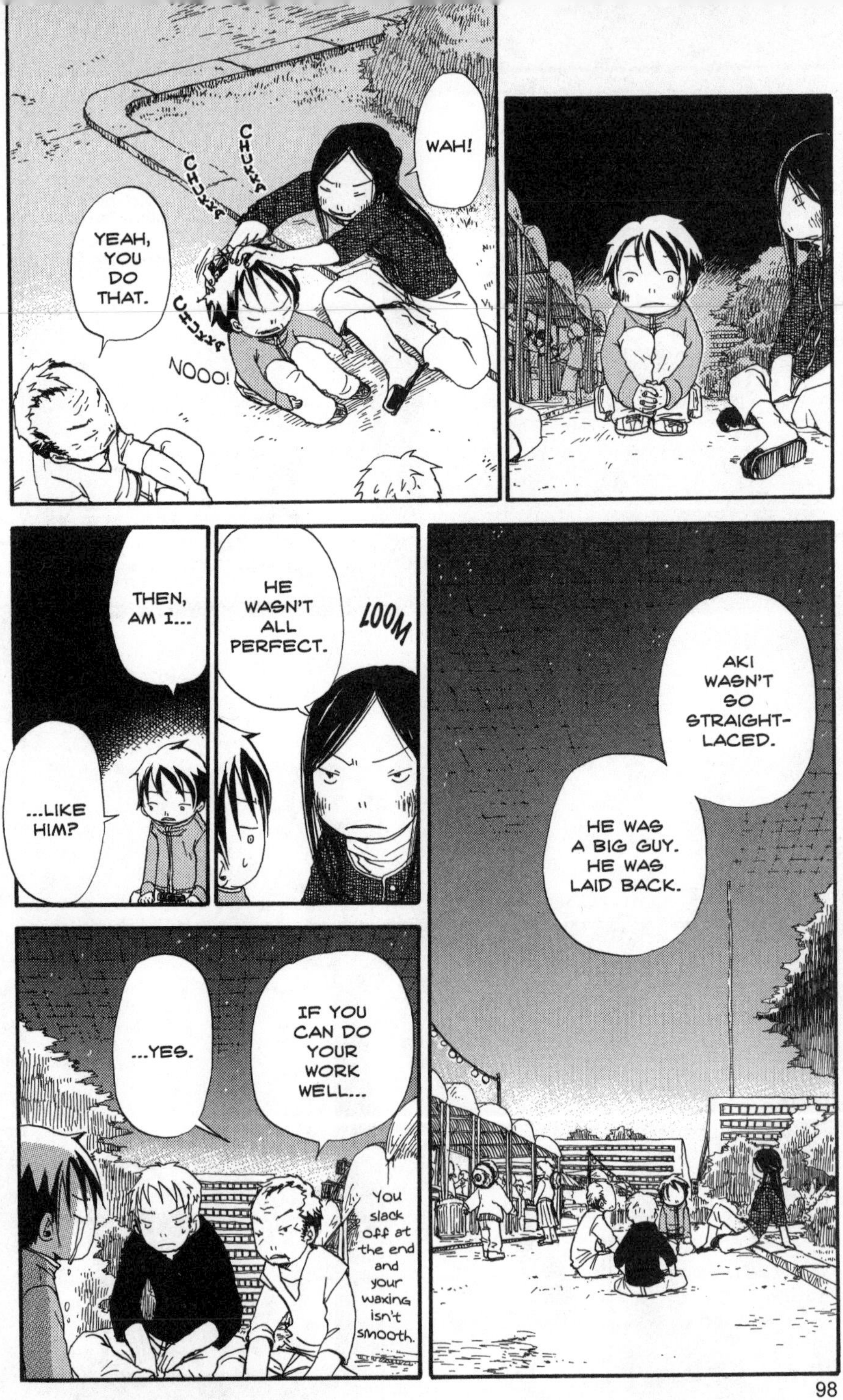
WAH!
CHUKKA
CHUKKA
YEAH, YOU DO THAT.
CHUKKA
NOOO!
AKI WASN'T SO STRAIGHT-LACED.
HE WAS A BIG GUY. HE WAS LAID BACK.
HE WASN'T ALL PERFECT.
LOOM
THEN, AM I...
...LIKE HIM?
IF YOU CAN DO YOUR WORK WELL...
...YES.
You slack off at the end and your waxing isn't smooth.

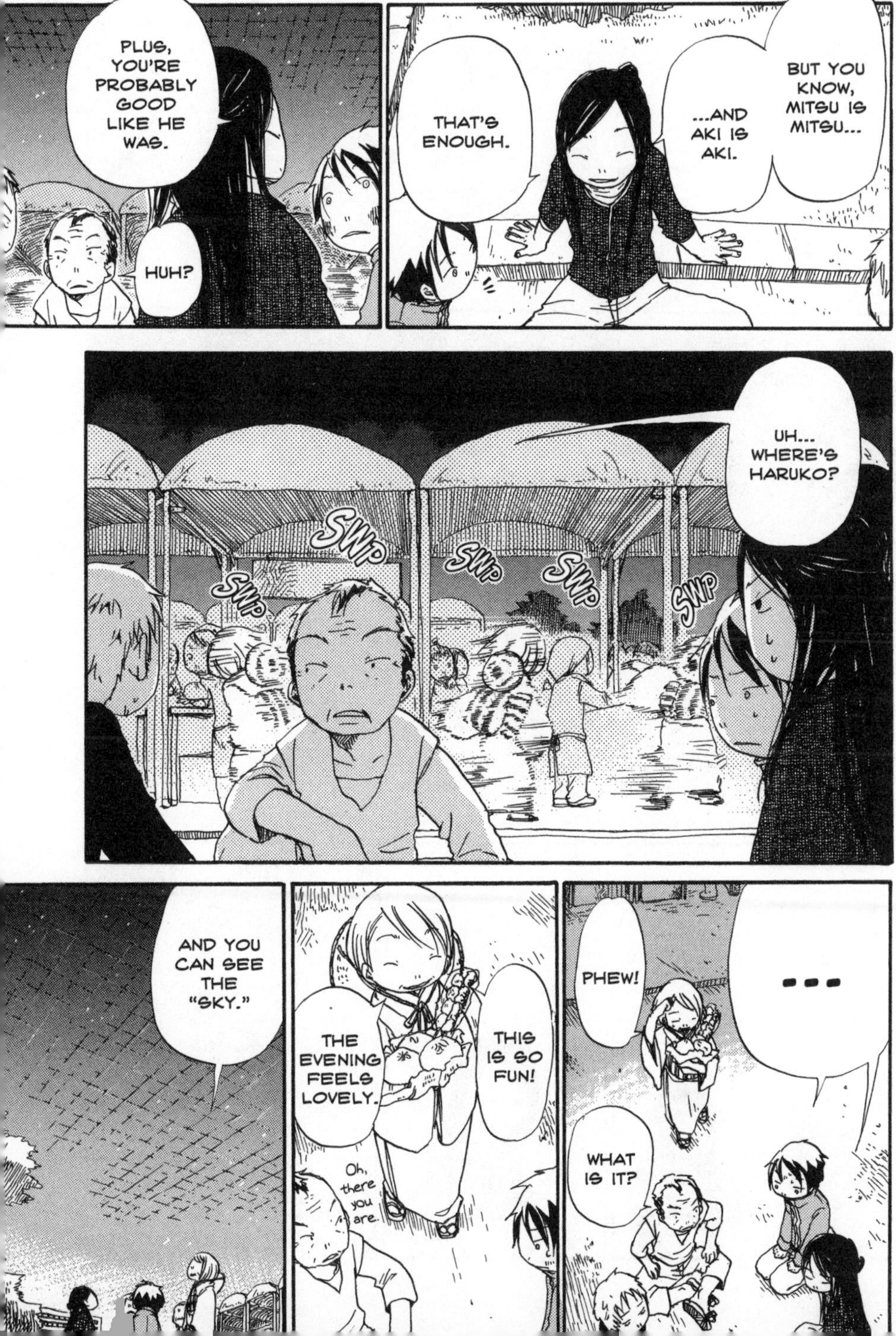
BUT YOU KNOW, MITSU IS MITSU...
...AND AKI IS AKI.
THAT'S ENOUGH.
PLUS, YOU'RE PROBABLY GOOD LIKE HE WAS.
HUH?
UH... WHERE'S HARUKO?
SWP
SWP
SWP
SWP
SWP
...
PHEW!
WHAT IS IT?
THIS IS SO FUN!
THE EVENING FEELS LOVELY.
Oh, there you are.
AND YOU CAN SEE THE "SKY."

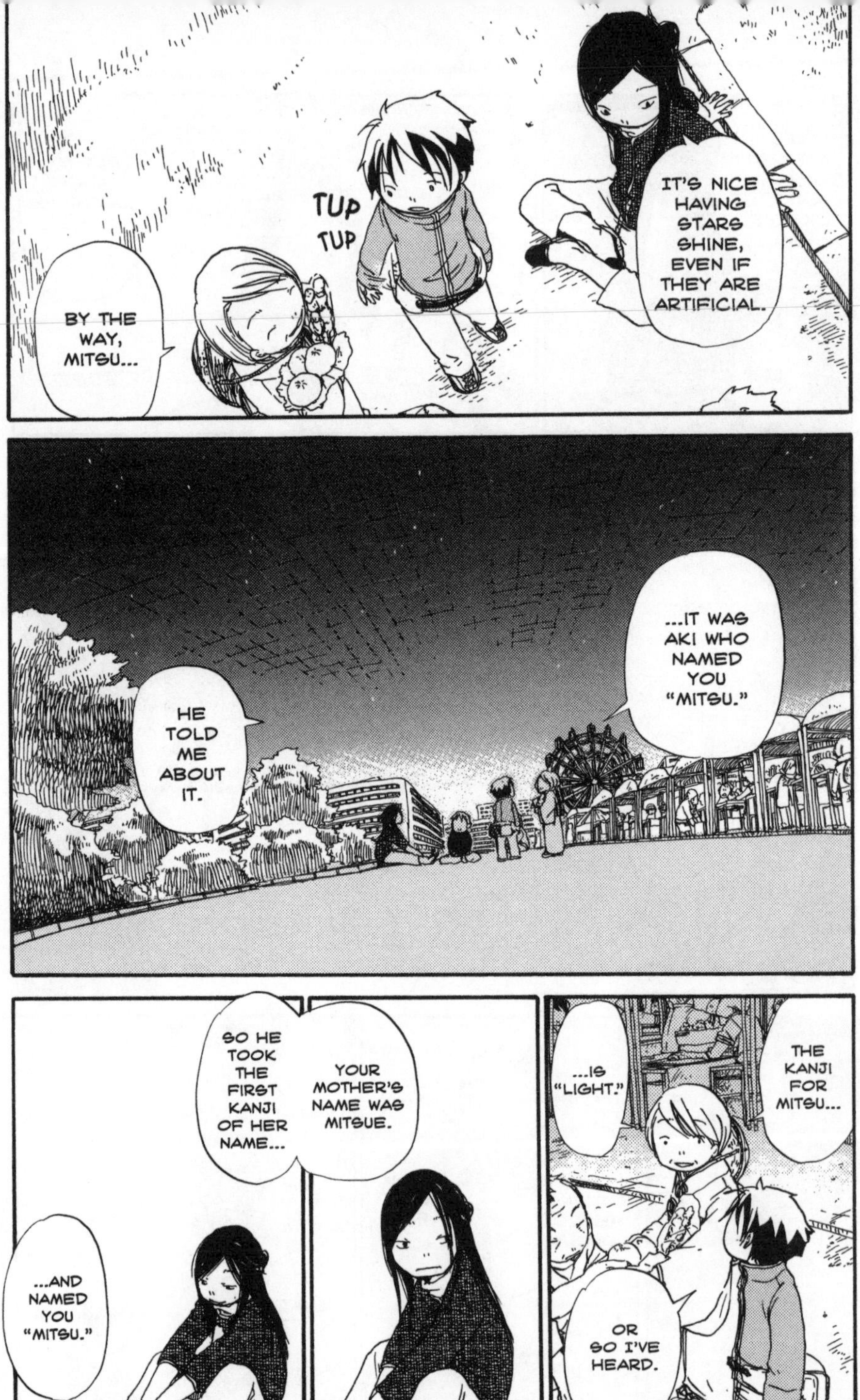
IT'S NICE HAVING STARS SHINE, EVEN IF THEY ARE ARTIFICIAL.
TUP TUP
BY THE WAY, MITSU...
...IT WAS AKI WHO NAMED YOU "MITSU."
HE TOLD ME ABOUT IT.
THE KANJI FOR MITSU...
...IS "LIGHT."
OR SO I'VE HEARD.
YOUR MOTHER'S NAME WAS MITSUE.
SO HE TOOK THE FIRST KANJI OF HER NAME...
...AND NAMED YOU "MITSU."

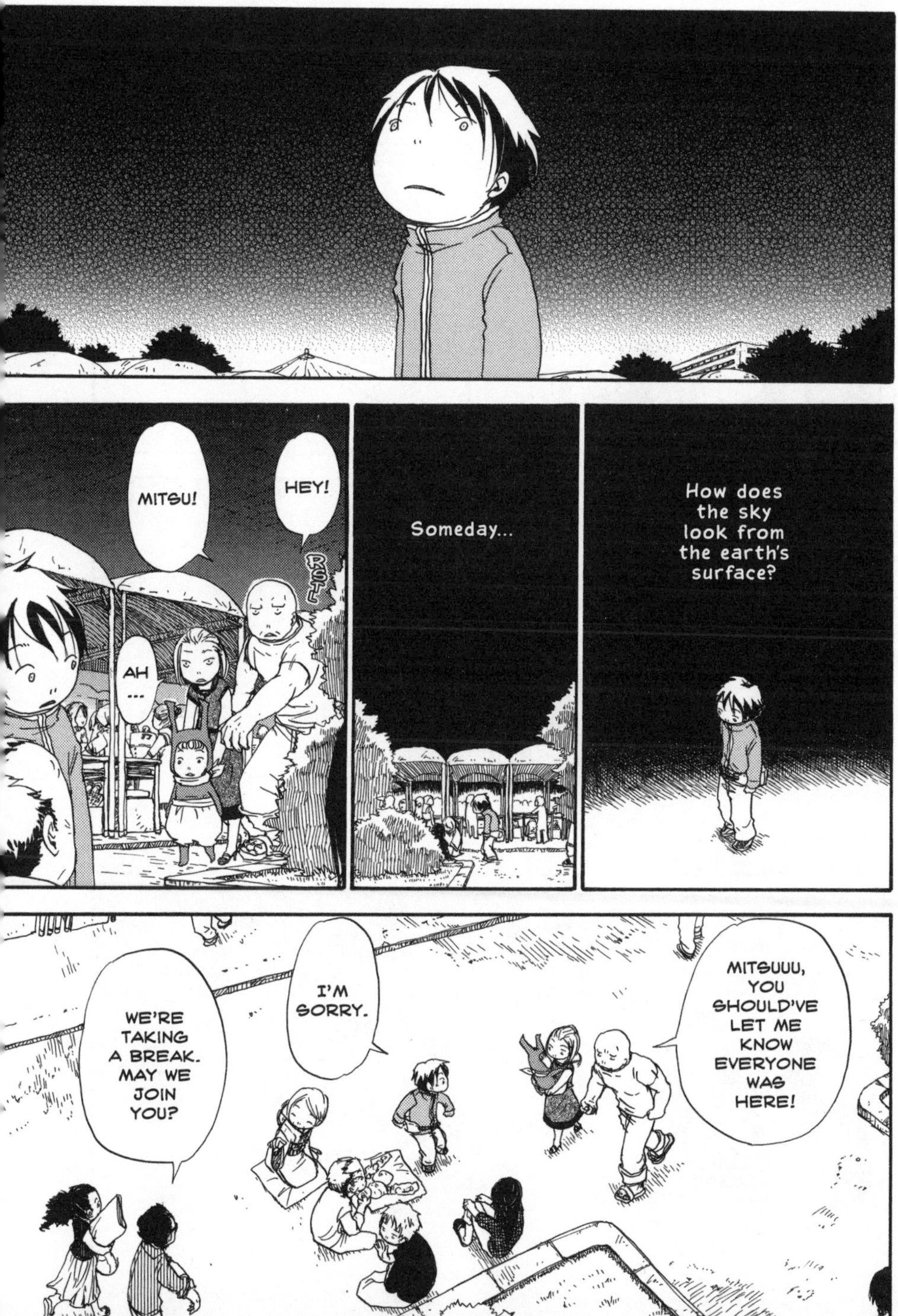
How does the sky look from the earth's surface?
Someday...
HEY!
RSTL
MITSU!
AH ...
MITSUUU, YOU SHOULD'VE LET ME KNOW EVERYONE WAS HERE!
I'M SORRY.
WE'RE TAKING A BREAK. MAY WE JOIN YOU?

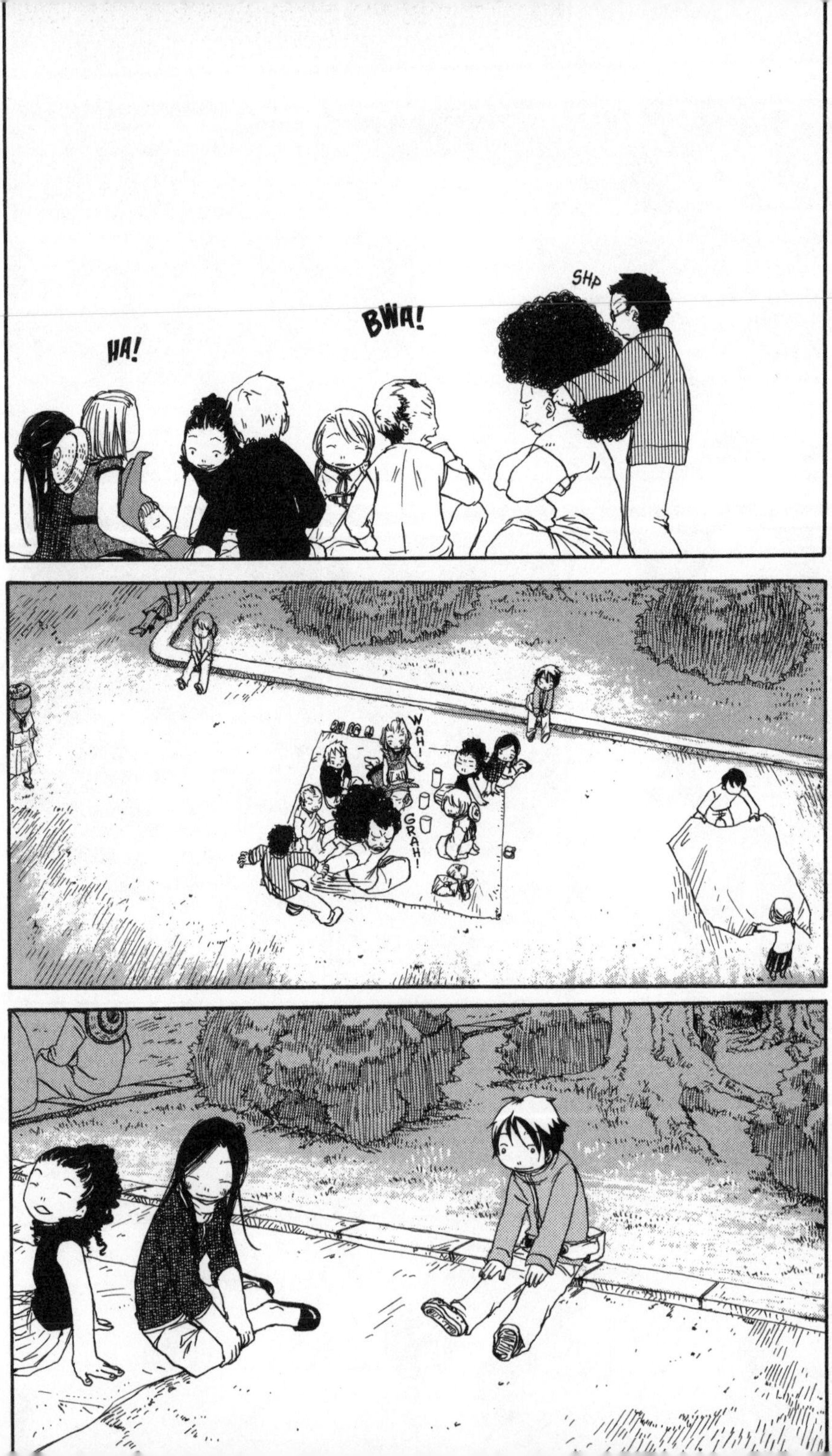
SHP
BWA!
HA!
WAH!
GRAH!

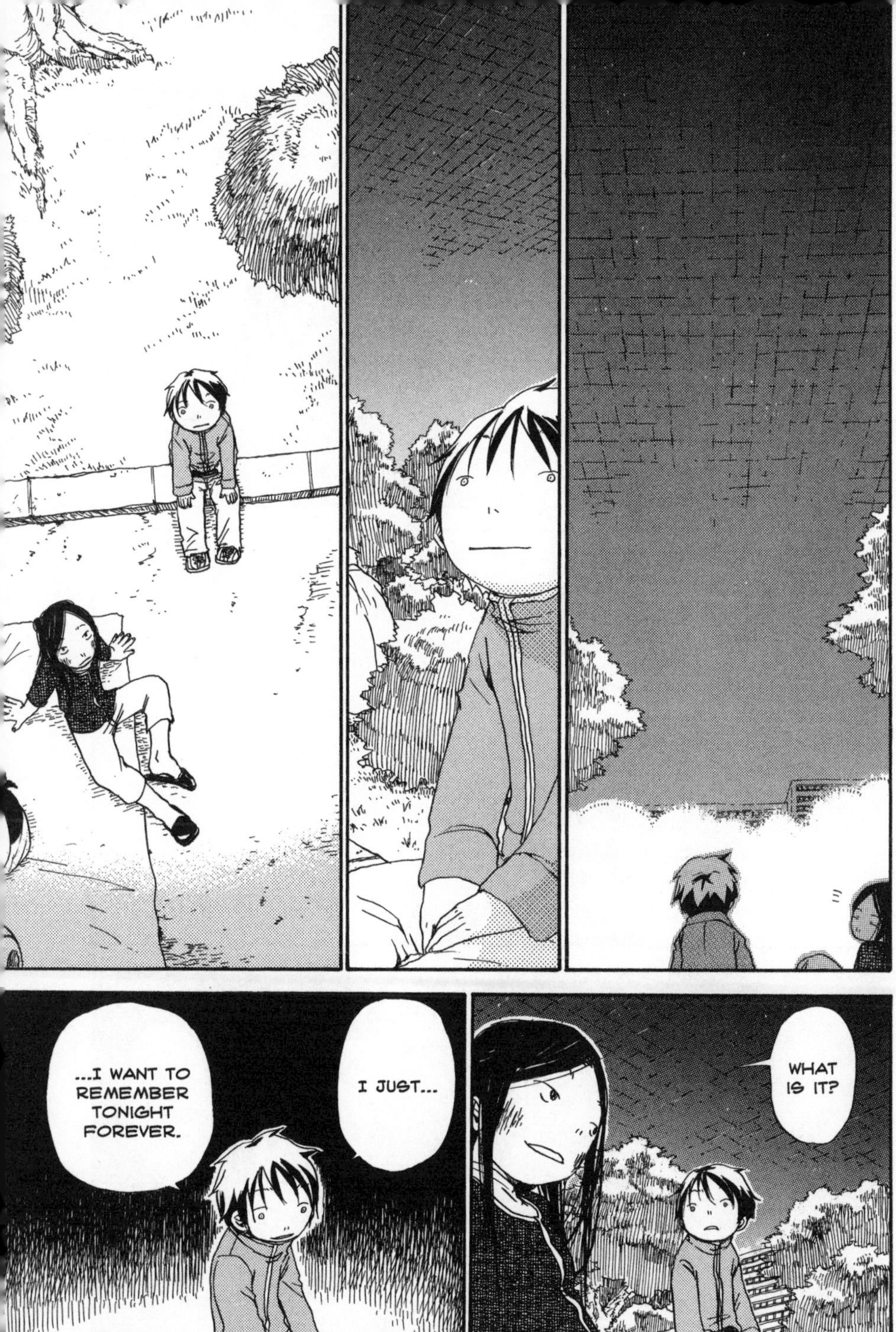
WHAT IS IT?
I JUST...
...I WANT TO REMEMBER TONIGHT FOREVER.

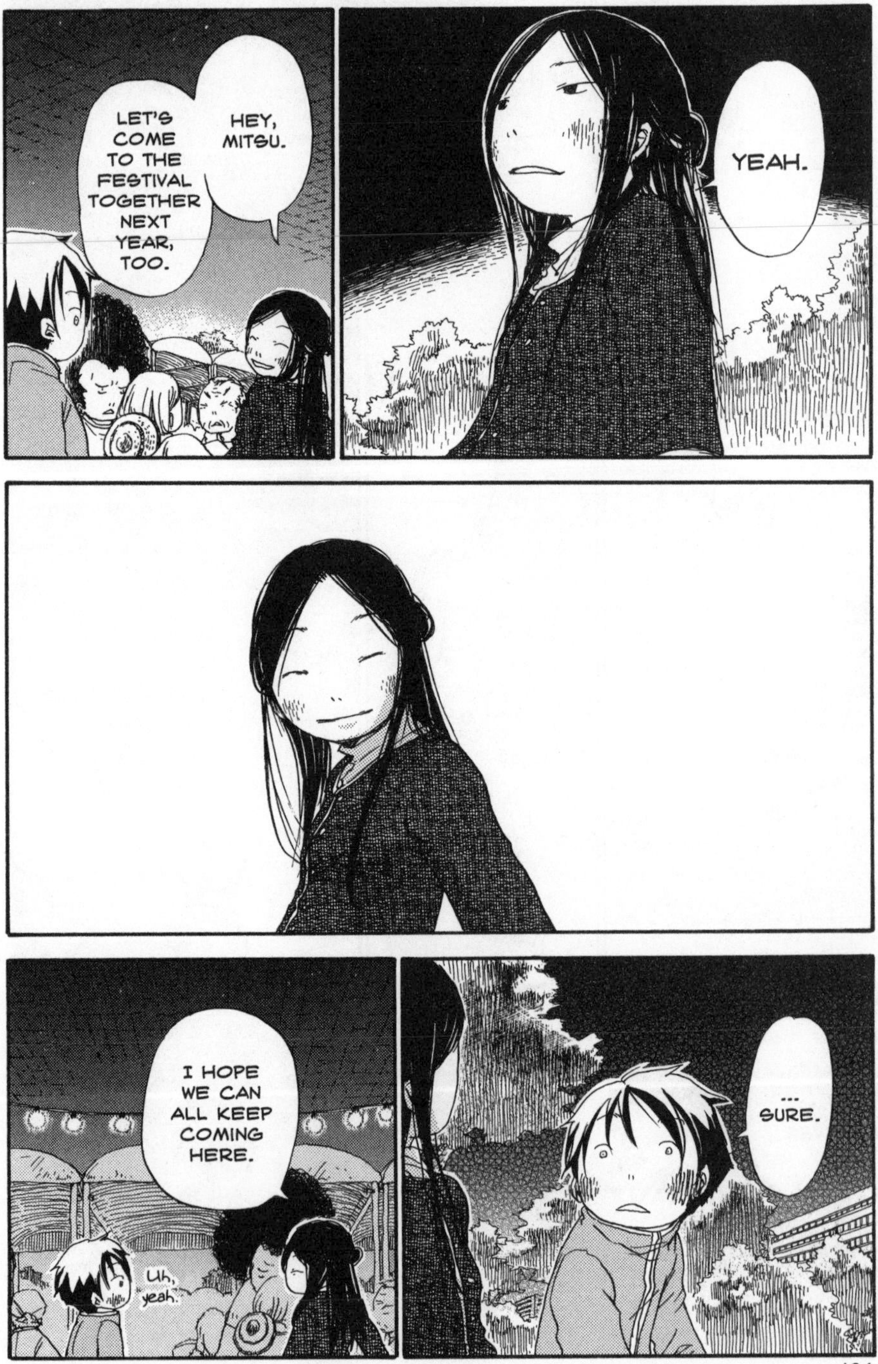
HEY, MITSU.
LET'S COME TO THE FESTIVAL TOGETHER NEXT YEAR, TOO.
YEAH.
I HOPE WE CAN ALL KEEP COMING HERE.
Uh, yeah.
... SURE.

floor 14: where I am now

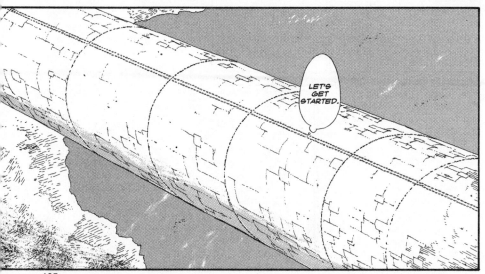

LET'S GET STARTED.

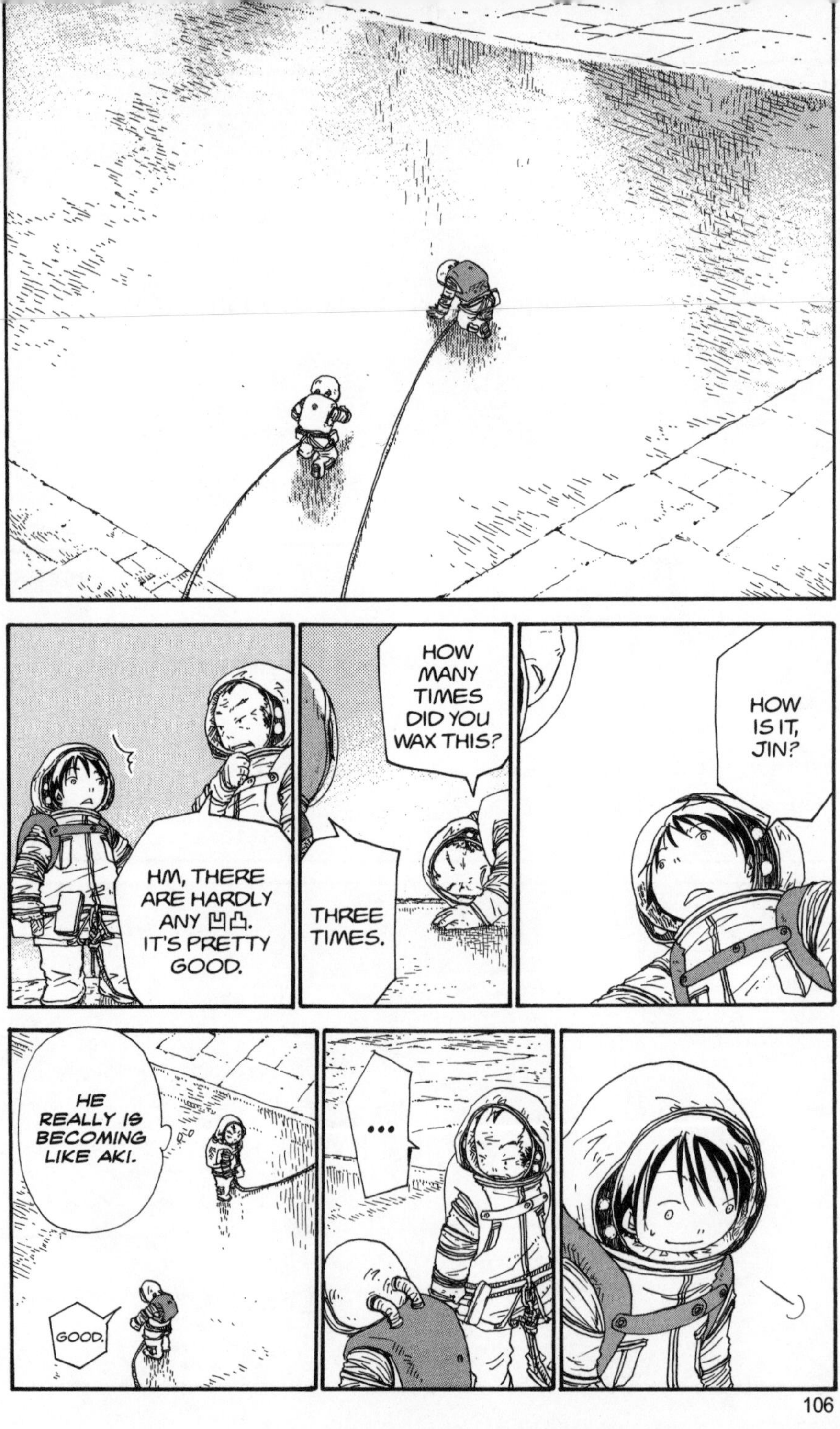
HOW IS IT, JIN?
HOW MANY TIMES DID YOU WAX THIS?
THREE TIMES.
HM, THERE ARE HARDLY ANY 凹凸. IT'S PRETTY GOOD.
...
HE REALLY IS BECOMING LIKE AKI.
GOOD.

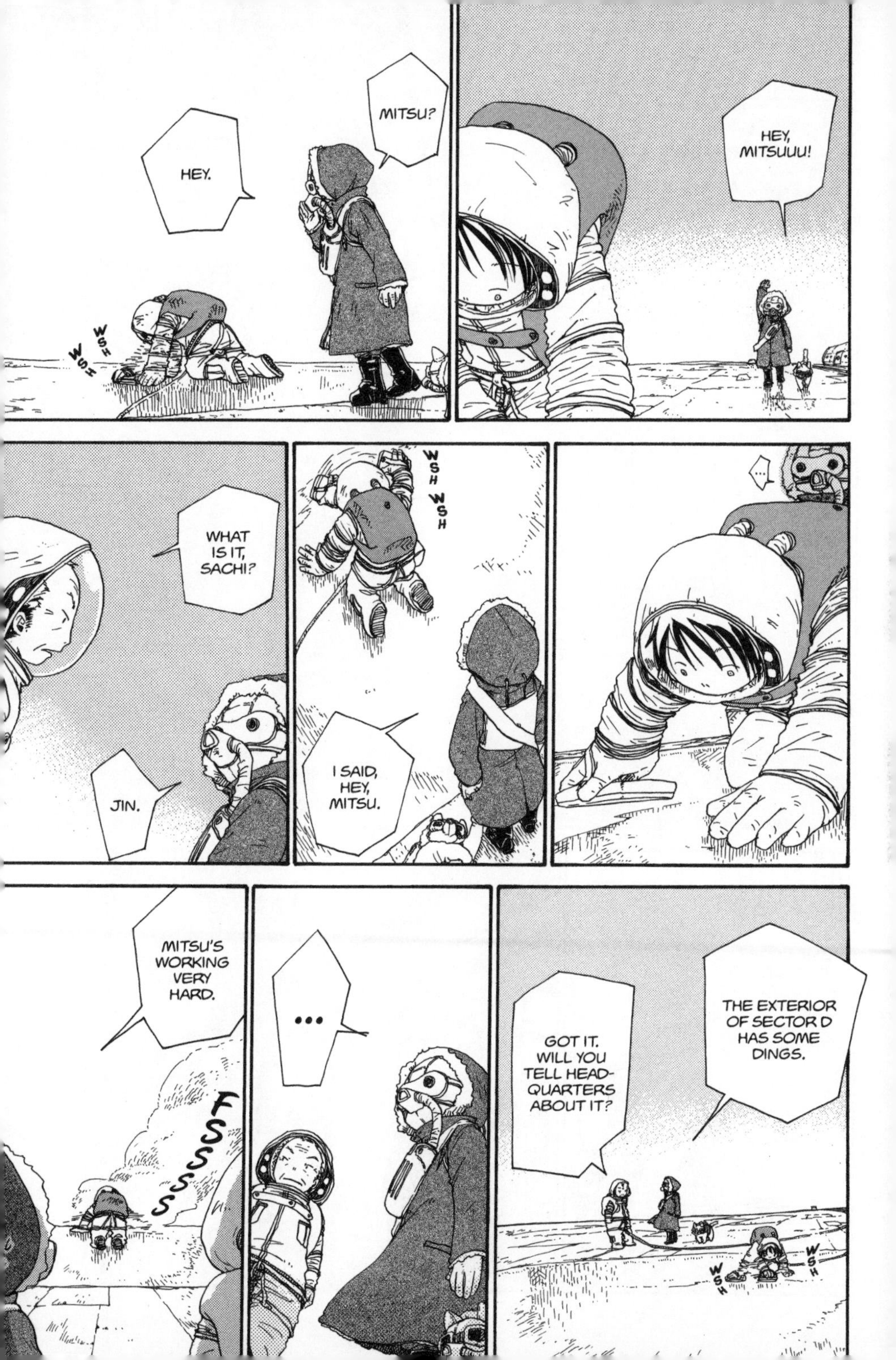
HEY, MITSUUU!
MITSU?
HEY.
WSH WSH
...
WSH WSH
I SAID, HEY, MITSU.
WHAT IS IT, SACHI?
JIN.
THE EXTERIOR OF SECTOR D HAS SOME DINGS.
GOT IT. WILL YOU TELL HEAD-QUARTERS ABOUT IT?
WSH WSH
...
MITSU'S WORKING VERY HARD.
FSSSSS

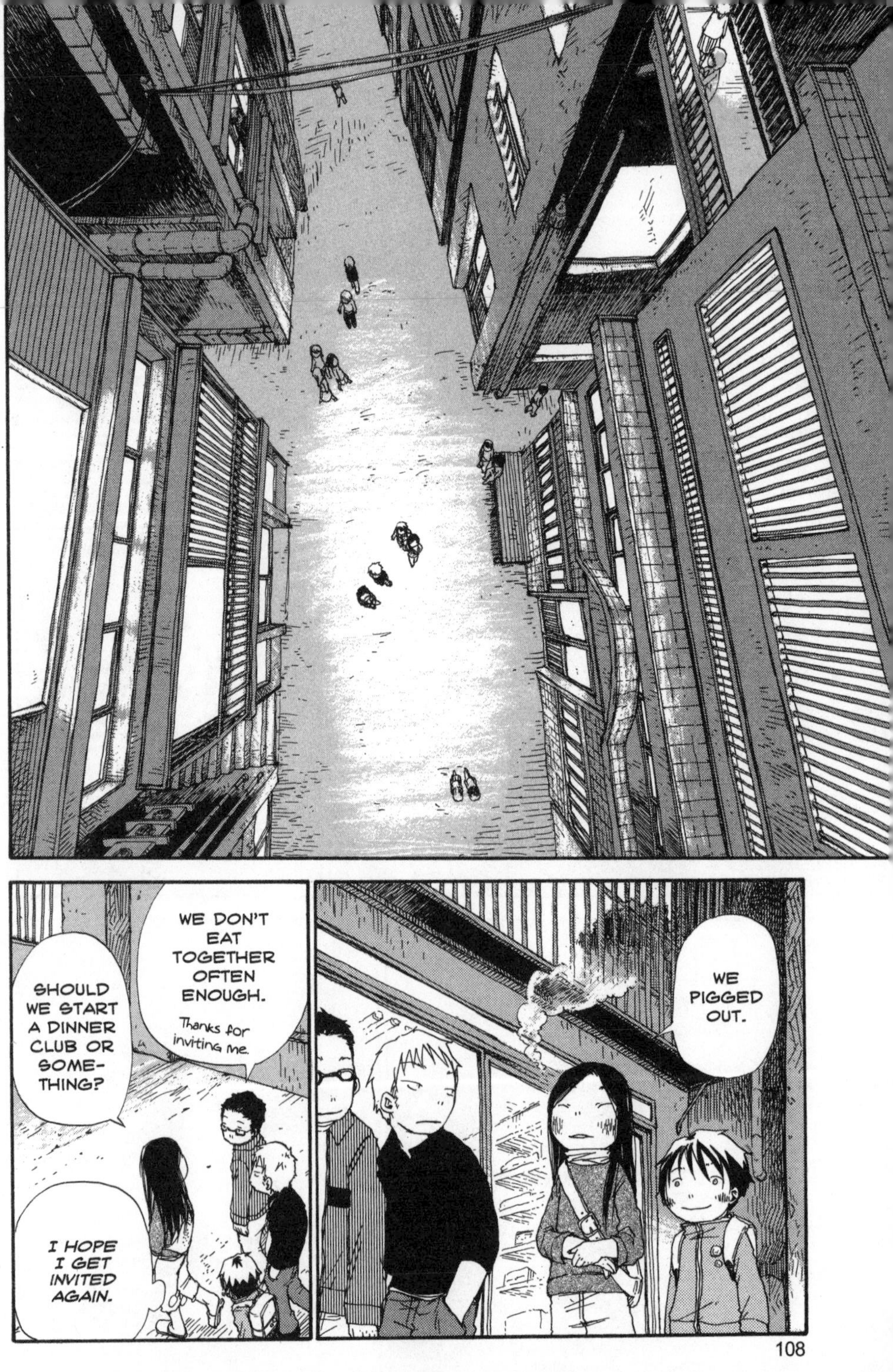
WE PIGGED OUT.
WE DON'T EAT TOGETHER OFTEN ENOUGH.
Thanks for inviting me.
SHOULD WE START A DINNER CLUB OR SOME-THING?
I HOPE I GET INVITED AGAIN.

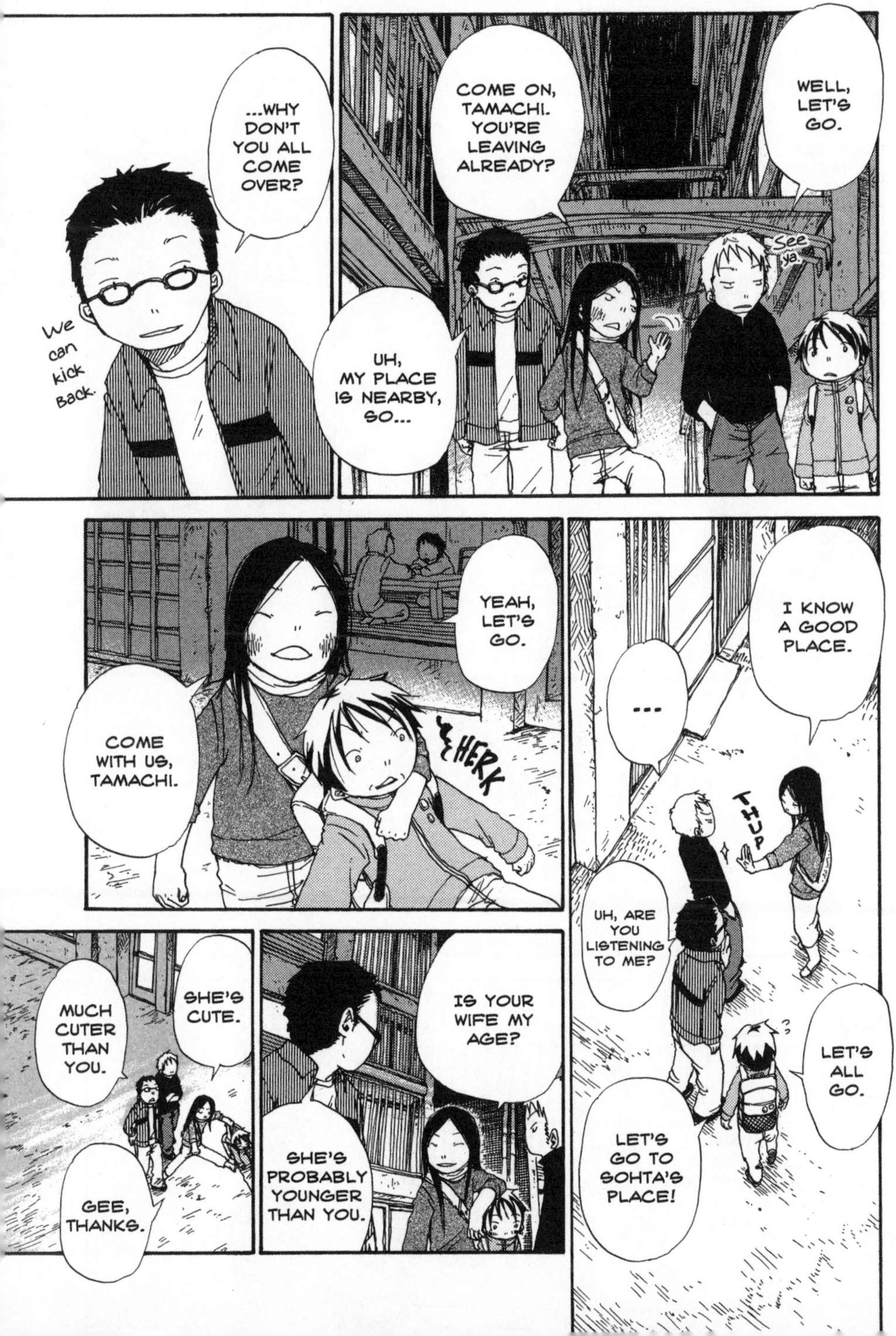
WELL, LET'S GO.
See ya.
COME ON, TAMACHI. YOU'RE LEAVING ALREADY?
UH, MY PLACE IS NEARBY, SO...
...WHY DON'T YOU ALL COME OVER?
We can kick back.
I KNOW A GOOD PLACE.
...
THUP
UH, ARE YOU LISTENING TO ME?
LET'S ALL GO.
LET'S GO TO SOHTA'S PLACE!
YEAH, LET'S GO.
HERK
COME WITH US, TAMACHI.
IS YOUR WIFE MY AGE?
SHE'S PROBABLY YOUNGER THAN YOU.
SHE'S CUTE.
MUCH CUTER THAN YOU.
GEE, THANKS.

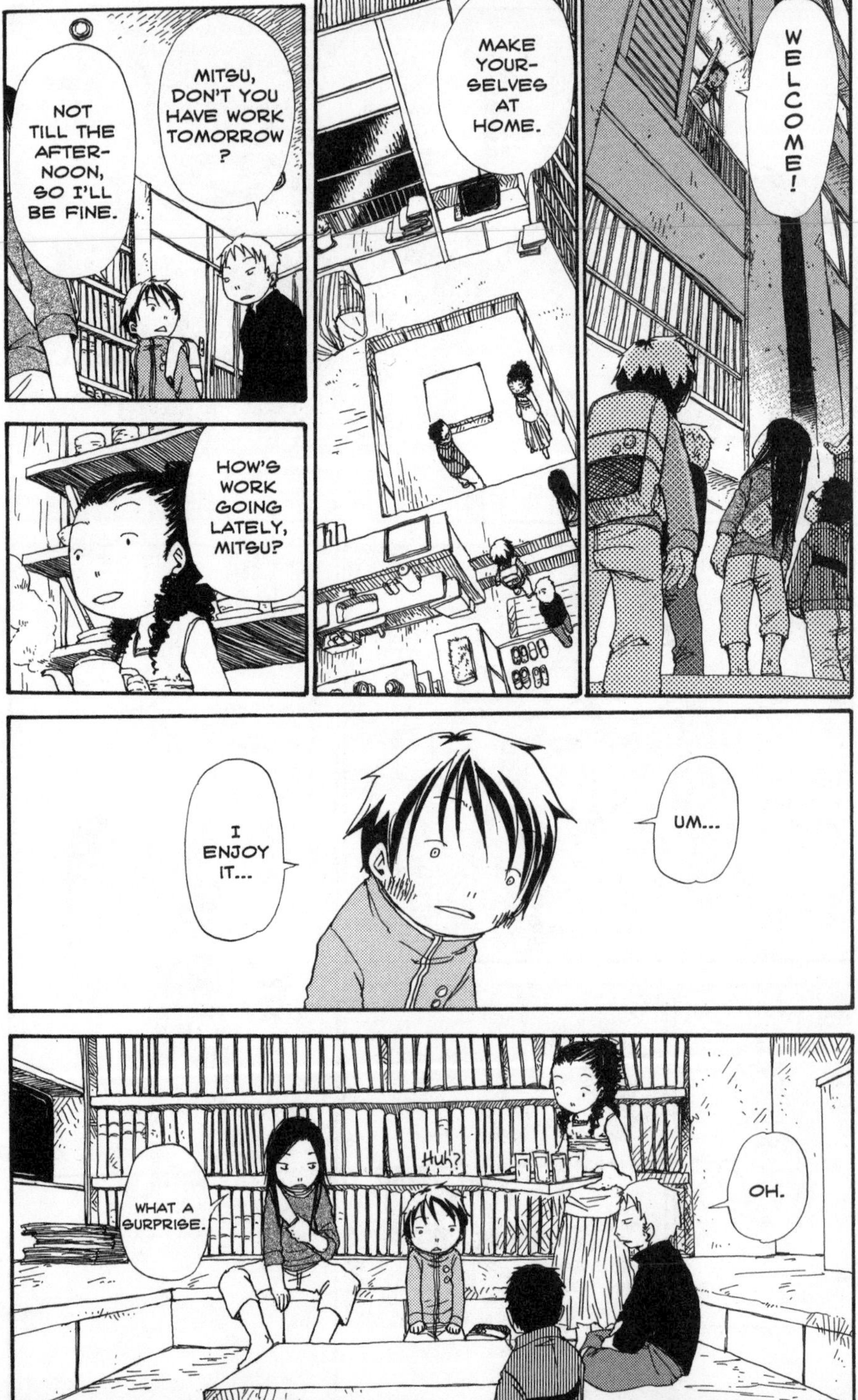
WELCOME!
MAKE YOURSELVES AT HOME.
MITSU, DON'T YOU HAVE WORK TOMORROW?
NOT TILL THE AFTERNOON, SO I'LL BE FINE.
HOW'S WORK GOING LATELY, MITSU?
UM...
I ENJOY IT...
OH.
Huh?
WHAT A SURPRISE.

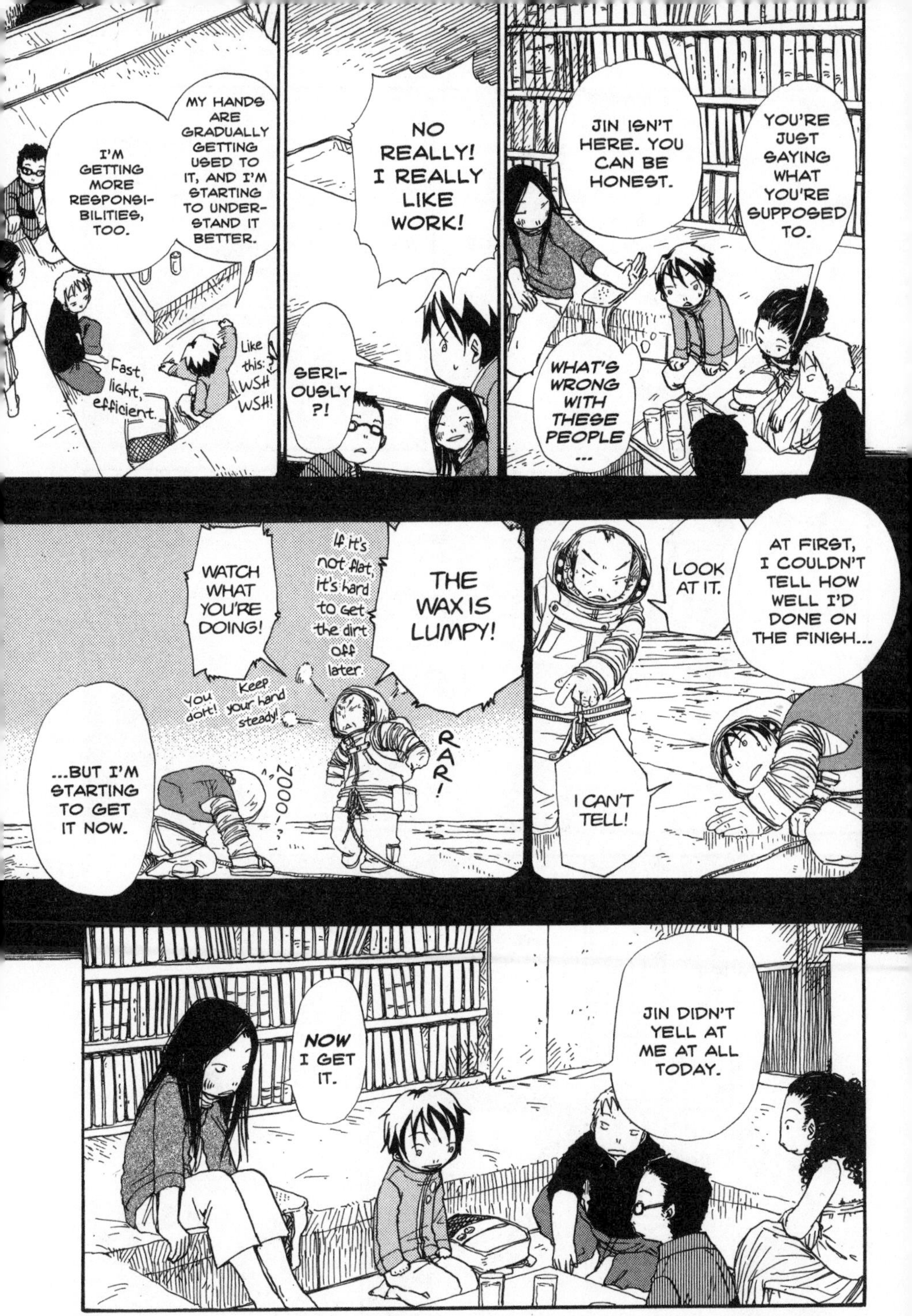
YOU'RE JUST SAYING WHAT YOU'RE SUPPOSED TO.
JIN ISN'T HERE. YOU CAN BE HONEST.
WHAT'S WRONG WITH THESE PEOPLE...
NO REALLY! I REALLY LIKE WORK!
SERIOUSLY?!
MY HANDS ARE GRADUALLY GETTING USED TO IT, AND I'M STARTING TO UNDERSTAND IT BETTER.
I'M GETTING MORE RESPONSIBILITIES, TOO.
Like this: WSH WSH!
Fast, light, efficient.
AT FIRST, I COULDN'T TELL HOW WELL I'D DONE ON THE FINISH...
LOOK AT IT.
I CAN'T TELL!
THE WAX IS LUMPY!
If it's not flat, it's hard to get the dirt off later.
RAR!
WATCH WHAT YOU'RE DOING!
Keep your hand steady!
You dolt!
ZOOO-
...BUT I'M STARTING TO GET IT NOW.
JIN DIDN'T YELL AT ME AT ALL TODAY.
NOW I GET IT.

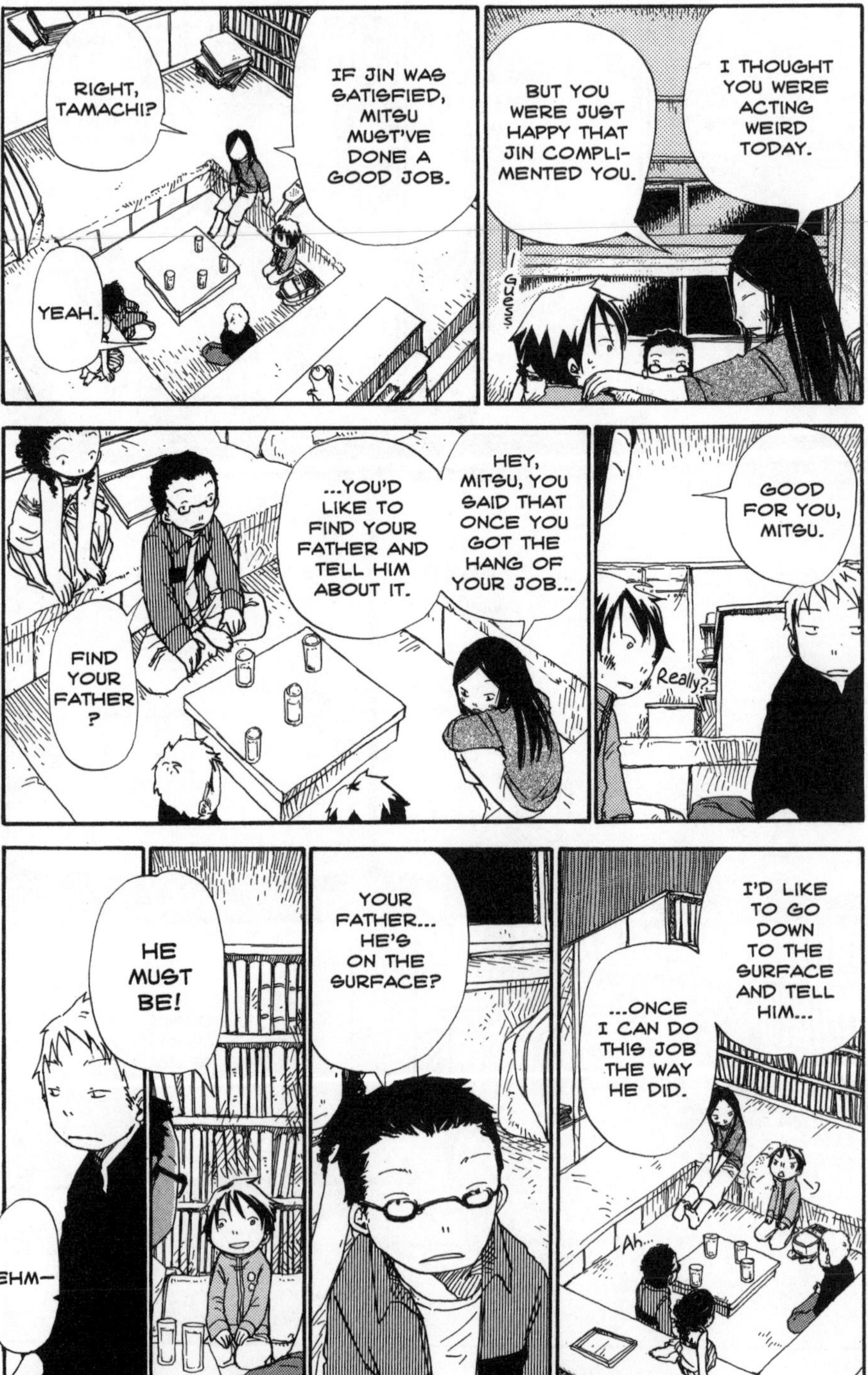
I THOUGHT YOU WERE ACTING WEIRD TODAY.
BUT YOU WERE JUST HAPPY THAT JIN COMPLIMENTED YOU.
I GUESS.
IF JIN WAS SATISFIED, MITSU MUST'VE DONE A GOOD JOB.
RIGHT, TAMACHI?
YEAH.
GOOD FOR YOU, MITSU.
Really?
HEY, MITSU, YOU SAID THAT ONCE YOU GOT THE HANG OF YOUR JOB...
...YOU'D LIKE TO FIND YOUR FATHER AND TELL HIM ABOUT IT.
FIND YOUR FATHER?
I'D LIKE TO GO DOWN TO THE SURFACE AND TELL HIM...
...ONCE I CAN DO THIS JOB THE WAY HE DID.
Ah...
YOUR FATHER... HE'S ON THE SURFACE?
HE MUST BE!
EHM—

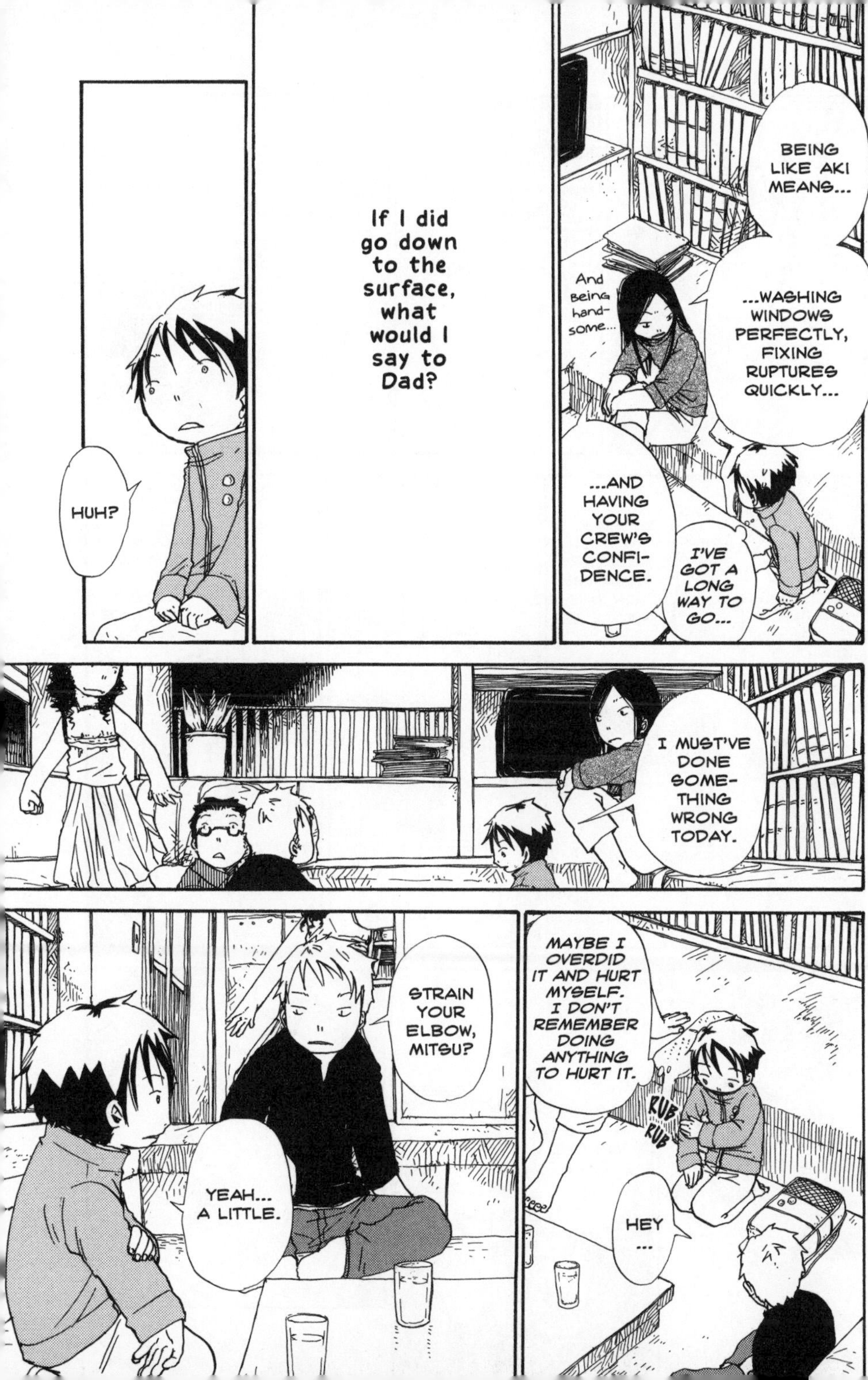
BEING LIKE AKI MEANS...
...WASHING WINDOWS PERFECTLY, FIXING RUPTURES QUICKLY...
And being hand-some...
...AND HAVING YOUR CREW'S CONFI-DENCE.
I'VE GOT A LONG WAY TO GO...
If I did go down to the surface, what would I say to Dad?
HUH?
I MUST'VE DONE SOME-THING WRONG TODAY.
MAYBE I OVERDID IT AND HURT MYSELF. I DON'T REMEMBER DOING ANYTHING TO HURT IT.
RUB RUB
HEY ...
STRAIN YOUR ELBOW, MITSU?
YEAH... A LITTLE.

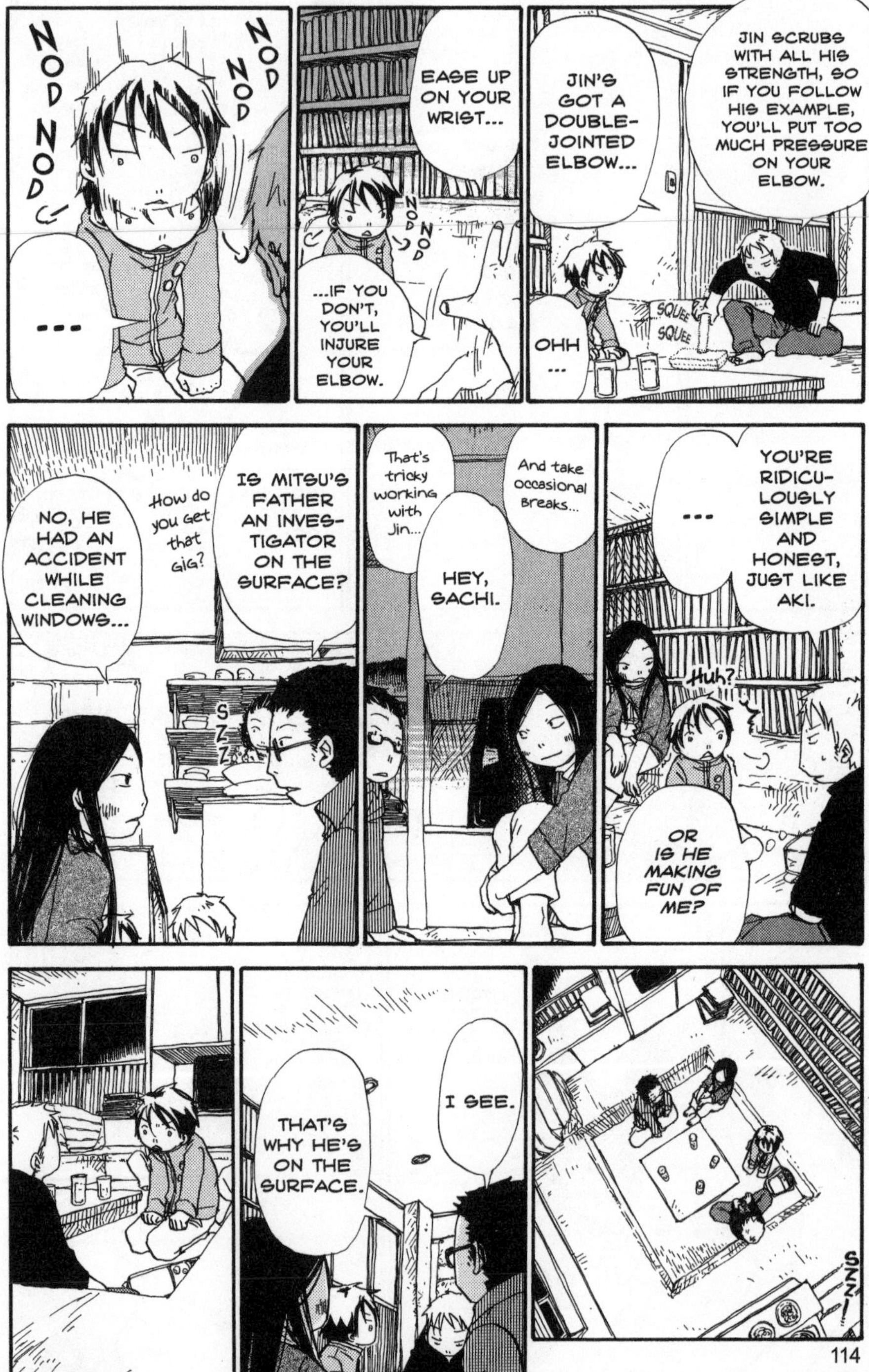
JIN SCRUBS WITH ALL HIS STRENGTH, SO IF YOU FOLLOW HIS EXAMPLE, YOU'LL PUT TOO MUCH PRESSURE ON YOUR ELBOW.
JIN'S GOT A DOUBLE-JOINTED ELBOW...
SQUEE SQUEE
OHH ...
EASE UP ON YOUR WRIST...
NOD NOD
...IF YOU DON'T, YOU'LL INJURE YOUR ELBOW.
NOD NOD
NOD NOD
...
YOU'RE RIDICULOUSLY SIMPLE AND HONEST, JUST LIKE AKI.
...
Huh?
OR IS HE MAKING FUN OF ME?
And take occasional breaks...
That's tricky working with Jin...
HEY, SACHI.
IS MITSU'S FATHER AN INVESTIGATOR ON THE SURFACE?
How do you get that gig?
NO, HE HAD AN ACCIDENT WHILE CLEANING WINDOWS...
SZZ
SZZ!
I SEE.
THAT'S WHY HE'S ON THE SURFACE.

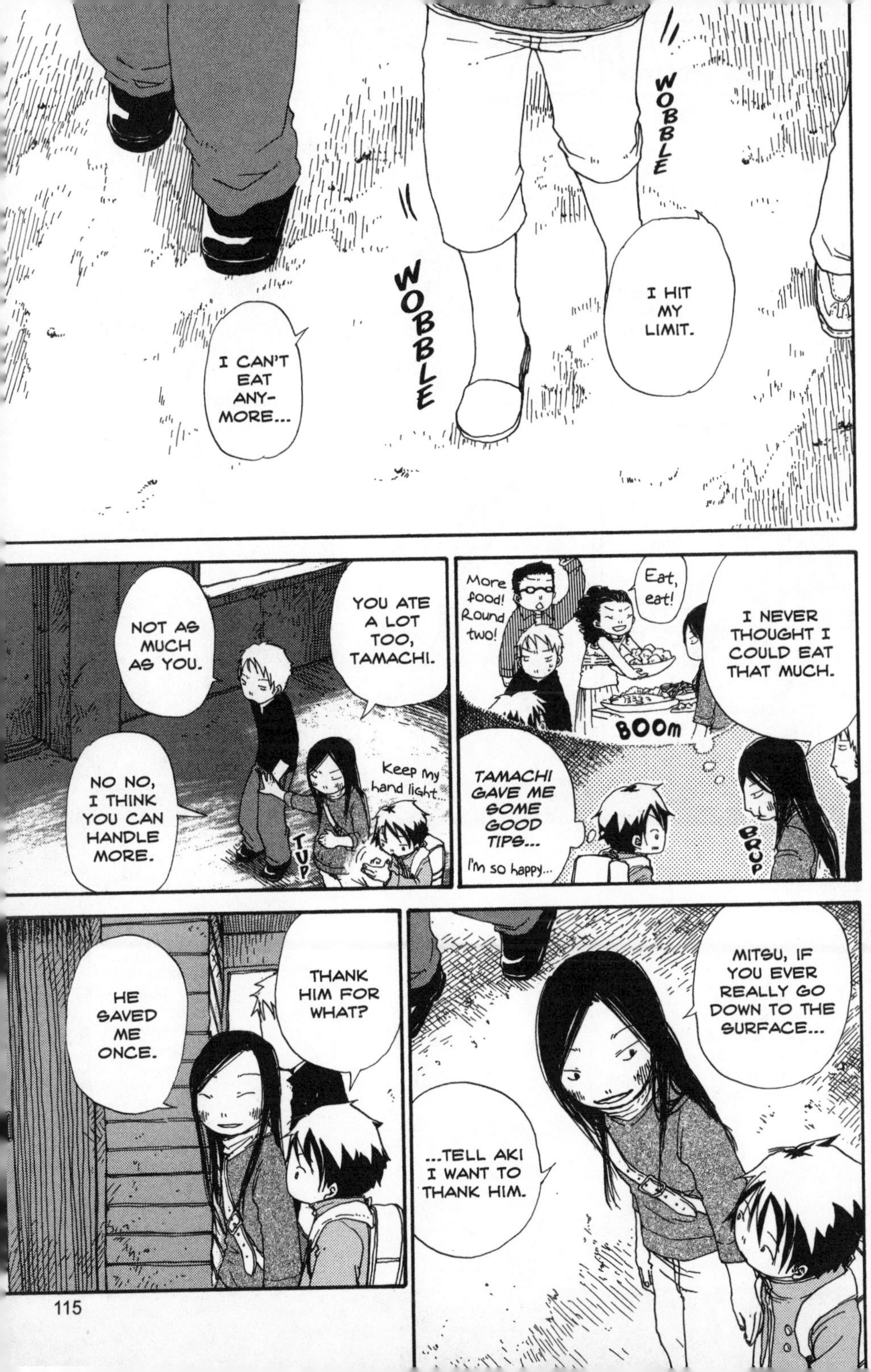
WOBBLE
I HIT MY LIMIT.
WOBBLE
I CAN'T EAT ANY-MORE...
I NEVER THOUGHT I COULD EAT THAT MUCH.
Eat, eat!
More food! Round two!
BOOm
BRUP
TAMACHI GAVE ME SOME GOOD TIPS...
I'm so happy...
YOU ATE A LOT TOO, TAMACHI.
NOT AS MUCH AS YOU.
Keep my hand light...
NO NO, I THINK YOU CAN HANDLE MORE.
TUP
MITSU, IF YOU EVER REALLY GO DOWN TO THE SURFACE...
...TELL AKI I WANT TO THANK HIM.
THANK HIM FOR WHAT?
HE SAVED ME ONCE.

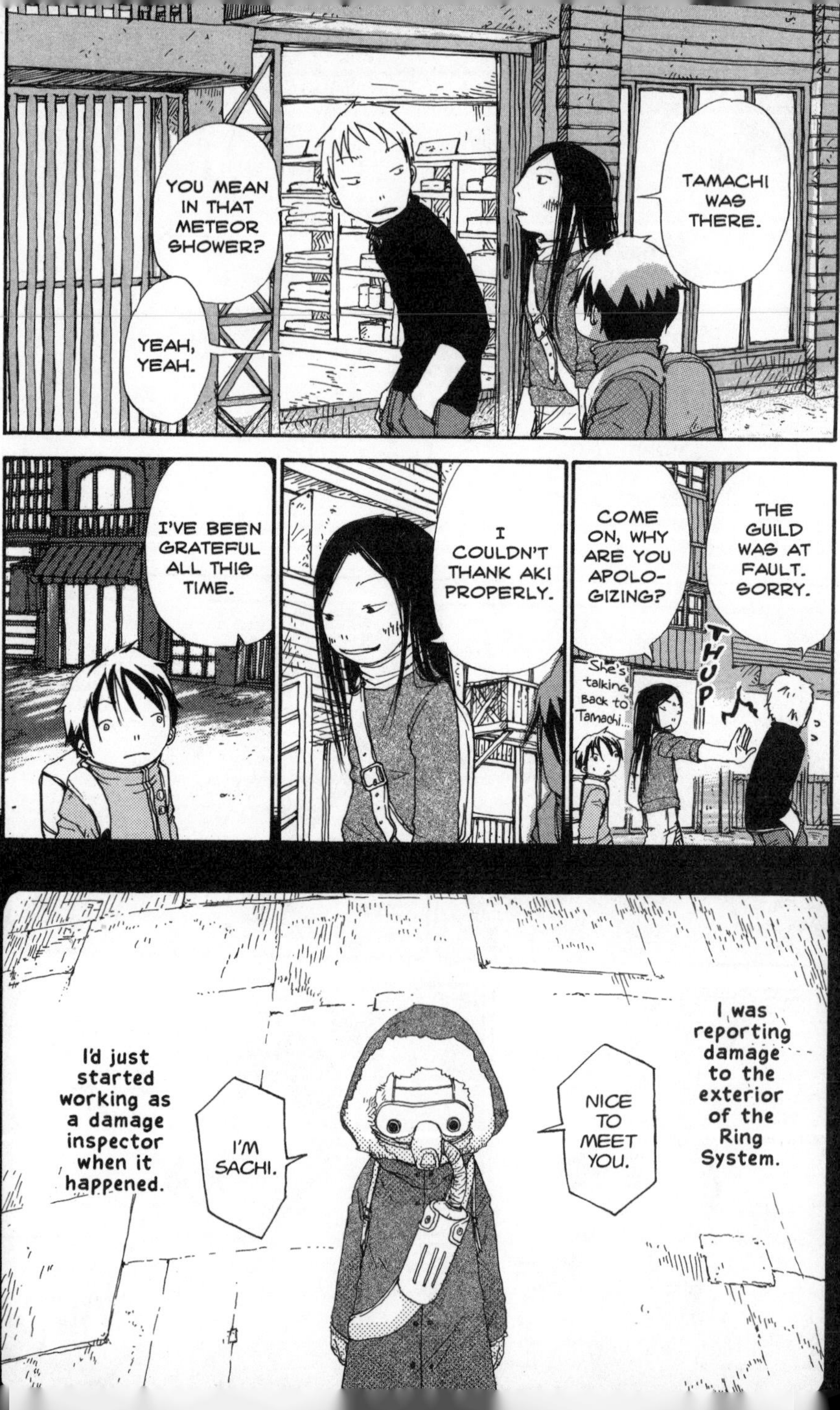
TAMACHI WAS THERE.
YOU MEAN IN THAT METEOR SHOWER?
YEAH, YEAH.
THE GUILD WAS AT FAULT. SORRY.
THUP
COME ON, WHY ARE YOU APOLOGIZING?
She's talking back to Tamachi...
I COULDN'T THANK AKI PROPERLY.
I'VE BEEN GRATEFUL ALL THIS TIME.
I was reporting damage to the exterior of the Ring System.
NICE TO MEET YOU.
I'M SACHI.
I'd just started working as a damage inspector when it happened.

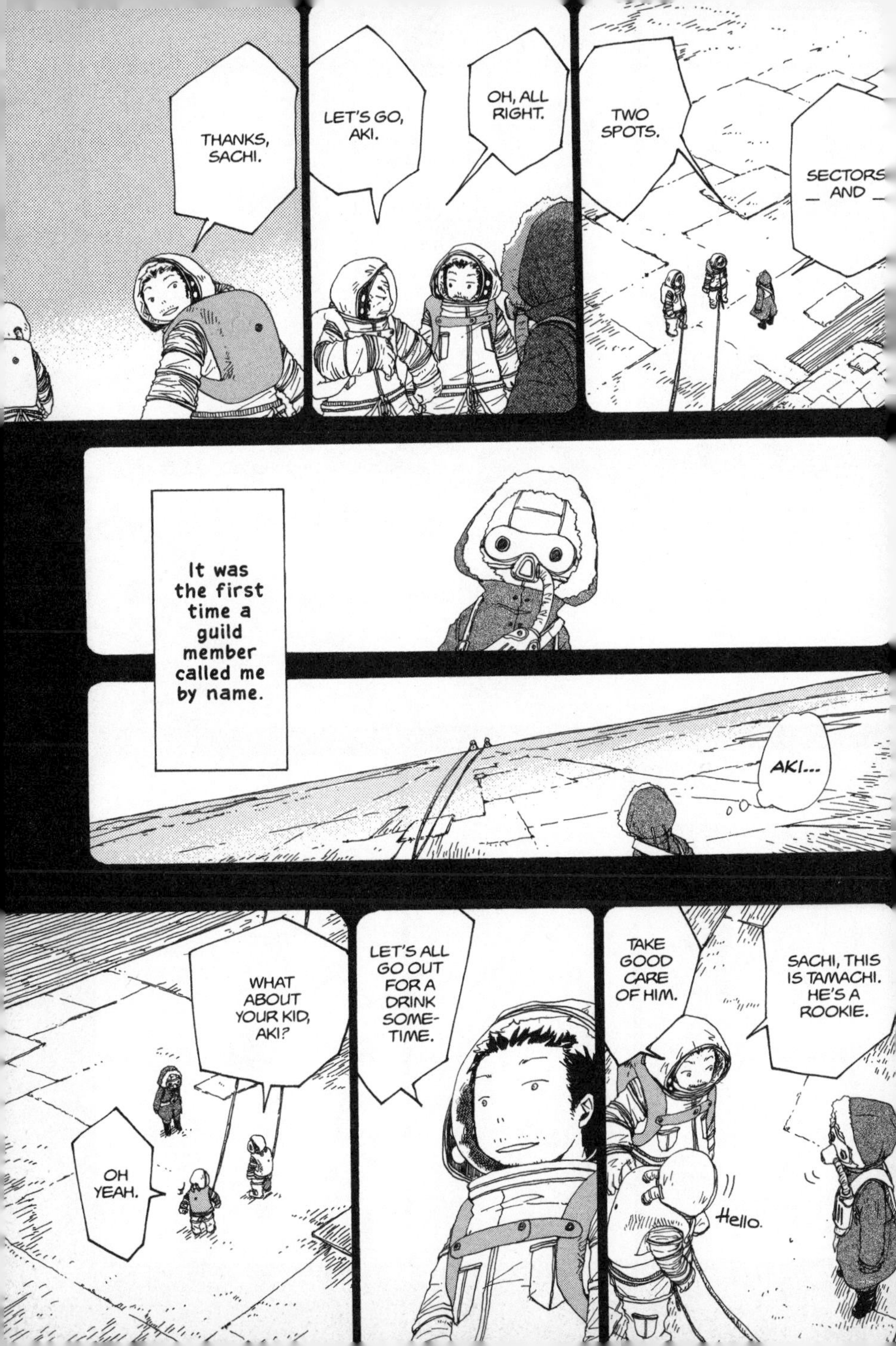
SECTORS _ AND _
TWO SPOTS.
OH, ALL RIGHT.
LET'S GO, AKI.
THANKS, SACHI.
It was the first time a guild member called me by name.
AKI...
SACHI, THIS IS TAMACHI. HE'S A ROOKIE.
TAKE GOOD CARE OF HIM.
Hello.
LET'S ALL GO OUT FOR A DRINK SOME-TIME.
WHAT ABOUT YOUR KID, AKI?
OH YEAH.

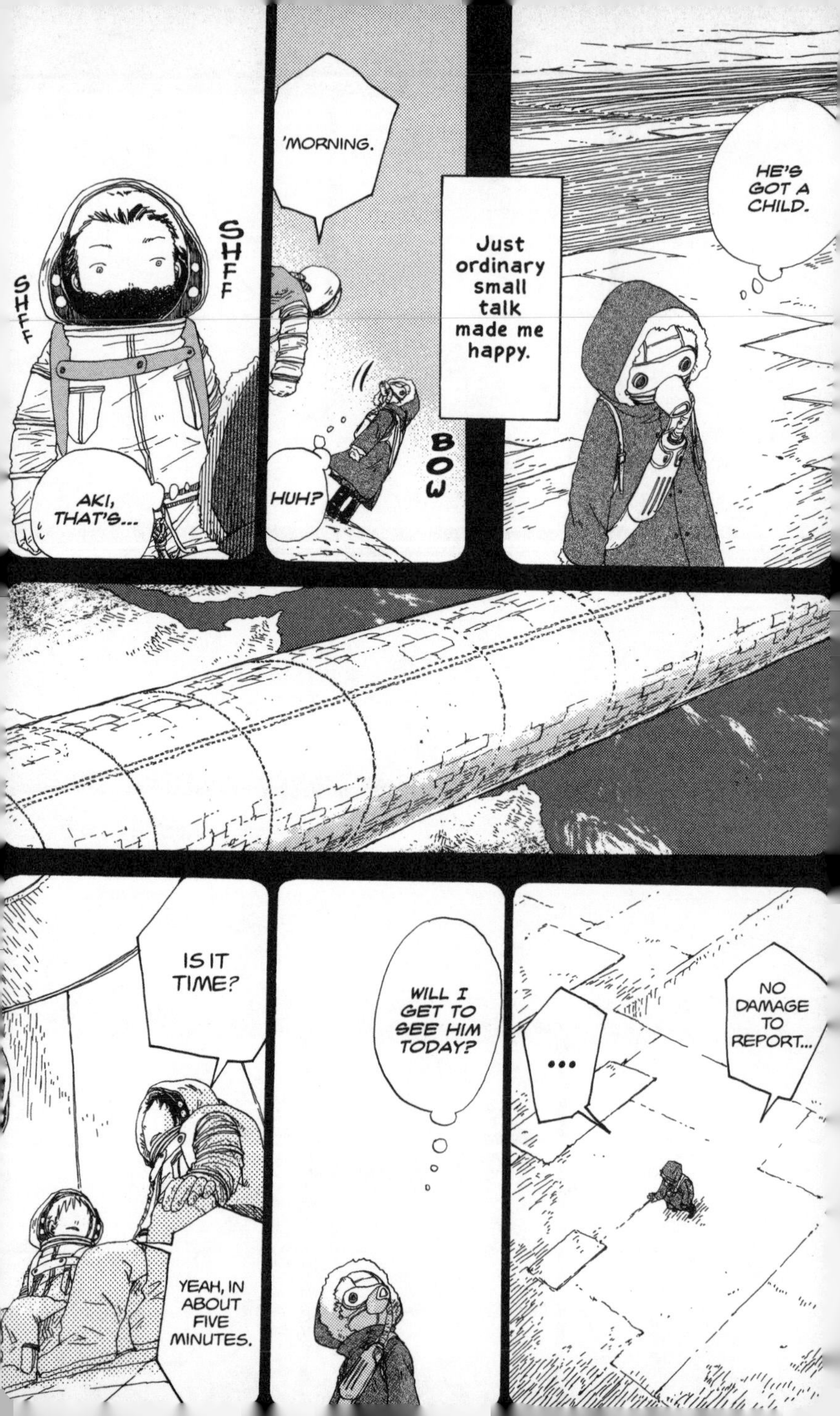
HE'S GOT A CHILD.
Just ordinary small talk made me happy.
'MORNING.
BOW
HUH?
SHFF
SHFF
AKI, THAT'S...
NO DAMAGE TO REPORT...
...
WILL I GET TO SEE HIM TODAY?
IS IT TIME?
YEAH, IN ABOUT FIVE MINUTES.

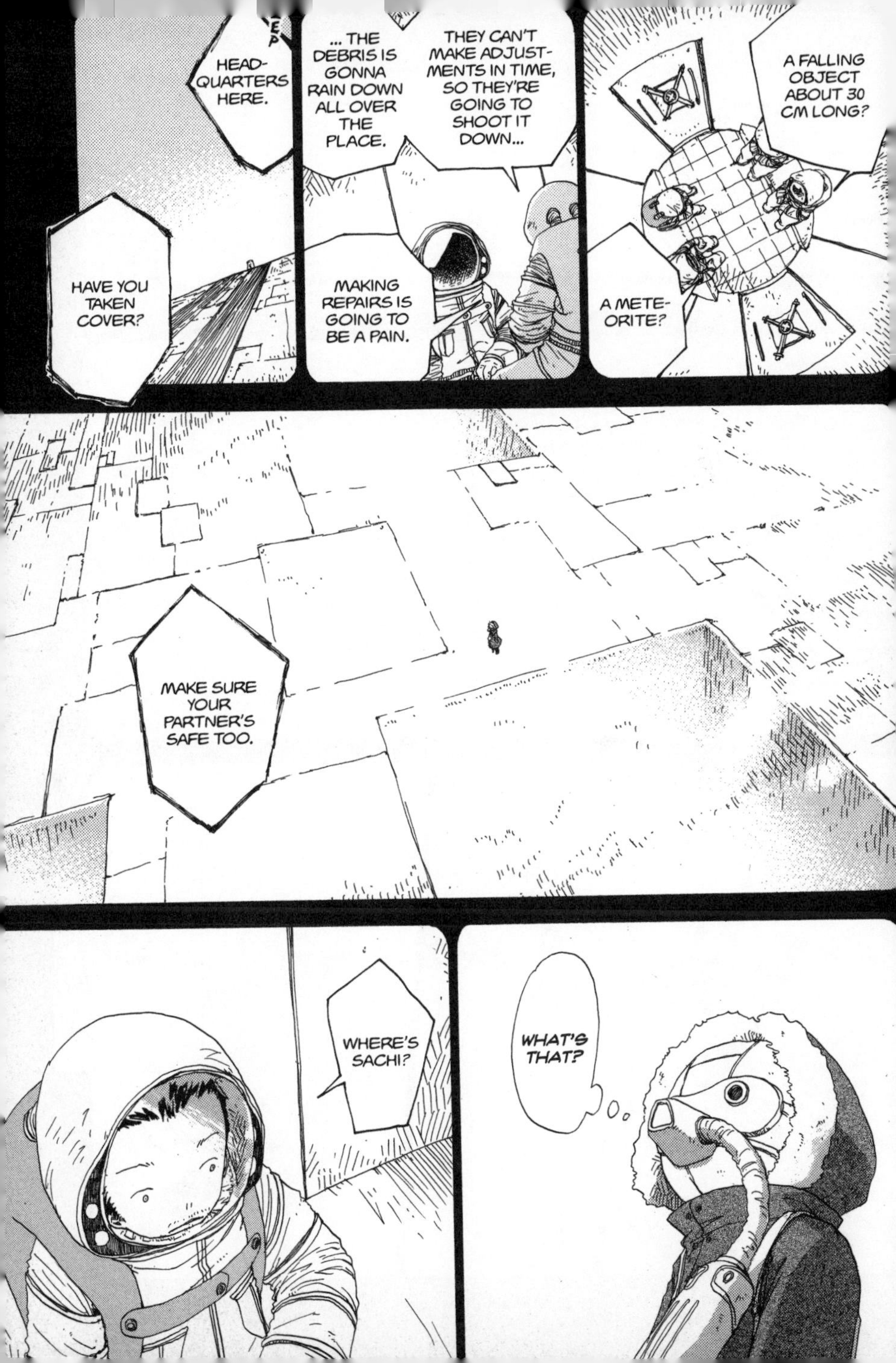
A FALLING OBJECT ABOUT 30 CM LONG?
A METEORITE?
THEY CAN'T MAKE ADJUSTMENTS IN TIME, SO THEY'RE GOING TO SHOOT IT DOWN...
... THE DEBRIS IS GONNA RAIN DOWN ALL OVER THE PLACE.
MAKING REPAIRS IS GOING TO BE A PAIN.
HEADQUARTERS HERE.
HAVE YOU TAKEN COVER?
MAKE SURE YOUR PARTNER'S SAFE TOO.
WHAT'S THAT?
WHERE'S SACHI?

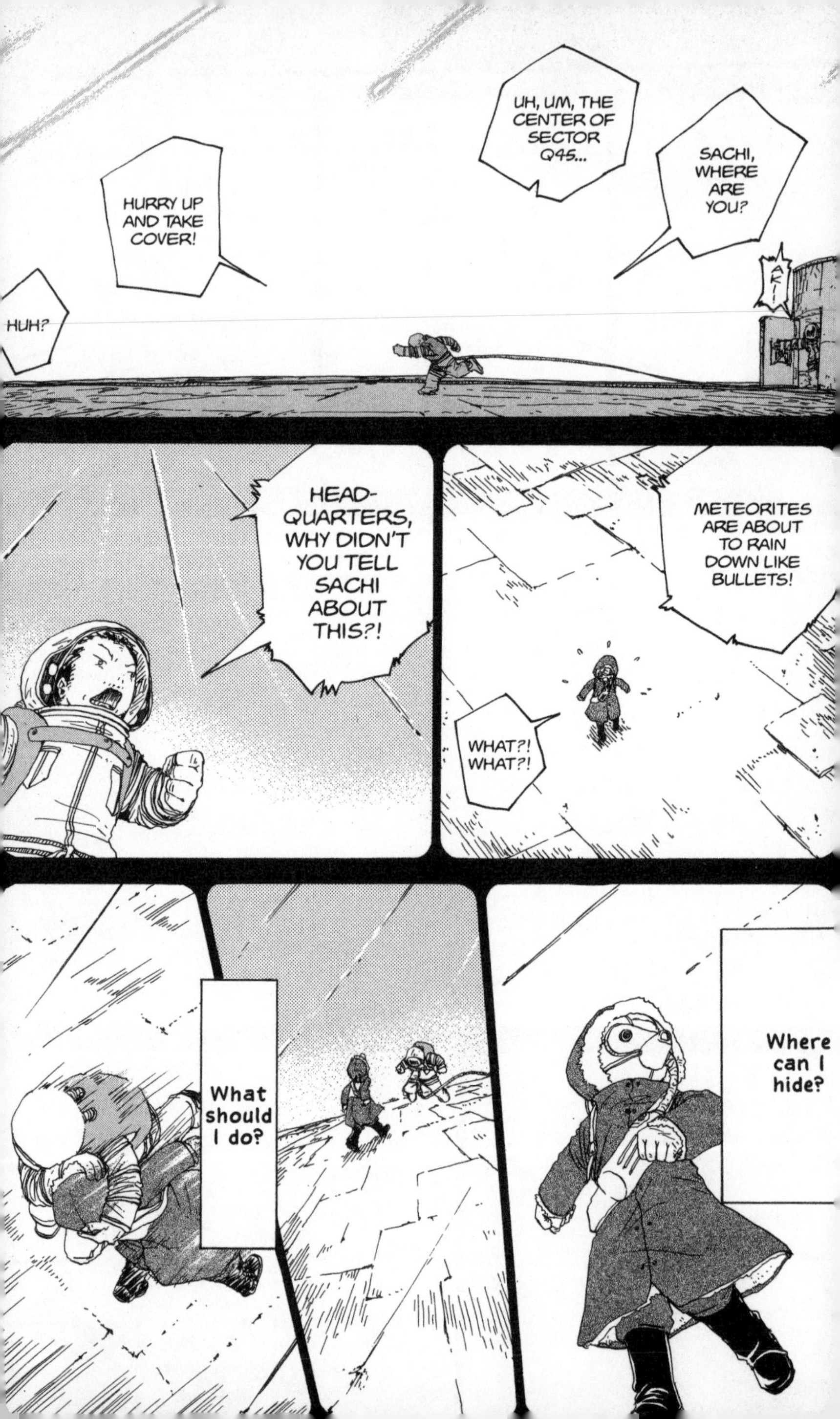
SACHI, WHERE ARE YOU?
UH, UM, THE CENTER OF SECTOR Q45...
AKI!!
HURRY UP AND TAKE COVER!
HUH?
METEORITES ARE ABOUT TO RAIN DOWN LIKE BULLETS!
WHAT?! WHAT?!
HEAD-QUARTERS, WHY DIDN'T YOU TELL SACHI ABOUT THIS?!
Where can I hide?
What should I do?

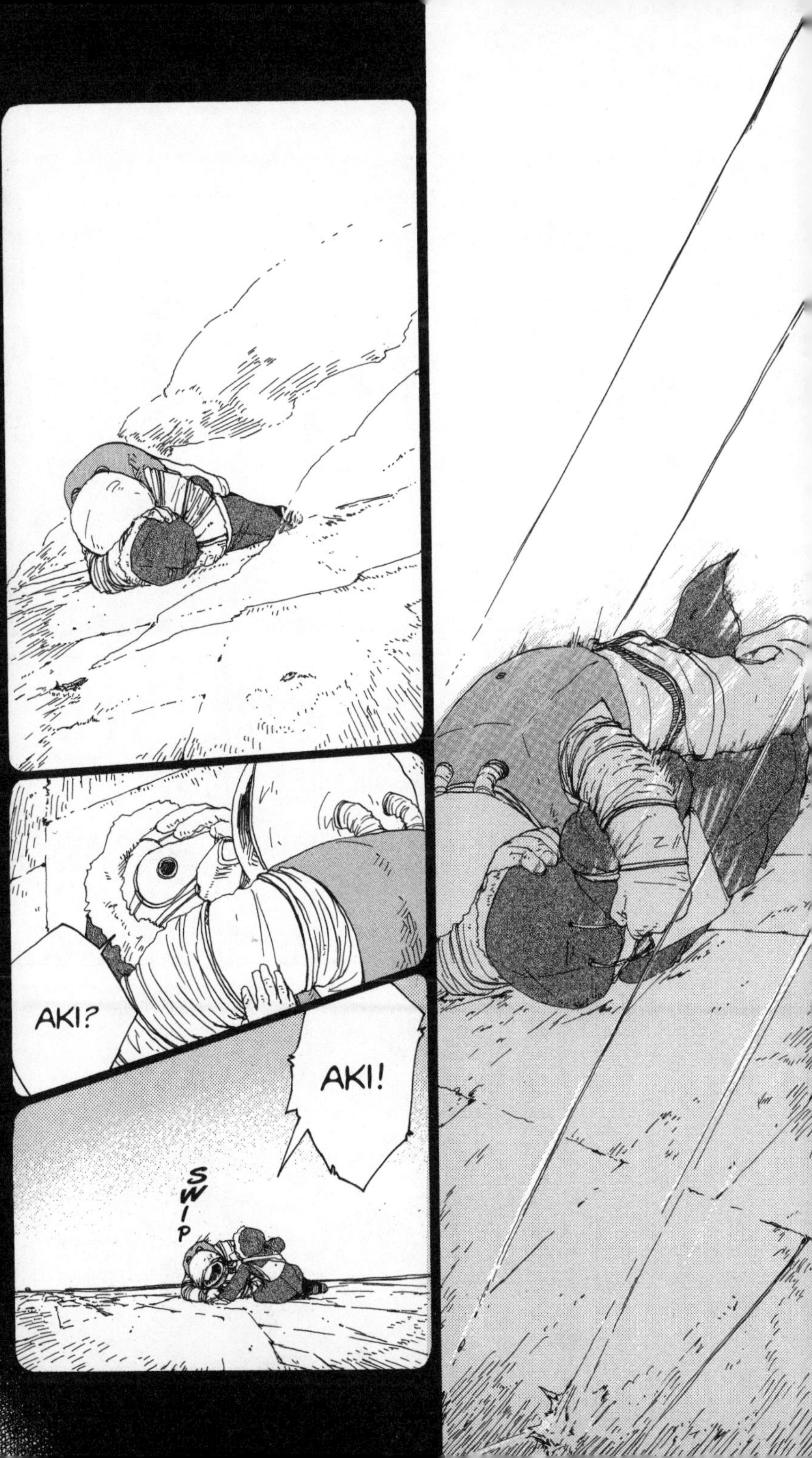
AKI?
AKI!
SWIP

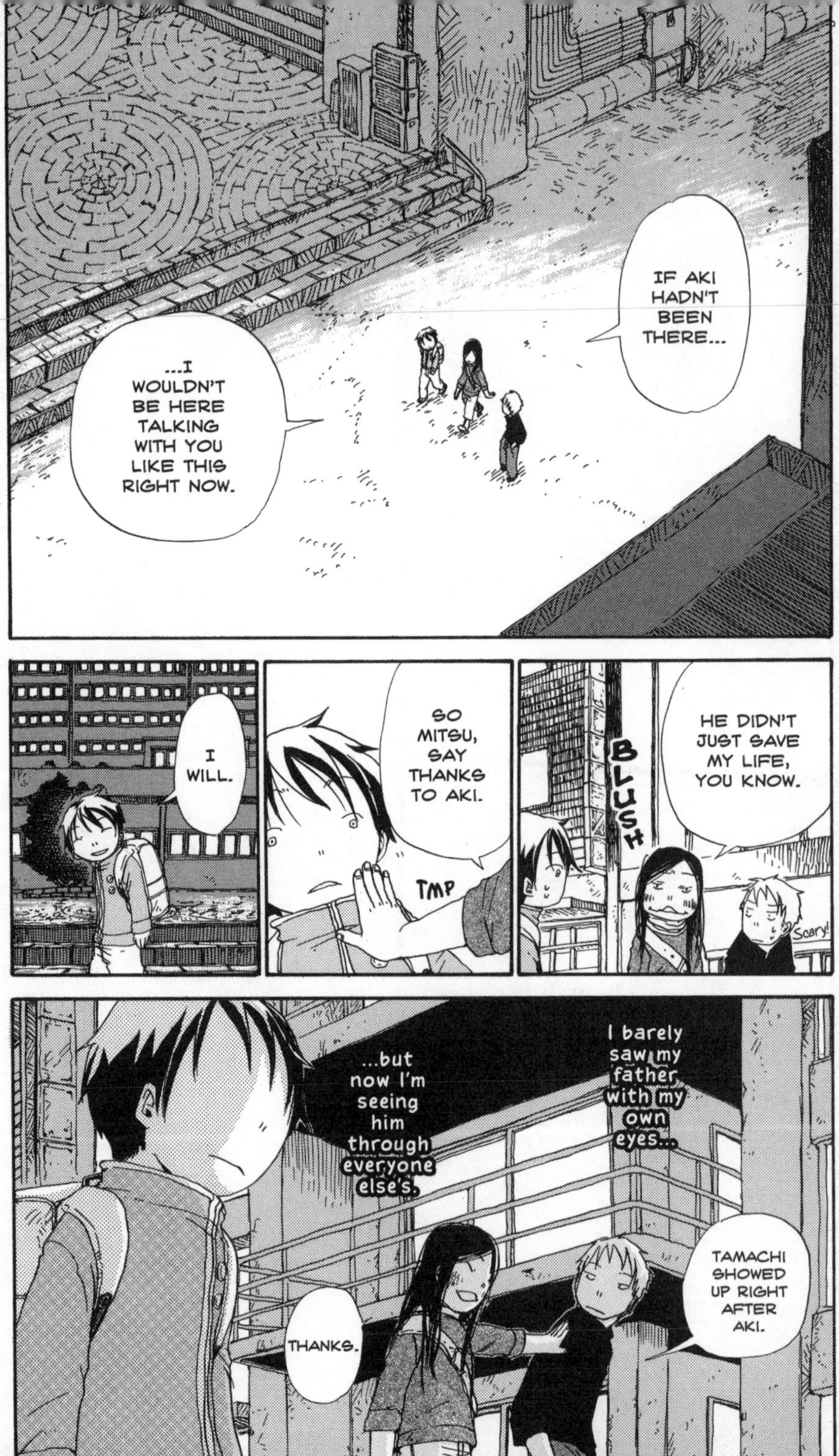
IF AKI HADN'T BEEN THERE...
...I WOULDN'T BE HERE TALKING WITH YOU LIKE THIS RIGHT NOW.
HE DIDN'T JUST SAVE MY LIFE, YOU KNOW.
BLUSH
Scary!
SO MITSU, SAY THANKS TO AKI.
TMP
I WILL.
I barely saw my father with my own eyes...
...but now I'm seeing him through everyone else's.
TAMACHI SHOWED UP RIGHT AFTER AKI.
THANKS.

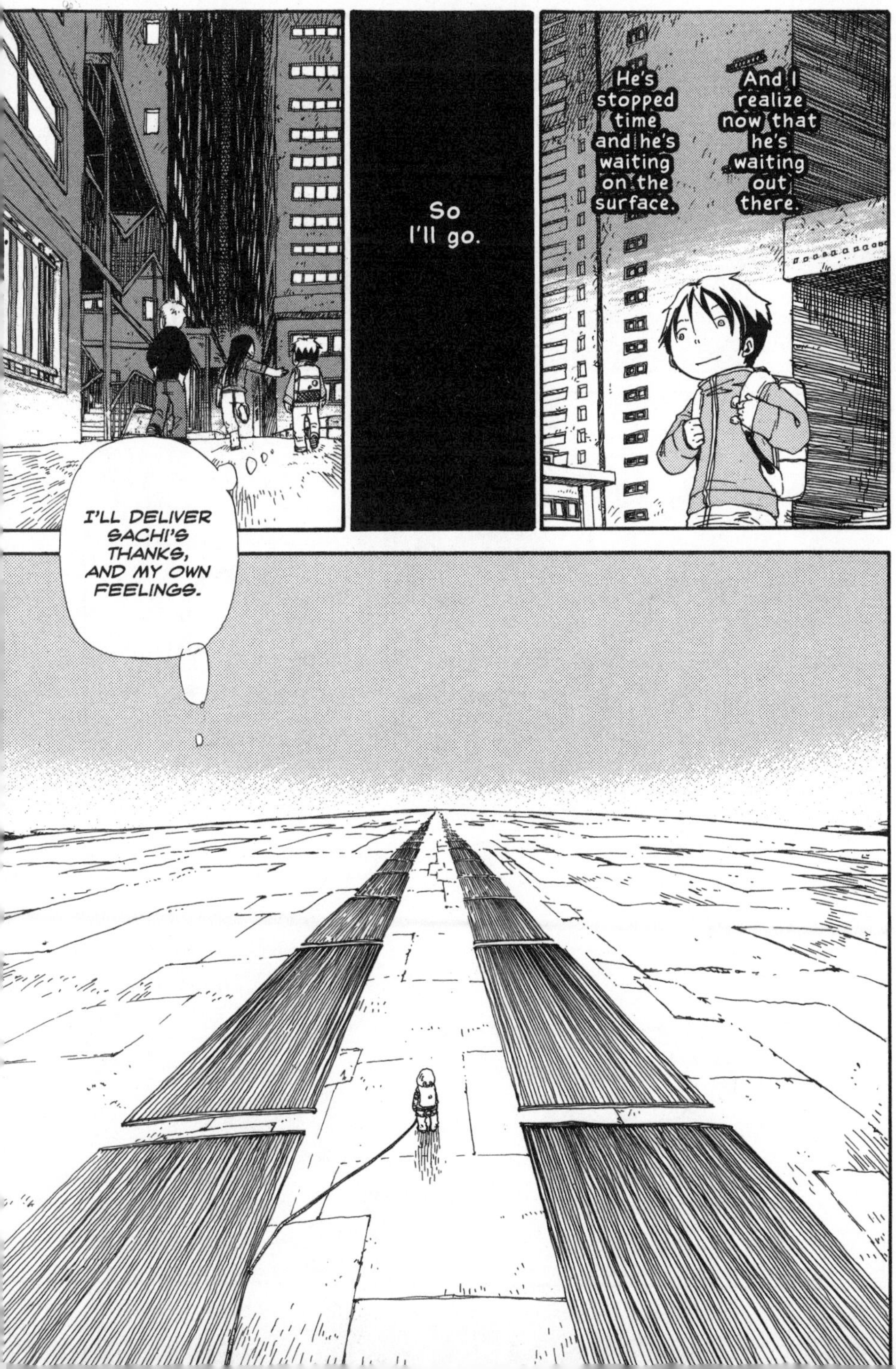
And I realize now that he's waiting out there.
He's stopped time and he's waiting on the surface.
So I'll go.
I'LL DELIVER SACHI'S THANKS, AND MY OWN FEELINGS.

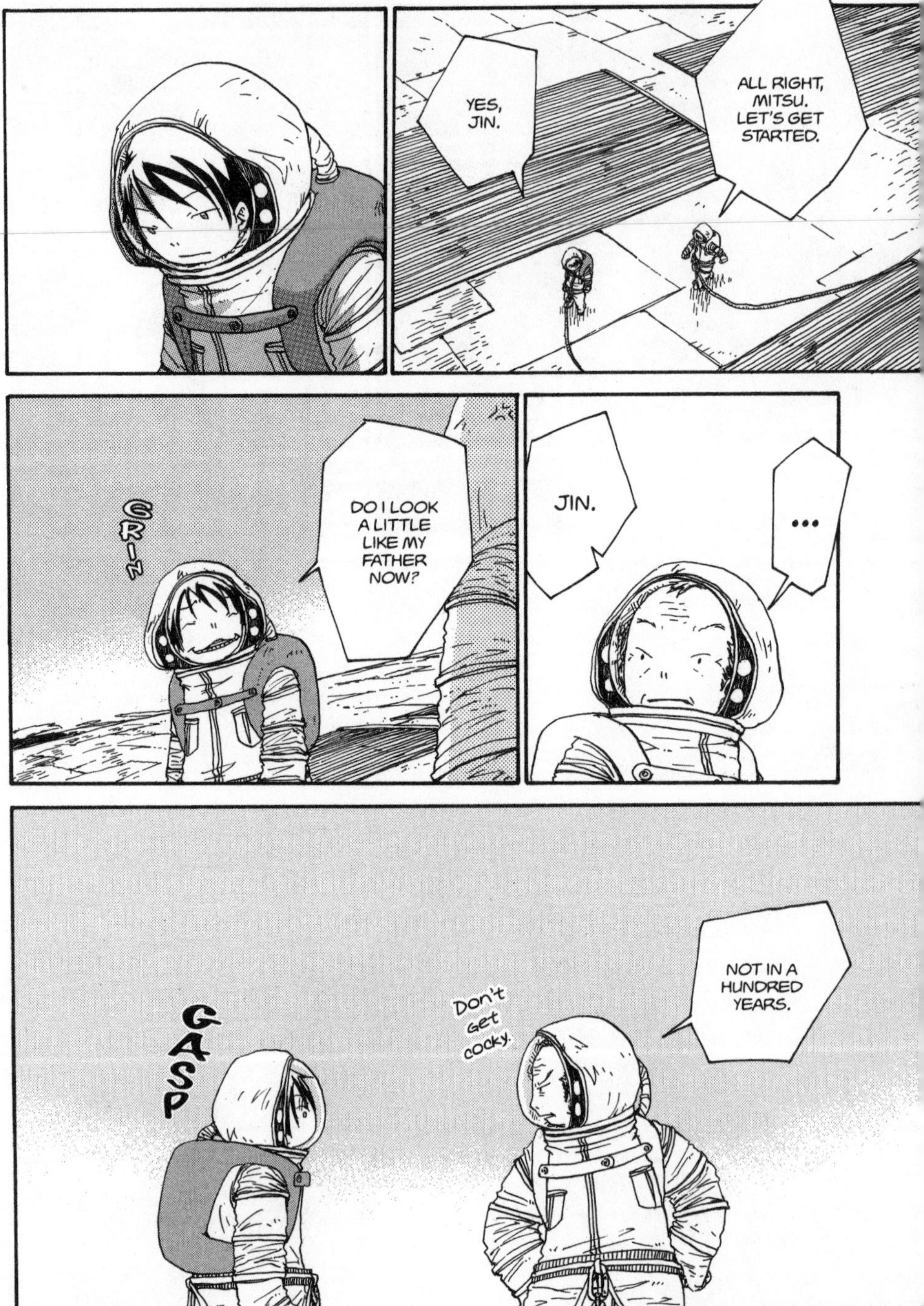
ALL RIGHT, MITSU. LET'S GET STARTED.
YES, JIN.
...
JIN.
DO I LOOK A LITTLE LIKE MY FATHER NOW?
GRIN
NOT IN A HUNDRED YEARS.
Don't get cocky.
GASP

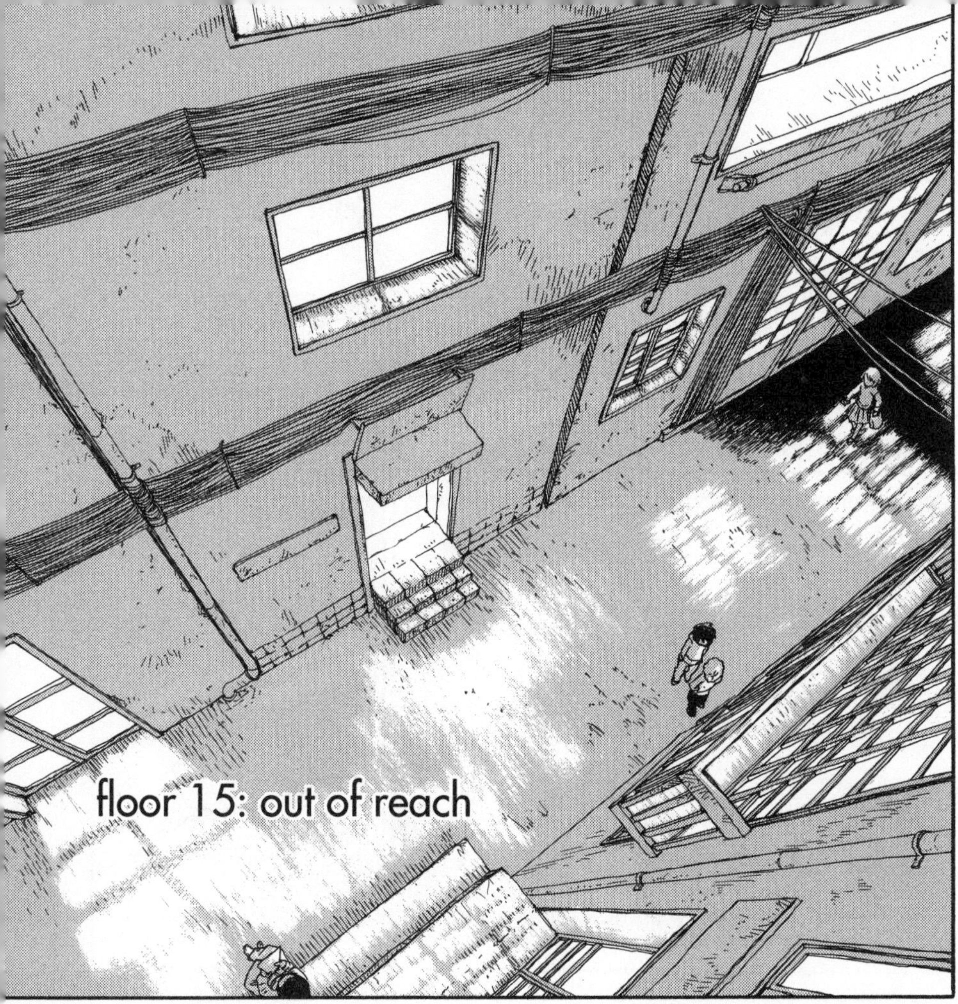
floor 15: out of reach

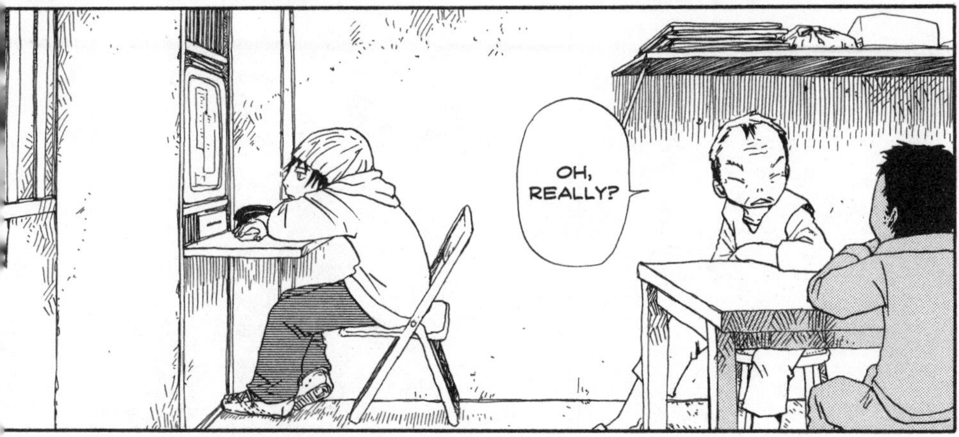
OH, REALLY?

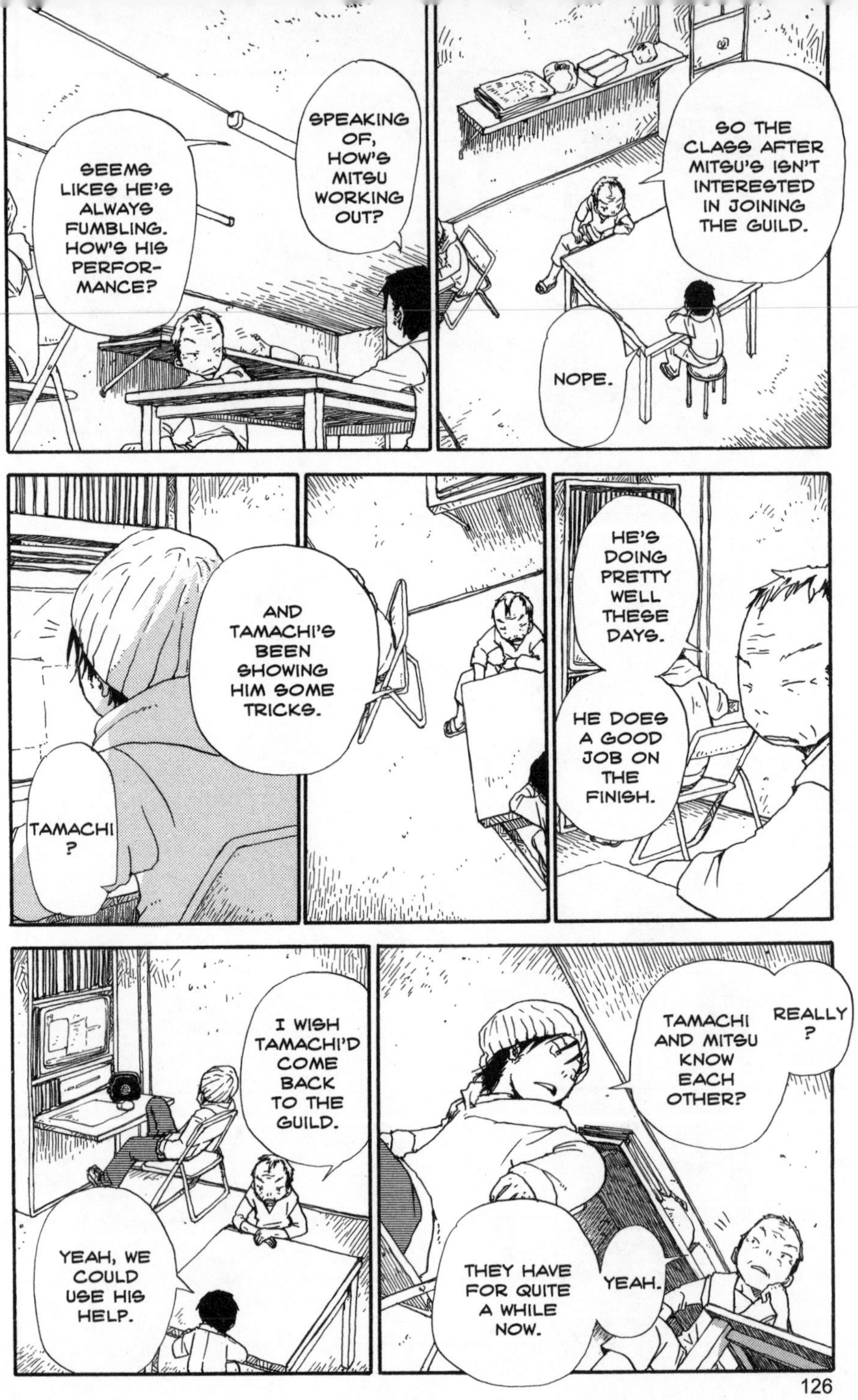
SO THE CLASS AFTER MITSU'S ISN'T INTERESTED IN JOINING THE GUILD.
NOPE.
SPEAKING OF, HOW'S MITSU WORKING OUT?
SEEMS LIKES HE'S ALWAYS FUMBLING. HOW'S HIS PERFORMANCE?
HE'S DOING PRETTY WELL THESE DAYS.
HE DOES A GOOD JOB ON THE FINISH.
AND TAMACHI'S BEEN SHOWING HIM SOME TRICKS.
TAMACHI?
REALLY?
TAMACHI AND MITSU KNOW EACH OTHER?
YEAH.
THEY HAVE FOR QUITE A WHILE NOW.
I WISH TAMACHI'D COME BACK TO THE GUILD.
YEAH, WE COULD USE HIS HELP.

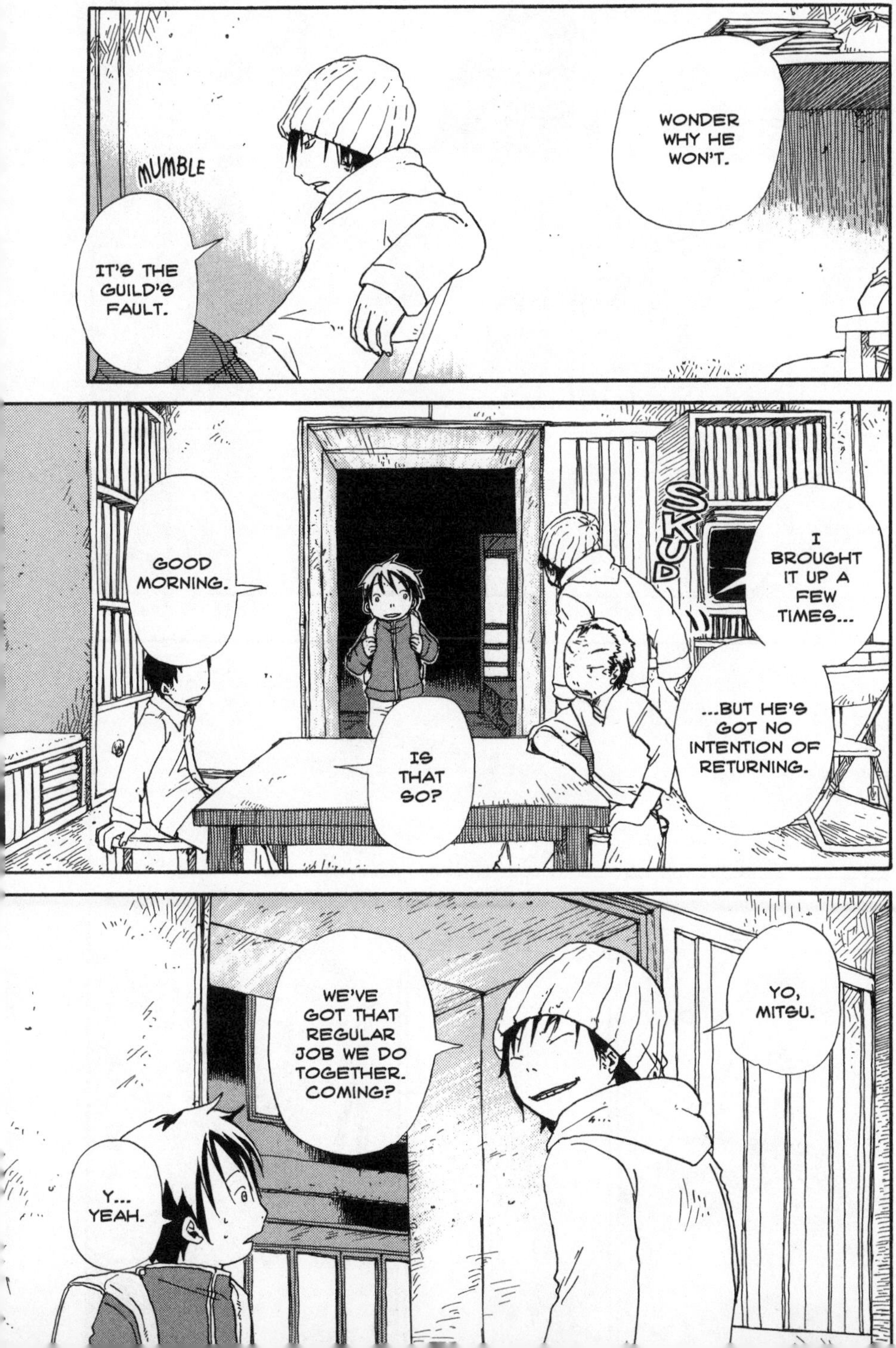
WONDER WHY HE WON'T.
MUMBLE
IT'S THE GUILD'S FAULT.
I BROUGHT IT UP A FEW TIMES...
SKUD
...BUT HE'S GOT NO INTENTION OF RETURNING.
GOOD MORNING.
IS THAT SO?
YO, MITSU.
WE'VE GOT THAT REGULAR JOB WE DO TOGETHER. COMING?
Y... YEAH.

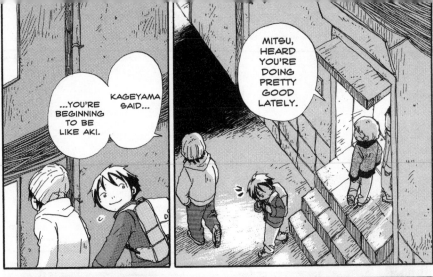

MITSU, HEARD YOU'RE DOING PRETTY GOOD LATELY.
KAGEYAMA SAID...
...YOU'RE BEGINNING TO BE LIKE AKI.
MUMBLE
LIKE HELL.
GLOW
MITSU, DON'T.
THUNK
FOCUS ON THE WINDOWS.

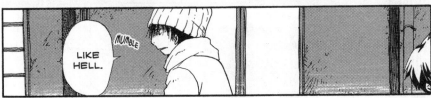

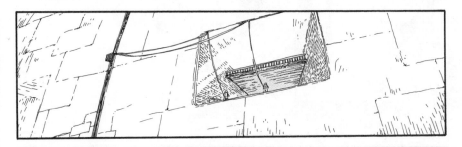

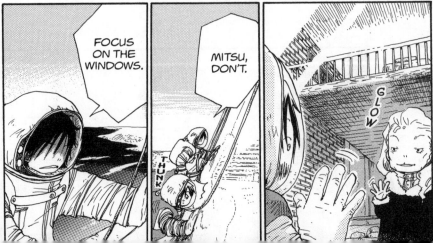

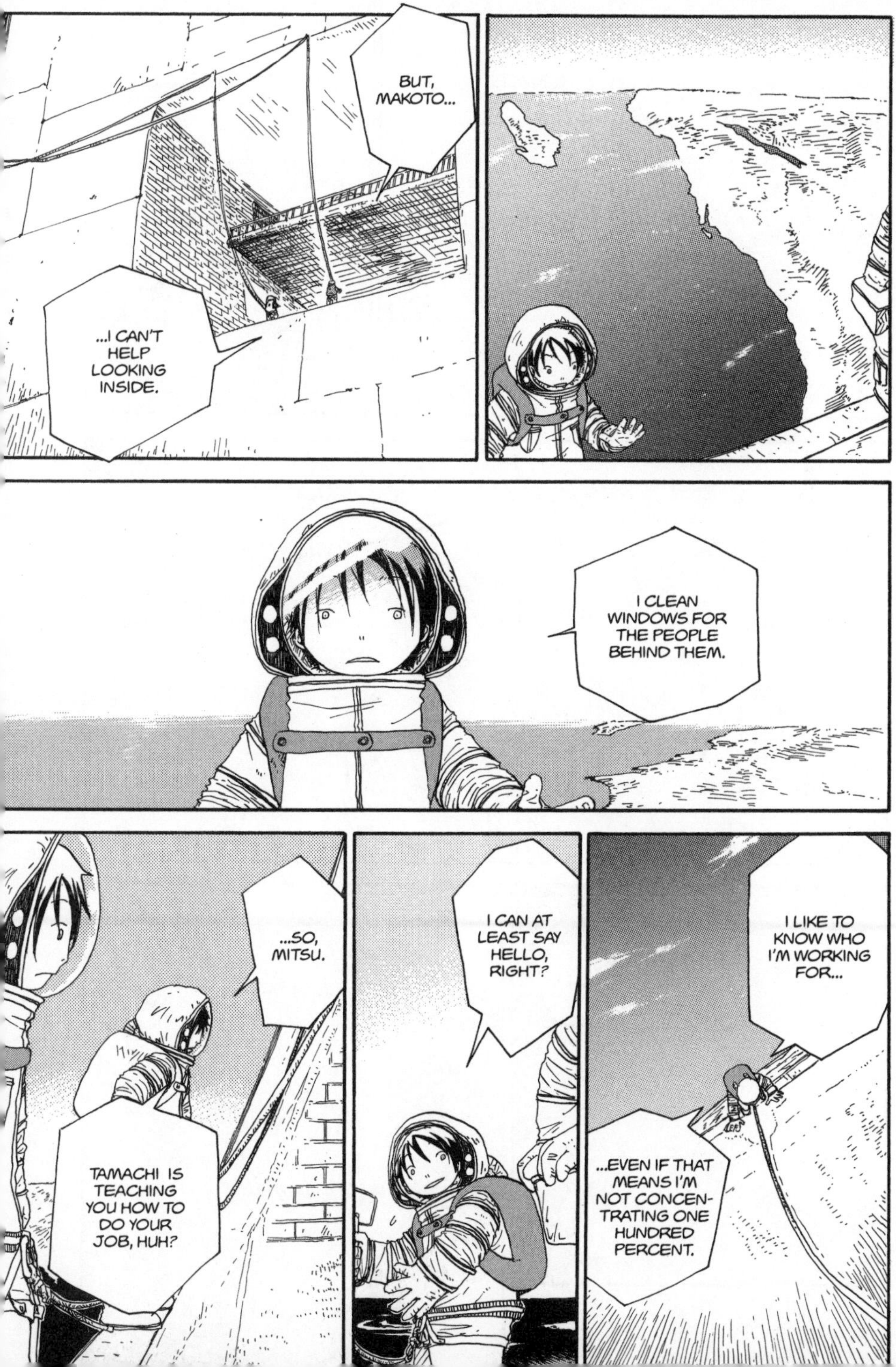
BUT, MAKOTO...
...I CAN'T HELP LOOKING INSIDE.
I CLEAN WINDOWS FOR THE PEOPLE BEHIND THEM.
I LIKE TO KNOW WHO I'M WORKING FOR...
...EVEN IF THAT MEANS I'M NOT CONCENTRATING ONE HUNDRED PERCENT.
I CAN AT LEAST SAY HELLO, RIGHT?
...SO, MITSU.
TAMACHI IS TEACHING YOU HOW TO DO YOUR JOB, HUH?

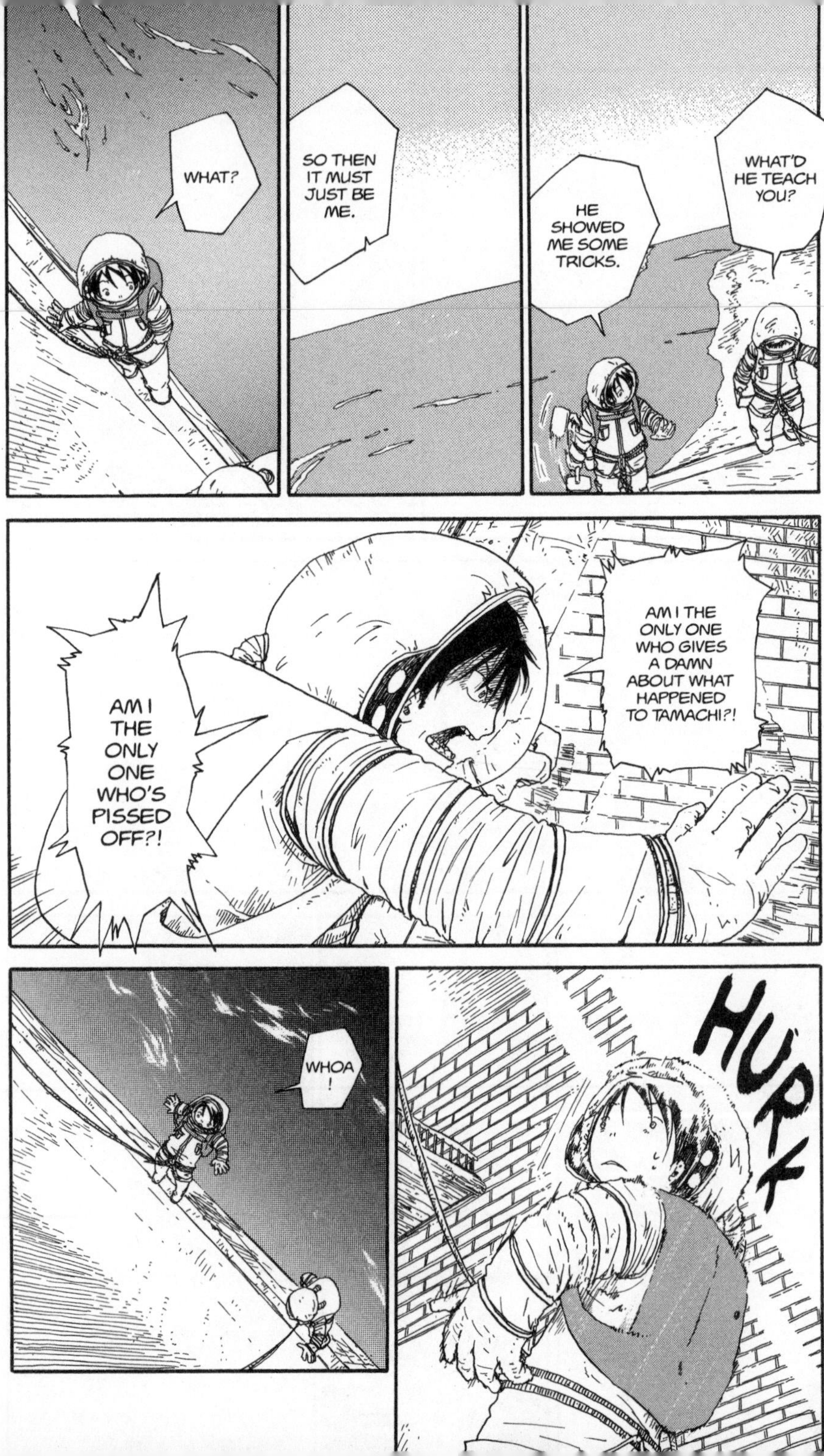
WHAT'D HE TEACH YOU?
HE SHOWED ME SOME TRICKS.
SO THEN IT MUST JUST BE ME.
WHAT?
AM I THE ONLY ONE WHO GIVES A DAMN ABOUT WHAT HAPPENED TO TAMACHI?!
AM I THE ONLY ONE WHO'S PISSED OFF?!
HURK
WHOA!

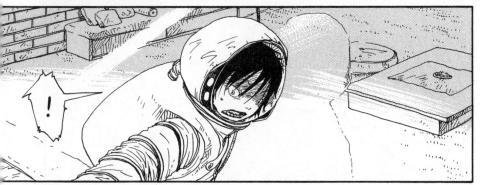

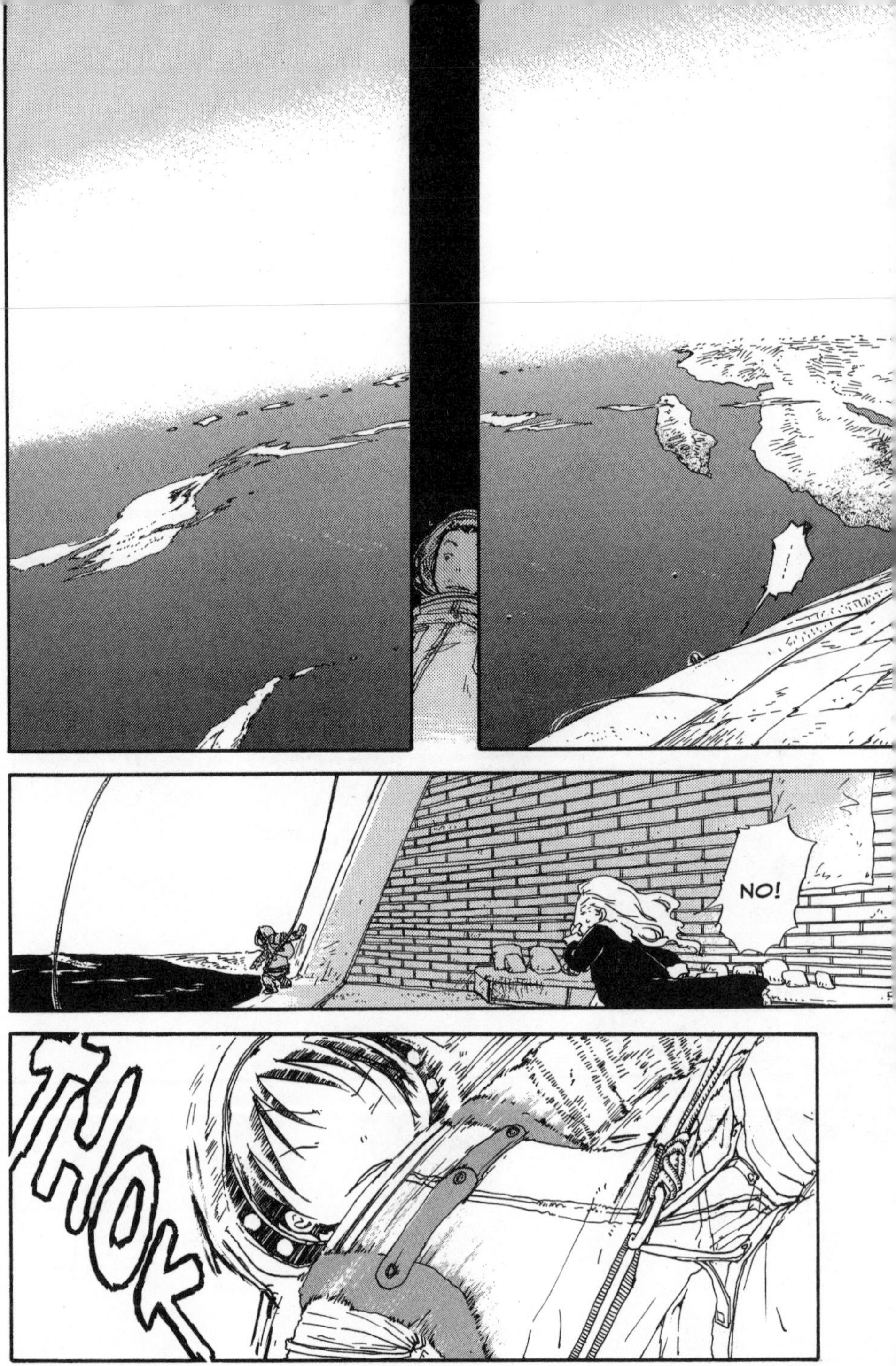
NO!
THOK

THE ROPE SAVED HIM.

THANK GOD!

FEEW

RIK RIK

FWOP

FWOP

TH...THAT WAS SCARY.

HAH HAH

WELL COME ON, GIVE HIM A HAND!

PHEW!

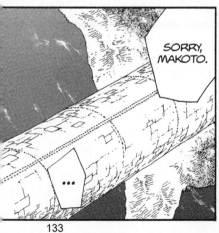

SORRY, MAKOTO.

•••

HUNH?

I WASN'T FOCUSING ENOUGH...

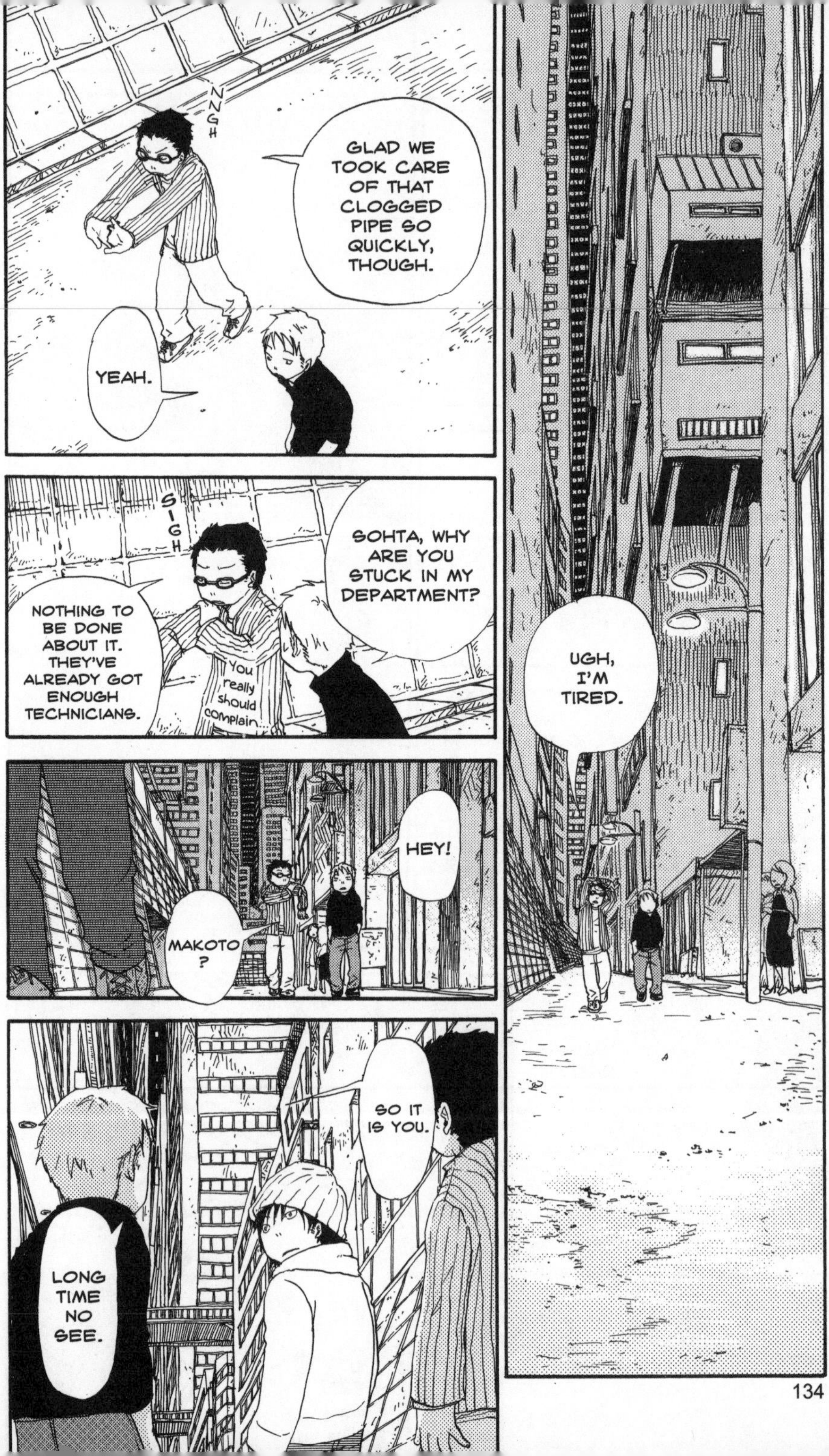
UGH, I'M TIRED.
NNGH
GLAD WE TOOK CARE OF THAT CLOGGED PIPE SO QUICKLY, THOUGH.
YEAH.
SOHTA, WHY ARE YOU STUCK IN MY DEPARTMENT?
SIGH
NOTHING TO BE DONE ABOUT IT. THEY'VE ALREADY GOT ENOUGH TECHNICIANS.
You really should complain...
HEY!
MAKOTO?
SO IT IS YOU.
LONG TIME NO SEE.

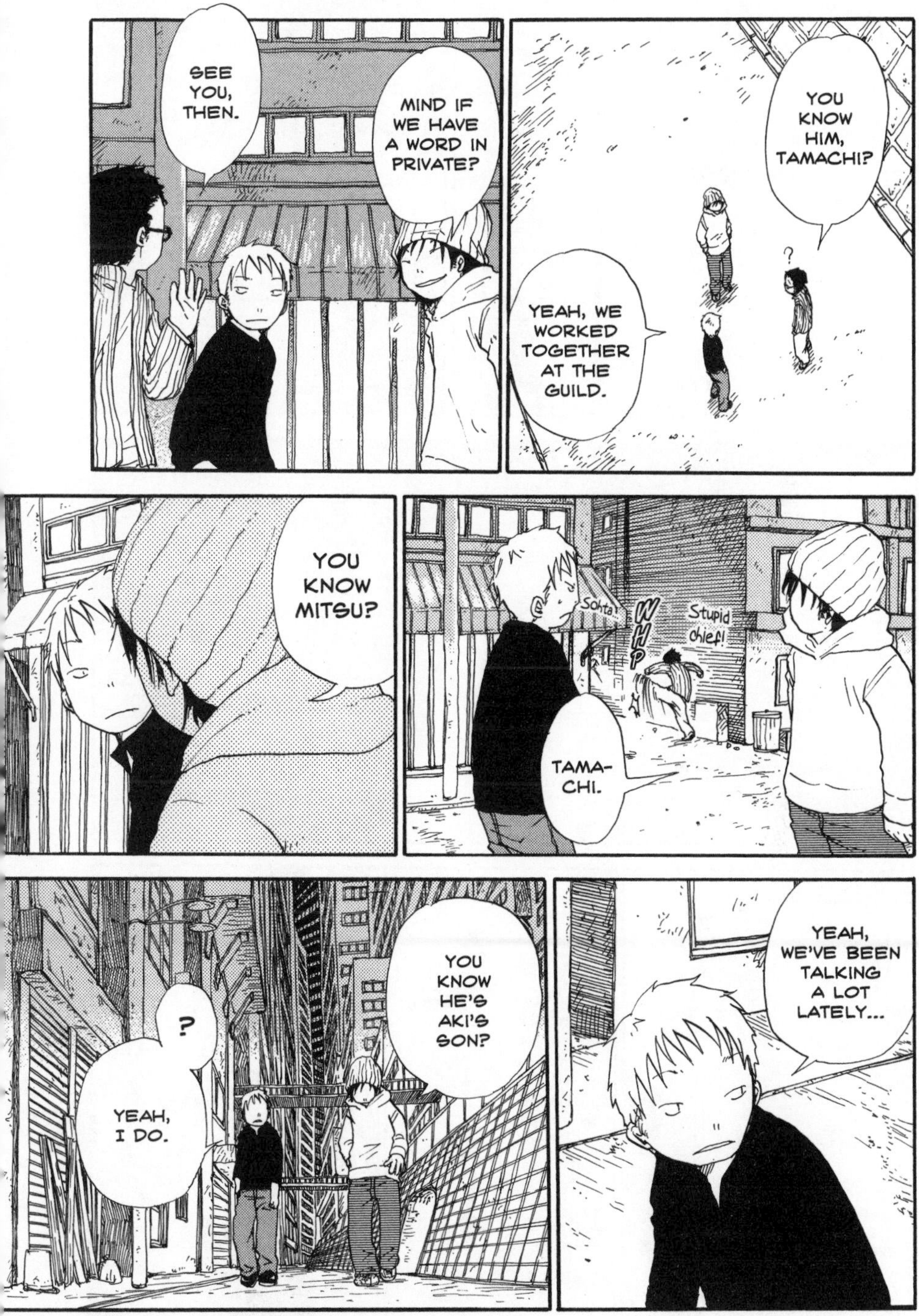
YOU KNOW HIM, TAMACHI?
YEAH, WE WORKED TOGETHER AT THE GUILD.
MIND IF WE HAVE A WORD IN PRIVATE?
SEE YOU, THEN.
Stupid chief!
WHP
Sohta!
TAMA-CHI.
YOU KNOW MITSU?
YEAH, WE'VE BEEN TALKING A LOT LATELY...
YOU KNOW HE'S AKI'S SON?
?
YEAH, I DO.

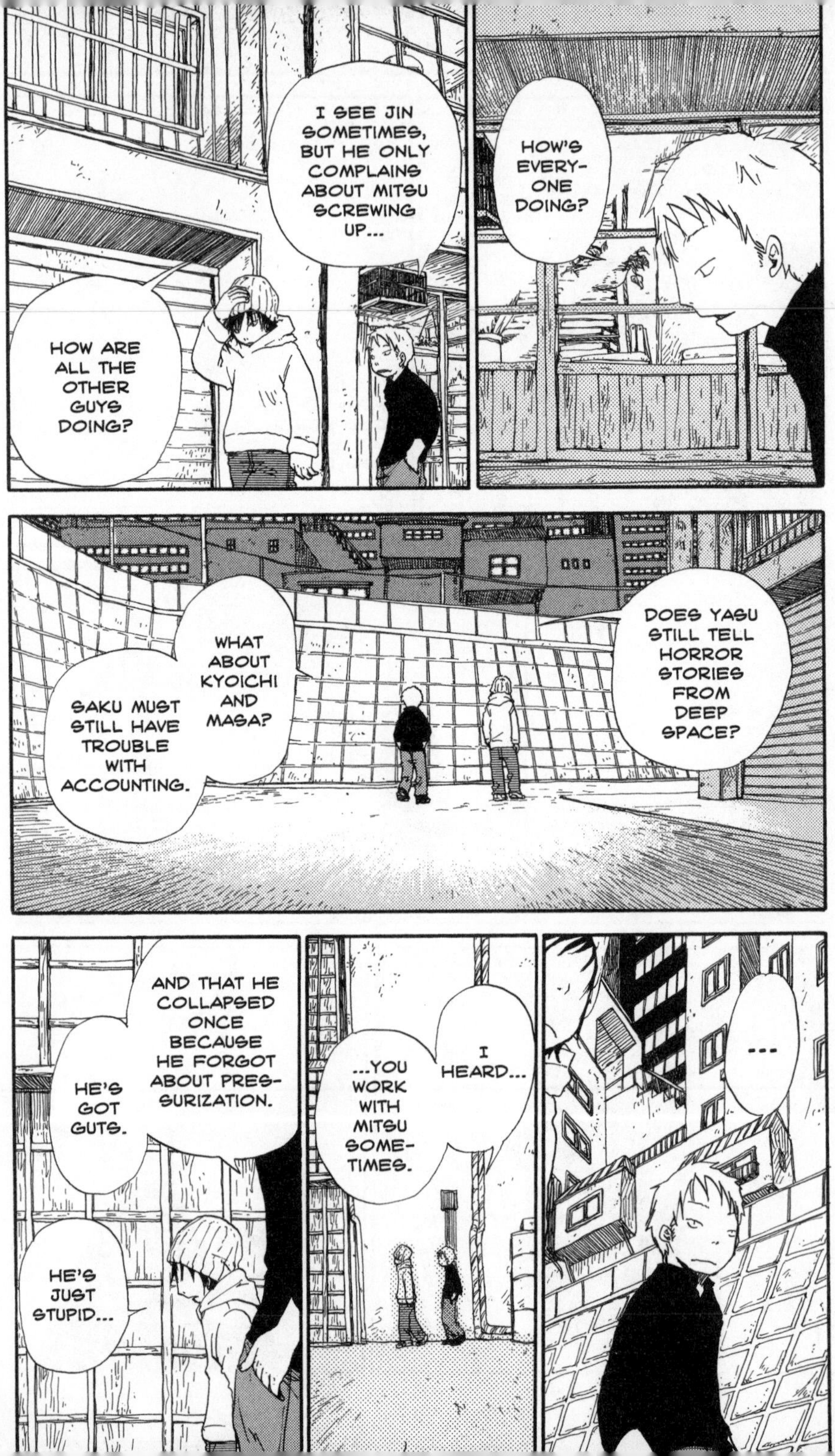
HOW'S EVERY-ONE DOING?
I SEE JIN SOMETIMES, BUT HE ONLY COMPLAINS ABOUT MITSU SCREWING UP...
HOW ARE ALL THE OTHER GUYS DOING?
DOES YASU STILL TELL HORROR STORIES FROM DEEP SPACE?
WHAT ABOUT KYOICHI AND MASA?
SAKU MUST STILL HAVE TROUBLE WITH ACCOUNTING.
...
I HEARD...
...YOU WORK WITH MITSU SOME-TIMES.
AND THAT HE COLLAPSED ONCE BECAUSE HE FORGOT ABOUT PRES-SURIZATION.
HE'S GOT GUTS.
HE'S JUST STUPID...

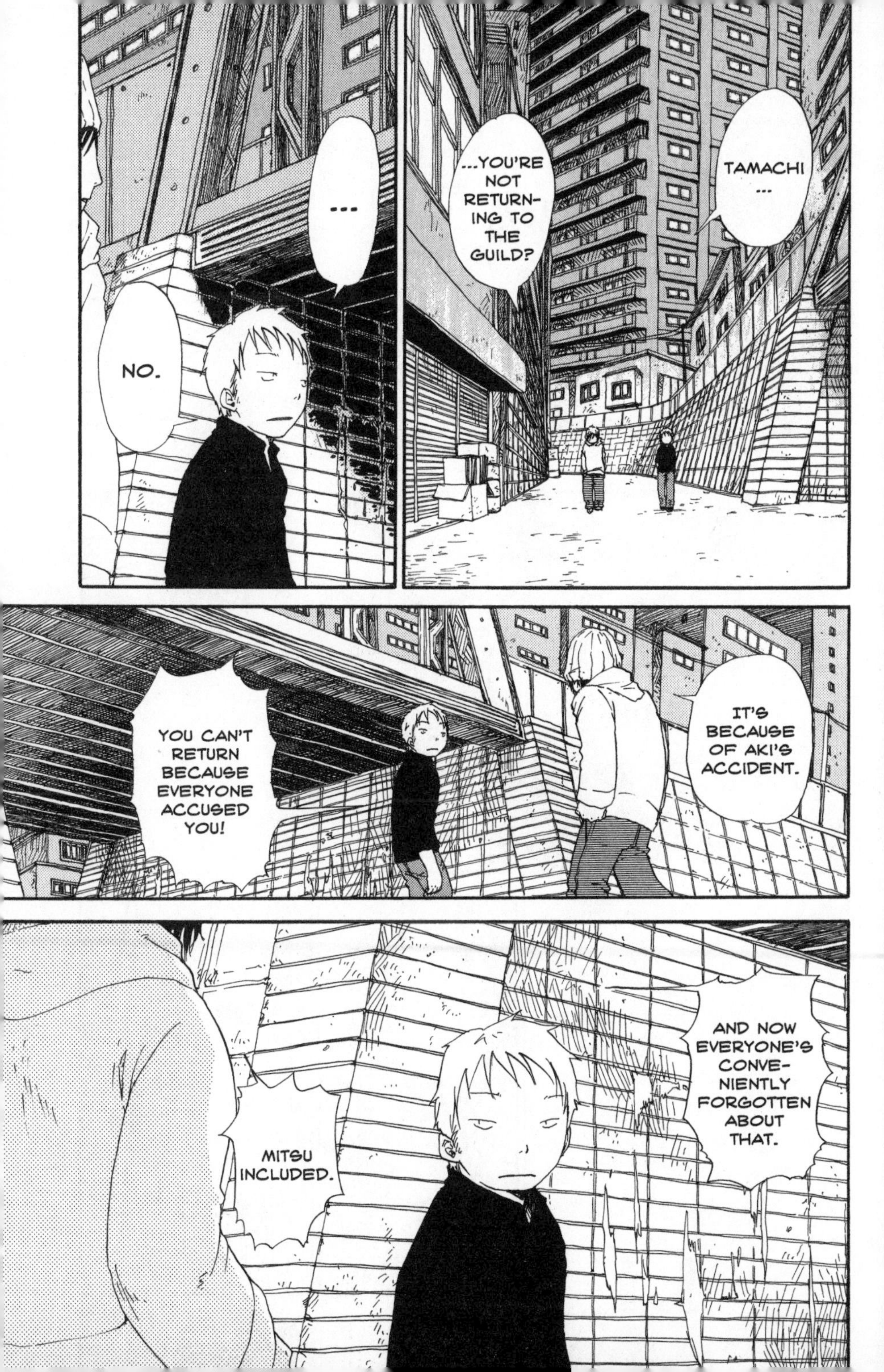
TAMACHI ...
...YOU'RE NOT RETURNING TO THE GUILD?
...
NO.
IT'S BECAUSE OF AKI'S ACCIDENT.
YOU CAN'T RETURN BECAUSE EVERYONE ACCUSED YOU!
AND NOW EVERYONE'S CONVENIENTLY FORGOTTEN ABOUT THAT.
MITSU INCLUDED.

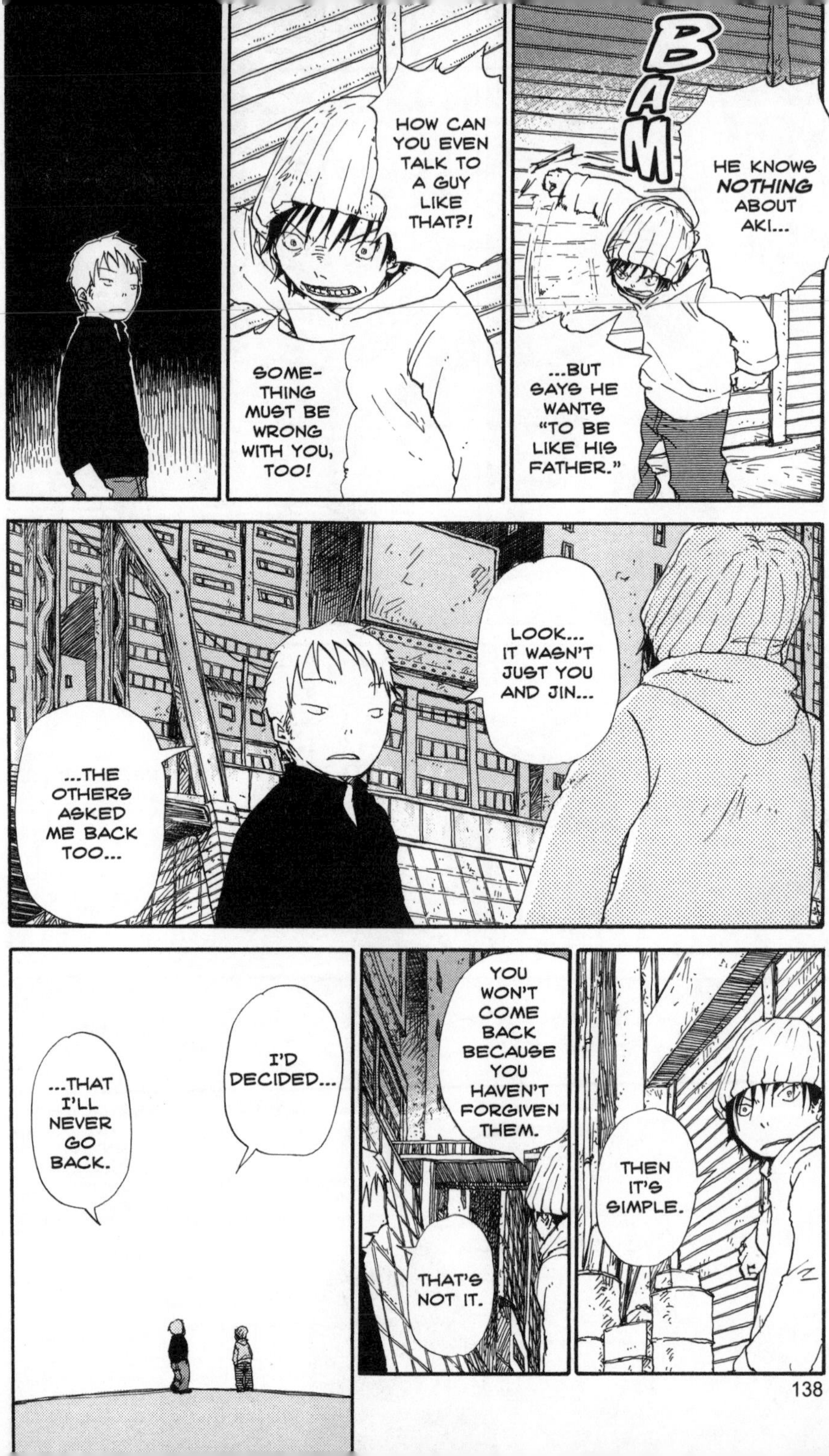
BAM
HE KNOWS NOTHING ABOUT AKI...
...BUT SAYS HE WANTS "TO BE LIKE HIS FATHER."
HOW CAN YOU EVEN TALK TO A GUY LIKE THAT?!
SOME-THING MUST BE WRONG WITH YOU, TOO!
LOOK... IT WASN'T JUST YOU AND JIN...
...THE OTHERS ASKED ME BACK TOO...
THEN IT'S SIMPLE.
YOU WON'T COME BACK BECAUSE YOU HAVEN'T FORGIVEN THEM.
THAT'S NOT IT.
I'D DECIDED...
...THAT I'LL NEVER GO BACK.

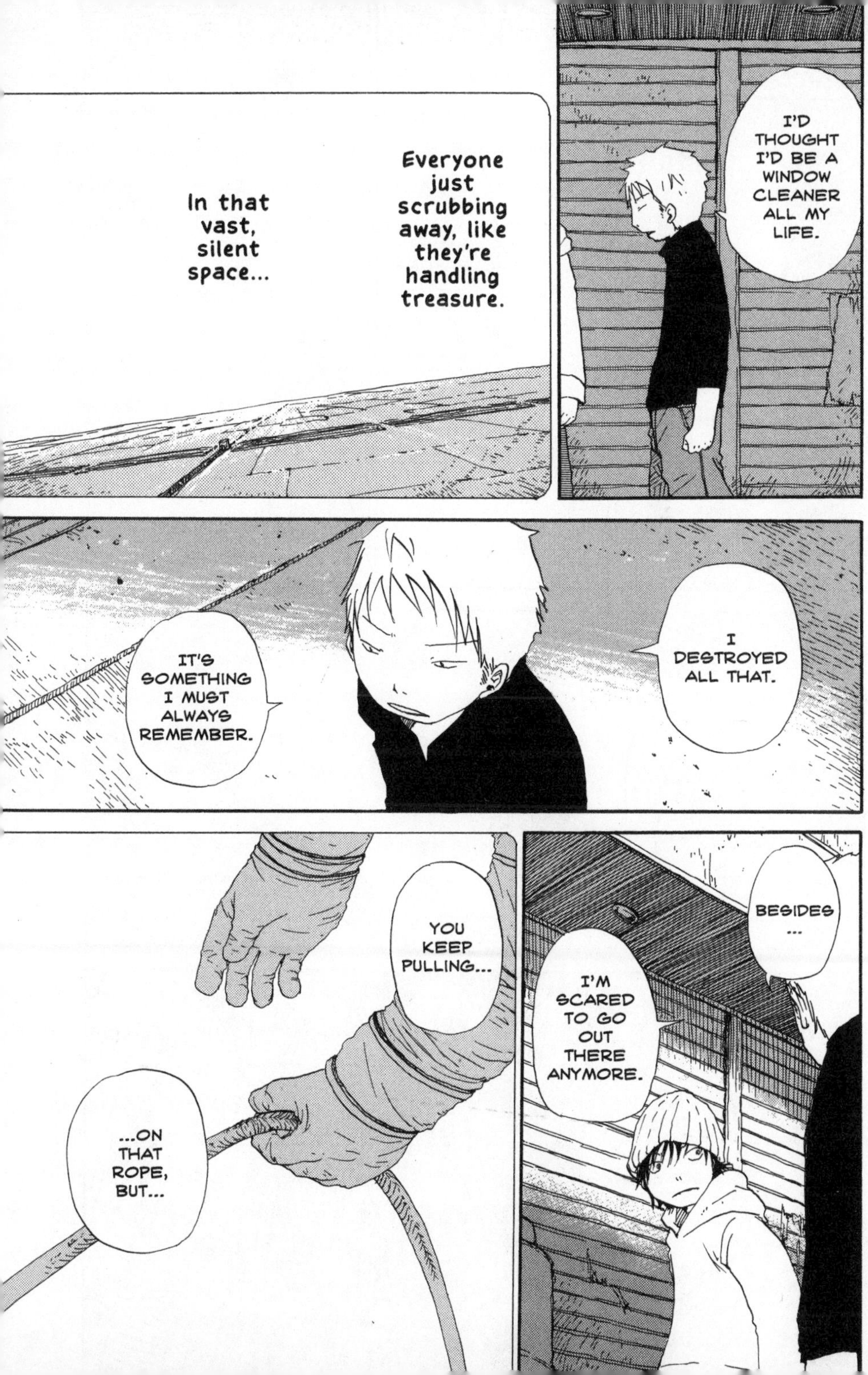
I'D THOUGHT I'D BE A WINDOW CLEANER ALL MY LIFE.
Everyone just scrubbing away, like they're handling treasure.
In that vast, silent space...
I DESTROYED ALL THAT.
IT'S SOMETHING I MUST ALWAYS REMEMBER.
BESIDES...
I'M SCARED TO GO OUT THERE ANYMORE.
YOU KEEP PULLING...
...ON THAT ROPE, BUT...

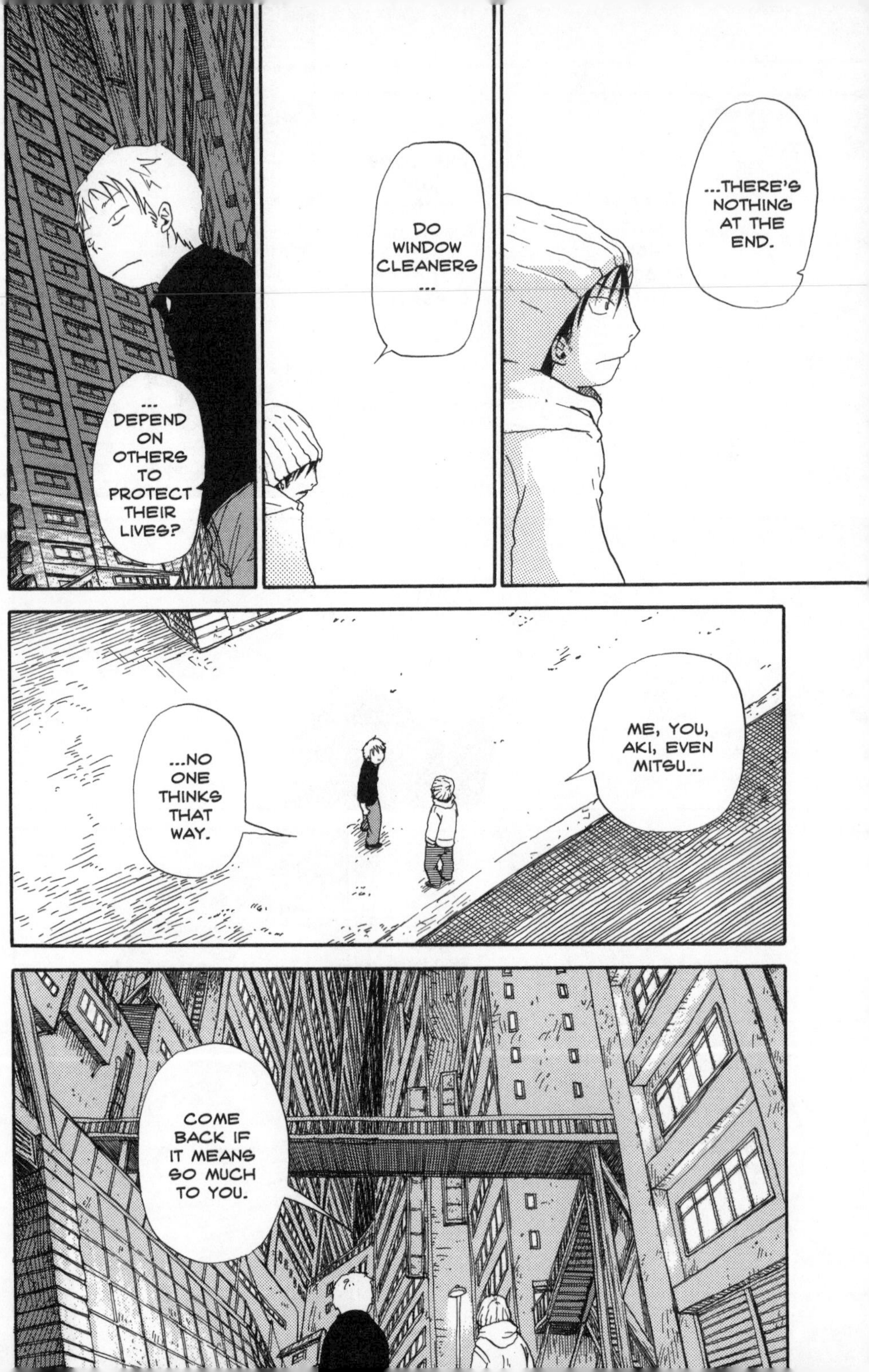
...THERE'S NOTHING AT THE END.
DO WINDOW CLEANERS ...
... DEPEND ON OTHERS TO PROTECT THEIR LIVES?
ME, YOU, AKI, EVEN MITSU...
...NO ONE THINKS THAT WAY.
COME BACK IF IT MEANS SO MUCH TO YOU.

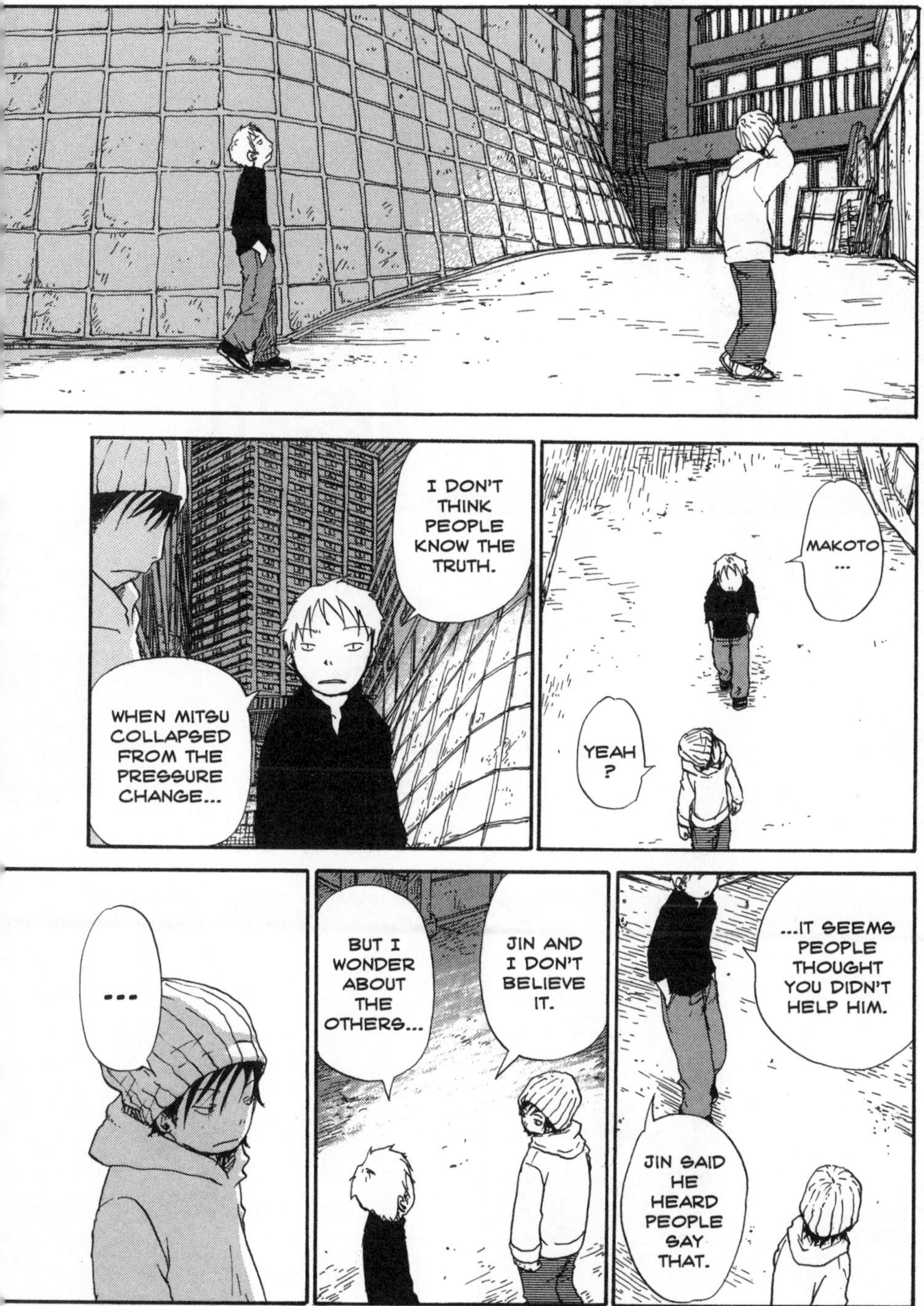
MAKOTO ...
YEAH ?
I DON'T THINK PEOPLE KNOW THE TRUTH.
WHEN MITSU COLLAPSED FROM THE PRESSURE CHANGE...
...IT SEEMS PEOPLE THOUGHT YOU DIDN'T HELP HIM.
JIN SAID HE HEARD PEOPLE SAY THAT.
JIN AND I DON'T BELIEVE IT.
BUT I WONDER ABOUT THE OTHERS...
...

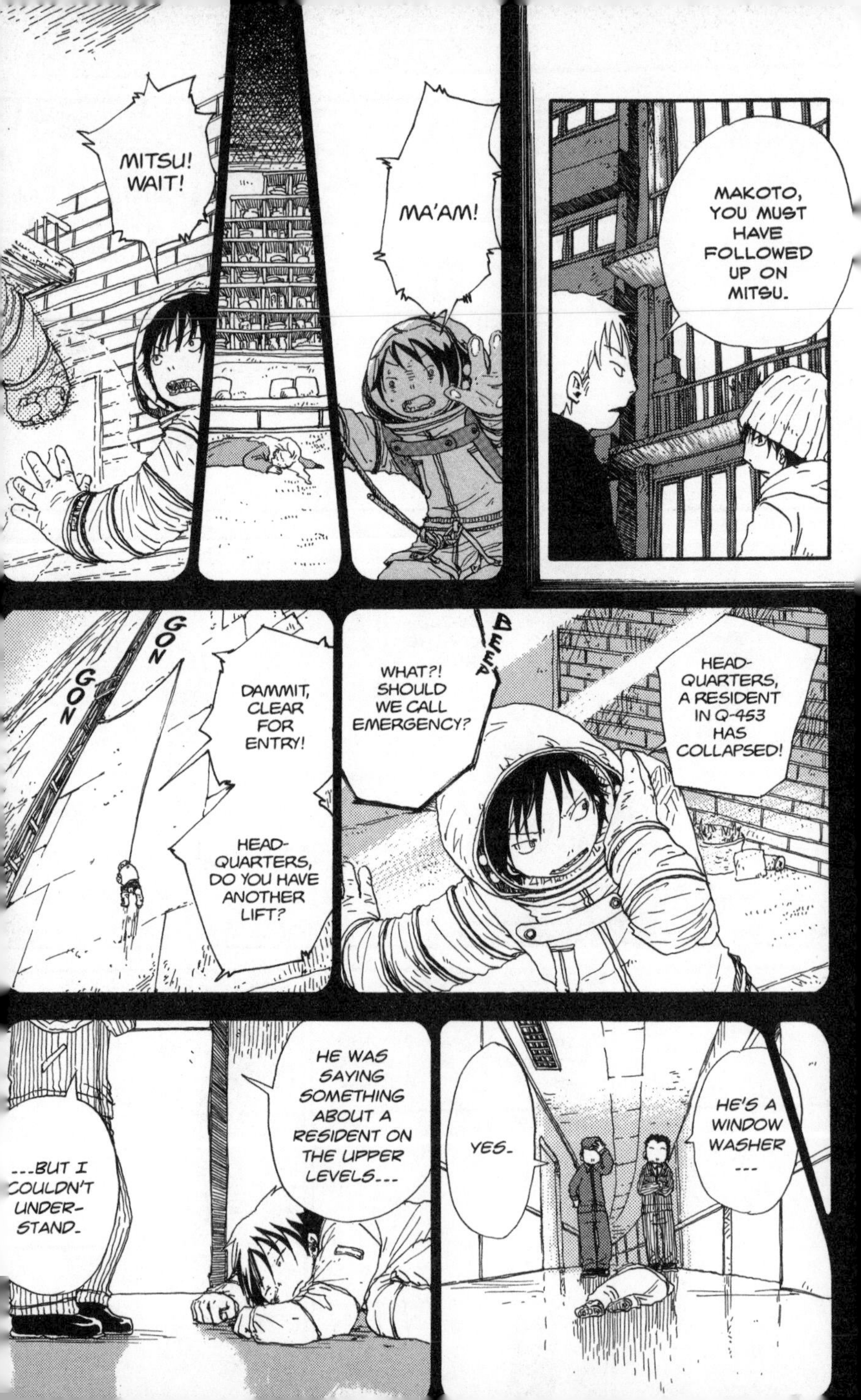
MAKOTO, YOU MUST HAVE FOLLOWED UP ON MITSU.
MA'AM!
MITSU! WAIT!
HEAD-QUARTERS, A RESIDENT IN Q-453 HAS COLLAPSED!
BEEP
WHAT?! SHOULD WE CALL EMERGENCY?
DAMMIT, CLEAR FOR ENTRY!
HEAD-QUARTERS, DO YOU HAVE ANOTHER LIFT?
GON
GON
HE'S A WINDOW WASHER...
YES.
HE WAS SAYING SOMETHING ABOUT A RESIDENT ON THE UPPER LEVELS...
...BUT I COULDN'T UNDER-STAND.

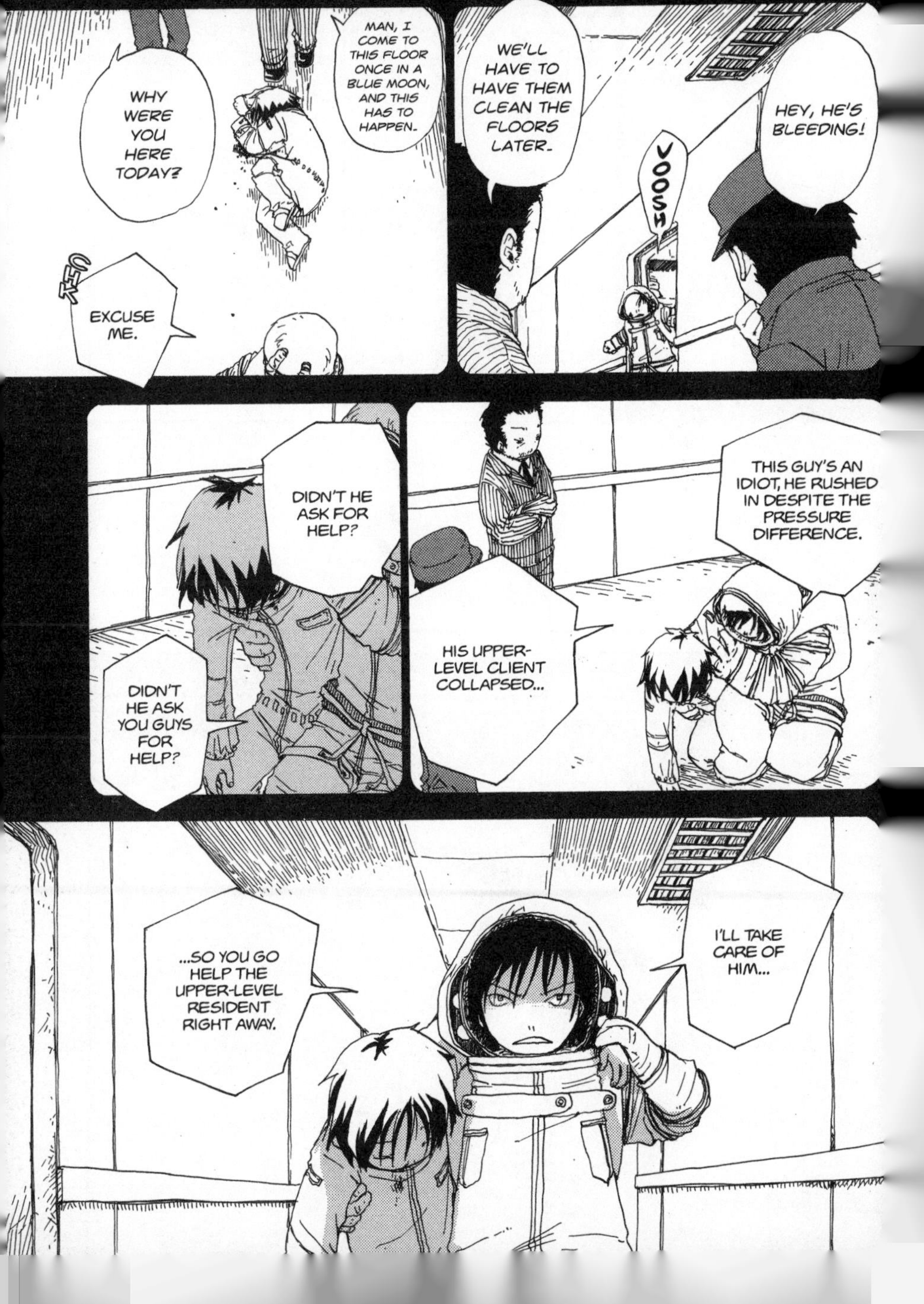
HEY, HE'S BLEEDING!
VOOSH
WE'LL HAVE TO HAVE THEM CLEAN THE FLOORS LATER.
MAN, I COME TO THIS FLOOR ONCE IN A BLUE MOON, AND THIS HAS TO HAPPEN.
WHY WERE YOU HERE TODAY?
CHK
EXCUSE ME.
THIS GUY'S AN IDIOT, HE RUSHED IN DESPITE THE PRESSURE DIFFERENCE.
HIS UPPER-LEVEL CLIENT COLLAPSED...
DIDN'T HE ASK FOR HELP?
DIDN'T HE ASK YOU GUYS FOR HELP?
I'LL TAKE CARE OF HIM...
...SO YOU GO HELP THE UPPER-LEVEL RESIDENT RIGHT AWAY.

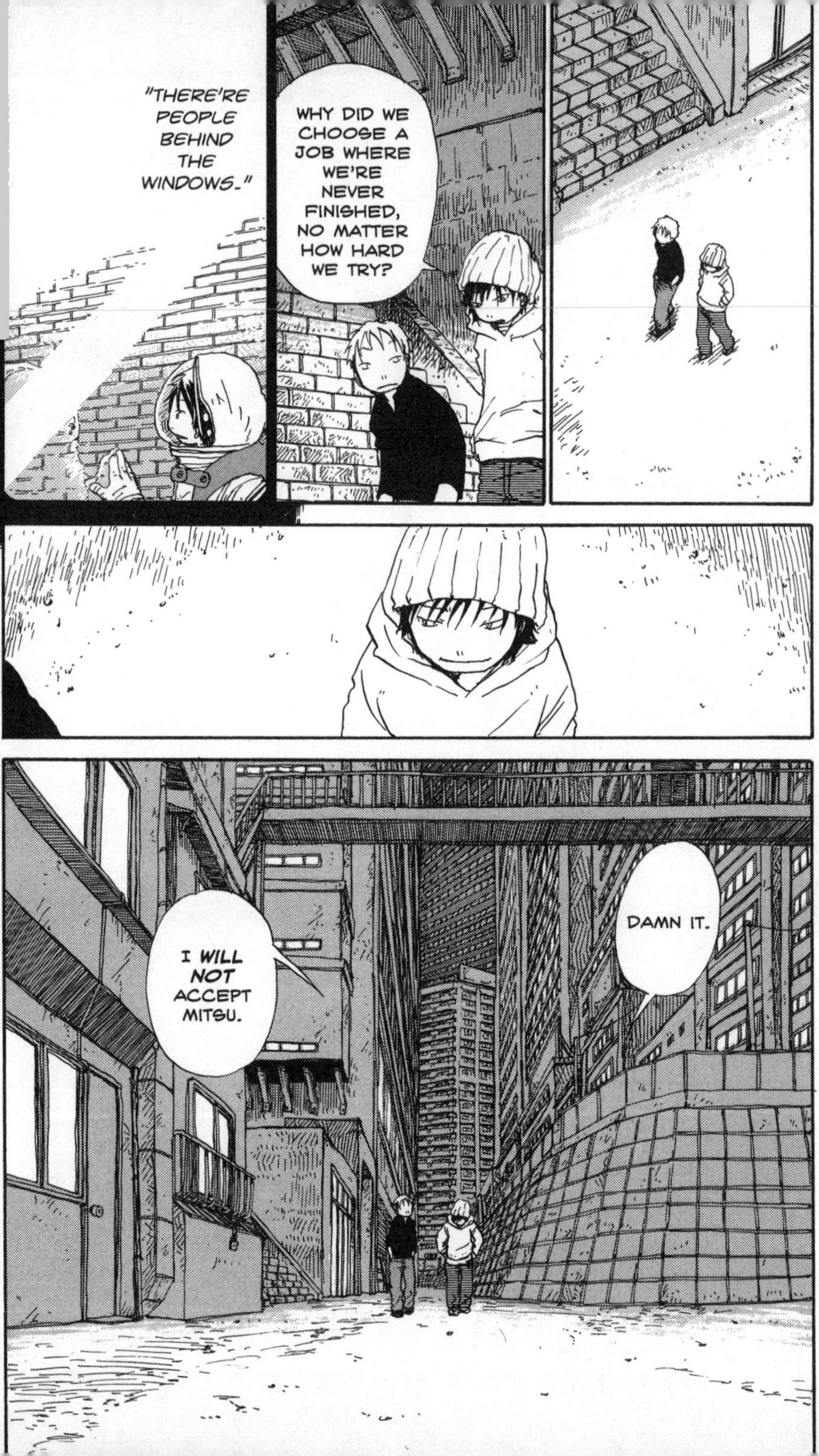
WHY DID WE CHOOSE A JOB WHERE WE'RE NEVER FINISHED, NO MATTER HOW HARD WE TRY?
"THERE'RE PEOPLE BEHIND THE WINDOWS."
DAMN IT.
I *WILL NOT* ACCEPT MITSU.

floor 16: glitter

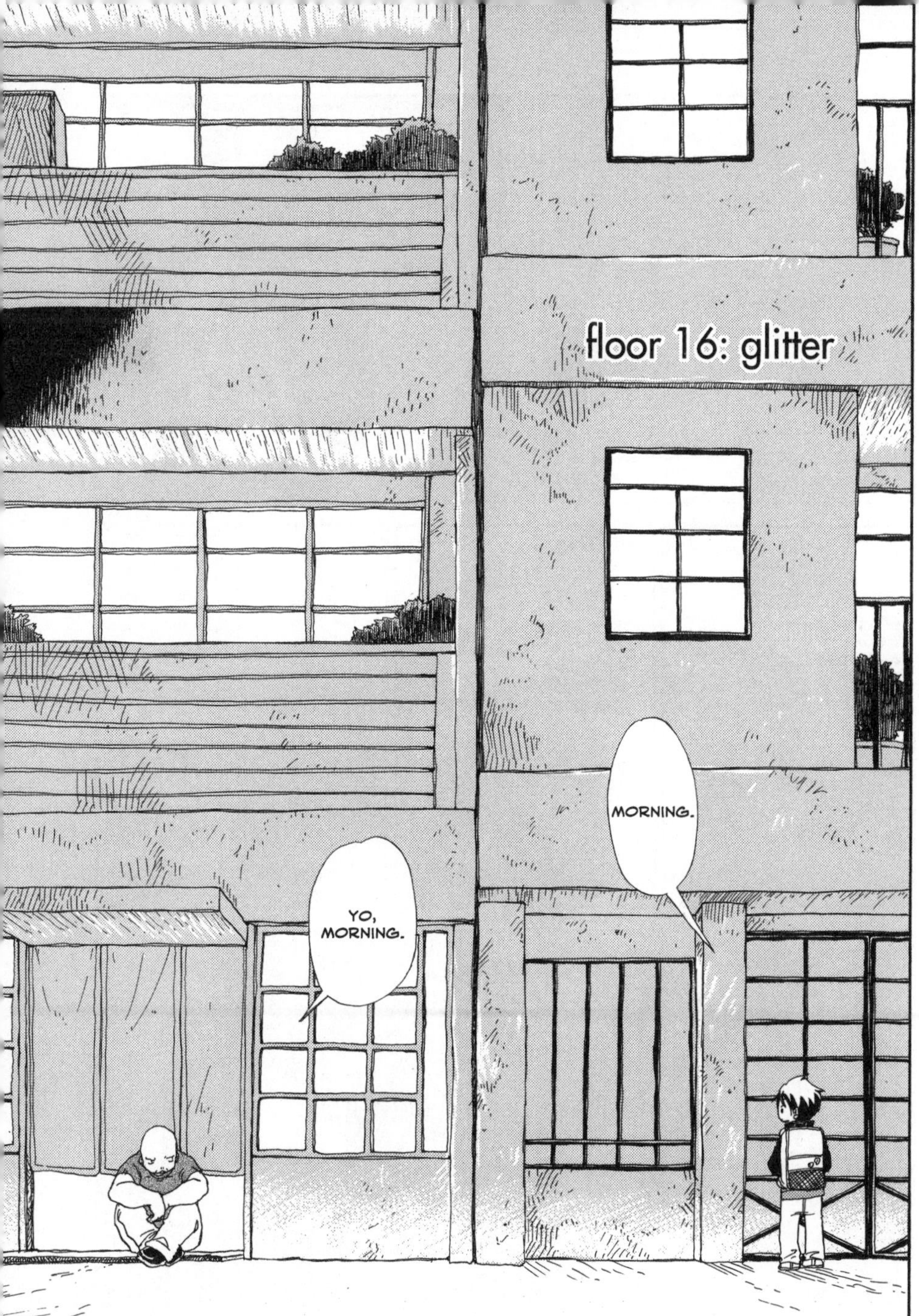
MORNING.
YO, MORNING.

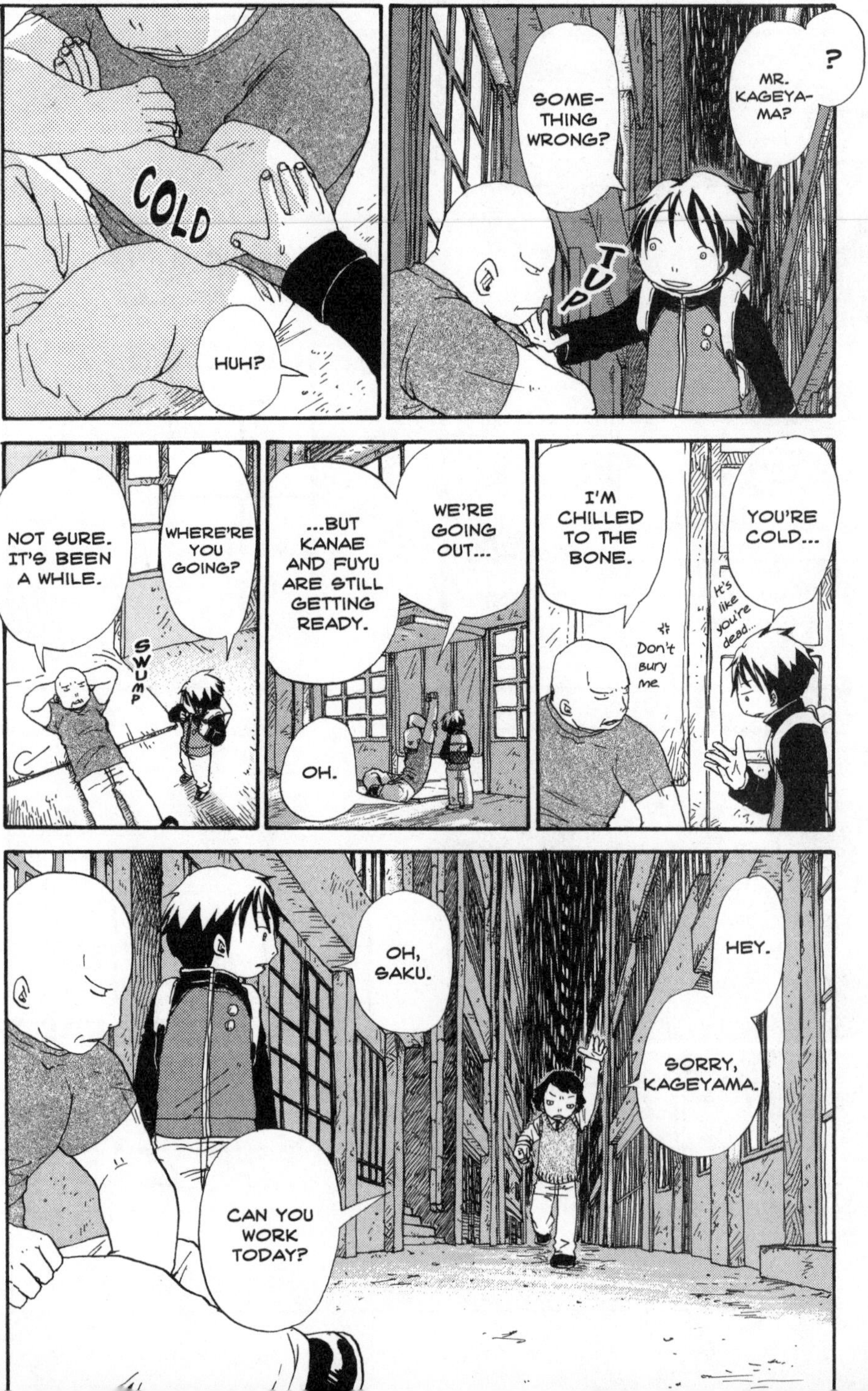
?
MR. KAGEYAMA?
SOMETHING WRONG?
TUP
COLD
HUH?
YOU'RE COLD...
It's like you're dead...
I'M CHILLED TO THE BONE.
Don't bury me.
WE'RE GOING OUT...
...BUT KANAE AND FUYU ARE STILL GETTING READY.
OH.
WHERE'RE YOU GOING?
NOT SURE. IT'S BEEN A WHILE.
SWUMP
HEY.
SORRY, KAGEYAMA.
OH, SAKU.
CAN YOU WORK TODAY?

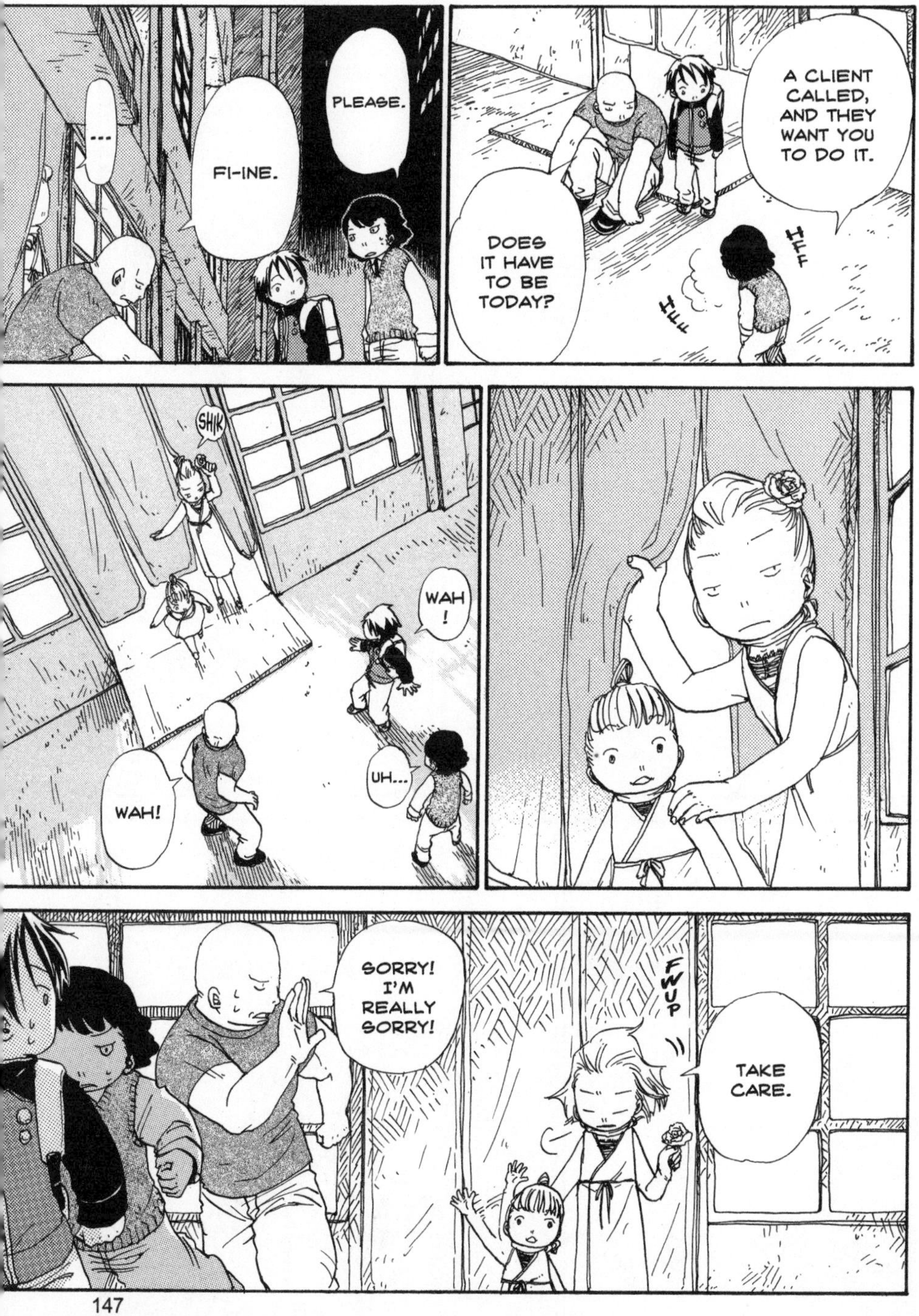
A CLIENT CALLED, AND THEY WANT YOU TO DO IT.
HFF
HFF
DOES IT HAVE TO BE TODAY?
PLEASE.
FI-INE.
...
SHIK
WAH!
UH...
WAH!
FWUP
TAKE CARE.
SORRY! I'M REALLY SORRY!

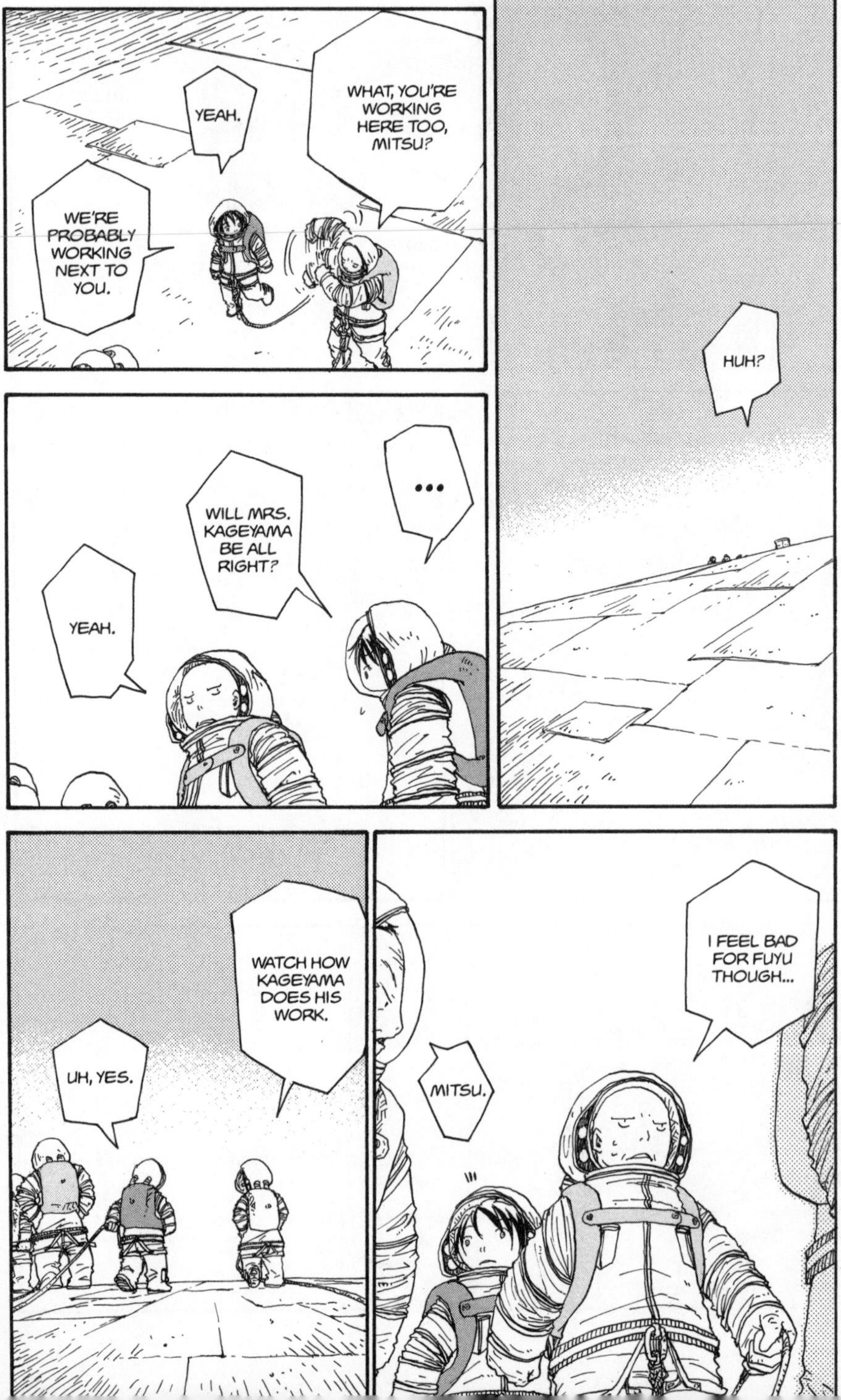
HUH?
WHAT, YOU'RE WORKING HERE TOO, MITSU?
YEAH.
WE'RE PROBABLY WORKING NEXT TO YOU.
...
WILL MRS. KAGEYAMA BE ALL RIGHT?
YEAH.
I FEEL BAD FOR FUYU THOUGH...
MITSU.
WATCH HOW KAGEYAMA DOES HIS WORK.
UH, YES.

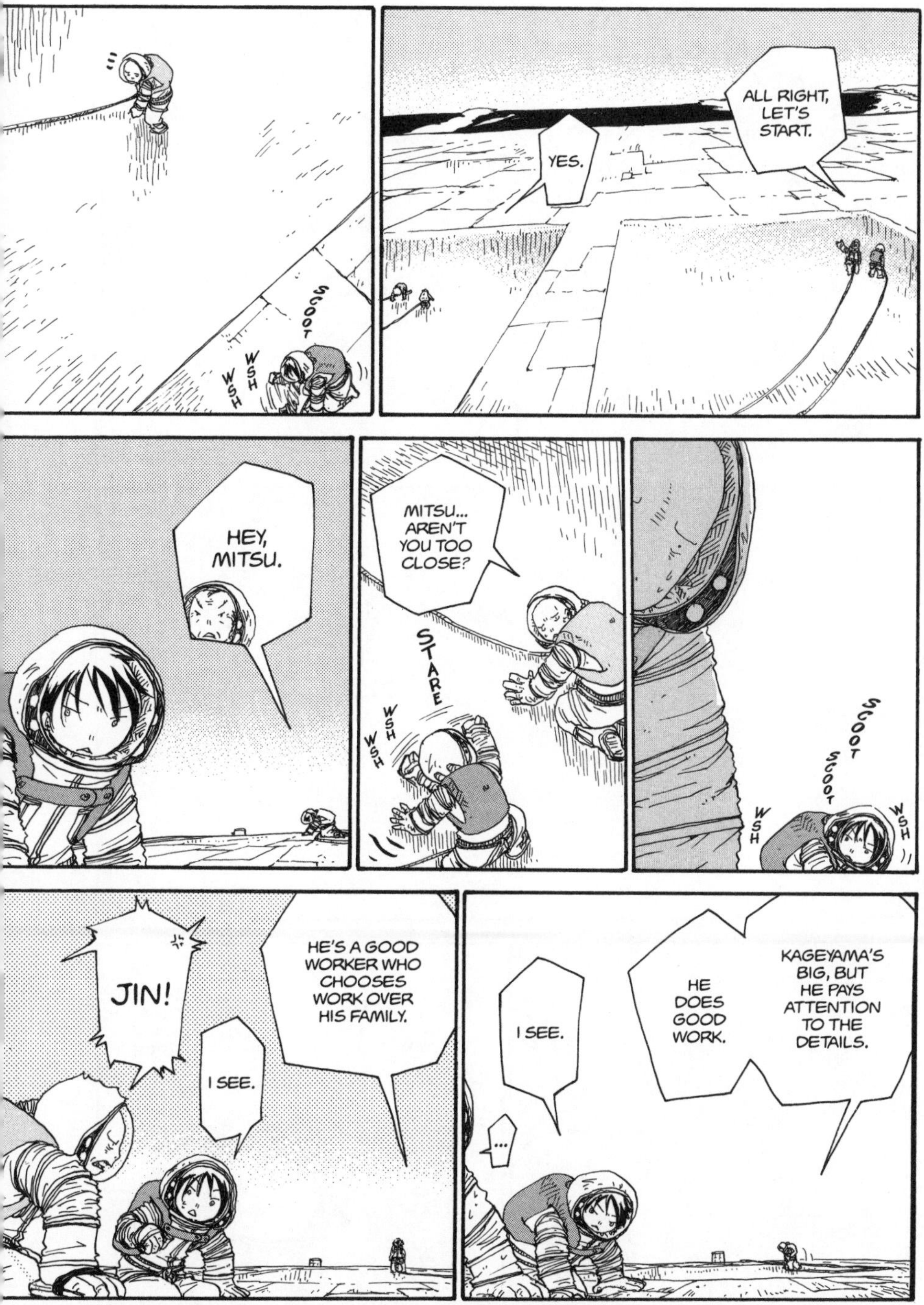
ALL RIGHT, LET'S START.
YES.
SCOOT
WSH WSH
SCOOT SCOOT
WSH
WSH
MITSU... AREN'T YOU TOO CLOSE?
STARE
WSH WSH
HEY, MITSU.
KAGEYAMA'S BIG, BUT HE PAYS ATTENTION TO THE DETAILS.
HE DOES GOOD WORK.
I SEE.
...
HE'S A GOOD WORKER WHO CHOOSES WORK OVER HIS FAMILY.
I SEE.
JIN!

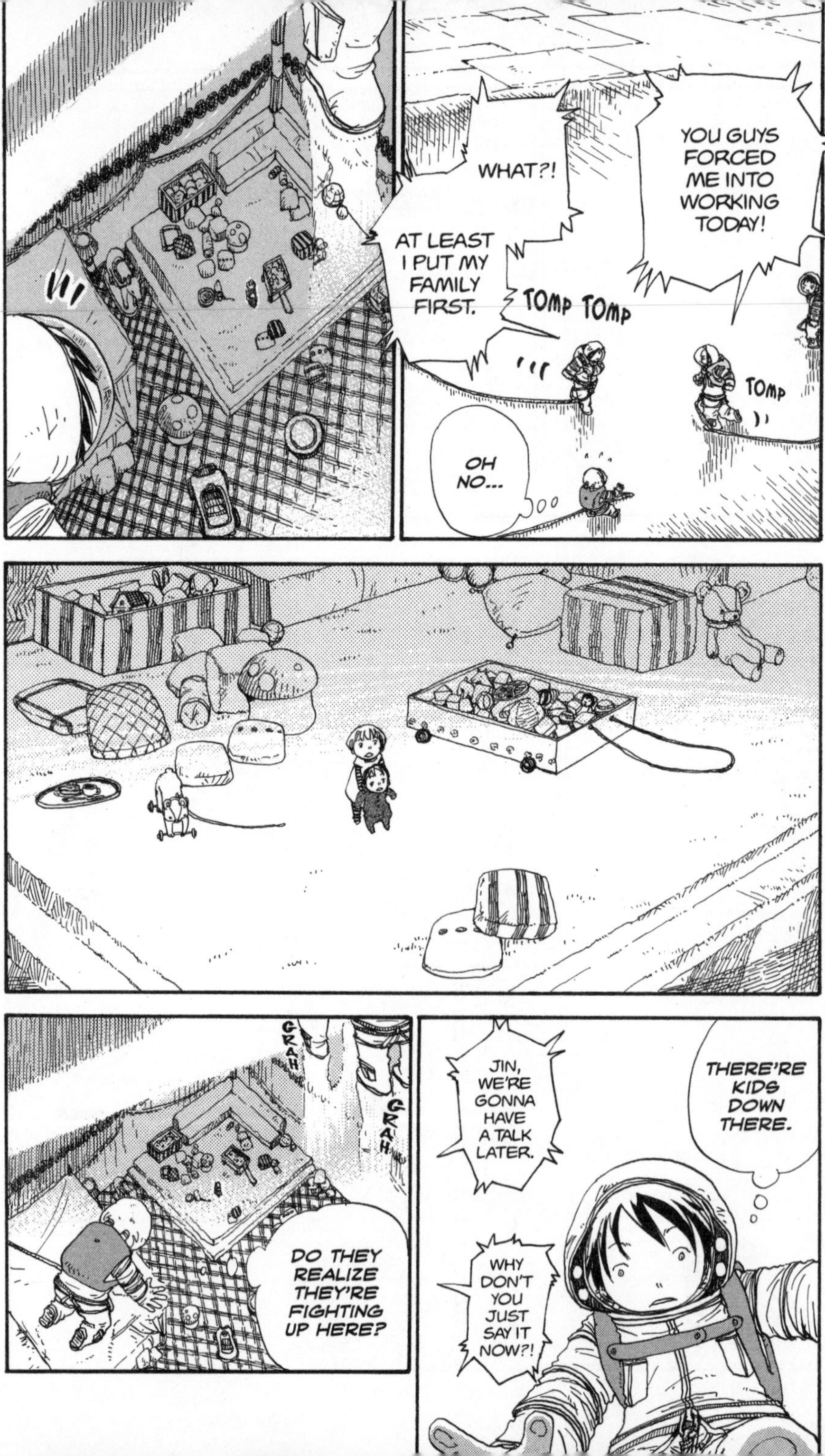
YOU GUYS FORCED ME INTO WORKING TODAY!
WHAT?!
AT LEAST I PUT MY FAMILY FIRST.
TOMP TOMP
TOMP
OH NO...
THERE'RE KIDS DOWN THERE.
JIN, WE'RE GONNA HAVE A TALK LATER.
WHY DON'T YOU JUST SAY IT NOW?!
GRAH
GRAH
DO THEY REALIZE THEY'RE FIGHTING UP HERE?

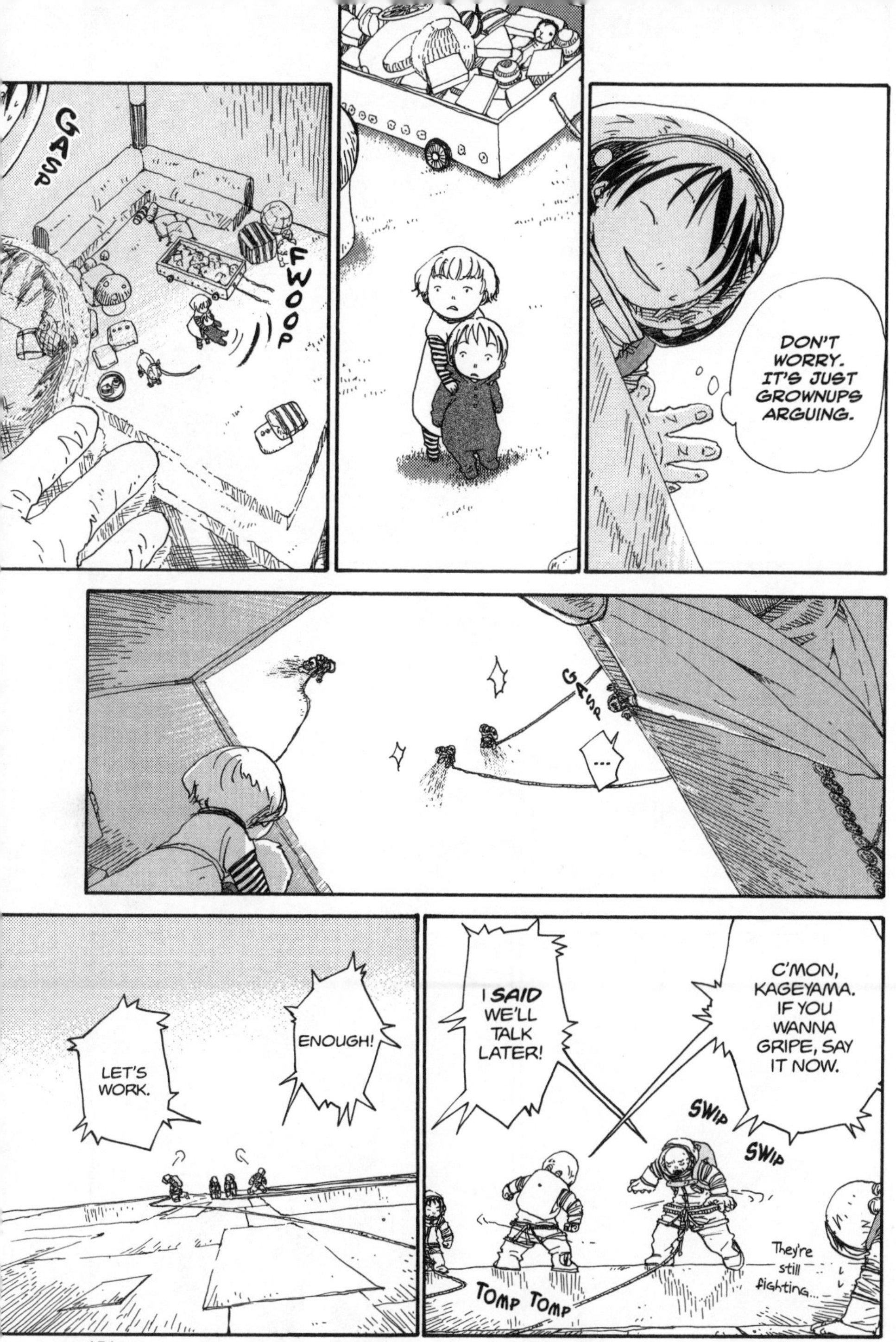
DON'T WORRY. IT'S JUST GROWNUPS ARGUING.
GASP
FWOOP
GASP
...
C'MON, KAGEYAMA. IF YOU WANNA GRIPE, SAY IT NOW.
I **SAID** WE'LL TALK LATER!
SWIP
SWIP
They're still fighting...
TOMP TOMP
ENOUGH!
LET'S WORK.

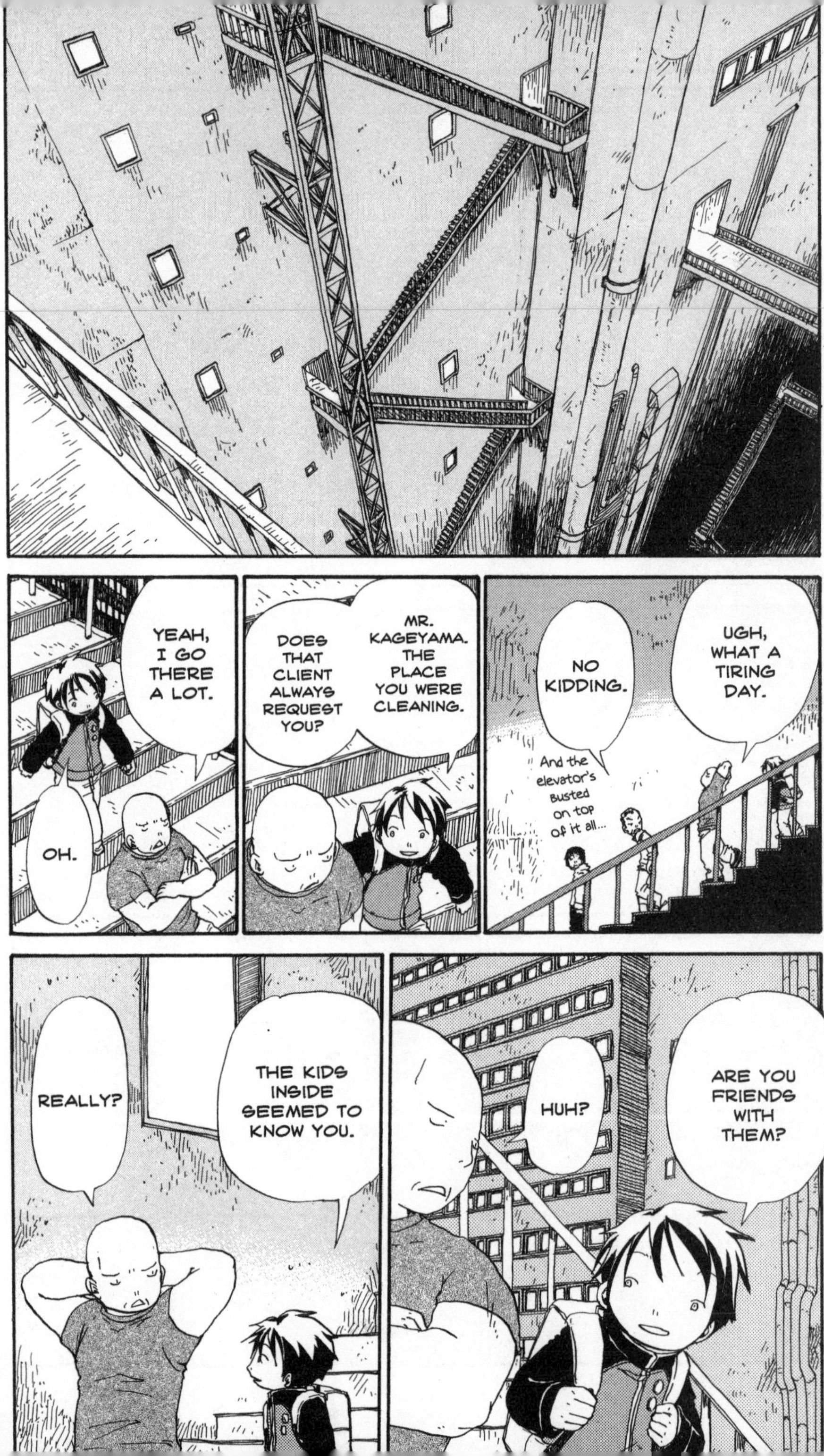
UGH, WHAT A TIRING DAY.
NO KIDDING.
And the elevator's Busted on top of it all...
MR. KAGEYAMA. THE PLACE YOU WERE CLEANING.
DOES THAT CLIENT ALWAYS REQUEST YOU?
YEAH, I GO THERE A LOT.
OH.
ARE YOU FRIENDS WITH THEM?
HUH?
THE KIDS INSIDE SEEMED TO KNOW YOU.
REALLY?

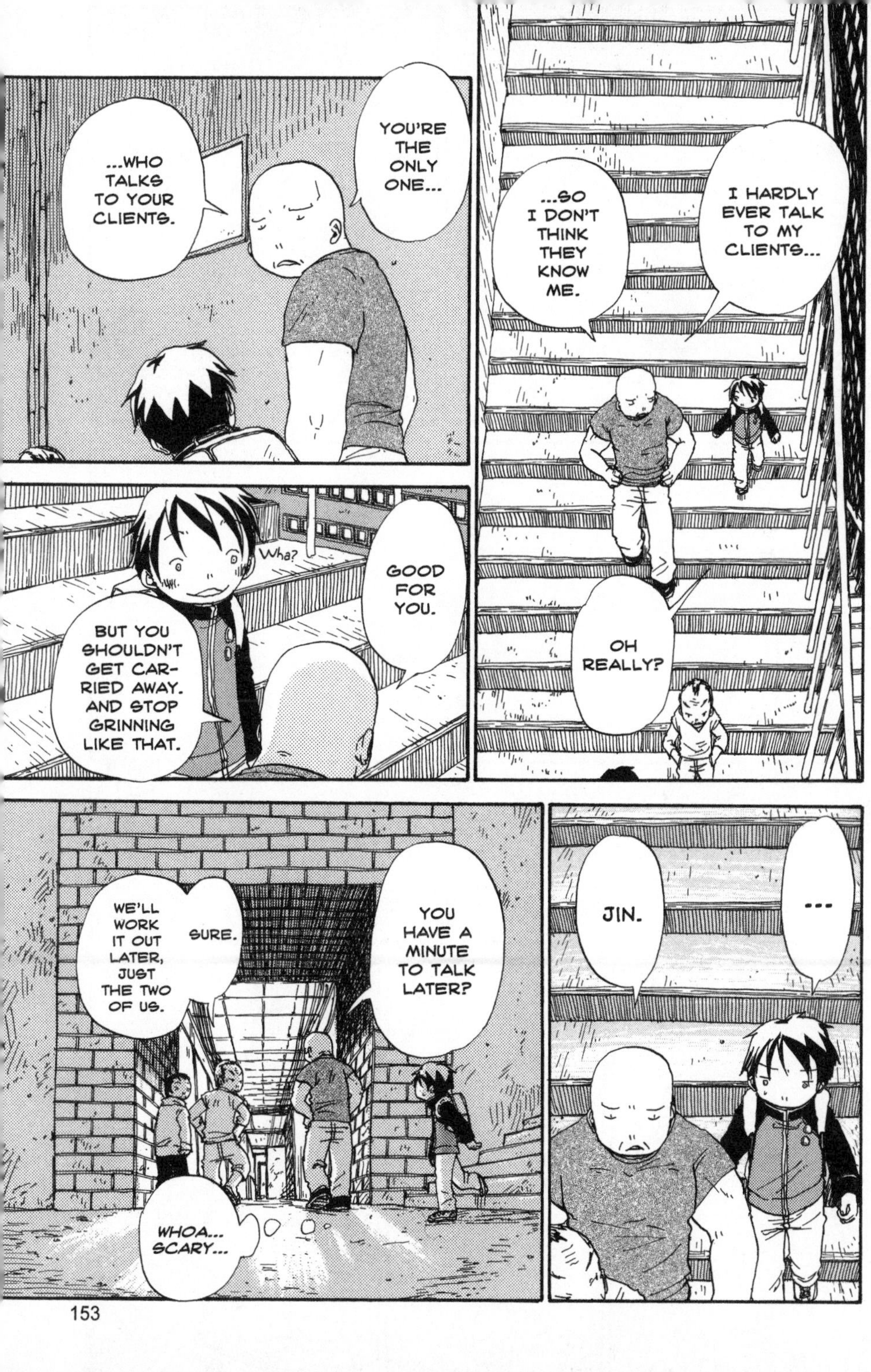
I HARDLY EVER TALK TO MY CLIENTS...
...SO I DON'T THINK THEY KNOW ME.
OH REALLY?
YOU'RE THE ONLY ONE...
...WHO TALKS TO YOUR CLIENTS.
GOOD FOR YOU.
Wha?
BUT YOU SHOULDN'T GET CAR-RIED AWAY. AND STOP GRINNING LIKE THAT.
...
JIN.
YOU HAVE A MINUTE TO TALK LATER?
SURE.
WE'LL WORK IT OUT LATER, JUST THE TWO OF US.
WHOA... SCARY...

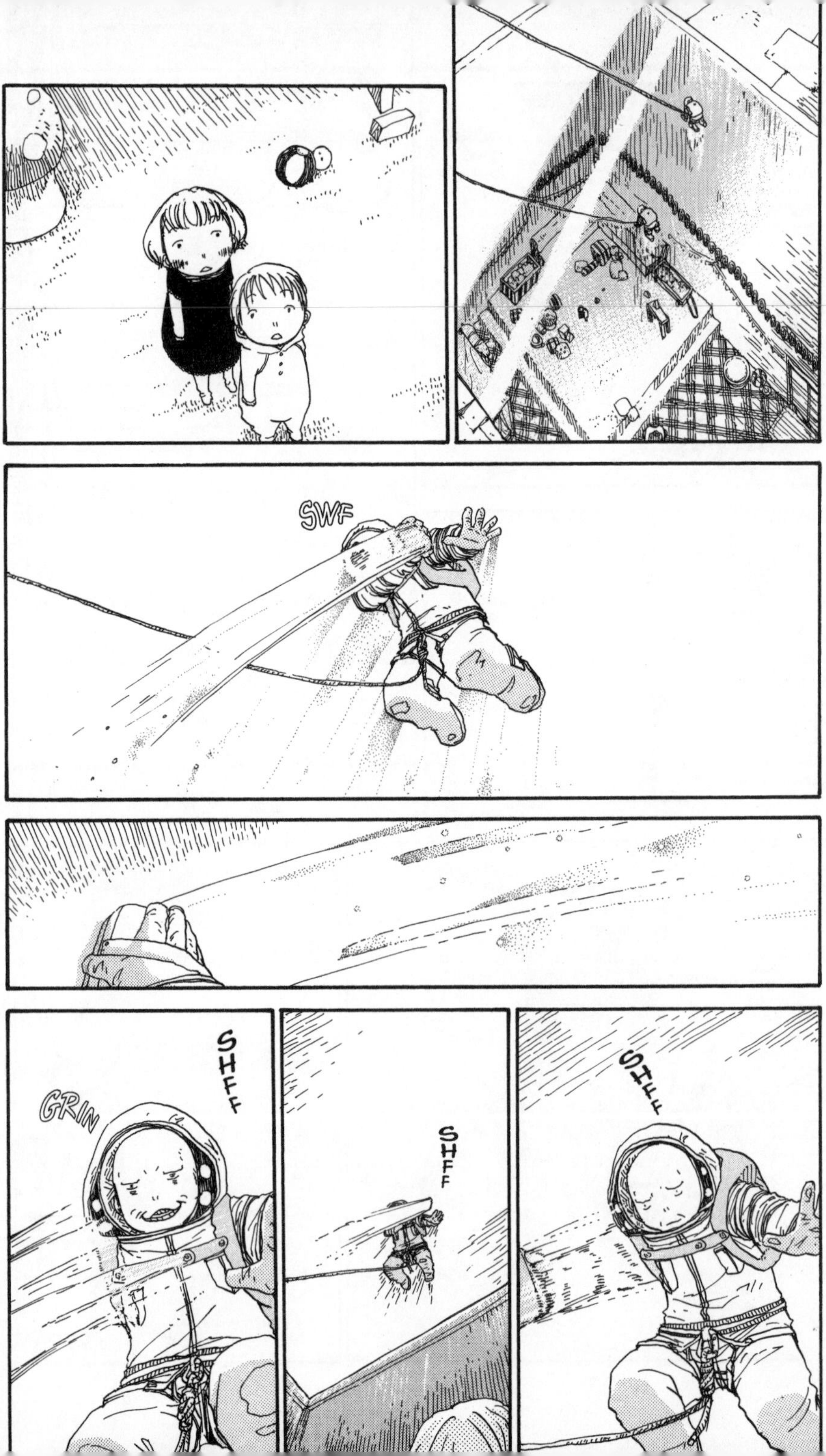
SWF
SHFF
SHFF
SHFF
GRIN

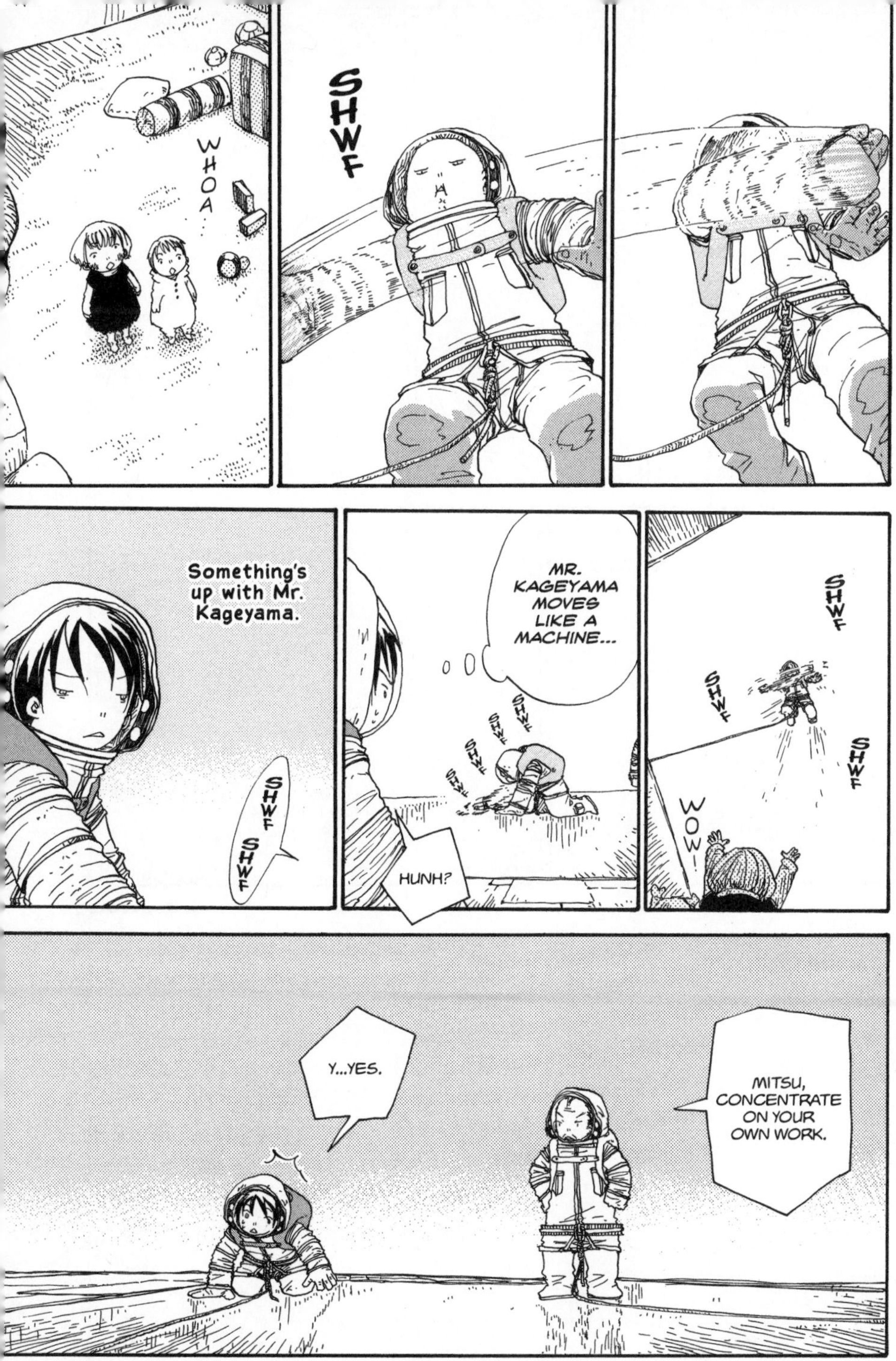
SHWF
WHOA...
SHWF
SHWF
SHWF
WOW!
MR. KAGEYAMA MOVES LIKE A MACHINE...
SHWF
SHWF
SHWF
SHWF
HUNH?
Something's up with Mr. Kageyama.
SHWF SHWF
MITSU, CONCENTRATE ON YOUR OWN WORK.
Y...YES.

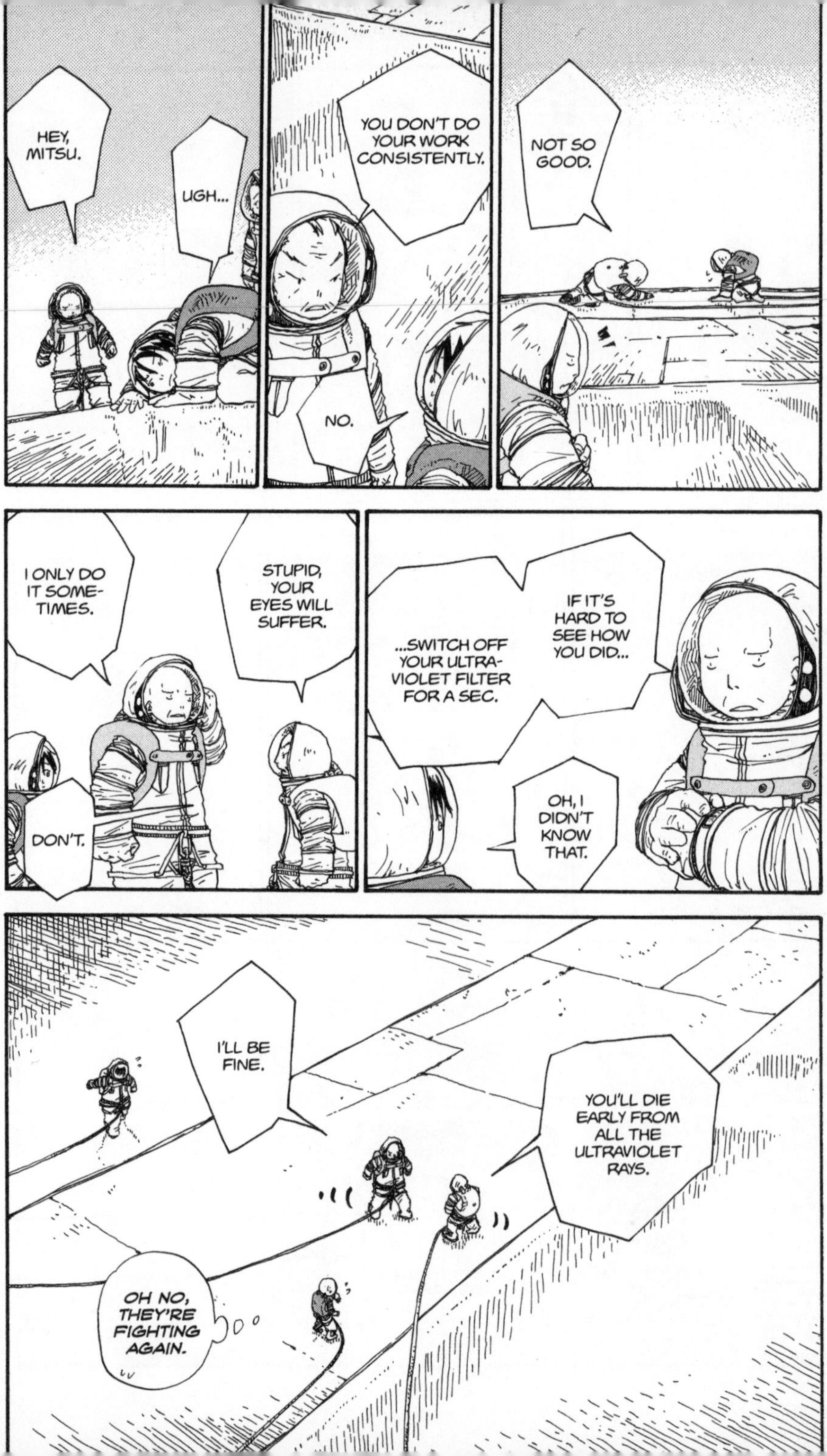
NOT SO GOOD.
YOU DON'T DO YOUR WORK CONSISTENTLY.
NO.
HEY, MITSU.
UGH...
IF IT'S HARD TO SEE HOW YOU DID...
...SWITCH OFF YOUR ULTRAVIOLET FILTER FOR A SEC.
OH, I DIDN'T KNOW THAT.
STUPID, YOUR EYES WILL SUFFER.
I ONLY DO IT SOMETIMES.
DON'T.
YOU'LL DIE EARLY FROM ALL THE ULTRAVIOLET RAYS.
I'LL BE FINE.
OH NO, THEY'RE FIGHTING AGAIN.

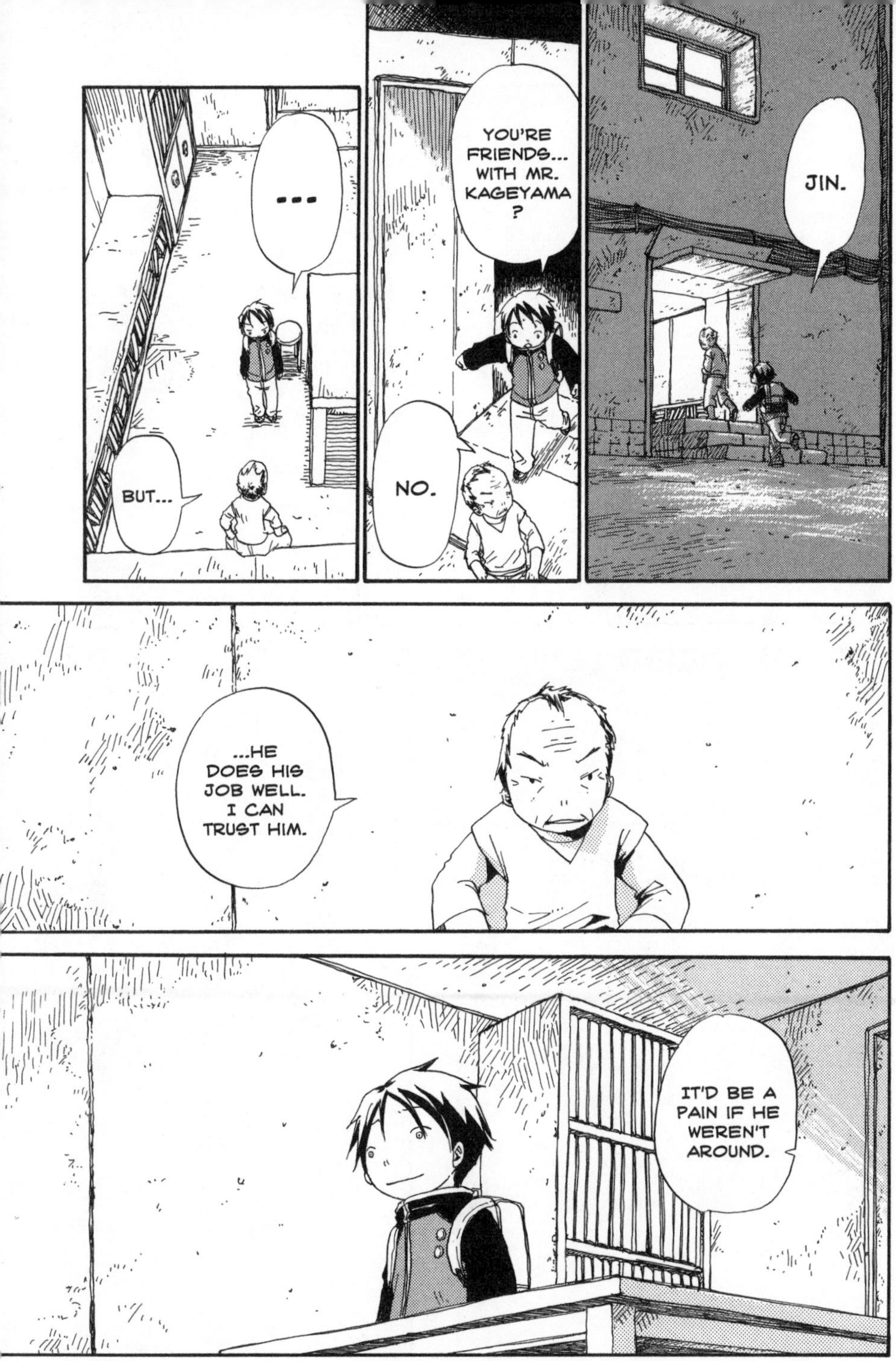
JIN.
YOU'RE FRIENDS... WITH MR. KAGEYAMA?
NO.
...
BUT...
...HE DOES HIS JOB WELL. I CAN TRUST HIM.
IT'D BE A PAIN IF HE WEREN'T AROUND.

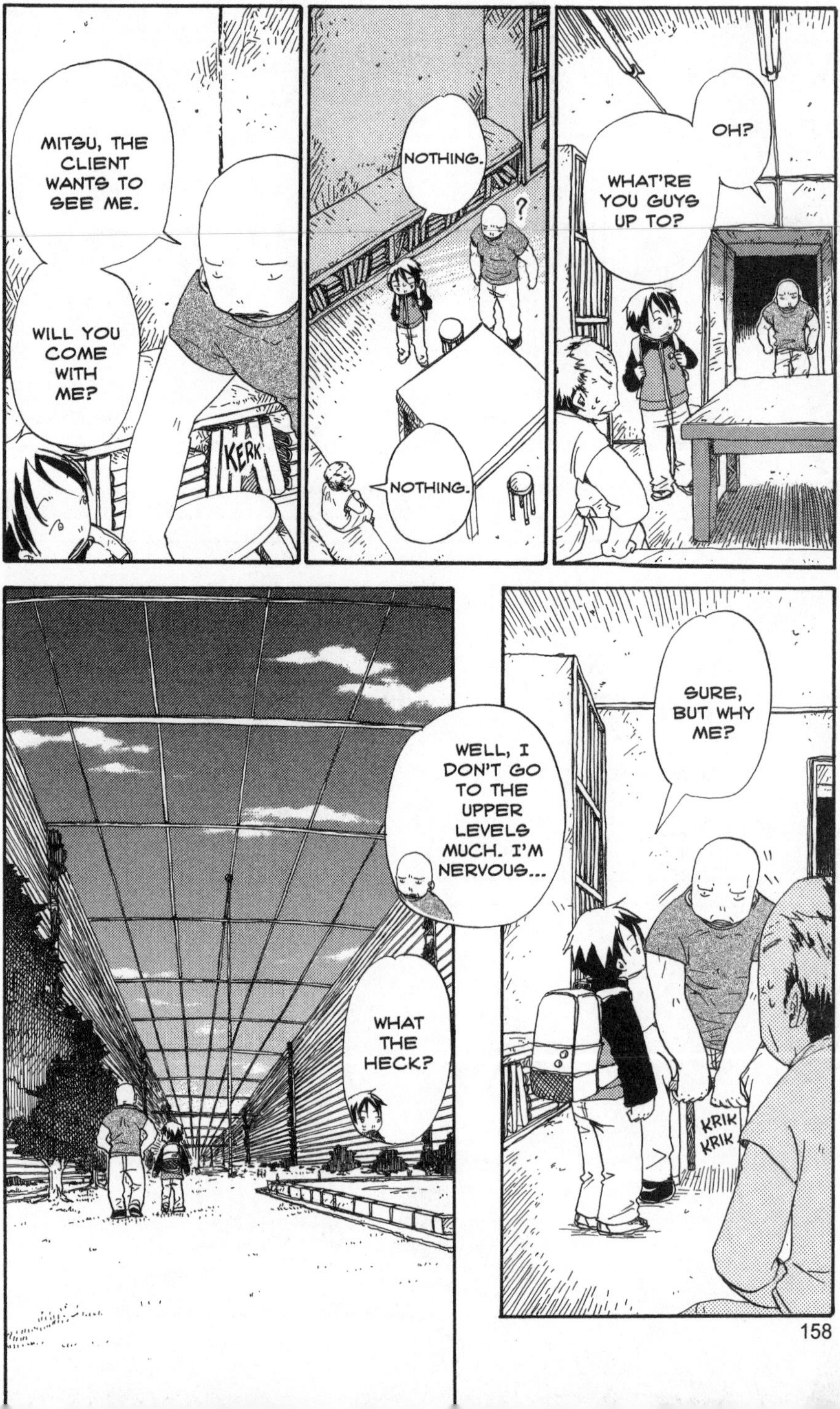
OH?
WHAT'RE YOU GUYS UP TO?
NOTHING.
NOTHING.
MITSU, THE CLIENT WANTS TO SEE ME.
WILL YOU COME WITH ME?
KERK
SURE, BUT WHY ME?
WELL, I DON'T GO TO THE UPPER LEVELS MUCH. I'M NERVOUS...
KRIK KRIK
WHAT THE HECK?

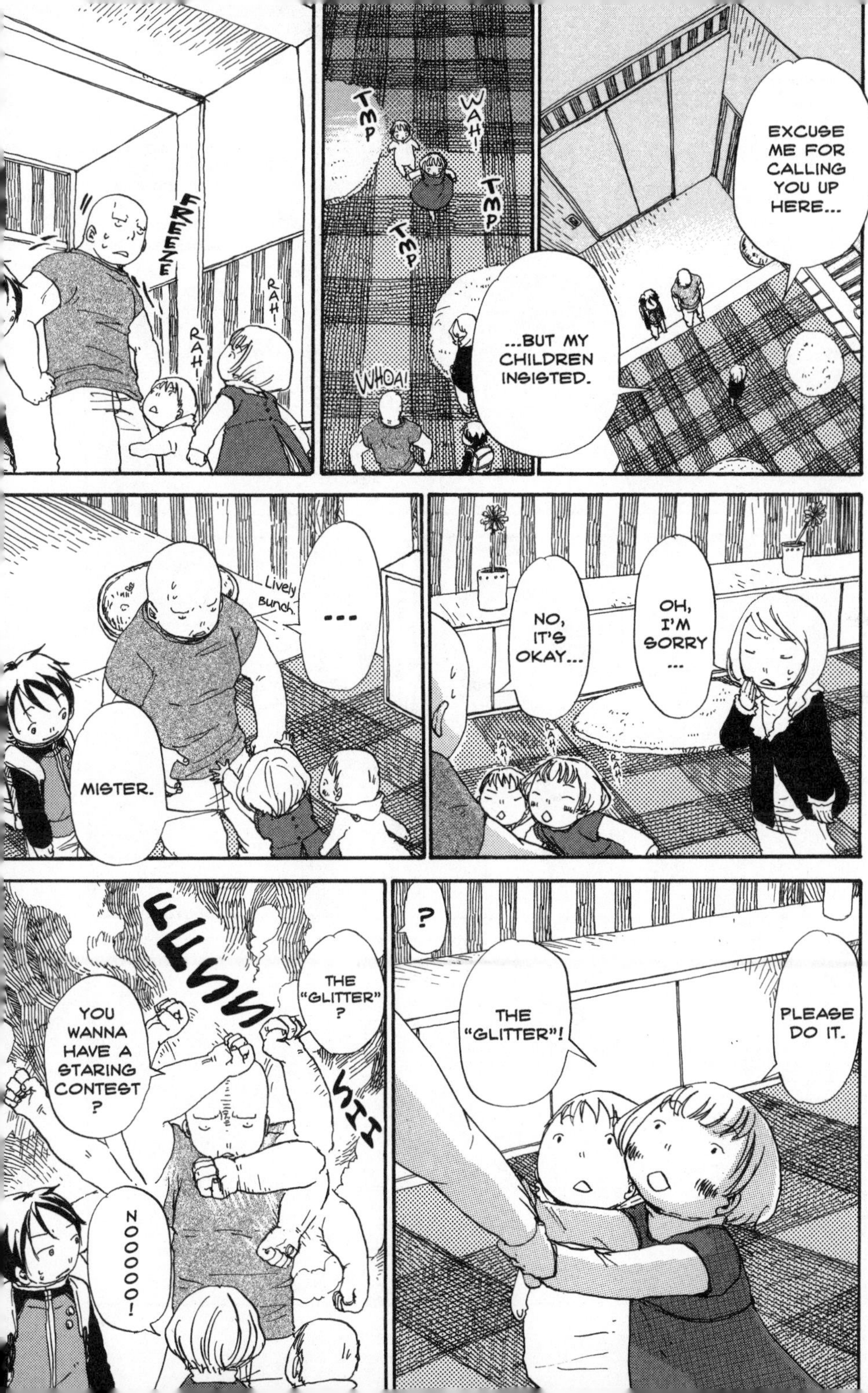
EXCUSE ME FOR CALLING YOU UP HERE...
...BUT MY CHILDREN INSISTED.
TMP
WAH!
TMP
TMP
WHOA!
FREEZE
RAH!
RAH!
OH, I'M SORRY ...
NO, IT'S OKAY...
RAH!
RAH!
RAH!
...
Lively bunch.
MISTER.
PLEASE DO IT.
THE "GLITTER"!
?
THE "GLITTER"?
FFSSSHH
YOU WANNA HAVE A STARING CONTEST?
NOOOOOO!

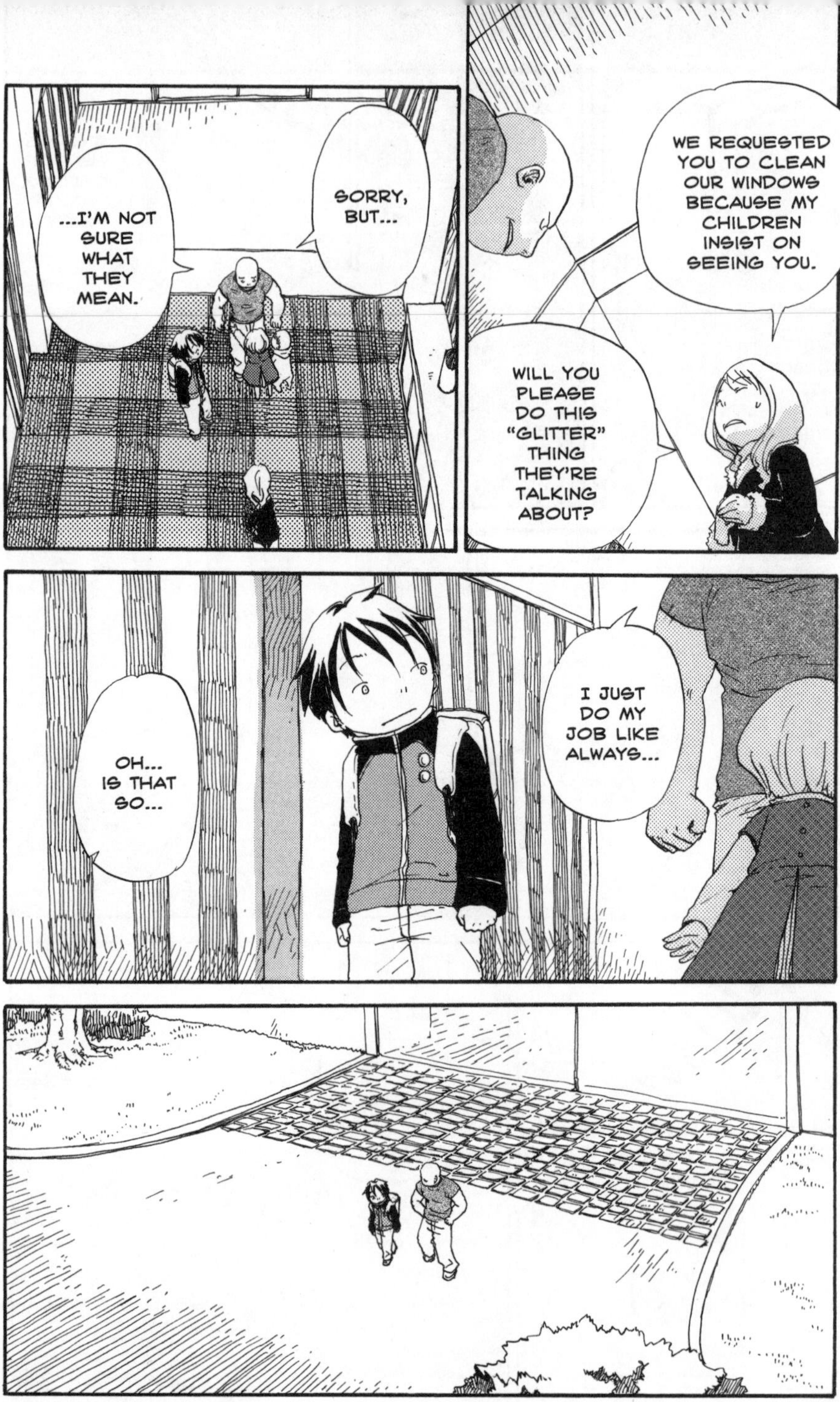
WE REQUESTED YOU TO CLEAN OUR WINDOWS BECAUSE MY CHILDREN INSIST ON SEEING YOU.
WILL YOU PLEASE DO THIS "GLITTER" THING THEY'RE TALKING ABOUT?
SORRY, BUT...
...I'M NOT SURE WHAT THEY MEAN.
I JUST DO MY JOB LIKE ALWAYS...
OH... IS THAT SO...

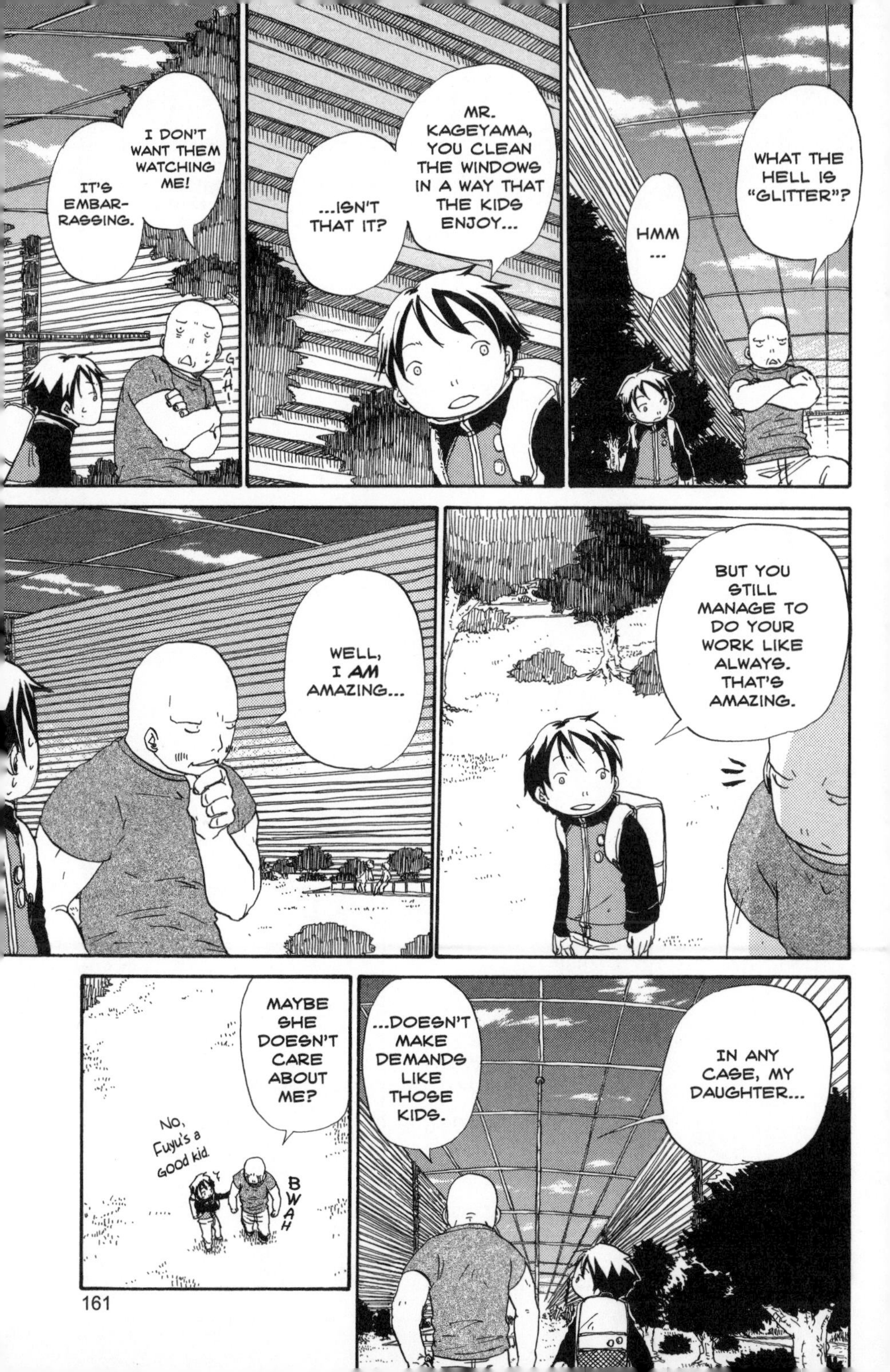
WHAT THE HELL IS "GLITTER"?
HMM...
MR. KAGEYAMA, YOU CLEAN THE WINDOWS IN A WAY THAT THE KIDS ENJOY...
...ISN'T THAT IT?
I DON'T WANT THEM WATCHING ME!
IT'S EMBAR-RASSING.
GAH!
BUT YOU STILL MANAGE TO DO YOUR WORK LIKE ALWAYS. THAT'S AMAZING.
WELL, I *AM* AMAZING...
IN ANY CASE, MY DAUGHTER...
...DOESN'T MAKE DEMANDS LIKE THOSE KIDS.
MAYBE SHE DOESN'T CARE ABOUT ME?
No, Fuyu's a good kid.
BWAH

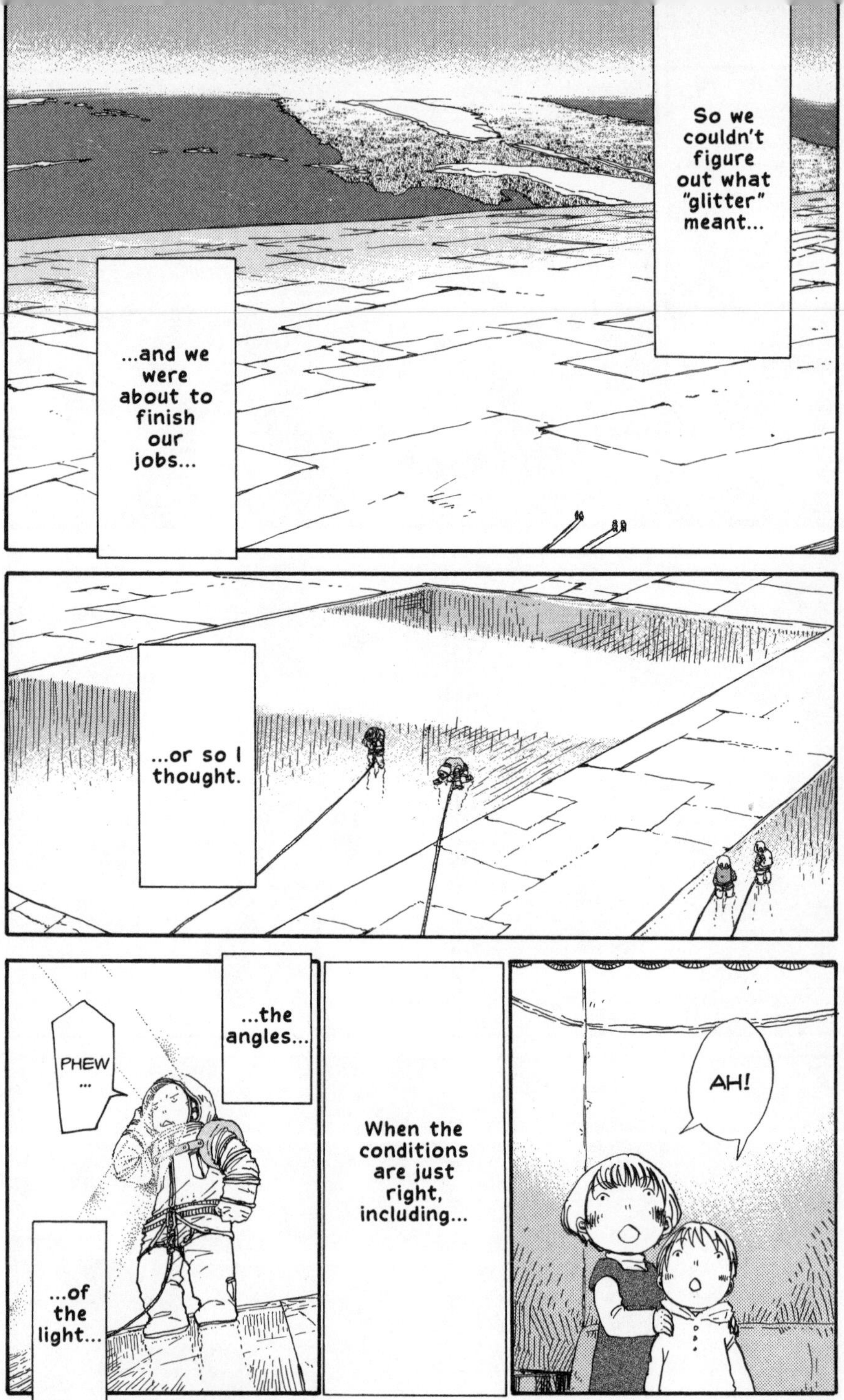
So we couldn't figure out what "glitter" meant...
...and we were about to finish our jobs...
...or so I thought.
AH!
When the conditions are just right, including...
...the angles...
PHEW ...
...of the light...

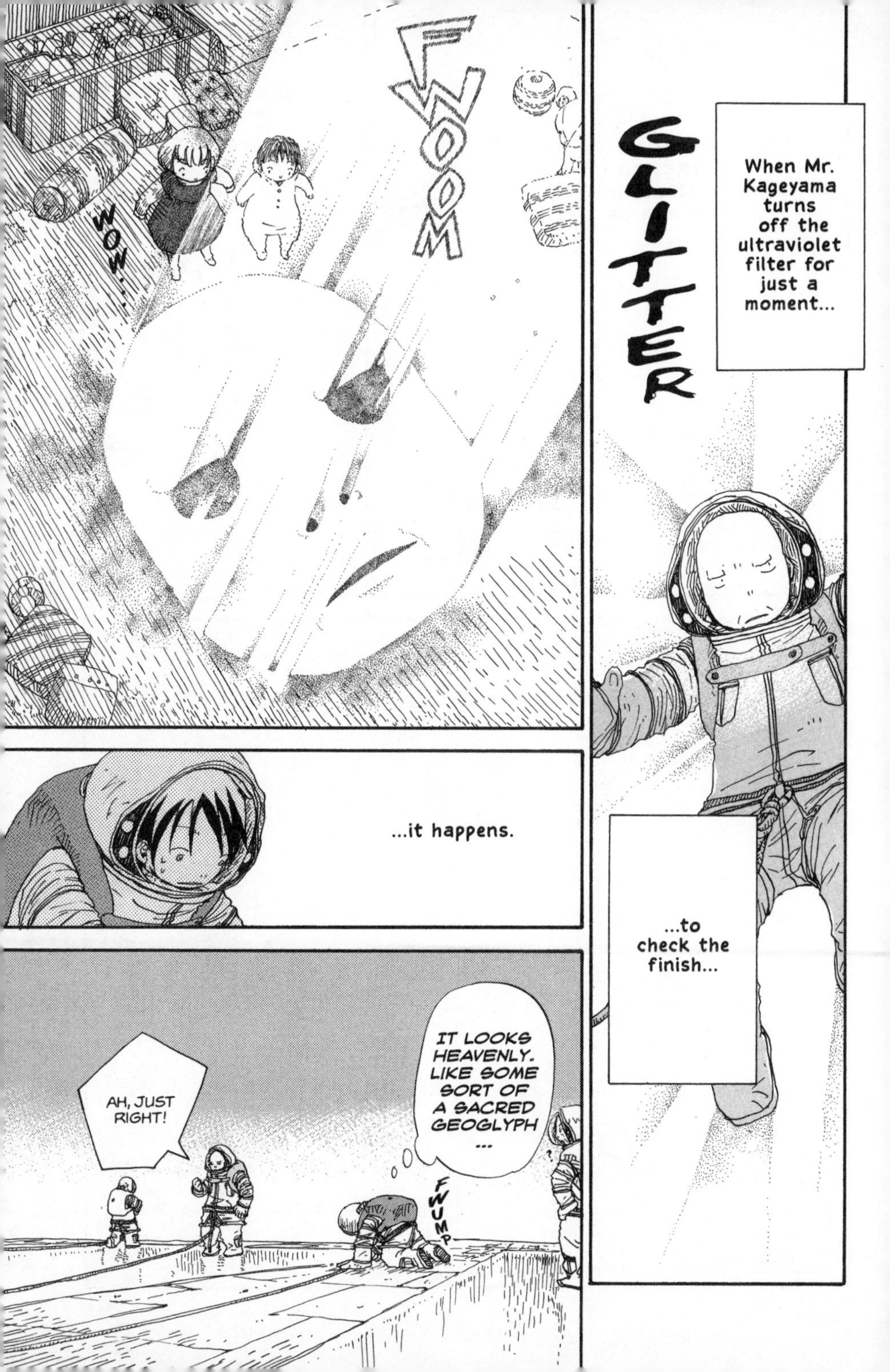
GLITTER
When Mr. Kageyama turns off the ultraviolet filter for just a moment...
...to check the finish...
FWOOM
WOW...
...it happens.
IT LOOKS HEAVENLY. LIKE SOME SORT OF A SACRED GEOGLYPH ...
FWUMP
AH, JUST RIGHT!

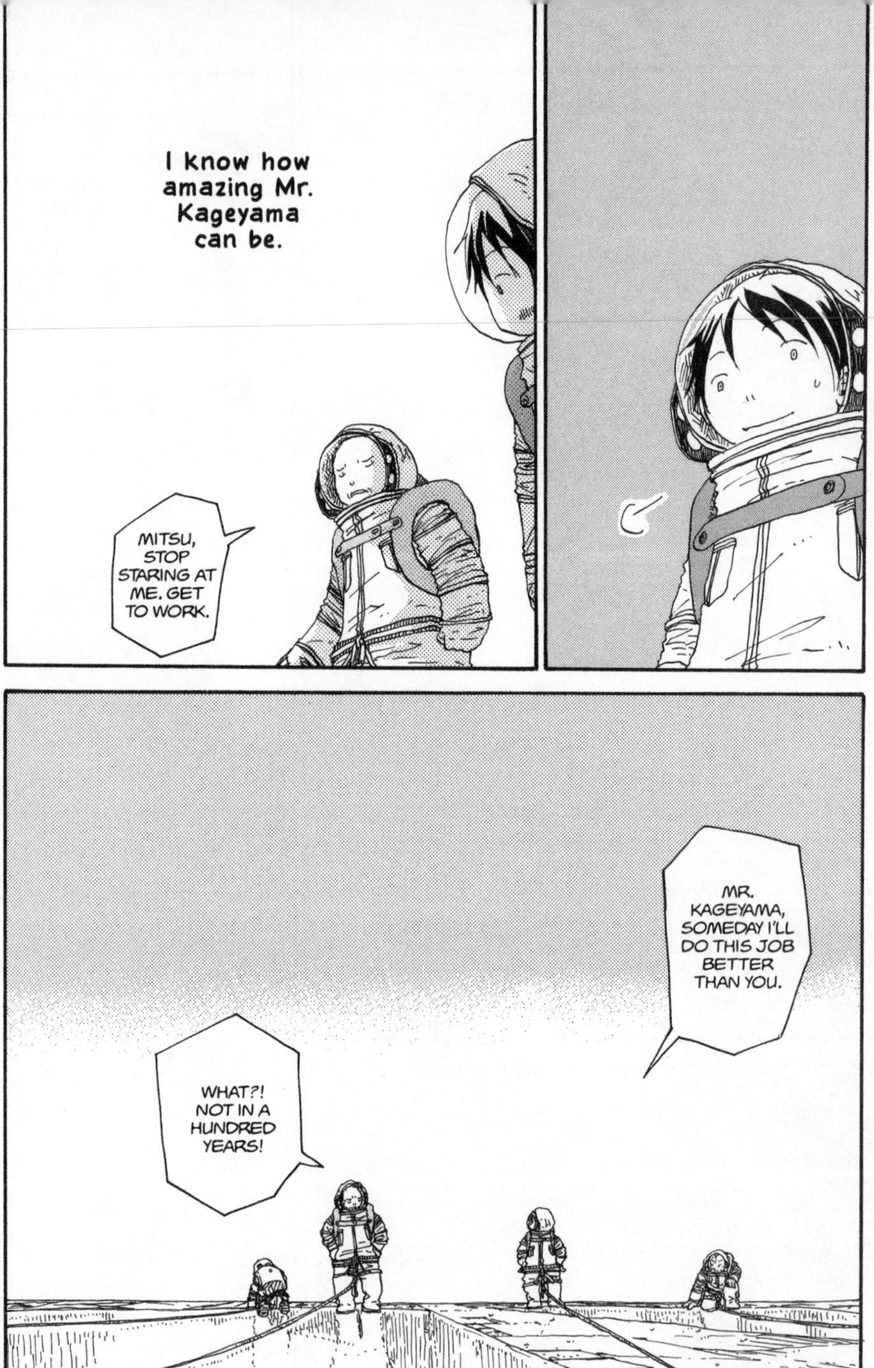
I know how amazing Mr. Kageyama can be.
MITSU, STOP STARING AT ME. GET TO WORK.
MR. KAGEYAMA, SOMEDAY I'LL DO THIS JOB BETTER THAN YOU.
WHAT?! NOT IN A HUNDRED YEARS!

floor 17: a room full of flowers

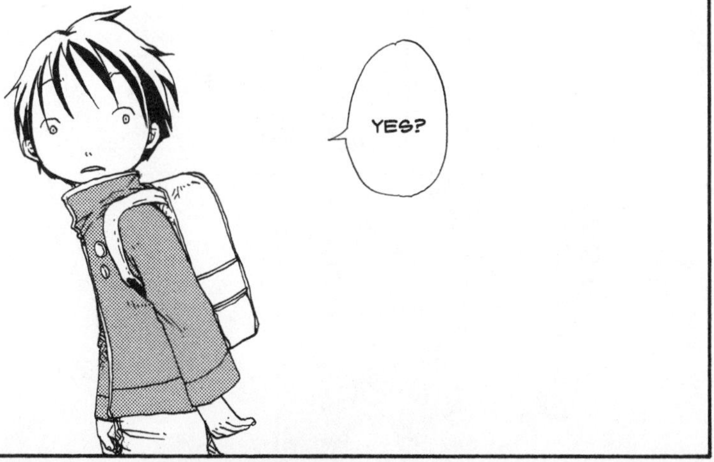
YES?

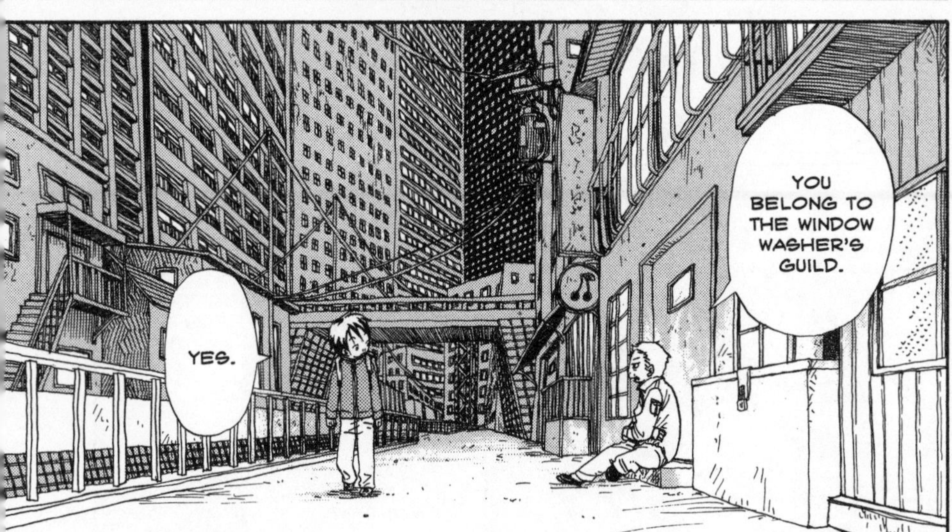
YOU BELONG TO THE WINDOW WASHER'S GUILD.
YES.

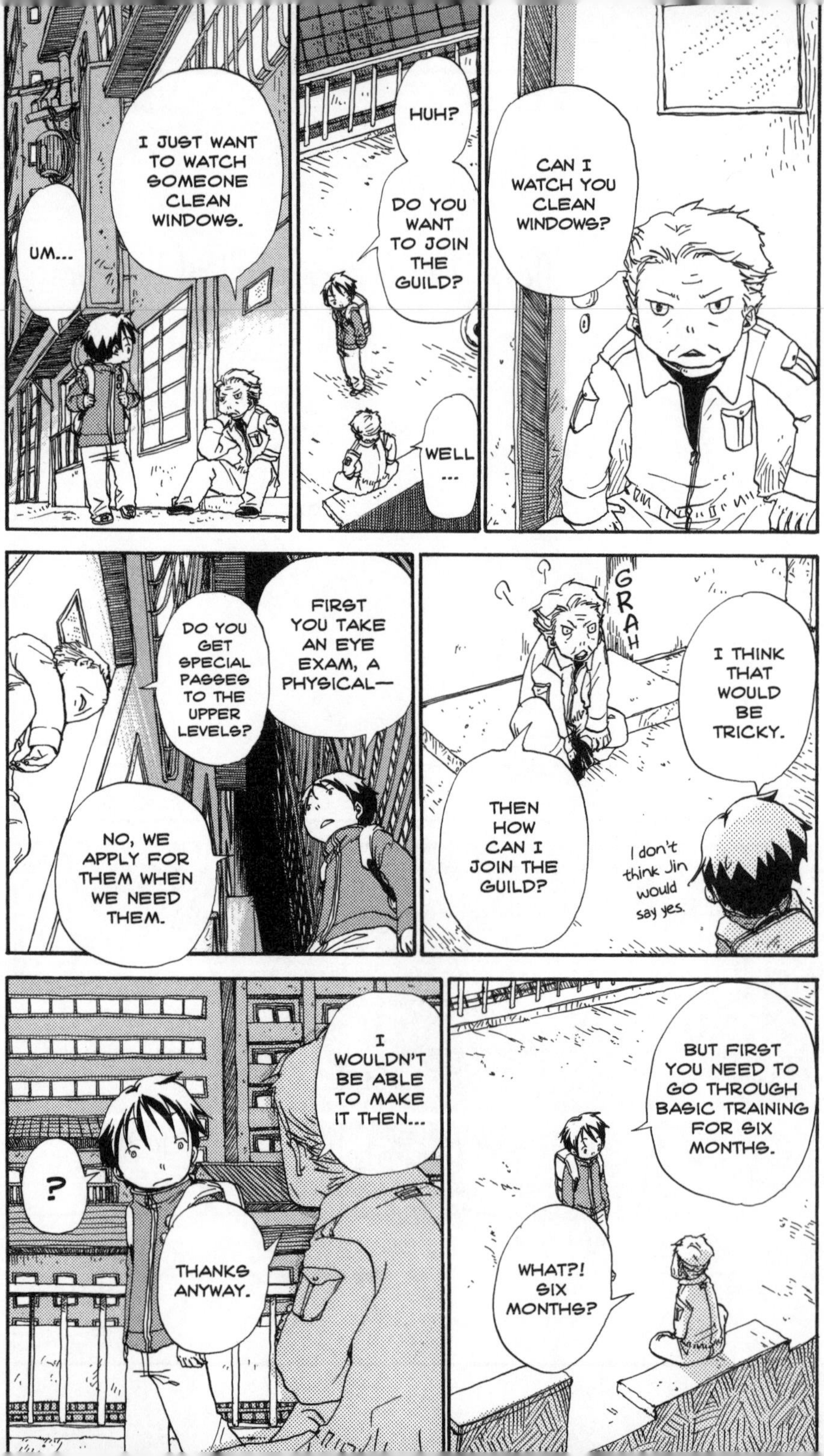
CAN I WATCH YOU CLEAN WINDOWS?
HUH?
DO YOU WANT TO JOIN THE GUILD?
WELL...
I JUST WANT TO WATCH SOMEONE CLEAN WINDOWS.
UM...
GRAH
I THINK THAT WOULD BE TRICKY.
THEN HOW CAN I JOIN THE GUILD?
I don't think Jin would say yes.
FIRST YOU TAKE AN EYE EXAM, A PHYSICAL—
DO YOU GET SPECIAL PASSES TO THE UPPER LEVELS?
NO, WE APPLY FOR THEM WHEN WE NEED THEM.
BUT FIRST YOU NEED TO GO THROUGH BASIC TRAINING FOR SIX MONTHS.
WHAT?! SIX MONTHS?
I WOULDN'T BE ABLE TO MAKE IT THEN...
?
THANKS ANYWAY.

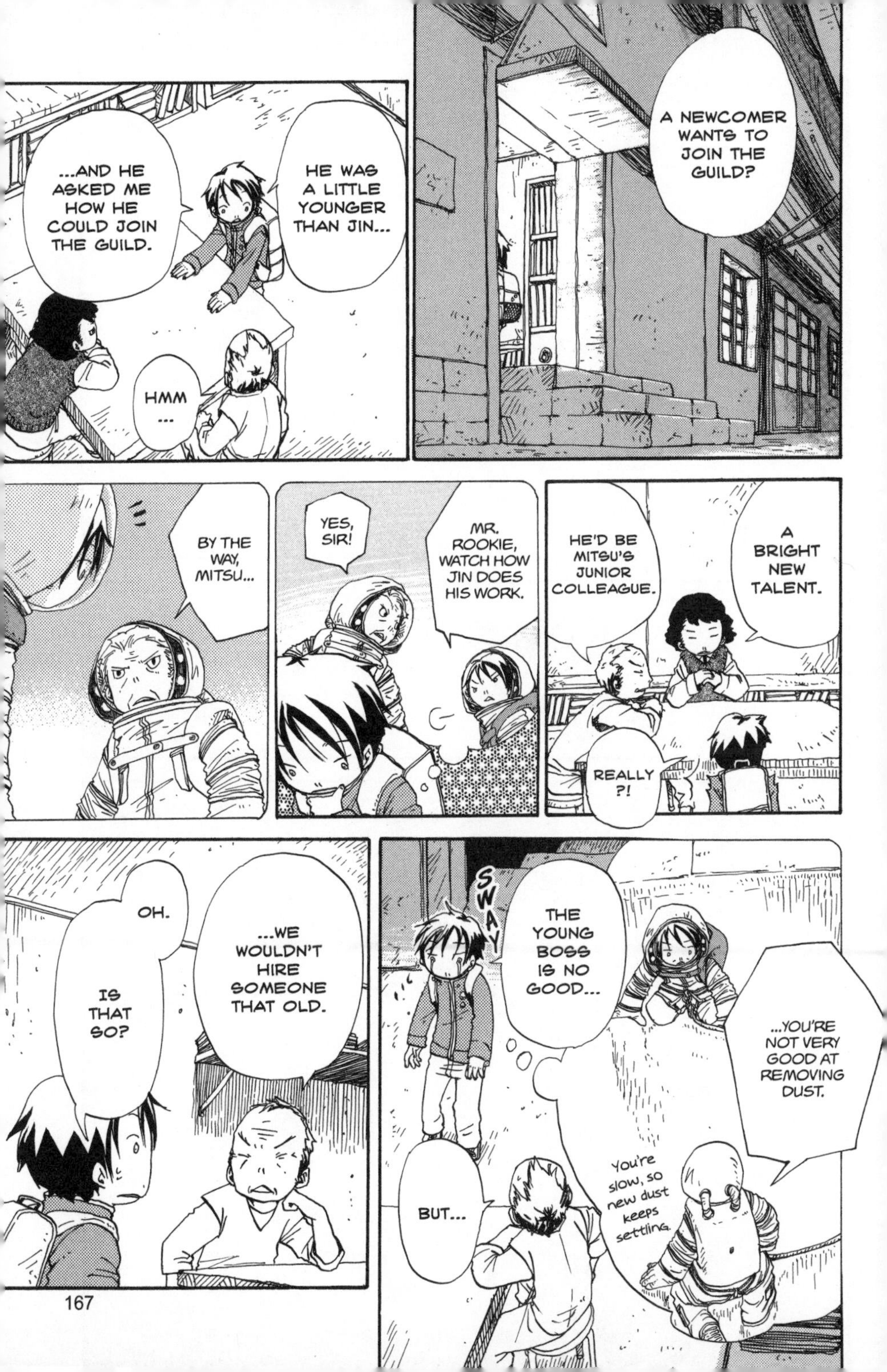
A NEWCOMER WANTS TO JOIN THE GUILD?
HE WAS A LITTLE YOUNGER THAN JIN...
...AND HE ASKED ME HOW HE COULD JOIN THE GUILD.
HMM ...
A BRIGHT NEW TALENT.
HE'D BE MITSU'S JUNIOR COLLEAGUE.
REALLY ?!
MR. ROOKIE, WATCH HOW JIN DOES HIS WORK.
YES, SIR!
BY THE WAY, MITSU...
...YOU'RE NOT VERY GOOD AT REMOVING DUST.
THE YOUNG BOSS IS NO GOOD...
SWAY
You're slow, so new dust keeps settling.
BUT...
...WE WOULDN'T HIRE SOMEONE THAT OLD.
OH.
IS THAT SO?

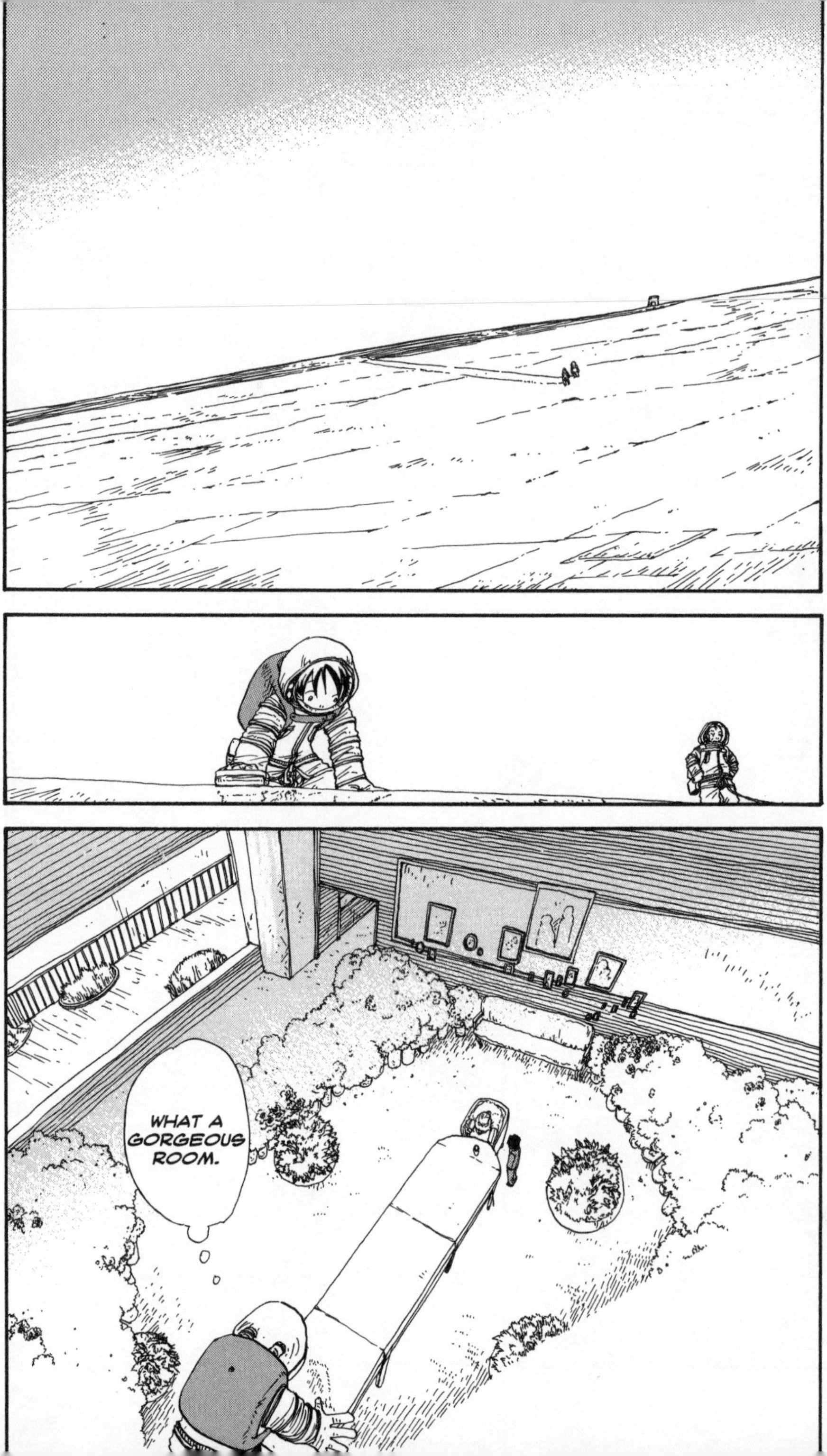
WHAT A GORGEOUS ROOM.

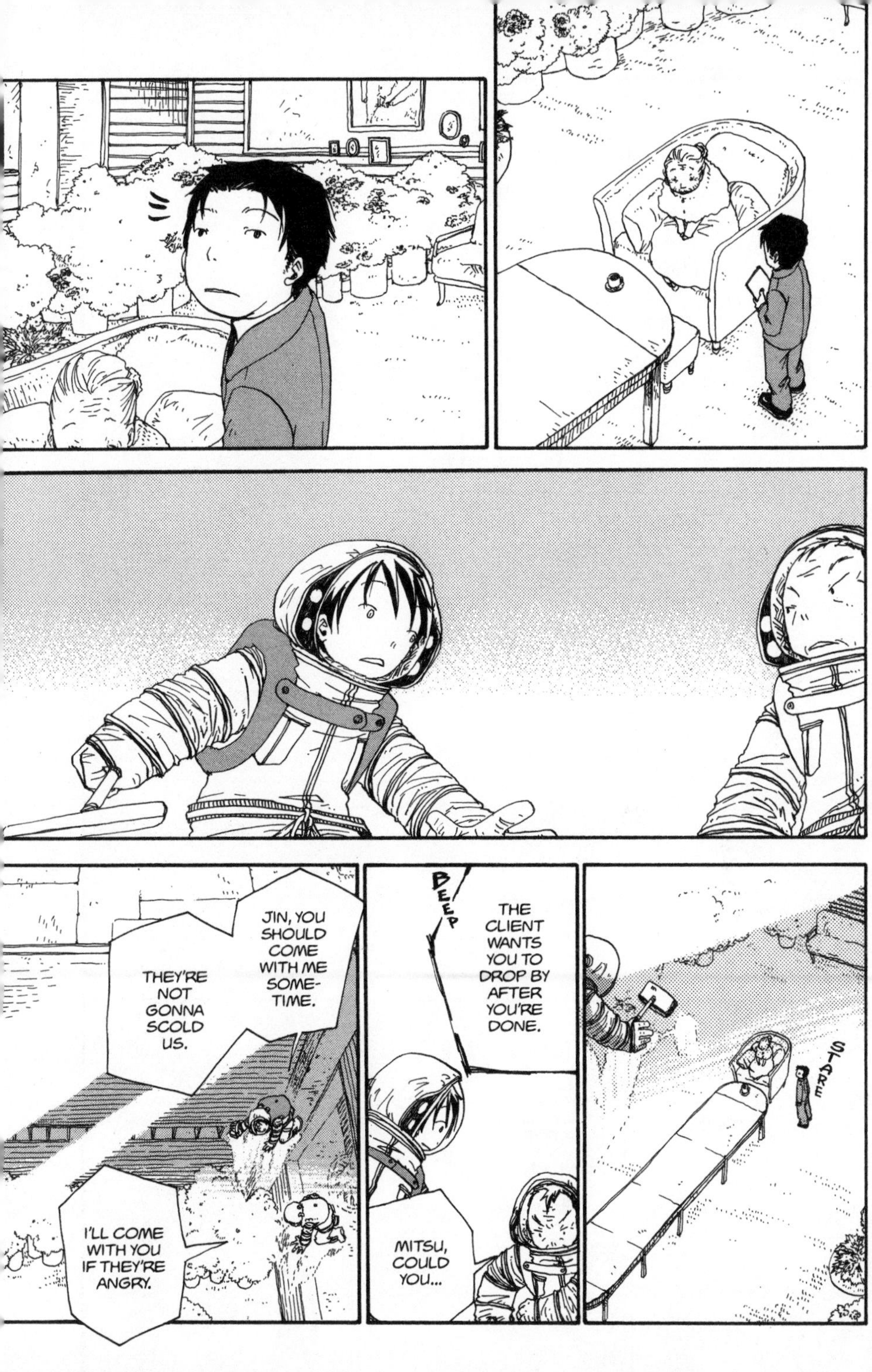
STARE
BEEP
THE CLIENT WANTS YOU TO DROP BY AFTER YOU'RE DONE.
MITSU, COULD YOU...
JIN, YOU SHOULD COME WITH ME SOME-TIME.
THEY'RE NOT GONNA SCOLD US.
I'LL COME WITH YOU IF THEY'RE ANGRY.

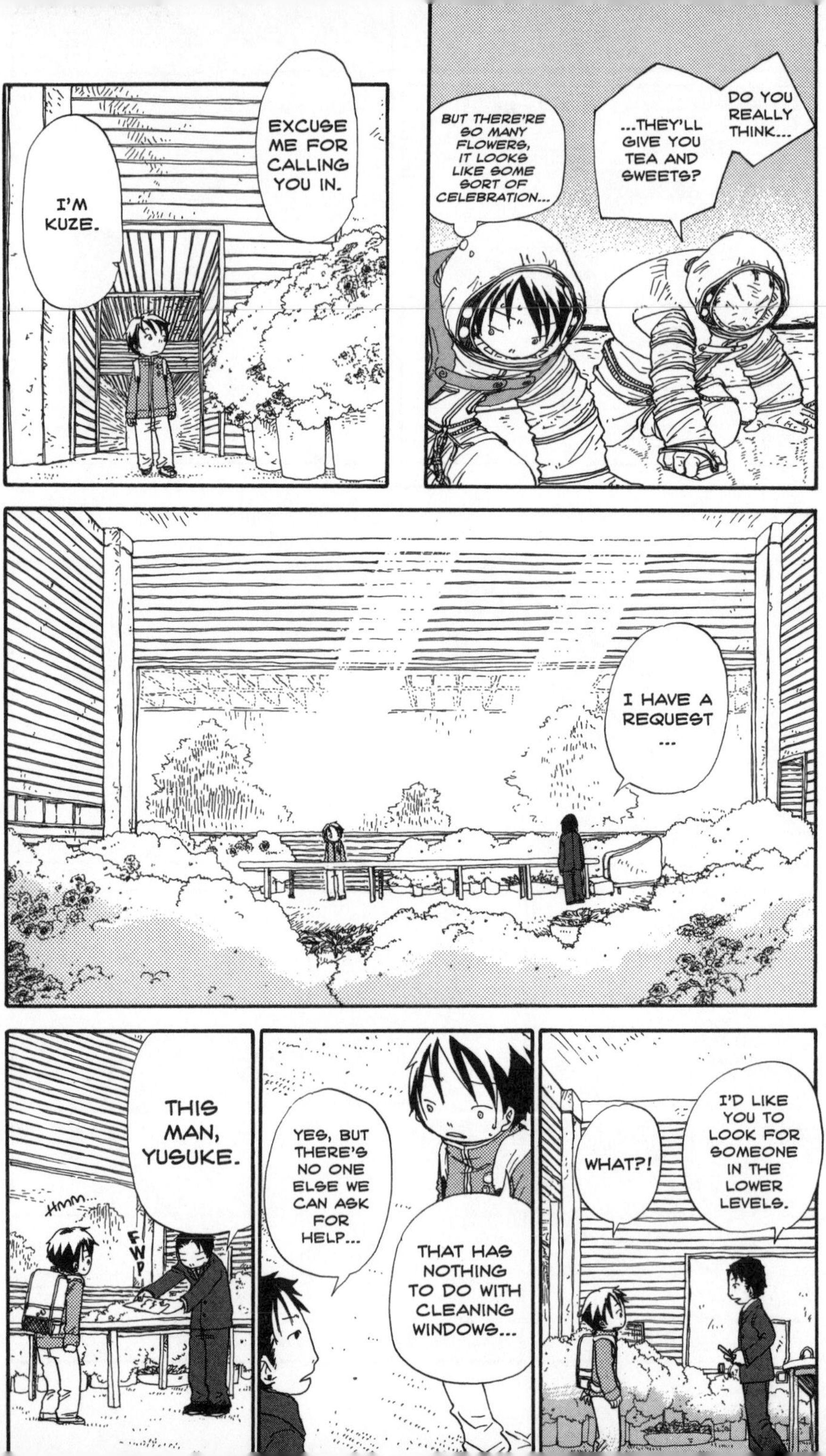
DO YOU REALLY THINK...
...THEY'LL GIVE YOU TEA AND SWEETS?
BUT THERE'RE SO MANY FLOWERS, IT LOOKS LIKE SOME SORT OF CELEBRATION...
EXCUSE ME FOR CALLING YOU IN.
I'M KUZE.
I HAVE A REQUEST ...
I'D LIKE YOU TO LOOK FOR SOMEONE IN THE LOWER LEVELS.
WHAT?!
THAT HAS NOTHING TO DO WITH CLEANING WINDOWS...
YES, BUT THERE'S NO ONE ELSE WE CAN ASK FOR HELP...
THIS MAN, YUSUKE.
FWP
HMM...

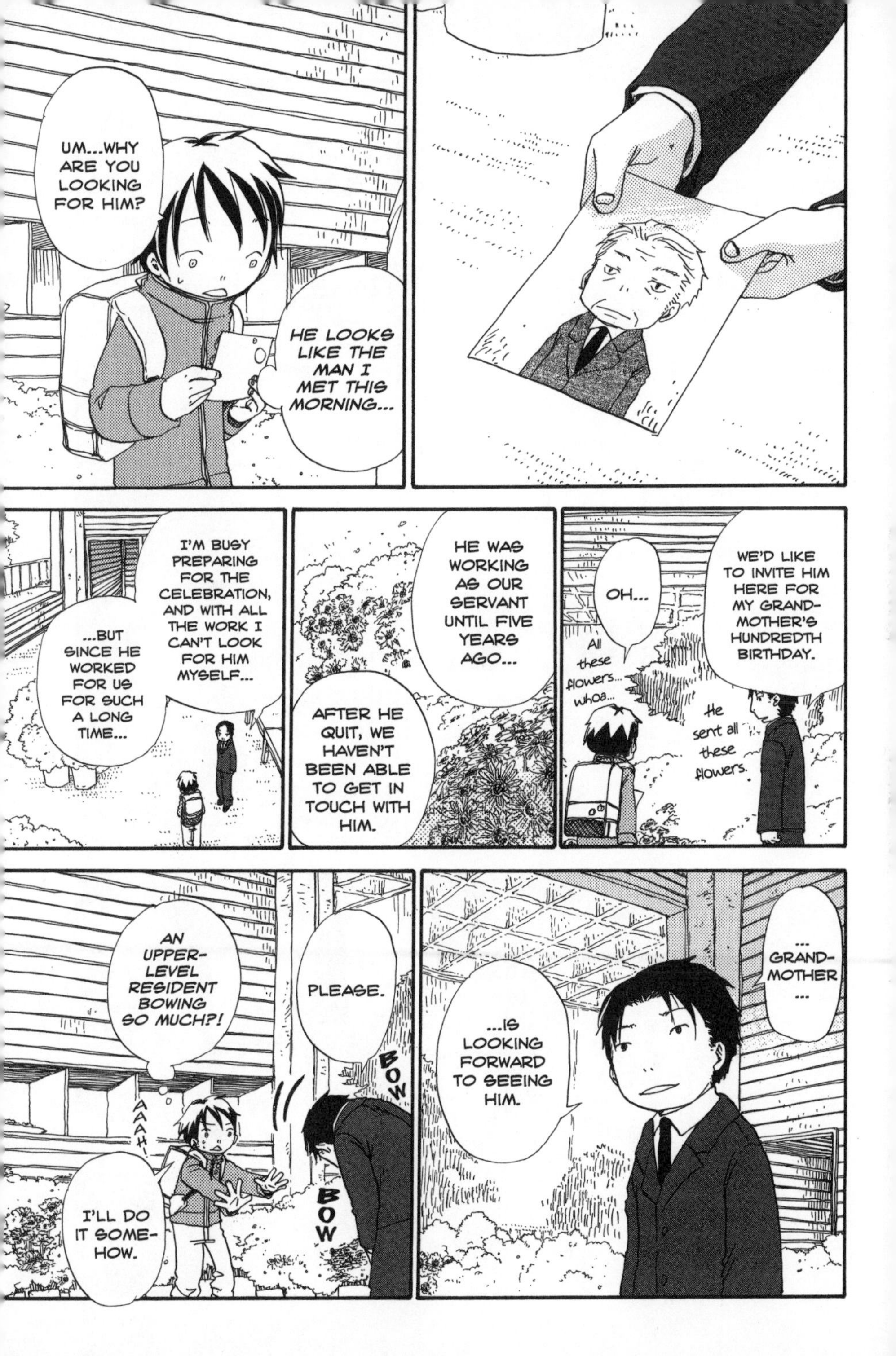
HE LOOKS LIKE THE MAN I MET THIS MORNING...
UM...WHY ARE YOU LOOKING FOR HIM?
WE'D LIKE TO INVITE HIM HERE FOR MY GRAND-MOTHER'S HUNDREDTH BIRTHDAY.
OH...
He sent all these flowers.
All these flowers... whoa...
HE WAS WORKING AS OUR SERVANT UNTIL FIVE YEARS AGO...
AFTER HE QUIT, WE HAVEN'T BEEN ABLE TO GET IN TOUCH WITH HIM.
I'M BUSY PREPARING FOR THE CELEBRATION, AND WITH ALL THE WORK I CAN'T LOOK FOR HIM MYSELF...
...BUT SINCE HE WORKED FOR US FOR SUCH A LONG TIME...
...GRAND-MOTHER...
...IS LOOKING FORWARD TO SEEING HIM.
PLEASE.
BOW
BOW
AN UPPER-LEVEL RESIDENT BOWING SO MUCH?!
AAAH!
I'LL DO IT SOME-HOW.

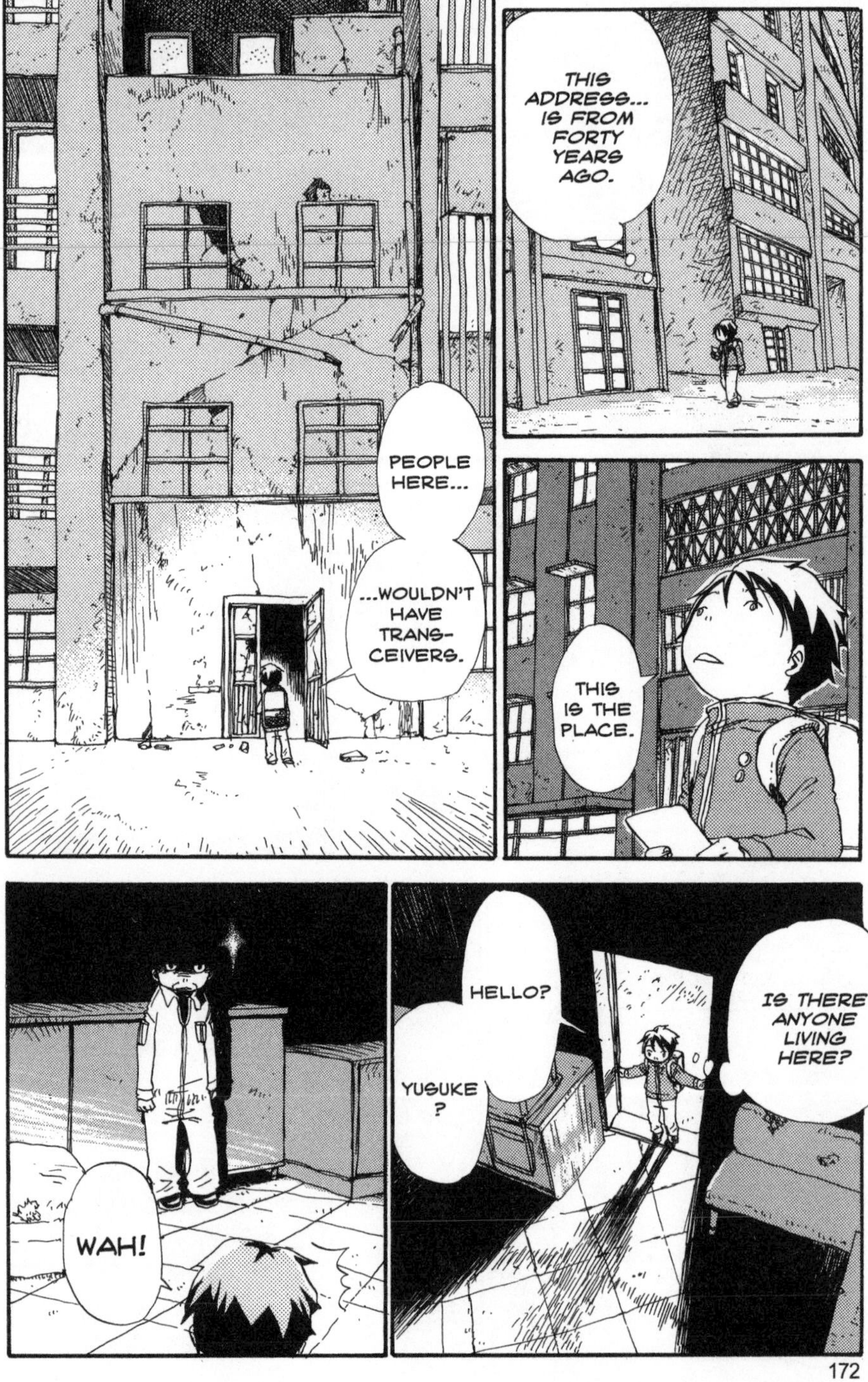
THIS ADDRESS... IS FROM FORTY YEARS AGO.
THIS IS THE PLACE.
PEOPLE HERE...
...WOULDN'T HAVE TRANS-CEIVERS.
HELLO?
IS THERE ANYONE LIVING HERE?
YUSUKE?
WAH!

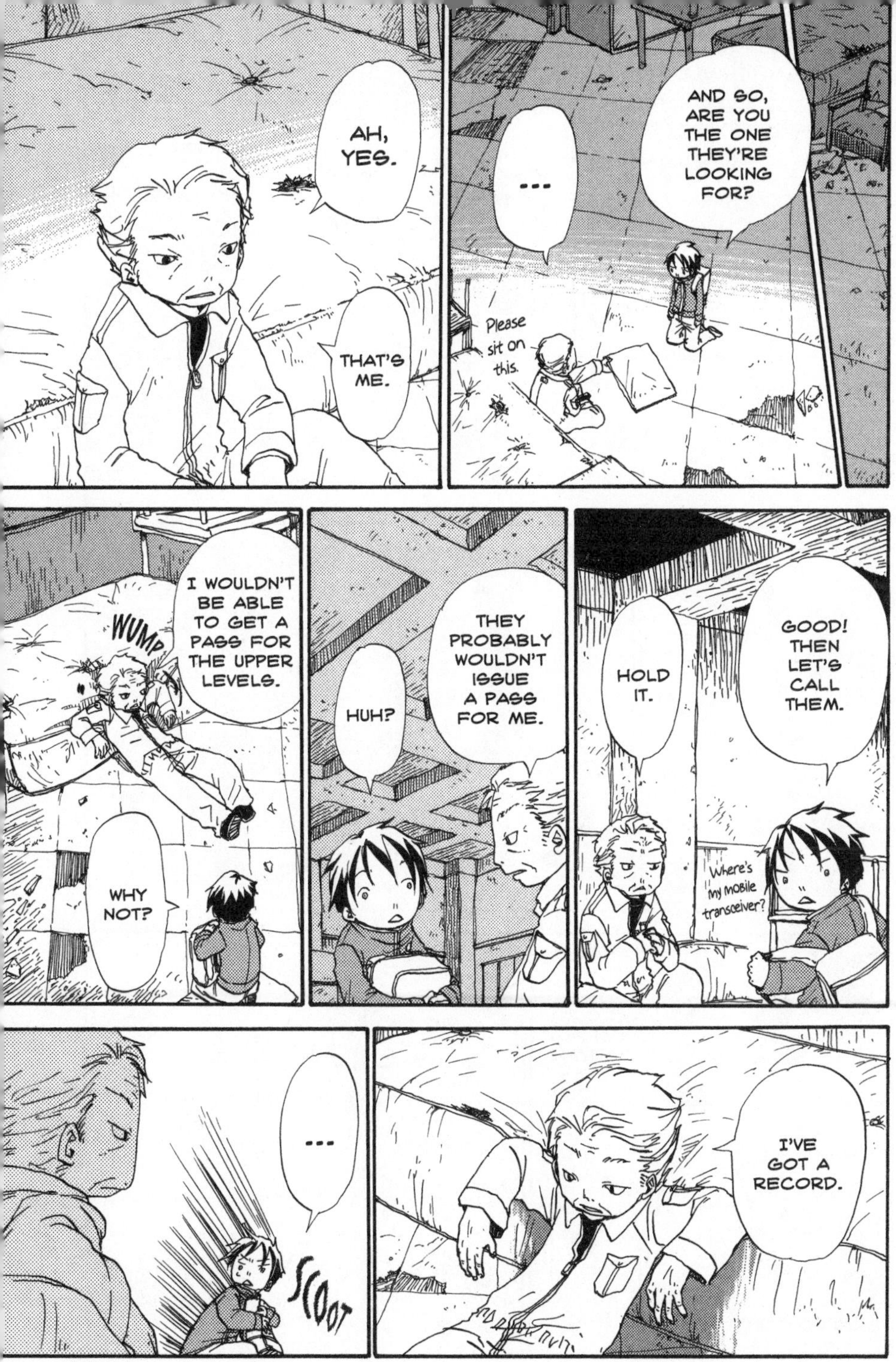
AND SO, ARE YOU THE ONE THEY'RE LOOKING FOR?
...
Please sit on this.
AH, YES.
THAT'S ME.
GOOD! THEN LET'S CALL THEM.
HOLD IT.
Where's my mobile transceiver?
THEY PROBABLY WOULDN'T ISSUE A PASS FOR ME.
HUH?
I WOULDN'T BE ABLE TO GET A PASS FOR THE UPPER LEVELS.
WUMP
WHY NOT?
I'VE GOT A RECORD.
...
SCOOT

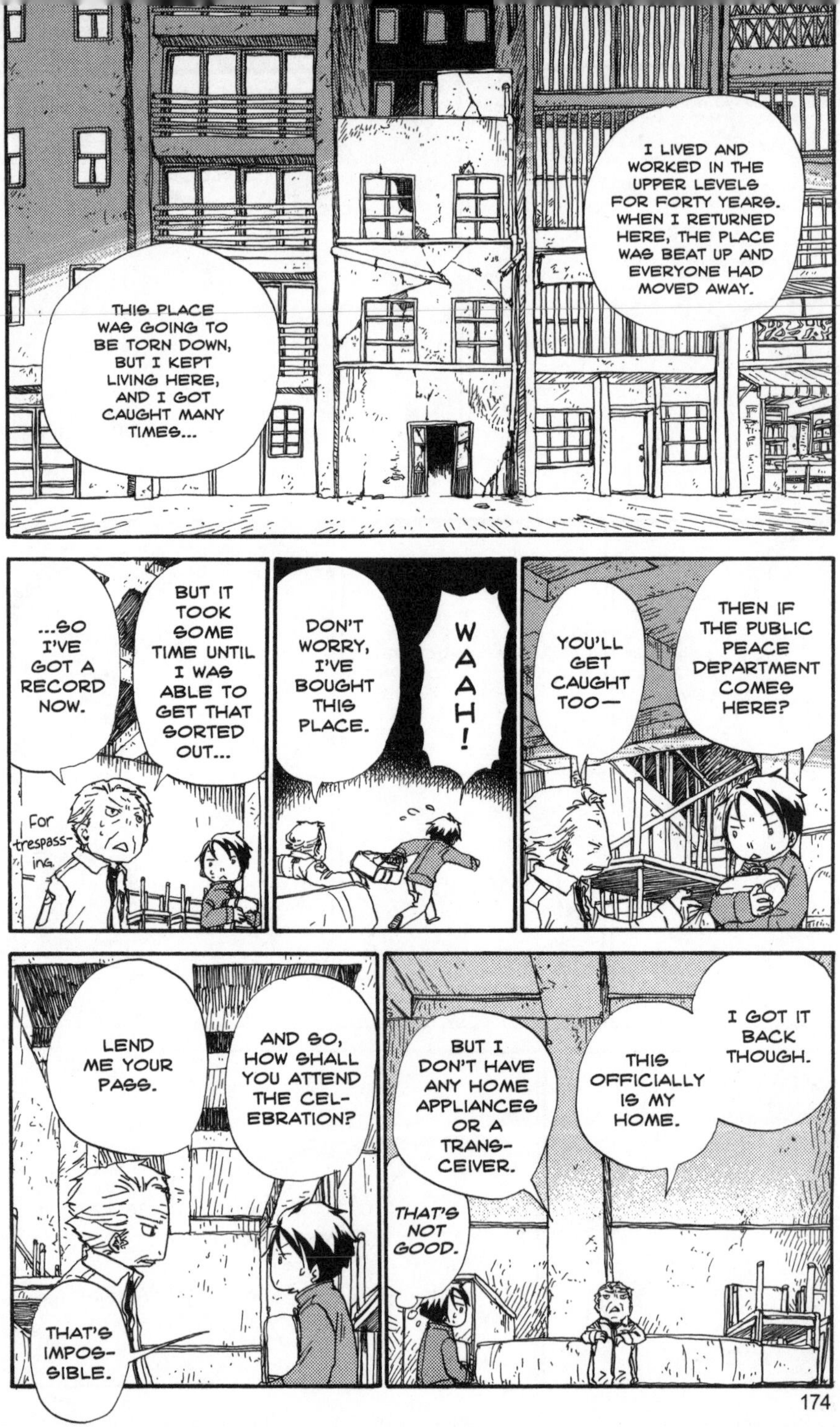
I LIVED AND WORKED IN THE UPPER LEVELS FOR FORTY YEARS. WHEN I RETURNED HERE, THE PLACE WAS BEAT UP AND EVERYONE HAD MOVED AWAY.
THIS PLACE WAS GOING TO BE TORN DOWN, BUT I KEPT LIVING HERE, AND I GOT CAUGHT MANY TIMES...
THEN IF THE PUBLIC PEACE DEPARTMENT COMES HERE?
YOU'LL GET CAUGHT TOO—
WAAH!
DON'T WORRY, I'VE BOUGHT THIS PLACE.
BUT IT TOOK SOME TIME UNTIL I WAS ABLE TO GET THAT SORTED OUT...
...SO I'VE GOT A RECORD NOW.
For trespass-ing.
I GOT IT BACK THOUGH.
THIS OFFICIALLY IS MY HOME.
BUT I DON'T HAVE ANY HOME APPLIANCES OR A TRANS-CEIVER.
THAT'S NOT GOOD.
AND SO, HOW SHALL YOU ATTEND THE CEL-EBRATION?
LEND ME YOUR PASS.
THAT'S IMPOS-SIBLE.

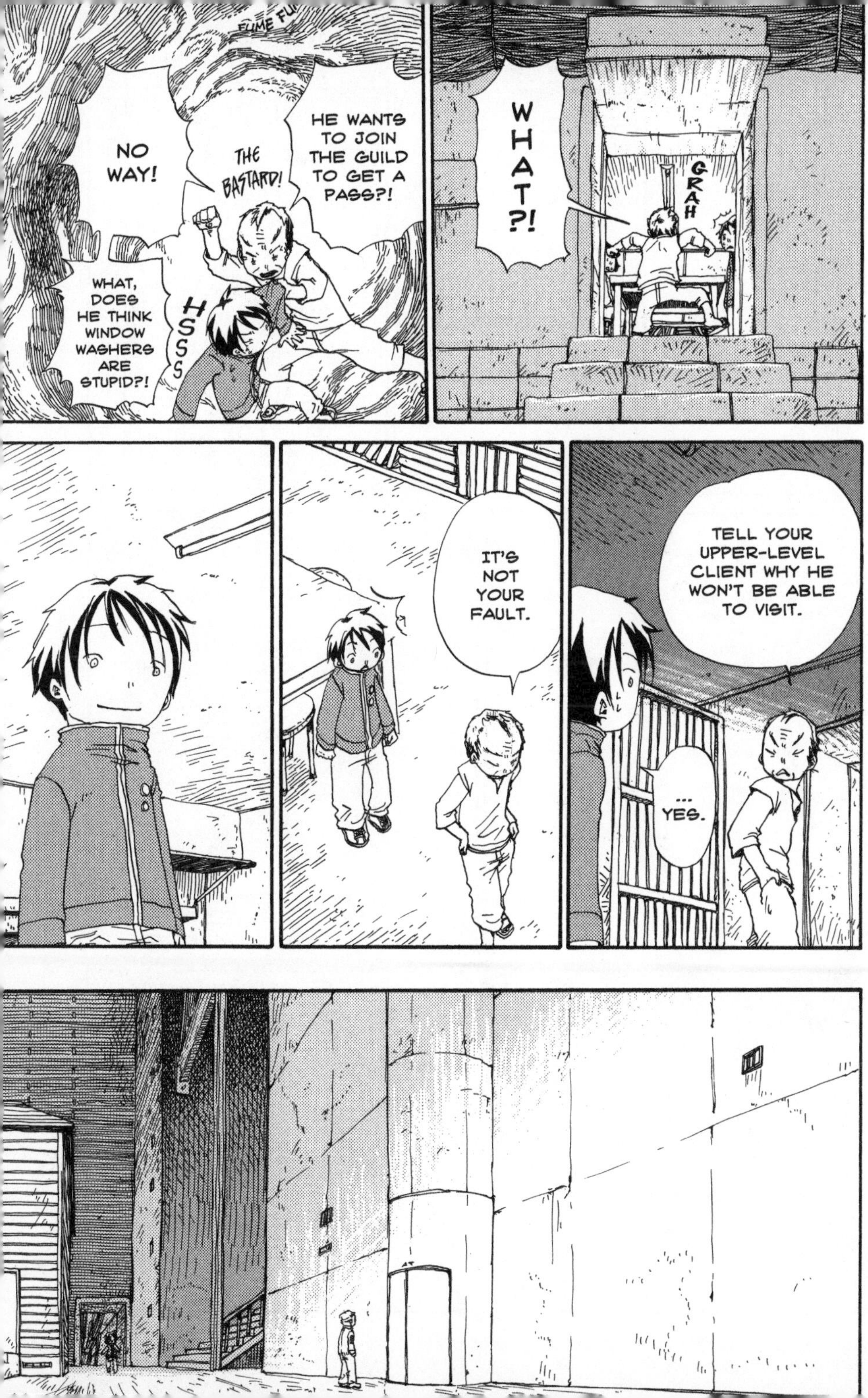
WHAT?!
GRAH
FUME FU
HE WANTS TO JOIN THE GUILD TO GET A PASS?!
THE BASTARD!
NO WAY!
HSSS
WHAT, DOES HE THINK WINDOW WASHERS ARE STUPID?!
TELL YOUR UPPER-LEVEL CLIENT WHY HE WON'T BE ABLE TO VISIT.
... YES.
IT'S NOT YOUR FAULT.

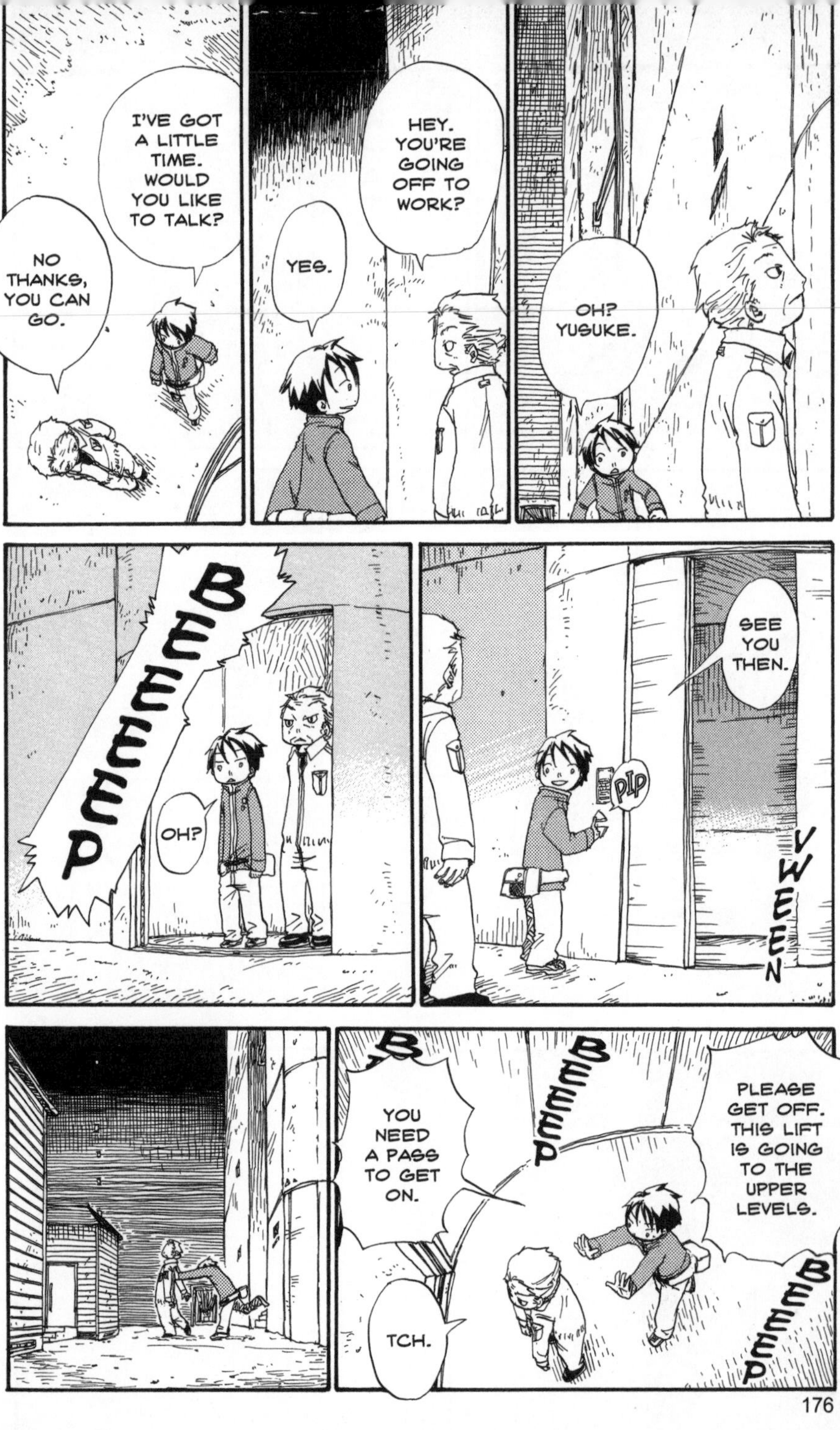
OH? YUSUKE.
HEY. YOU'RE GOING OFF TO WORK?
YES.
I'VE GOT A LITTLE TIME. WOULD YOU LIKE TO TALK?
NO THANKS, YOU CAN GO.
SEE YOU THEN.
PIP
VWEEN
BEEEEEEP
OH?
PLEASE GET OFF. THIS LIFT IS GOING TO THE UPPER LEVELS.
BEEEEP
BEEEEP
YOU NEED A PASS TO GET ON.
TCH.

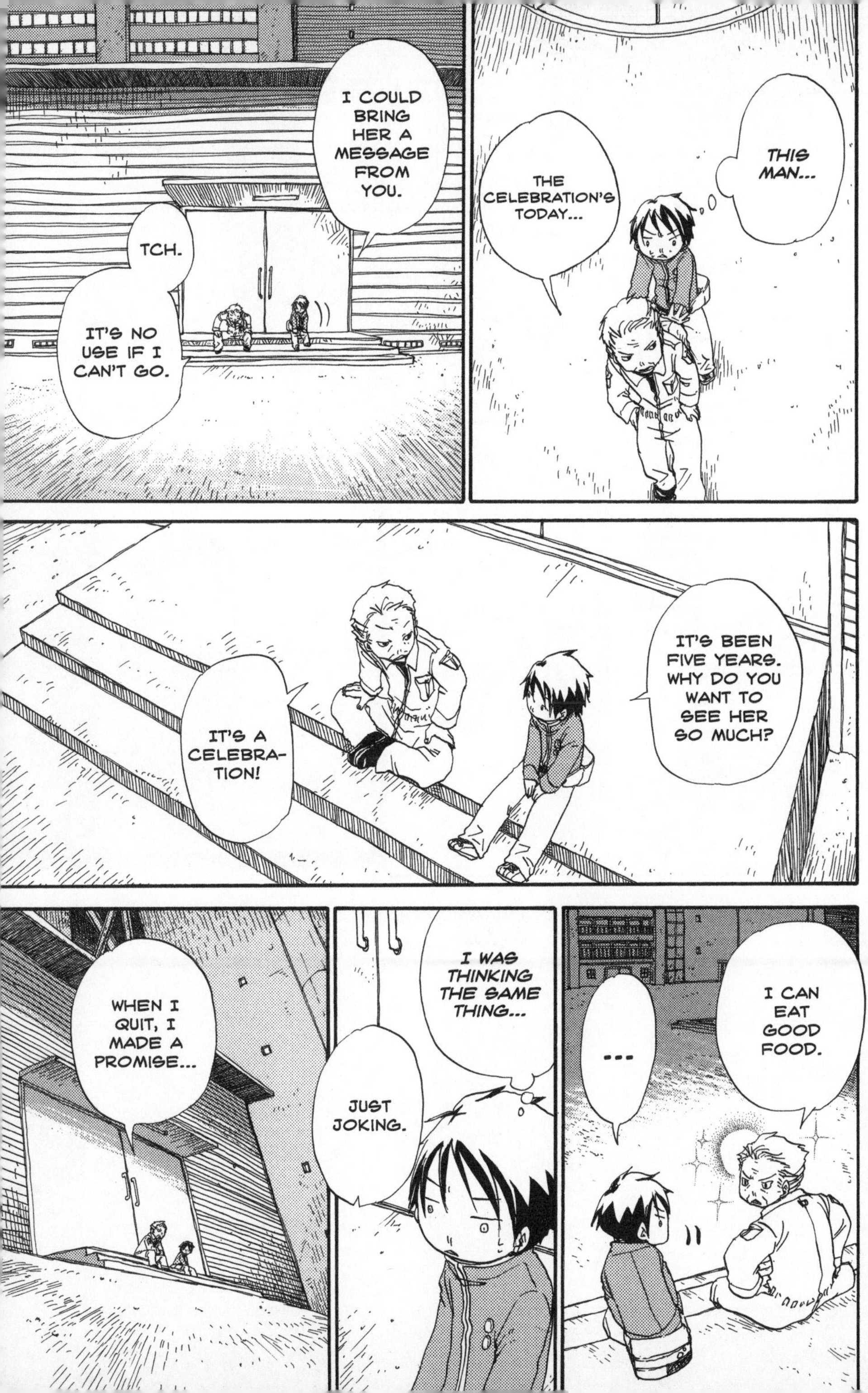
THIS MAN...
THE CELEBRATION'S TODAY...
I COULD BRING HER A MESSAGE FROM YOU.
TCH.
IT'S NO USE IF I CAN'T GO.
IT'S BEEN FIVE YEARS. WHY DO YOU WANT TO SEE HER SO MUCH?
IT'S A CELEBRATION!
I CAN EAT GOOD FOOD.
...
I WAS THINKING THE SAME THING...
JUST JOKING.
WHEN I QUIT, I MADE A PROMISE...

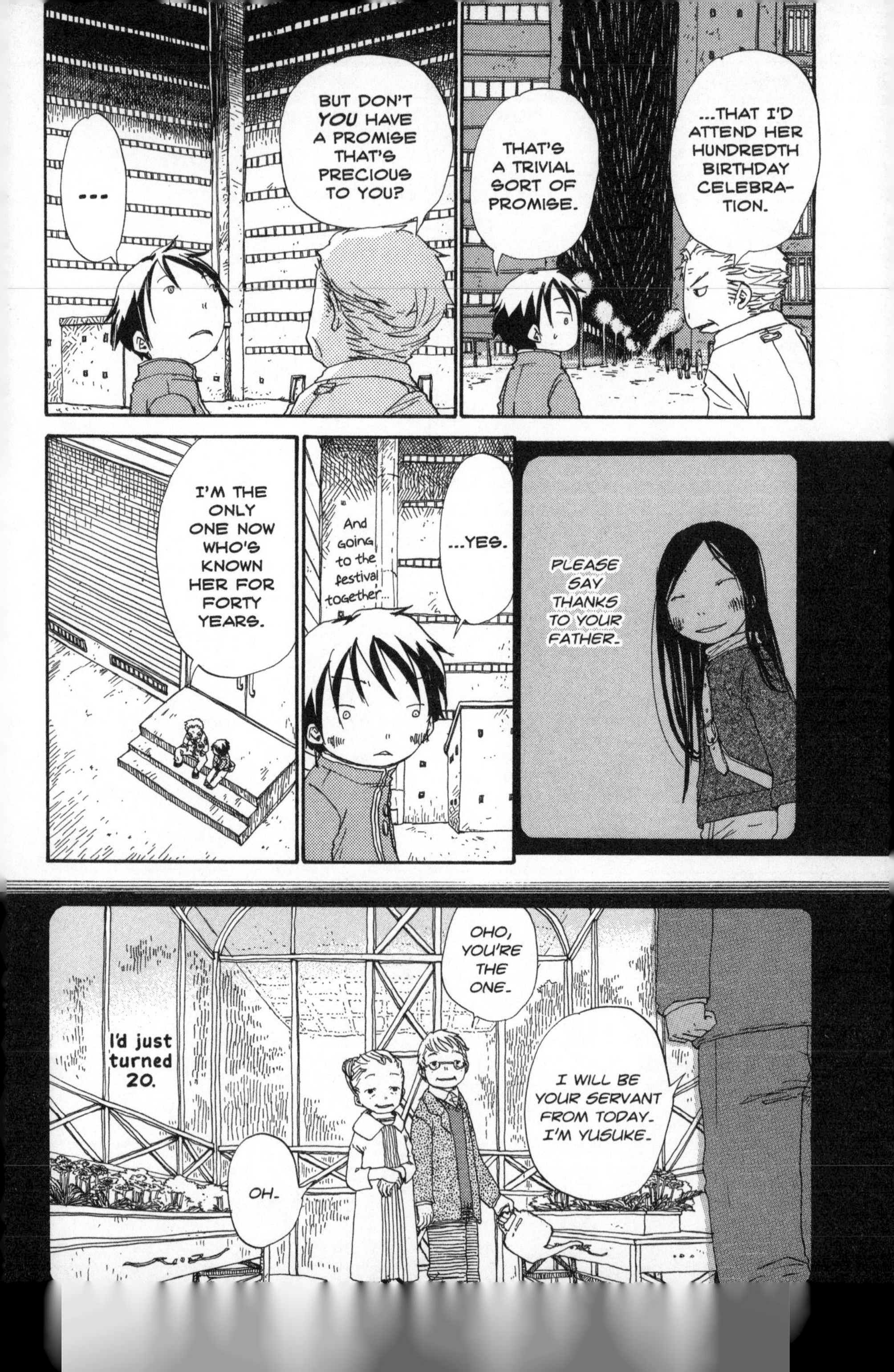
...THAT I'D ATTEND HER HUNDREDTH BIRTHDAY CELEBRA-TION.
THAT'S A TRIVIAL SORT OF PROMISE.
BUT DON'T *YOU* HAVE A PROMISE THAT'S PRECIOUS TO YOU?
...
PLEASE SAY THANKS TO YOUR FATHER.
...YES.
And going to the festival together...
I'M THE ONLY ONE NOW WHO'S KNOWN HER FOR FORTY YEARS.
OHO, YOU'RE THE ONE.
I WILL BE YOUR SERVANT FROM TODAY. I'M YUSUKE.
I'd just turned 20.
OH.

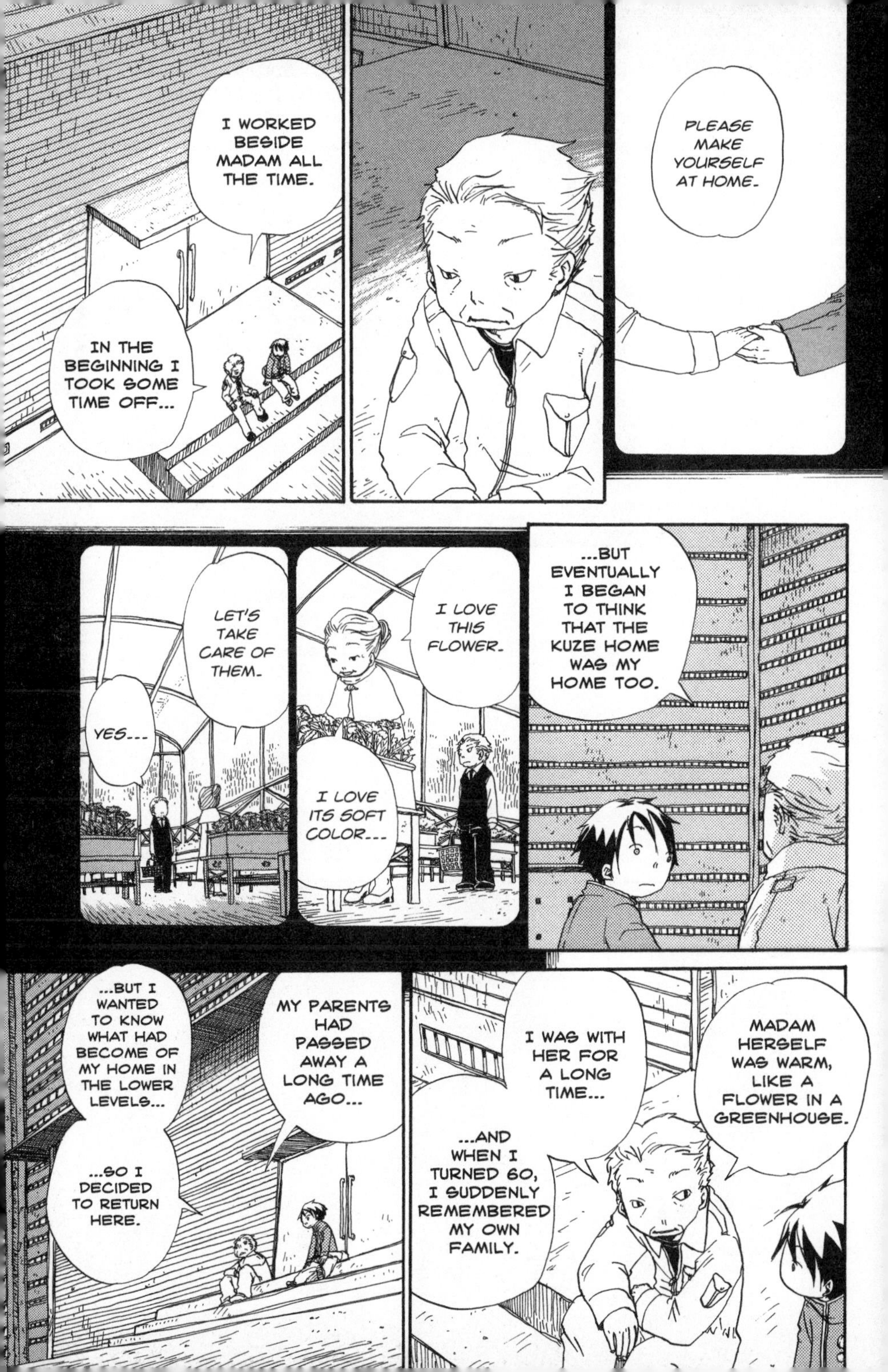
PLEASE MAKE YOURSELF AT HOME.
I WORKED BESIDE MADAM ALL THE TIME.
IN THE BEGINNING I TOOK SOME TIME OFF...
...BUT EVENTUALLY I BEGAN TO THINK THAT THE KUZE HOME WAS MY HOME TOO.
I LOVE THIS FLOWER.
I LOVE ITS SOFT COLOR...
LET'S TAKE CARE OF THEM.
YES...
MADAM HERSELF WAS WARM, LIKE A FLOWER IN A GREENHOUSE.
I WAS WITH HER FOR A LONG TIME...
...AND WHEN I TURNED 60, I SUDDENLY REMEMBERED MY OWN FAMILY.
MY PARENTS HAD PASSED AWAY A LONG TIME AGO...
...BUT I WANTED TO KNOW WHAT HAD BECOME OF MY HOME IN THE LOWER LEVELS...
...SO I DECIDED TO RETURN HERE.

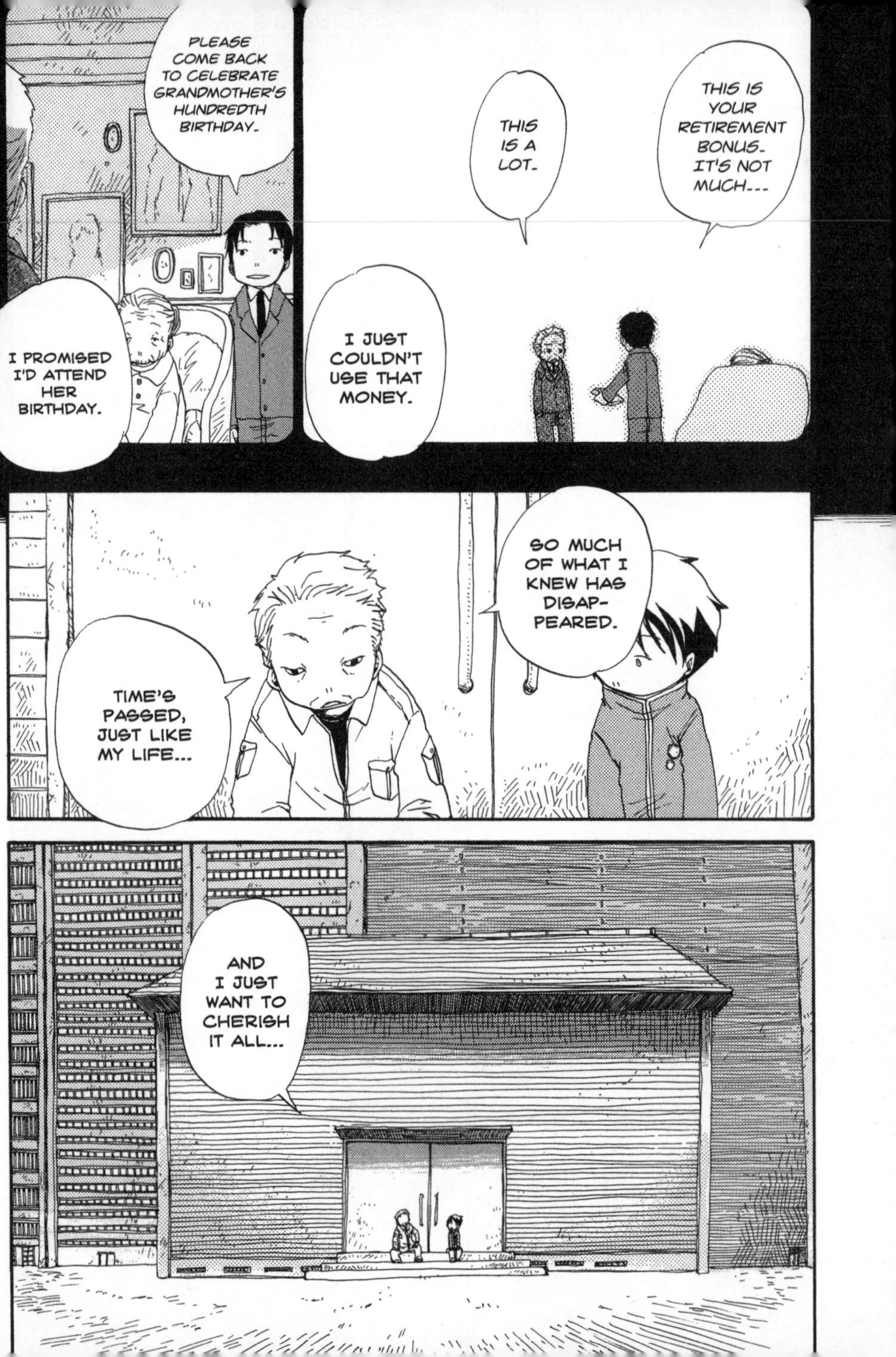
THIS IS YOUR RETIREMENT BONUS. IT'S NOT MUCH...
THIS IS A LOT.
I JUST COULDN'T USE THAT MONEY.
PLEASE COME BACK TO CELEBRATE GRANDMOTHER'S HUNDREDTH BIRTHDAY.
I PROMISED I'D ATTEND HER BIRTHDAY.
SO MUCH OF WHAT I KNEW HAS DISAP-PEARED.
TIME'S PASSED, JUST LIKE MY LIFE...
AND I JUST WANT TO CHERISH IT ALL...

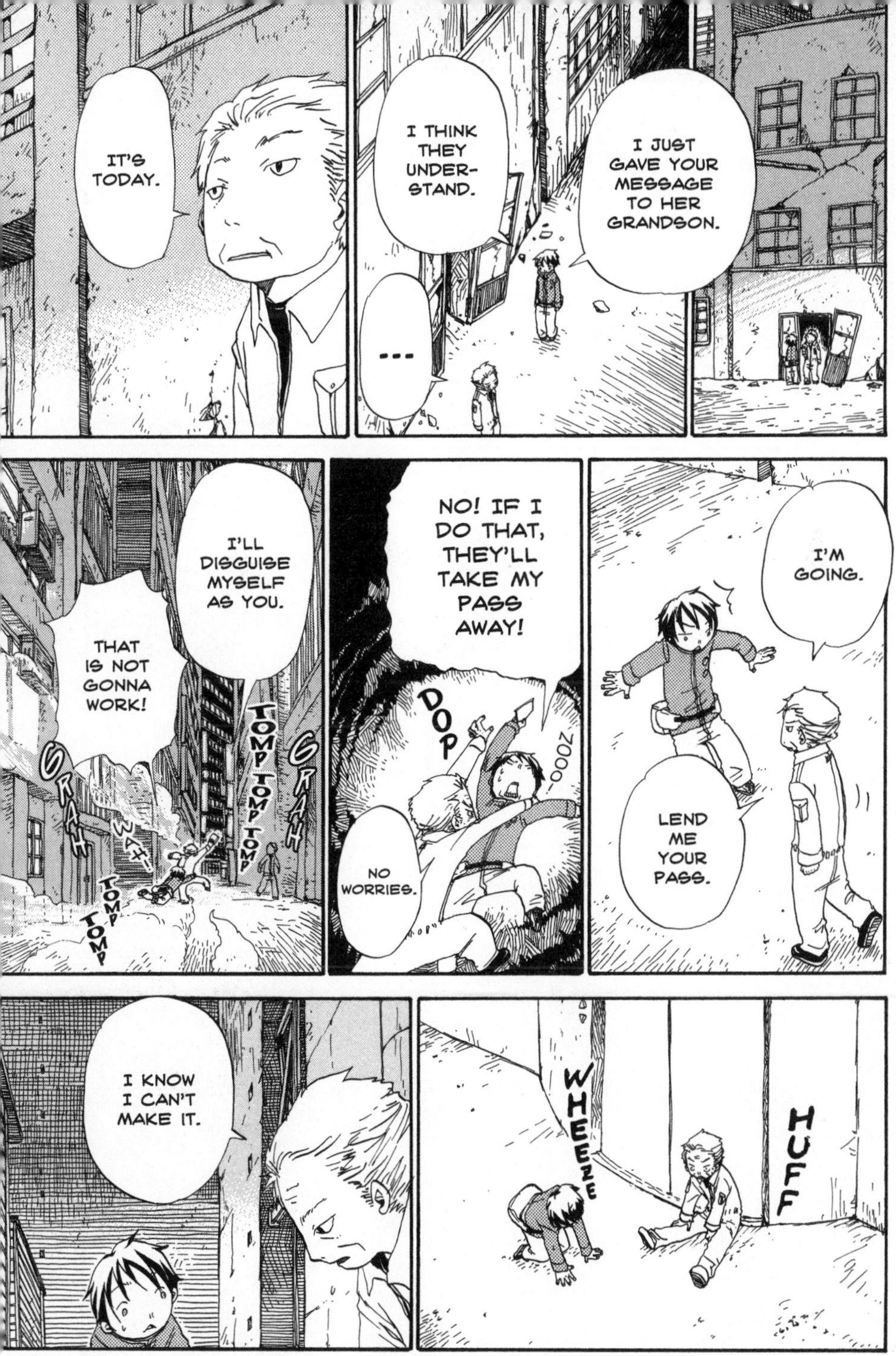

I JUST GAVE YOUR MESSAGE TO HER GRANDSON.
I THINK THEY UNDERSTAND.
...
IT'S TODAY.
I'M GOING.
LEND ME YOUR PASS.
NO! IF I DO THAT, THEY'LL TAKE MY PASS AWAY!
DOP
NO WORRIES.
I'LL DISGUISE MYSELF AS YOU.
GRAAH
TOMP TOMP TOMP TOMP
THAT IS NOT GONNA WORK!
GRAAH
WAH!
TOMP TOMP TOMP
HUFF
WHEEZE
I KNOW I CAN'T MAKE IT.

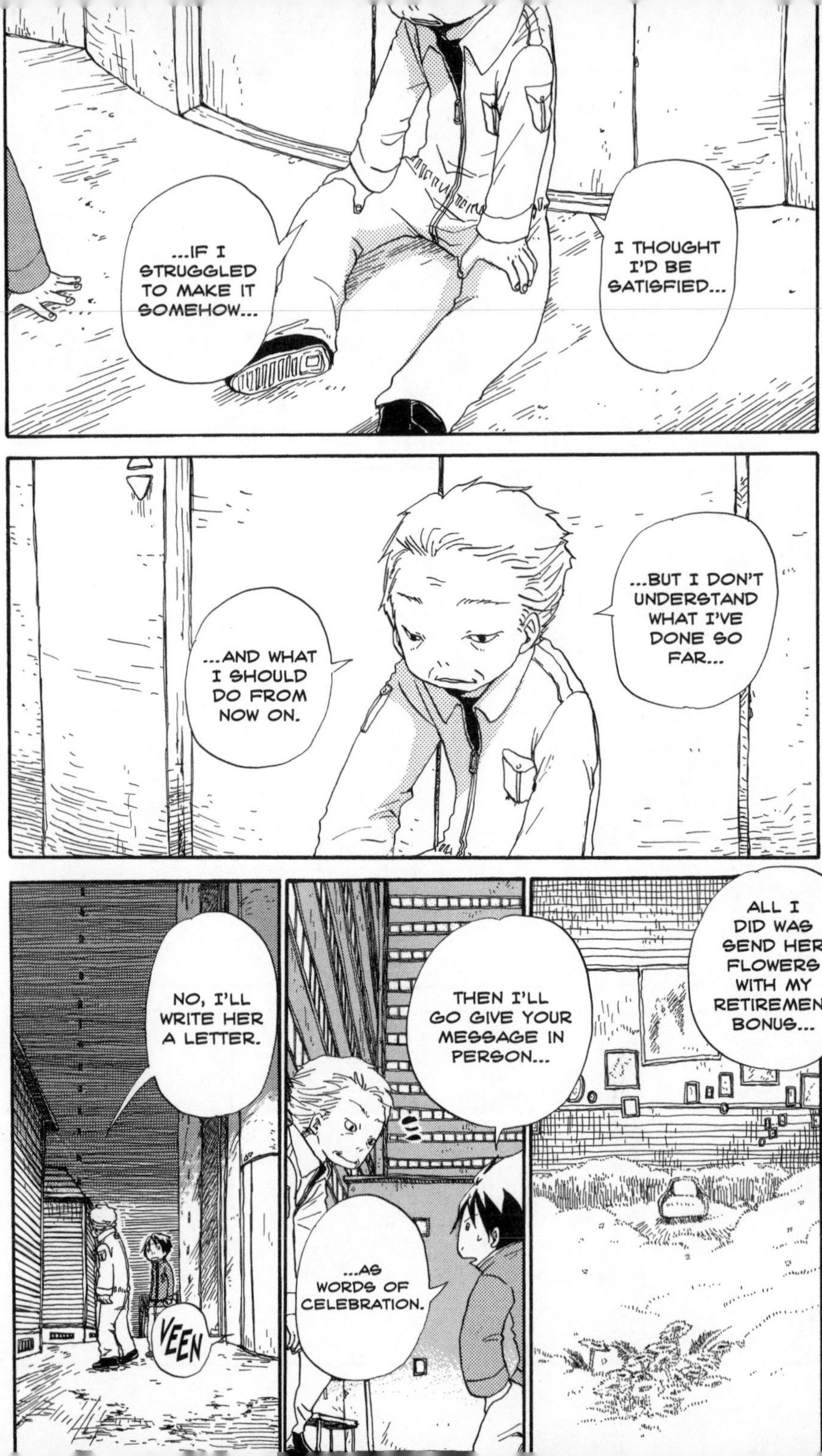
I THOUGHT I'D BE SATISFIED...
...IF I STRUGGLED TO MAKE IT SOMEHOW...
...BUT I DON'T UNDERSTAND WHAT I'VE DONE SO FAR...
...AND WHAT I SHOULD DO FROM NOW ON.
ALL I DID WAS SEND HER FLOWERS WITH MY RETIREMENT BONUS...
THEN I'LL GO GIVE YOUR MESSAGE IN PERSON...
...AS WORDS OF CELEBRATION.
NO, I'LL WRITE HER A LETTER.
VEEN

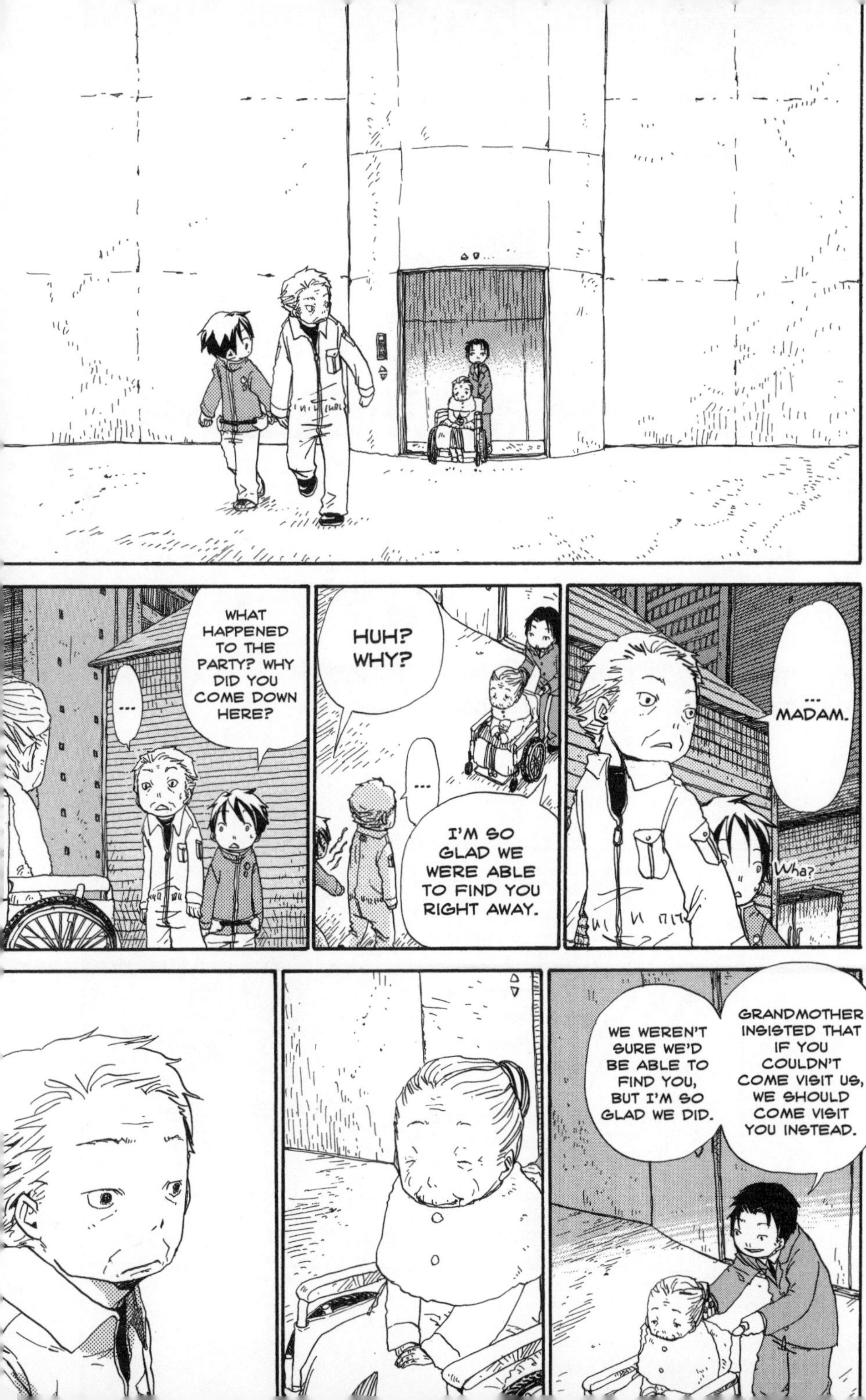
... MADAM.
Wha?
HUH? WHY?
...
I'M SO GLAD WE WERE ABLE TO FIND YOU RIGHT AWAY.
WHAT HAPPENED TO THE PARTY? WHY DID YOU COME DOWN HERE?
...
GRANDMOTHER INSISTED THAT IF YOU COULDN'T COME VISIT US, WE SHOULD COME VISIT YOU INSTEAD.
WE WEREN'T SURE WE'D BE ABLE TO FIND YOU, BUT I'M SO GLAD WE DID.

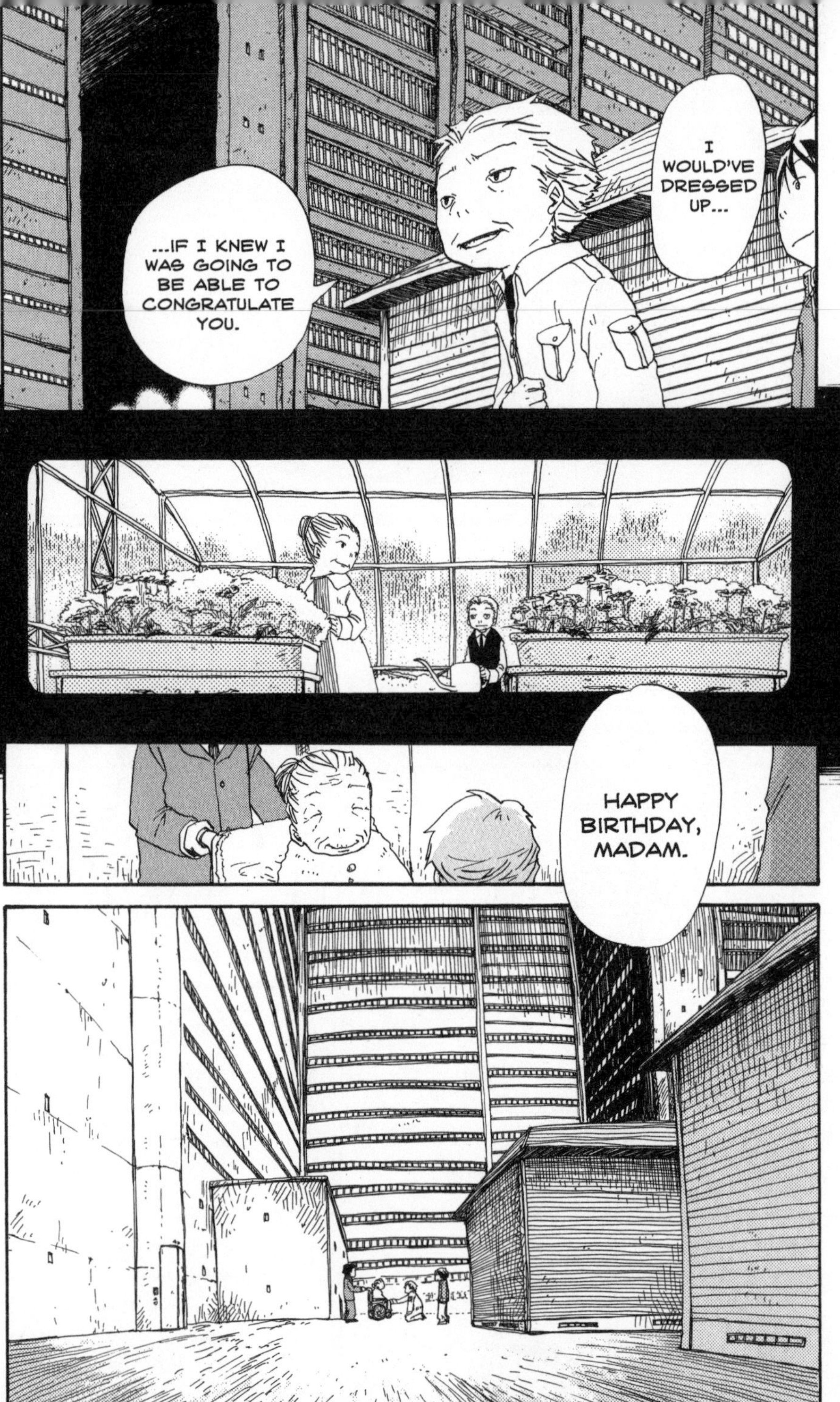
I WOULD'VE DRESSED UP...
...IF I KNEW I WAS GOING TO BE ABLE TO CONGRATULATE YOU.
HAPPY BIRTHDAY, MADAM.

in the loft

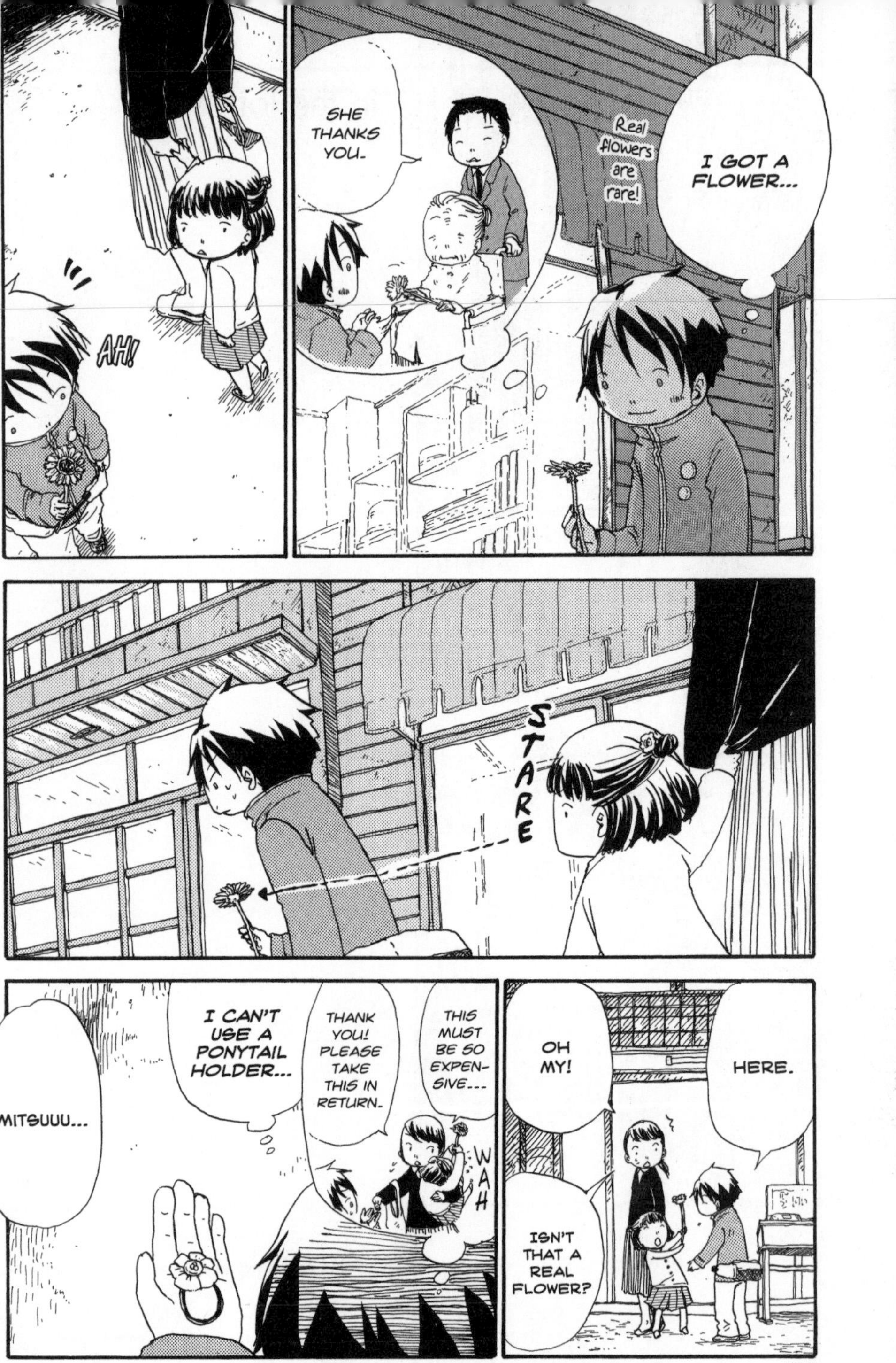
I GOT A FLOWER...
Real flowers are rare!
SHE THANKS YOU.
AH!
STARE
HERE.
OH MY!
ISN'T THAT A REAL FLOWER?
THIS MUST BE SO EXPENSIVE...
THANK YOU! PLEASE TAKE THIS IN RETURN.
WAH
I CAN'T USE A PONYTAIL HOLDER...
MITSUUU...

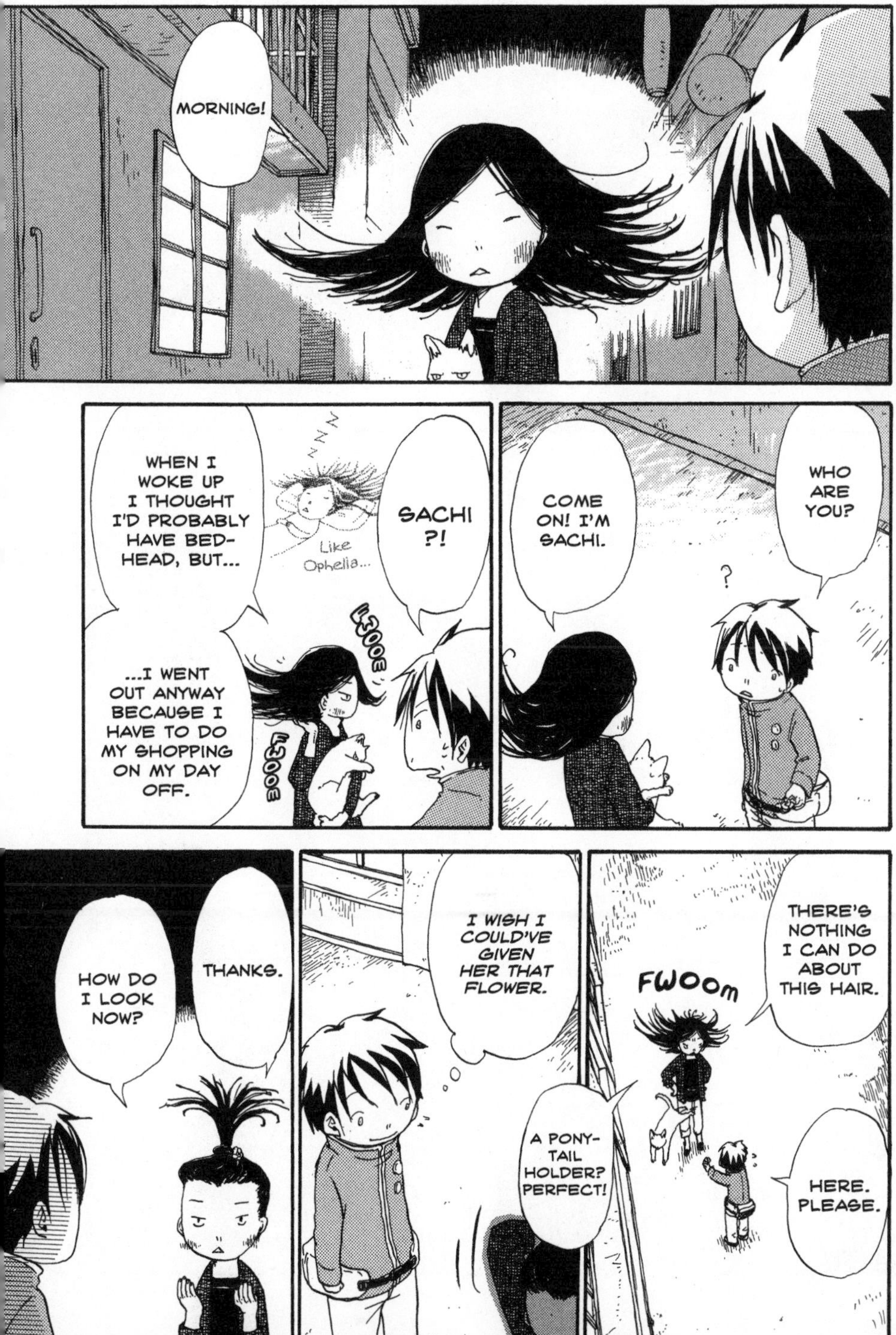
MORNING!
WHO ARE YOU?
COME ON! I'M SACHI.
?
SACHI ?!
Like Ophelia...
WHEN I WOKE UP I THOUGHT I'D PROBABLY HAVE BED-HEAD, BUT...
FWOOM
FWOOM
...I WENT OUT ANYWAY BECAUSE I HAVE TO DO MY SHOPPING ON MY DAY OFF.
THERE'S NOTHING I CAN DO ABOUT THIS HAIR.
FWOOm
HERE. PLEASE.
I WISH I COULD'VE GIVEN HER THAT FLOWER.
A PONY-TAIL HOLDER? PERFECT!
THANKS.
HOW DO I LOOK NOW?

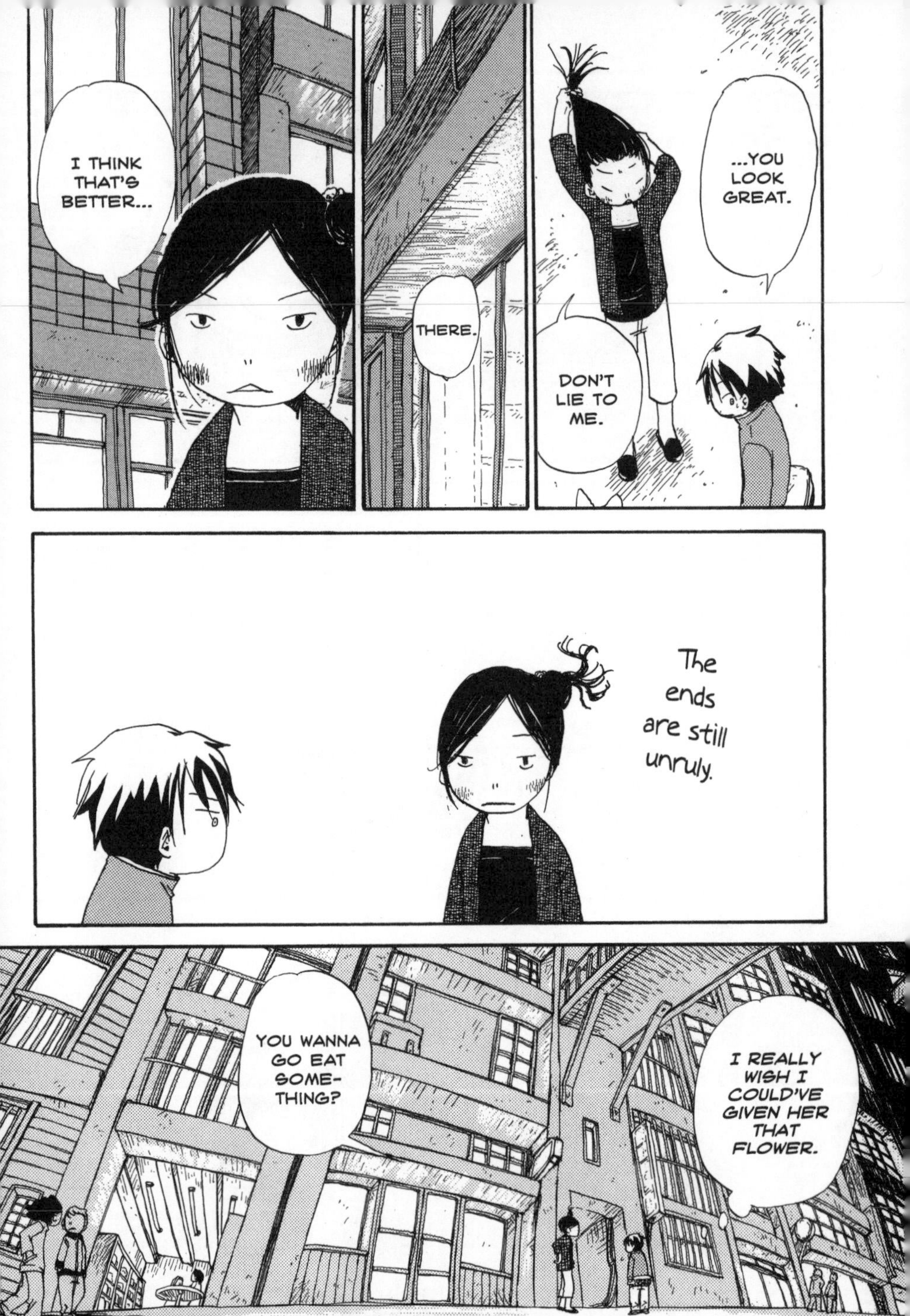
...YOU LOOK GREAT.
DON'T LIE TO ME.
THERE.
I THINK THAT'S BETTER...
The ends are still unruly.
I REALLY WISH I COULD'VE GIVEN HER THAT FLOWER.
YOU WANNA GO EAT SOME-THING?

Thanks to Hideki Egami, Mami Hirai, Megumi Kasai, Fumika, Kinozuka, and to you, for reading.

THE END OF SATURN APARTMENTS 2

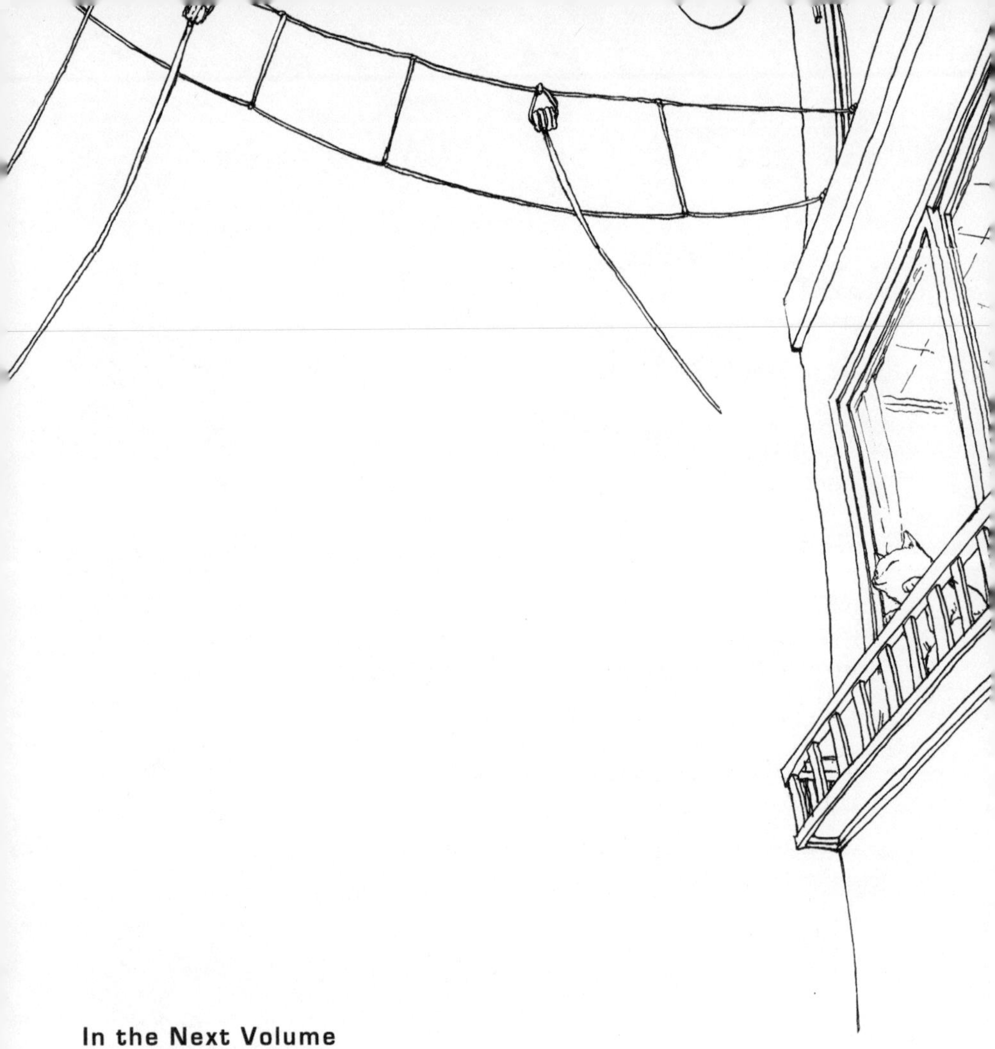

In the Next Volume

Mitsu meets two new clients, both lonely in their own ways. Meanwhile, his work ethic catches the eye of other employers. Sohta, already overqualified for his job at the power plant, gets demoted due to nepotism and channels his frustration toward the surface of the earth. Another day, another dollar for the workforce of Saturn Apartments.

saturn apartments

SATURN APARTMENTS
Volume 2
VIZ Signature Edition

Story and Art by **HISAE IWAOKA**

© 2006 Hisae IWAOKA/Shogakukan
All rights reserved.
Original Japanese edition "DOSEI MANSION" published by SHOGAKUKAN Inc.

Design of original Japanese edition by Kei Kasai

Translation/Matt Thorn, Tomo Kimura
Touch-up Art & Lettering/Eric Erbes
Design/Yukiko Whitley
Editor/Daniel Gillespie

Printed in Canada

Published by VIZ Media, LLC
P.O. Box 77010
San Francisco, CA 94107

10 9 8 7 6 5 4 3 2 1
First printing, November 2010

VIZ SIGNATURE
www.sigikki.com

www.viz.com

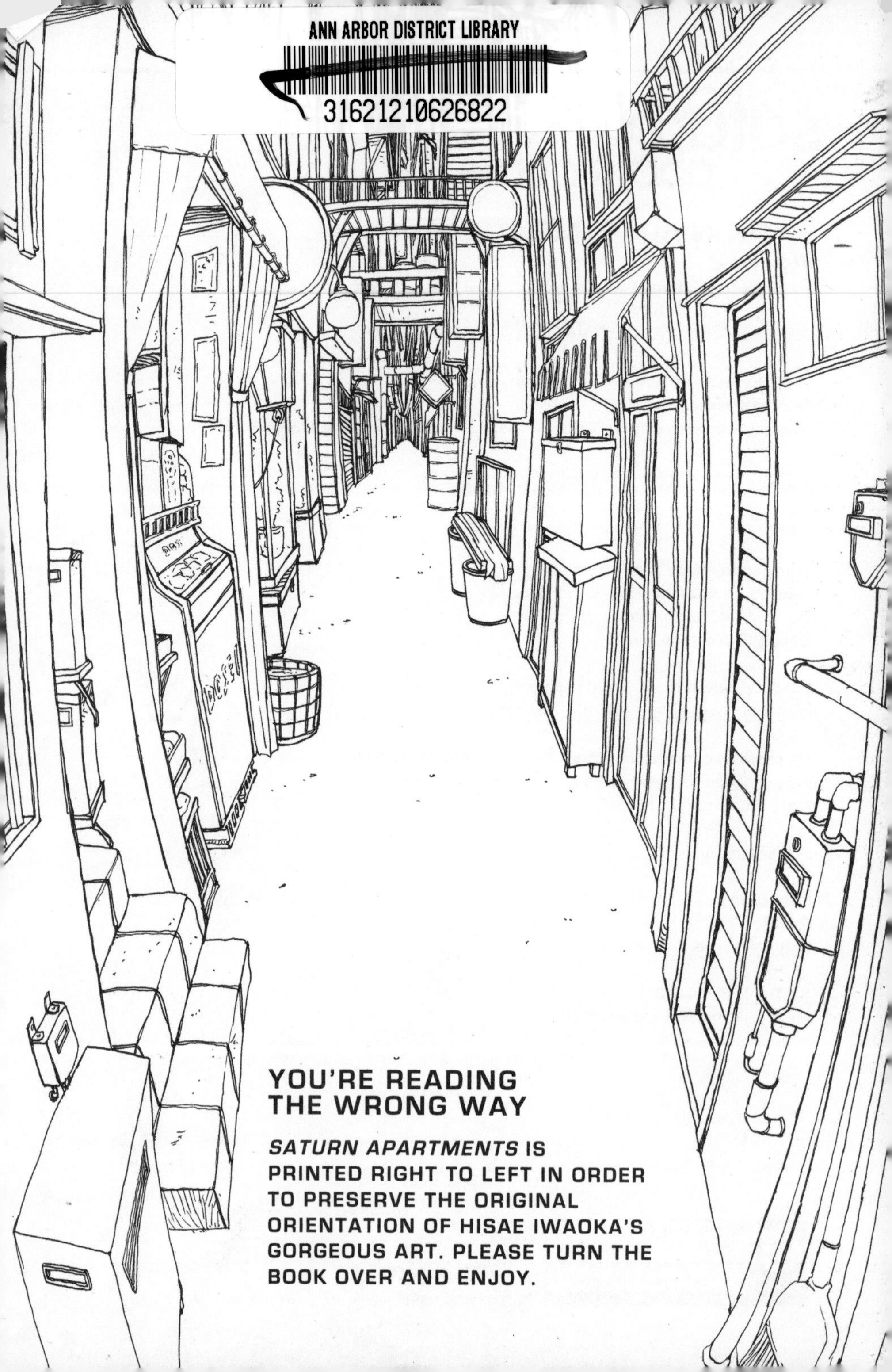

YOU'RE READING THE WRONG WAY

SATURN APARTMENTS IS PRINTED RIGHT TO LEFT IN ORDER TO PRESERVE THE ORIGINAL ORIENTATION OF HISAE IWAOKA'S GORGEOUS ART. PLEASE TURN THE BOOK OVER AND ENJOY.